A Public Records Primer
And Investigator's Handbook
1995 California Edition

CALIFORNIA
A Public Records Primer &
INVESTIGATOR'S HANDBOOK

1995 Edition

By Don Ray

Newly Added:

☑ Public Records Databases

☑ District Attorneys

☑ Case Studies

☑ Workers Comp. Appeals Boards

☑ 1,000s of updated listings

Copyright, 1989, 1990, 1991, 1992, 1995 by Don Ray. All rights reserved. The reproduction or utilization of this work or any part thereof in any form or by any electronic, mechanical, or other means, now known or hereafter invented, including electrostatic copying, photocopy and recording, and in any information storage and retrieval system is forbidden without prior written permission.

ENG Press
P.O. Box 4375
Burbank, CA 91503-4375
(818) THE-NEWS -- (818) 843-6397
Fax: (818) 843-3223
ISBN 0-9629552-3-X (Formerly 0-9629552-1-3 and 0-9629552-0-5)
Printed in the United States of America

First Printing, April 1989
Second Printing, June 1989
Third Printing, January 1990
Fourth Printing, First Revision, May, 1991
Fifth Printing, Second Revision, September, 1992
Sixth Printing, Third Revision, March, 1995

Table of Contents

Acknowledgments 7

Introduction to the 1995 Edition 9

Chapter 1: The Investigative Strategy 11

Chapter 2: Investigating Yourself 19

Chapter 3: The Human Factor 33

Chapter 4: Case Studies 41

Chapter 5: How to Use this Book 61

Chapter 6: Non-Governmental Resources 63

Chapter 7: Database Resources 67

Chapter 8: Other Resources 73

Chapter 9: Municipal Records 77

Chapter 10: County Records 79

Chapter 11: California State Records 89

Chapter 12: Federal Records 113

Chapter 13 Genealogical Resources 127

Appendix A: Municipal Office Listings 131

Appendix B: County Office Listings 223

Appendix C: California Public Records Act . 265

Index 279

Acknowledgments

There isn't anyone in my circle of friends who hasn't contributed in some form to this book—some contributed labor, some money, others helped me keep my sanity. Others gave me ideas, critiques, criticism or polite suggestions. Still others helped me with copy editing, proofreading or just plain inspiration. If I missed anybody, tell me now and I'll add you to the update.

Artineh Havan deserves a lot more than I paid her for updating most of this edition. She gave up much of her spring break to do all-nighters to get the book pasted up for the printer. She's the greatest!

This edition wouldn't be possible if my mother, Doris Quinn, hadn't volunteered to help me raise the printing money. She and her friends Marian and Ron Pearson hand addressed thousands of fliers. Special thanks also to Jeanne McCollum for also addressing, licking stamps and mailing hundreds of fliers.

Bill Thomas came up with the cover design and helped with copy editing. Mary Winkleman Velgos provided graphics consultation. And again, Dr. Gary Shumway was there waiting to handle much of the printing and binding. Tom Cheng of Copy U.S. in Anaheim stuck his neck out for me. Thanks also to Bill Bastian of Media West in Santa Fe Springs for his fine work printing the cover.

Don Holland proved his friendship dozens of times while I struggled to get the book completed. He shot the cover photo (which I insisted be lighted as it was), helped me with the proofing, repeatedly mailed or faxed me valuable information I included in the book and helped me stay afloat. Thanks, Don!

Cindi Ishigaki also pitched in to get the book to the printer. And again, her folks kept me well fed when my cupboards were bare. Elmer Romero helped with the difficult last-minute paste-up.

Others who helped out: Gladis Howard, Dianne Toomey, Dalia Aref, Victor Cook, Dianne Heath, Nadine Bunn, Vilma Garcia, David Ritchie, Tom Newmark, Chris Sisley, Drew Sullivan, Milvia Ponce, Carrie Gaston, Patricia Khachadoorian, Donna Gengenagel, Dale Martin, Dave Holland, Margaret Davis, Toni LaMaritate, Michelle Anton, Melanie Paek, Karl Voss, Paige Harrigan, Bob Ginger, Derek Beverly, Carolyn Garner, Alan Schlein, Ernest Garcia, Ron Farmer, Sharon Fagan and Anna Hronis-Cesar.

Introduction to the 1995 Edition

A lot has changed since the last edition of *A Public Records Primer and Investigator's Handbook*.

Voter registration records aren't nearly as accessible. The Republicans have taken over. Rodney King is now a millionaire. Michael Jackson and O.J. Simpson have had to spend millions. The elevation of the San Fernando Valley has changed. The Great California Drought has officially ended. And in 2 1/2 years, Don Ray has aged about 15.

What had started off as a lecture handout and later became a book has done to its author what three ex-wives and 10 children does to any average, mortal man. The only difference is I don't get visitation rights. I know what you're saying. "At least he doesn't have three ex-wives hounding him for alimony." That's true. I just have several hundred sworn police officers rehearsing the line, "I ordered a book from you months ago and you have the right to remain silent."

What a nightmare! Did I mention the kidney stones? For six weeks I tape recorded my wailing and moaning in hopes I could sell realistic background sounds to Lamaze classes. The pains finally passed but, unfortunately, the stones still haven't.

Here's a good one. I broke a story that caused more money to be spent on a single news story than has ever been spent in history. The words "Michael Jackson is under investigation" triggered more spending by the news media than has been spent on most wars. I spent a month trying to make phone contact with a friend in the remote state of Punjab in India. When I finally reached her I told her I'd broken the biggest entertainment story of the decade. She replied, "What story? Michael Jackson?"

I only tell you this so that I can lament about the fact that I was probably the only journalist that didn't cash in on the story. People told me afterwards that I could have sold my story to one of the TV tabloids for at least $50,000. I learned to reply, "Virtue, though in rags, will keep me warm!" Looking back I wonder why I'm freezing today. I guess I'm one of the few holdouts who still believe that honesty and hard work will eventually pay off. It's lonely here in Peasant Flats.

Despite he fact this book has nearly been the death of me, I promised myself I was going to make this edition more readable and more entertaining and throw in some case studies people could relate to. I paid a price for the update—about an additional month of being without a completed book in hand.

As I write this, I'm not sure I'll have the strength to do another update. If you have either lots of money or lots of ambition, make me an offer. This book would be a guaranteed money maker for someone with enough capital to properly market and distribute it. If I took the advice written in every book I've read on self-publishing or on starting a business I would never have even started. They all predicted that without credit, capital or collateral it's impossible. The fact that you're reading this book is proof that it is possible. But oh what a price you pay.

What's clear is that there is a need for a book like this. What's amazing is that in the six years I've published the book, no one has stepped in to produce a book that can compete with this one. That's probably why I keep updating the book—everybody keeps clamoring for it.

What you're going to find is that some of the numbers and addresses have already changed. I have to assume you're qualified enough to call *directory assistance* for the changes. With each printing of the book I'll be correcting those entries I learn about, so feel free to let me know of anything that's changed.

Also, you can help assure there will be another edition next year (or shortly thereafter) if you encourage others to buy the book. Better yet, invite me to put on a presentation in your city. Or, if you run across an incredible news story you can share with me, give me a call. As a freelance journalist, I survive by my ability to come up with stories that news outlets will pay me to write or produce. As long as I'm surviving, I'll make sure this book is updated.

Enjoy.

The Investigative Strategy
How to think through an investigation.

With all the fanfare and hype it was hard to believe it was just a carnival act. When the performer came out I expected lions, tigers or elephants. Instead he came out with nothing more than a brick. But this, he pointed out, was no ordinary brick. This was a *trained* brick! And true to his promise, every time the man gave a command, the brick responded accordingly.

Astounding, you say? Far from it. As it turns out, the only command the man actually gave the brick was, "Stay!" And it did, without faltering. After I thought about it for a while, I realized that that's what we ask most of a brick—to stay. The more a brick stays where it is, the more we like it.

There have been other uses for bricks. I was stationed in Detroit shortly after that city's riots in the late 1960s and some of the former participants still referred to a brick as a "two-by-four-by-eight." Placed in proper context it went something like, "Lay one finger on my car and I'll hit you up side the head with a two-by-four-by-eight!"

But no matter how hard one tries, it's impossible to train the brick to hurl itself in the direction of salmon's head. In reality, the brick can be an effective tool (or weapon) only if you know how to use it properly.

This book is a lot like that brick. It also will stay—with or without your command. It could also produce a small lump if you used it to hit someone upside the head. But you'd still have to hurl it yourself. The point is, this book is a great tool and a great building block in your investigation, but, it ain't gonna solve the mystery for you. Furthermore, it ain't even gonna tell you specifically how to solve your mystery. You're going to have to do that yourself. If you're over, say, age 35 you may remember this oft-repeated notice:

Crest has been shown to be an effective decay preventive dentifrice that can be of significant value when used in a conscientiously applied program of oral hygiene and regular professional care.

I tend to think of it more as a disclaimer than as an alluring ad. It really warns you that the product is no good if you don't use it, good if you do, and even better if you use it properly and in conjunction with other stuff. That could also be said of this book. Maybe I should have printed this on the cover:

A Public Records Primer and Investigator's Handbook *has been shown to be an effective information gathering reference and guide that can be of significant value when used in a conscientiously applied program of creative thinking, thorough legwork, great people skills, astute interpretation, attention to detail and incredible persistence.*

This book can't think, or make phone calls, or befriend a county clerk, or tell you when someone has lied on a public document, or wake you up early enough to be first in line at county recorder's office. It's a lot like your toothpaste. It won't apply itself to your brush. You have to. And if you don't, your teeth will have cavities. If you wait for this book to solve all of your mysteries, your investigation will have cavities of its own.

An effective investigator should always think through an investigation before diving in. Assess what you already know, what you ultimately need to know and what pieces of information will help you along the way.

Need to find a trucker who witnessed an accident? His name is John Smith? You could shout his name in your home or office and hope he can hear you. Or you could hit the streets and go door-to-door asking for him. Within a day or two you'd probably find a John

Smith—but not the John Smith you're looking for. You could even open the phone book and start calling every John Smith listed there—but there's a good chance you still wouldn't find the right John Smith. You will have wasted a lot of time and energy. It's better to first ask yourself some questions before diving into an investigation.

What do I already know? You know he's in his 40s, he drives some kind of a truck—an 18-wheeler. He mentioned to someone he was going to stop along the way last July 20th and visit his mother in Lone Pine. You know he used his bowling ball to smash open a car window and free the person trapped inside. He also had a big, slobbering St. Bernard with him.

What do I ultimately need to know? You need to know where he is or how to reach him.

What pieces of information will help me along the way? Certainly some identifying information would be great, such as his date of birth, Social Security number or driver's license number. Knowing merely what city he lives or works in would be a start. Or at least, you'd like to find someone who knows him.

Unfortunately, you don't know enough to dive into public records and quickly identify your John Smith. And unless the police on the scene of the accident somehow wrote down his vehicle license or driver's license number, you're not likely to get any of the key identifying numbers.

Always ask yourself, "Who would know?" In this case you can focus on finding a woman at least in her 60s (old enough to have a son in his 40s), divorced or widowed (he wasn't visiting his *parents*, so there's probably no father living there), probably with the last name of Smith and living in Lone Pine. If you find his mother, she surely knows how to reach her son. You could check with the bowling alley nearest to Lone Pine and hope someone remembers a John Smith who drives a truck and has a St. Bernard and visits his mother in Lone Pine. Or, you could check with truck stops in Lone Pine and hope someone there can remember the guy with the St. Bernard. Maybe there's someone in Lone Pine who knows the dog. The local kennel? The Humane Society? A St. Bernard breeder in town? The local pet store? Or maybe someone from the accident scene can remember something more about that truck that stopped. A company name? The type of cargo?

In this case, you should probably start calling all of the Smiths in Lone Pine until you find someone who knows of a Smith woman with a trucker son who lives out of town. Chances are you'd find someone who would give you the mother's name. Mothers will almost always give you their children's phone numbers. And even if you can't reach his mother, someone in her neighborhood knows everything. At the very least you could probably learn in what city the son lives and possibly his wife's name or the name of the company for which he drives.

No luck? Then whip out your copy of *A Public Records Primer and Investigator's Handbook.* Look up Lone Pine in the *Municipalities* section starting on page 131. You find that, even though it's not an incorporated city, it's listed as an unincorporated part of Inyo County. There's a listing there, however, for the local chamber of commerce. You might call them and ask about the nearest bowling alley, truck stops, animal regulation people, kennels and pet stores. When you call, don't forget to ask them if they know the right Mrs. Smith.

Next, you might want to turn to the *Counties* section of your book starting on page 223. Now you can call the county tax assessor to find out about properties owned by women with the last name of Smith. You can check with the county recorder to find out if maybe there was a John Smith married there within the past, say, 20 years. Or maybe he was born there. The recorder might just check birth certificates going back 40 to 50 years. In smaller counties they often provide such help. Before the laws changed in 1995 you could call the registrar of voters and have someone there look up John Smith. Now you might want to call the Municipal Court in nearby Independence to see if they have any records on a John Smith there.

There is no newspaper listed under Lone Pine in the Municipalities section, so you might look for the largest nearby city in Inyo County by looking again in the Counties section. You find that Bishop is where the County Clerk is located, so you can return to the Municipalities section of your book and look up Bishop. There you find the local paper, the *Review Herald.* If you call there and ask for "the morgue"—where all the newspaper clips and indices are kept—they might pull all stories written about any John Smith. Maybe one of those stories relates also to trucks or bowling or St. Bernards or heroes or a mother in Lone Pine.

Don't forget to check with the sheriff's station there in Lone Pine. It's also listed in the County section. Deputies often point investigators, journalists, genealogists or other researchers in the right direction. The folks at the chamber of commerce can tell you which high schools serve the area. There's a good chance the school or the nearest public library will have back issues of the yearbook. Yes, sometimes a kind soul will actually search a few years for you. If they found a John Smith, it could provide you with a picture (although a dated picture) and a clue as to the year he was born. Maybe he's pictured with friends or teammates. Maybe an old friend still lives nearby and knows where he is—or maybe knows someone who might know.

The chances are that if your John Smith ever lived in Lone Pine—or for that matter in Inyo County—you probably would have found him or someone who would know where he is.

"Nothing in the world can take the place of persistence. Talent will not—nothing is more common than unsuccessful people with talent. Genius will not—unrewarded genius is almost a proverb. Education will not—the world is full of educated derelicts. Persistence and determination alone are omnipotent. The slogan "press on" has solved and always will solve the problems of the human race."

I've had an old, tattered, yellow copy of this quotation on my wall for close to 20 years. I only recently discovered it to be from the mouth of President Calvin Coolidge. Apparently, persistence worked for him. The search for John Smith, as outlined above, is an example of planned persistence. Before you even begin to dig, you can plan a focused and persistent search. There's no doubt persistence will eventually reward you. In fact, the person going door-to-door asking for John Smith would, given enough time, surely find the John Smith in question—or at least his elderly grandchildren. In a race between two persistent people, the more efficient one will almost always win.

The late writer Dorothy Parker best described it years ago—at a time when her wisdom and wit would not have been overshadowed by today's paranoiac political correctness:

You can lead a horticulture, but you can't make her think.

Okay, stop your screaming. It's not about women. It's about people who are unable or unwilling to synthesize information. The truth is that very few students were taught or are currently being taught how to think. They're taught to memorize. And after the exam or the degree, they dump the information—they reformat the disk of their computer-like mind to make way for the next transient information that will take up room and board in their overworked brains.

People who aren't taught how to think will never pick up this art form—that is unless thinking becomes absolutely necessary to survive. The term "street wise" refers to people who, even with little or no formal education, have been forced to use their wits to survive. Too often the spoon fed never learn to cook. If the silver spoon should be taken away they will either search for someone else with a silver spoon, they will somehow learn to cook or they will surely die.

In the investigative world today, the silver spoon is the computer. Like a nanny, it delivers each byte already prepared, processed and ready to swallow. Don't ask what it's made of, from where it comes or how it gets here—just swallow and pray the food is not tainted or contaminated.

Today's computers and databases, like nannies, do everything for you without you having to think. And in the process, they're nourishing a new breed of investigator—be it journalistic, governmental, private or academic—who can consume and process astounding amounts of information without ever really knowing what it's made of, from where it comes or how it gets here—and even worse—whether or not it's inaccurate, stolen or otherwise contaminated.

It's getting dangerously easy to obtain information. And almost everybody is being invited (if not coerced) to take a spin on the Internet. Mark my words. Soon the elite, longtime users of the Internet and the information superhighway will watch their medium of communication go the route of the CB radio channels of the 1970s. They'll see what was once a sleek superhighway become clogged, littered and graffitied. Millions of untrained newcomers are already invading the phone lanes with keyboards constantly pounding out "breaker breaker, good buddy, keep your hard drive a'spinnin'."

But it's a fact of life—the seasoned, veteran investigators of the past can no longer survive without becoming computer literate. Conversely the young techno-investigators of today—the ones born with a silver mouse in their hands—will not progress beyond mediocrity without learning how it was done before the term *on line* referred only to the place New Yorkers stood to get theater tickets.

I've had a chance to gather information both ways—I've spent years in the darkened, musty basements poring over dusty, archived records, and I've also "surfed the databases" without ever leaving my office. I can see the world of investigations from both sides and I'm sure of one thing—you need to know both how to squeeze the most efficiency out of that computer and you need to know how to read and interpret the documents the computer helps you locate.

In Chapter 4, see how other investigative people have solved information problems using a variety of tools. Digest some of their victories and defeats. In each scenario, there are important lessons, tips and warnings. In each case study you'll be able to see one or more common elements—creative thinking, thorough legwork, good people skills, astute interpretation, attention to detail and persistence. There's another element common to most of the cases—*a positive belief that we'll score*—that we will, indeed, nail down the information.

It's a state of mind similar to that of a martial artist who visualizes his or her hand on the other side of the thick, wooden board. The board is not a barrier, but rather an insignificant obstacle. Those who see the board as a barrier will smash their hand into a solid piece of wood and go no further. Similarly, investigators who believe they can't get the information won't.

I've worked with some people who I believe subconsciously embrace the obstacle, thinking "If I can't get access to the information I won't have to work with it." Or they'll spend the entire afternoon awaiting a return phone call from the only person they called upon for information. There's always someone else who has the answer.

For me, the question is never, "I wonder *if* I'll get the information." Rather, I'm always saying to myself, "Hmm, I know I'm going to get the information. I wonder *how* I'll end up doing it—and how quickly."

Certainly, the tools on hand will enhance the effectiveness of he investigation. To familiarize you with the some important tools I've thrown in two chapters you'll find very helpful. Chapter 7 outlines some of the more useful commercial databases to which you may want to subscribe. It will also list some of the more useful CD-ROMs available. And in Chapter 8, you'll find listings of people, companies or organizations who are anxious to help you with your investigation.

THIS SPACE FOR RENT
To have your ad printed here in future printings,
Call (818) THE-NEWS

Investigating Yourself
An introduction to public records

A positive, "I-can-do-it" attitude works best if you are constantly working on building and improving your information-gathering skills. If you don't have a lot of experience, try practicing on yourself. Think for a moment of all the ways in which you interact with government at various levels—in how many places your name shows up on public records. Then, spend a day retrieving copies of the documents that relate to you. It will be a good investigative exercise as well as a sobering reminder of how very vulnerable you are.

But first, take a minute to get an understanding of the whole concept of public records. What are they? They're documents, lists, printouts, affidavits, court cases, licenses, certificates, photographs, maps, computer data, reports and much more. What they have in common is that there's a law or regulation or statute or court ruling that makes them available for public inspection.

Basically, they're available because the U.S. Constitution, the Bill of Rights, the federal Freedom of Information Act, the California Public Records Act (see Appendix C), hundreds of other statutes and scads of court decisions say the people have the right to know how the government ("Of the people, by the people, for the people") functions. By viewing records at all levels of government, the people can determine how tax money is being spent, how many people are voting in a certain household, which judges are letting the crooks go and which ones are hanging the innocent.

The records show you how much money in contributions certain elected officials are getting from various interest groups and how much property tax the mayor's brother-in-law is paying. They show you who the true owner is of the land the state wants to take over for that new highway and whether that shady mechanic, dentist or private investigator is really qualified and licensed.

Public records allow you to make better decisions on the stocks you buy, the airlines you fly, the companies you do business with and even the person you might want to marry.

But what about privacy? Aren't I protected? Yes, but it's a double-edged sword. The price we pay for an open government is often public disclosure of those things that may affect others. It's important at times to know if someone is qualified to vote or to drive or to practice medicine. And there are times when we need to know for sure when someone was born or married or that they're really divorced. Someone declaring bankruptcy could easily affect us as could the fact that someone is being sued or is accused of committing a crime.

Many government records regarding individuals are kept very private—those records that are the most personal in nature, such as income tax, Social Security information, medical records and welfare information. You can avoid the generation of many records by choosing to avoid the privileges. No law requires you to vote or drive or own real property or file law suits or get married or commit a crime. There's a constant battle raging between privacy and the public's right to know. Both are essential in a democracy.

If reading this book makes you paranoid, there's help available. A group called the Privacy Rights Clearinghouse in San Diego is ready to mail you, fax you or modem you valuable information on how to protect yourself from the people, companies or organizations who are bent on prying into your personal life. The folks there will be tickled to send you one or more of their handy publications. Get all the details on Page 76.

To do a practice investigation on yourself, start with local government. Before your home was built, someone had to obtain a variety of permits from some sort of city or county Building and Safety Office. There may be permits that allowed demolition of a previous structure, grading permits, permits for laying the foundation, the carpentry, electrical and plumbing, etc. Any improvements to your home also required permits—the swimming pool, the add-on den or extra bedroom. You may also find that permits were required for a security alarm system. There's a myriad of permits and most of them are public record.

Step over to another desk and look at business licenses. You may have your own business—or maybe you had to get a permit for that garage sale last summer. And somewhere at or near the city level is the office that keeps track of your dog, Ed (three proofreaders have objected to me using the name "Ed" for a dog. What's the big deal? If the "Ed" here causes you to lose concentration or makes you want to kill yourself or someone else, please, scratch out "Ed" and replace it with "Fido" or "Spot"). If you paid for a license, the file is probably public. If you didn't, but went ahead and got Ed a rabies vaccination, a copy of that certificate is probably on file where they keep pet licenses.

Do you have a library card? You'll find that the information on your library card is *not* public record. In the United States, you are free to read whatever you wish without anyone monitoring you. However, if you fail to pay your overdue book fines, *that information* is open to public inspection. Generally, you'll find that when you break some kind of a rule, the public has more of a right to inspect the file—to make sure the government is enforcing the rules equally. Wouldn't want the mayor's son to get away with not paying his overdue book fines, now would you?

Now step over to the elections desk. If you've ever run for a city office, there will be a file on you. In fact, if you've ever contributed to any city or school board candidate or to any political action committee or ballot measure, you'll be part of that particular file.

Before you step outside city limits you might also want to visit your local police. Been arrested? Called for the police? That's right, it's public record. Not all of it, but the police pretty much have to tell you who they've arrested (including date of birth, address, description and more), where they're being held and what their bail arrangements are (See the California Public Records Act, Government Code section 6254.f(1) & (2) on page 268). After all, we live in a country where there's not supposed to be police secretly arresting folks they don't particularly like. This openness is an important part of the checks and balances on government power. Also, the police have to tell you quite a bit about each call for assistance—where, why, who called and when they responded. Another check on the power of government.

Now zip over to your county offices and see how popular you are. If you register to vote, there are certain people who can look at the affidavit you completed that day outside the supermarket. Up until January 1, 1995, anyone could view it. Now just government folks, people running for office or campaigning for some cause, researchers and journalists can look at it. That also applies to the precinct roll — the listing, by address, of everyone who votes at your polling place.

There are also campaign contribution reports filed with the Registrar of Voters—reports for ballot measures, political action committees and all countywide offices, including judges, county supervisors, sheriffs and district attorneys. offices, They're always open for inspection by the public. You'll also find campaign financing reports for wannabees from your county seeking statewide office—such as the State Assembly, State Senate, Board of Equalization, Secretary of State, Attorney General and even Governor. If you either ran for one of those offices or contributed to one of the candidates, you're on file. A side note. If you live in Los Angeles County or San Francisco City/County you're lucky. All candidates for statewide office—regardless of the counties in which they reside and filed campaign statements—must also file in Los Angeles and San Francisco. It's sort of a convenience for people who want to research on a statewide basis.

Walk across the hall or across the street (or if you're in some large counties, across town) to the office of the County Assessor. If you own your own home or any other property in the county, you'll probably be listed as the assessee of the property. Pull that file and the corresponding map book and see how much information is available to anyone. While you're there you can check to see how much property tax your nasty neighbors are paying. Wouldn't want them getting a break. In fact, that's the very reason the files are open to public inspection. Isn't it great to live in America? By the way, if you own the house in which you're living, you're entitled to a tax break. It's called the Homeowner's Exemption. It's not automatic—you have to apply for it. If you haven't, now's a good time to do it. It'll save you a couple hundred bucks on your property tax bill. If you want to reward me for this information, I'll take cash or checks. My address is plastered all over this book. Don't underestimate the Homeowner's Exemption—it can help you determine whether or not the owner is occupying the house.

Okay, now check in with the Tax Collector to make sure you're paid up—another public file. You might also check with either the Assessor or the Tax Collector about *unsecured* property. One of those two offices are probably responsible for keeping track of taxable things that aren't "secured" to the ground the way real estate is—things such as large boats, big old machinery and airplanes and such. The county wants a piece of that tax action too—and part of the file is public record.

Now on to the gold mine of county records—the County Recorder. It's usually broken down into two main camps—the Vital Records branch and the Grantor-Grantee branch. Start with Vital Records. The folks there keep track of birth, marriage and death certificates. If you think you were born in that county, you (and anyone else) can buy a copy of your birth certificate. If you think you were married in that county, you (and usually anybody else, I'll explain) can buy a copy of your marriage certificate. If you think you died in that county you *cannot* buy a copy of your death certificate—because you're dead! Of course, anybody else can buy it, frame it, display it or even paper their bathroom walls with it (my, what did you do to so alienate everyone?).

About that marriage certificate stuff—there's a way you can get married and not generate a public record file. In California, men and women who have lived together "as husband and wife" (that means if you spent one night together in the same bed and "did it") you may get married without a blood test (darn lotta good it'd do now!), without a waiting period (you didn't wait before, why wait now?) and without any public record. It's a law designed to protect you from all those "holier than thou" folks you've been lying to for the past six years (and maybe for the last three kids). This way they won't read about you in the Vital Records column in the local rag. Your secret will be safe with the County Recorder.

About the only way someone can learn about your indiscretion is to go to the County Recorder already armed with your exact names and the exact date of the *Confidential Marriage* in that county. If someone provides the Recorder with precisely the right information, the Recorder must say, "Uh huh. That's right. Those two folks were, indeed, married on that date in this county." But the Recorder still can't show them or give them a copy of your marriage certificate. You, of course, are authorized to buy a copy of your own

Confidential Marriage Certificate—that is if you're into that kind of self torture.

Now remember, there's lots of good information available on each birth, marriage and death certificate. You can learn about people's parents, dates of birth, places of birth, places of employment, religious affiliations, ministers, addresses, doctors, best friends, prior births, prior marriages—all kinds of good junk. Go on, order a copy of your own (some counties won't give it to you over the counter—they insist on mailing it) and keep it handy. You never know when you may need to prove you were born in order to get that job or that passport or sign up for welfare or something.

Over in the other corner of the County Recorder's office is the Grantor-Grantee section (I once gave my investigative reporting students a walking tour of the Los Angeles Civic Center and one student was most excited about experiencing what she thought was the "Grand Tour, Grand Tea section. She ended up disappointed). "Grantor-grantee" relates to civil documents that one person (the grantor) hands over to another person (the grantee). They voluntarily give a copy of the document to the recorder as a permanent record. There are zillions of types of documents on file there, but most of them are deeds and other property transfer documents.

This has led to a common misconception. Since the *seller* of a piece of property grants the deed to the *buyer* of that property, people conclude that *grantor* always means *seller* and *grantee* always means *buyer*. And so when unsophisticated (or unenlightened) investigators go looking to see what property someone owns, they look only in the index marked *grantee*, because they want to know what property that person received. Don't fall for it my friends! *Sellers* can be *grantees* also. And *buyers* can be *grantors*. Yes, it's confusing. It has to be—government offices are designed that way. Suppose the *seller* of the property (the *grantor* of the deed) decides to carry a second mortgage on behalf of the *buyer* (the *grantee* of the deed). Well, to do this, the *buyer* must now give to the *seller* a document that promises he or she will pay back this loan. Thus, the *buyer* now becomes the *grantor* of the *deed of trust* and the *seller* becomes the *grantee* of that same deed of trust. So you see, both parties are both *grantor* and *grantee*.

Why should you care? Because if you're interested in someone's assets, you should also be interested in how much money that person has borrowed to get the property they own. Rule of thumb? Always run any name you're searching through both the *grantor* and the *grantee* index. In many counties the indices are cross referenced.

These indices will lead you to actual copies of the documents filed there. Always remember, there's really no government agency requiring people to have these documents recorded. It's a service provided by the county for people who don't trust other folks to not alter civil documents. In this case, the government is the only party some people trust.

There are more than just deeds and deeds of trust on file at the County Recorder. Look for *reconveyances* (notices that a deed of trust is paid off), *powers of attorney* (someone allowing someone else to act legally on their behalf), *mechanics liens* (something a contractor slaps on your property when you don't pay the bill. A *lien* is an outstanding debt that someone has to pay back before their property can be sold), *tax liens* (same as above except the government does the slapping and receiving), *notices of foreclosure* (you didn't make those monthly payments and now the sharks are circling), *notices of sale*, (too late now, they're going to sell your house out from under you—to those sharks), and scads of other documents. Go look yourself up.

And while you're there, there's another obscure, but really cool place people's names show up—in notary publics' log books. You won't find them exactly there in the Recorder's office, but that's where you start. Look for the notary's seal and signature at the bottom of almost any document filed in the Grantor-Grantee section. The notary is the person who witnessed the signature of whoever signed the document. He or she then filled in a bunch of stuff in his or her Notary's Log Book. It included the type of document, the name of the person signing, his or her address, driver's license number and, if it was done recently, the actual thumb print of the person who signed the document. Cool, huh? To see this log book you first have to track down the notary. Since you're at the County Recorder's office, try looking up the notary's name in the Grantor-Grantee index. He or she may have recorded a bond of some sort as a protection against some unintentional error. That recorded bond might very well include the address and phone number of the notary. If not, the County Clerk probably maintains a listing of all the notaries public in your county. If that fails, the Secretary of State in Sacramento keeps the definitive listing of all notaries.

By law, the notary must allow you to view and/or copy the particular line item in question. If the log book is filled or the notary's commission has expired, the notary must return the book to either the County Clerk or the Secretary of State.

Speaking of the County Clerk. Step over to that office and you'll find indices of recent Marriage Licenses. It's good to look here in case someone proposed but didn't follow through. Also, the County Clerk keeps copies of recent *fictitious name statements* (some people still refer to them as *DBAs*—as in *doing business as*). Maybe you once tried running your own business and someone told you you had to file one of these. Legally, it's a public declaration that someone or some organization is doing business using a name other than the legal name. Example—Don Ray is *doing business as* ENG Press. In this case, Don Ray is the *legal entity*—a person, and ENG Press is the *fictitious name*. There really is no legal entity named ENG Press. In this case the legal entity is a person.

But not just *people* have to file *fictitious name statements.* If a *corporation,* a *general partnership,* a *limited partnership,* a *husband and wife partnership,* a business trust or *an unincorporated association other than a partnership* does business using any name other than its legal name, that legal entity must take out an ad in a local newspaper and declare to the world (or at least anyone in the county who reads legal notices) who's really behind the operation. That newspaper ad and the original application remain on file for at least seven years. You can usually find the file using either the true name of the entity or its fictitious name.

The County Clerk is also the clerk of the Superior Court. You may find your name in one of the files there. If you've ever been sued for a lot of money or sued someone for a lot of money you'll find the *civil case file* here—replete with all the accusations, denials, exhibits and rulings. Or maybe you'll find your *divorce file* here—again, often chock-full with the kind of mud-slinging and personal tidbits you wouldn't want others to see. You probably don't have a *probate file* here, but your late parents or grandparents might. In this file you'll generally find the *last will and testament,* a great inventory of the family, everything the deceased person owed, everything he or she owned and who ended up with it all. It's always a great file to look at if you're looking for someone. Remember, *where there's a will, there's a relative.*

I hope there's not a criminal file on you here, but it's possible. Everyone with a file at the Superior Court was either *indicted* or was held over for trial by a *municipal court* judge. Although much of the file is no longer open for inspection, there is still a lot of information available. Don't overlook it.

Another file in which you may find your name is a *Reciprocal Enforcement Support Law* file (*RESL*). This is a case where an ex-husband (or ex-wife occasionally) is ordered to pay alimony or child support but instead skips town and ends up in another county or state. This federal law requires the District Attorney in the county where the non-paying scum is living to collect the money from the slimeball and ship it to the District Attorney in the county where the innocent, struggling former significant other is living. Then that D.A. gives him or her the money. You'll find both ex-hubby and ex-wife listed in files at both ends—along with tons of personal information. Fathers, for the sake of your privacy, pay up!

Don't leave that County Courthouse—there's more. At the Municipal Court you'll find *civil case files* similar to those at superior court—except the dollar amounts are smaller. You'll find even smaller cases at the Small Claims Court. Don't overlook these files. If you're listed in one of the indices here, you're either a person who was so angry at someone doing you wrong that you were willing to put yourself through self-inflicted abuse to nail the creep—or someone believes you're the creep who did them wrong.

If you were the plaintiff, there's a good chance you won the case but never collected a dime. That happens to a lot of people. And while it's certainly bad news for the person who hasn't collected following the judgment, it could be great news for the investigator who's also looking for the party that didn't pay up. Do you want to find someone who'll gladly talk about someone else? Check the Small Claims Court for someone who sued your subject, won the case but didn't collect. It's almost guaranteed they'll hand over more valuable dirt on that scoundrel than you could find in a month. For some reason, non-collecting winners in Small Claims Court never seem to let go of their anger. Many continue monitoring the other party for years.

Don't leave the courthouse yet. Your name still might show up in either Municipal Criminal Court or Traffic Court. Just being arrested won't result in you going to court. The City Attorney or the county's District Attorney must decide to charge you with a misdemeanor. Then you'd be *arraigned* before a real live judge or a *commissioner* (that's a trusted, experienced lawyer wearing judge's training wheels). To be *arraigned* is to have a judge or commissioner tell you clearly what you're being charged with and then ask you how you plead. Whether or not you plead guilty, you'll probably end up in municipal court at a later date to be either sentenced or tried. As with the Superior Court criminal records, Municipal Court criminal records are open for inspections, but the clerk will remove many of the more juicy documents unless you're an attorney, a police person or the person charged.

Traffic Court files are still fairly open. This is a good resource for finding someone's home address. You can actually view the citation the traffic officer wrote up and imagine the person you're investigating sitting, humiliated in traffic, with the bright lights from the top of the police care alternately turning the driver's face red, then white, then red and then white.

There's more stuff at the county level, but you can't spend the rest of your life digging through files. Now you should look at what files include your name at the state level. Most likely is the Department of Motor Vehicles. Your vehicle licensing information and your own driver's license (and driving record) are available in one form or another to just about anyone. Whether they deal directly with DMV or go through some authorized contractor, they can learn most everything except your home address. In fact, even that is not completely secure. You might think about getting a post office box. It'll slow down the curious a little bit—but not too much. Don't forget that motorcycles, trucks and trailers show up in the DMV files.

Look in the white pages of your phone book for a local number for the Department of Consumer Affairs. This agency is broken up into mini-agencies—each one responsible for licensing and monitoring various professionals who service Californians in a variety of ways. There's an office overseeing mechanics, another for hairdressers, one for psychologists, others for private investigators, veterinarians, nurses, funeral directors, dentists, contractors, geologists, tax preparers, architects, appliance repair people and more. If you're in one of these professions, anyone can call up for basic identifying information.

If you sell products or services you may also have a *Resale Permit* issued by the Board of Equalization. Some of the information in its files is public record. Or you might be on file at the Department of Real Estate or the Department of Insurance or the Banking Department if you are in one of those fields. If you were ever injured at work, certain folks can go to the Workers Compensation Appeals Board and view your file. If you were born or married in California, you're definitely on file at the Statewide Office of Vital Statistics. If you went to prison, people can learn about your stay and your parole by calling the folks at the Department of Corrections. And if you ran for statewide office or contributed to someone who ran, you'll be on file with the Fair Political Practices Commission and possibly the Secretary of State.

But the Secretary of State doesn't just handle elections. That office also keeps track of nearly every corporation doing business in California. Anyone can look up the corporation's status, get a copy of the *Articles of Incorporation* and view, or buy a copy of, the annual *Statement of Officers*.

Another desk at the Secretary of State keeps track of *Uniform Commercial Code* (*UCC*) filings. These are declarations made by people or other legal entities who borrow money by putting tangible equipment up as collateral. To prevent you from offering the same collateral to more than one lender, you must file papers with the Secretary of State's UCC office. That way potential lenders can look you up to ensure they're not being hoodwinked. This is a great place to find someone's assets—or at least their Social Security Number and address.

Still at the office of the Secretary of State—*Limited Partnership* papers. Don't get excited about this one—unless you are a limited partner. Some politicians pulled some strings back in the 1980s that allowed people to invest as limited partners and not show up on public record. This policy really stinks—especially if you're trying to find out who truly owns some property. Write your assembly member and state senator.

You probably won't find yourself on file at the Secretary of State's office of Limited Liability Companies, because this branch is practically brand new. A limited liability company is sort of a hybrid of a corporation and a partnership. It offers certain tax and liability advantages the others don't have—plus it's very easy to form. You'll find that there is a considerable amount of information available to members of the public. However, when we've called the office, some people have insisted that practically everything on file there is confidential. Their attorneys have assured us, however, that the files are quite open for inspection and copying.

I already told you about the Secretary of State's Notary Public office—remember? Refresher: Notaries are commissioned at this office. The staff here will help you find the notary public who witnessed the signatures on whatever recorded document you found.

The Secretary of State is going to have more information about you—that is if you ever ran for public office, were appointed to any government controlled commission, or had a government job where you had authority to disperse public funds or decide on land usage. These people are required to complete a *Statement of Economic Interest* each year. They must file this declaration at both the local level (where they work) and with the Secretary of State. This is a disclosure designed to prevent conflicts of interest. We wouldn't want the city's purchasing officer to buy computers only from the company in which he owns thousands of shares of stock. On the *Statement of Economic Interest* the person tells the world how much money he or she has in the bank, what stocks they own, what property, what loans they've given out and received, what corporate boards they sit on and what gifts they've received. A great file.

Don't give up your search without visiting the federal agencies. You're likely to show up on U.S. District Court if you've ever been arrested and charged with a federal crime, filed for bankruptcy or been a creditor to someone else who filed for bankruptcy, applied for U.S. citizenship or been a plaintiff or defendant in a civil action in U.S. District Court.

There's another federal court you may have visited—U.S. Tax Court. Anyone who takes their case to this court is offering the public a rare opportunity to look into their personal finances. Otherwise, your income tax files are private.

Other federal agencies with whom you may have had contact? If you have a post office box that you use for business, some of the information on your *Post Office Box Application* is open to the public. Also, *Bulk Mail Permits* and *Metered Mail* information can be traced back to you or your company.

If you're a former member of the armed services, your file is probably housed at the National Personnel Records Center in St. Louis. You're also on file with the branch of the military you were in—even if you were a reservist or a member of the National Guard. Even if you were a civilian employee for the federal government, your personnel file is kept at another office in St. Louis.

The Federal Election Commission keeps track of money you contributed to people running for federal office. The Federal Aviation Administration in Oklahoma City has information about the plane you may own or about your pilot's license. The Federal Communications Commission keeps track of your *Radio Operator's License*. If you are a big wheel in a publicly held corporation, you may be able to read about yourself in the files of the Securities and Exchange Commission. And finally, when you die, the Social Security Administration will gladly tell anyone who calls their toll-free number exactly when you died and where you were buried.

If you were to actually conduct the search I've just outlined, you would have more than enough experience to be hired by any attorney or private investigator as a field investigator. You would have more public records experience than ninety percent of government investigators, half the private investigators and probably half the journalists in California.

On many occasions I've found, in public record files, information about people that they, themselves didn't even know. In a demonstration of public records I was the first to inform a police lieutenant that her husband had filed for divorce against her many years before. Apparently he never served her with the papers and she never found out. In another demonstration I located the father-in-law of a student I was back grounding. He had died 13 years earlier of alcohol-related problems. His death certificate indicated he had died at his place of residence—a downtown Los Angeles homeless mission. Before disclosing this to the rest of the class, I called the student and asked her if she had any problems with me discussing her father-in-law.

"Heavens no," she replied. "Say anything about him you like. My husband and I don't even know where he is. Haven't seen him in 15 years."

You might just learn something about yourself.
Happy hunting!

Don Ray in Person!
Bring the expert to you!

Things have changed!
New procedures
New Databases
New resources
New Laws
Tips
Strategies

Don Ray only wishes he were this skinny ⇨

Don Ray can train,
He can entertain!
Book 'em today.

Thousands of criminal investigatiors, journalists, private investigators, genealogists and librarians have improved their investigative skills while smiling through Don Ray's lively, humorous and energetic presentations.

To book him, Call (818) THE-NEWS.

The Human Factor
How *your* attitude can set the tone for success.

Just knowing where to find public records will not ensure success. In researching yourself you have a big advantage—you know the existence of most of the material, and you pretty much know where it is. Also, since your name is on all the documents, there should be little resistance on the part of the custodians pf tje recprds to show you those documents.

There will be times, however, when you don't know exactly what you're looking for, where it might be and what it means if you do get your hands on it. At that moment, you will be at the mercy of the government employee behind the counter. And it's that person who can make or break you. Why? Because that person has the power—and you don't.

It's a lot like going to a restaurant and acting like a pompous, demanding ass. I once dined with such a pompous, demanding ass. He's dead now, so I could probably name him. But I won't. In the very unlikely event that someone in the world liked him, I would hate to be so disrespectful as to name him—although as I describe his demeanor, anyone who may have suffered through a restaurant meal with him will surely cringe, grit their teeth and moan in memory of the tortuous experience.

I swear I'll never forget it. As we entered the upscale, Century City restaurant, he interrupted the only-slightly canned greeting by the hostess.

"Good afternoon. Welcome. Will there be just two . . . ?"

He waved off her words as if they were written on a blackboard. "Don't give me that crap," he snapped. "The last time I was here I ordered ice cream for dessert. Instead some idiot brought me some God-awful crap. Listen, I want you to go to the manager right now and find out if they're still serving that cheap, stale, frozen concoction and trying to pass it off as ice cream."

That was just the beginning. The bastard was so bellicose ("bellicose" is similar to "belligerent"—but an educated friend told me "belligerent" applies to agression between two nations. Countries are belligerent, people are bellicose. Bear with me, I only have about a half dozen $10-words and I rarely get a chance to whip them out. Maybe later I'll get to use "ensconced" or "adjure.")—anyway, he was so bellicose that I was afraid to eat *my* food for fear the servers would poison us *both*.

That's what servers can do when you get them angry—they can put stuff in your food. Maybe not poison, but certainly something disgusting. I once worked as a short order cook and I heard stories. In fact, I was once tempted, but I chickened out. But the point is, the server and the cook both have power over you. So don't mess with them! A flight attendant once confessed to me that she had, on several occasions, been forced to "deal with" unruly, drunken, pompous asses by putting one drop of a particular liquid substance in their drink. She claims (and others have confirmed) that one drop of this liquid (which many women keep in their purses for its intended use) will send the person running to the lavatory within an hour and, as she put it, "keep them running for the next 24 hours."

I can tell you that one meal with a pompous, demanding ass was an experience I never want to repeat. I spent more than an hour sitting at the same table as that pitiful little man as he took out all of his self hate on everyone around him. I was embarrased for both of us. I wouldn't be surprised if our waitress never came back to work again. As we left, I pretended to forget something at the table and discreetly slipped the waitress $10 for her pain and suffering.

"You deserve a lot more," I told her. "I'm so sorry."

"Thanks," she said. "But you had to sit with the jerk." In truth, I doubt that she sabotaged his food, but I'm sure many servers have been tempted. I'm sure that if someone would have poisoned him, no jury in the world would have convicted that waiter or waitress.

What most pompous asses don't realize is that the act of snapping one's fingers to get the attention of a server can easily be translated into, "Waiter, please spit in my food!" I cannot in good taste translate for you into English what banging a water glass with a fork means. My message here is *never mess with anyone who handles your food*. While we're at it, *never mess with anyone who handles your anesthesia*. When traveling, *never mess with anyone who handles your luggage*. Ticketing personnel can project the warmest of smiles as they re-route your Las Vegas-bound suitcase to Hong Kong. Don't laugh, it happens every day. In television news we live by the credo: *never mess with anyone who handles your videotape*. And when it comes to investigative research, *never mess with anyone who handles your public record files*.

This is really important. For just a moment, imagine what a day is like in the life of a clerk behind the counter at a government office. Imagine scores of angry, confused, impatient, frustrated and sometimes marginally imbecilic patrons finally locating that typically poorly marked counter in that equally poorly signed building across the street from that war-zone parking structure whose stairwells double at night as men's restrooms. By the time they find the counter they've usually developed a case of PDS *(Patience Deficit Syndrome)*.

The clerk behind the counter has seen it all—dozens of times a day for maybe two decades. He or she may no longer need to or want to look the patron in the eye. The clerk will dutifully retrieve what someone asks him or her to retrieve. And unless the patron asks for more, the clerk will probably not offer more. On the other hand, if the patron manages to press the wrong buttons, the custodian may decide to invoke one or more of the ten unofficial excuses for not finding your file. You won't find these in writing. They've been passed on from bureaucrat to bureaucrat for at least six centuries during secret initiation ceremonies in the back room of some seafood restaurant. Until this very moment, I believe they've never been written down—at least in modern English (I guess I can say good-bye to any chances of ever working for the government again). For the first time ever, here they are:

1. You've come to the wrong office. That file's at the 2nd Street Archives (which, by the way, doesn't exist).

2. The person in charge of that file is off today.
3. You don't have the authority to see that file.
4. I'm on my break. (This one has variations. I once worked at the post office alongside a lazy, but admittedly clever employee. One day a supervisor observed us chatting in the break room for the second time in less than an hour. "Oh, I can explain it," said my associate. "You see, the first time you saw us we were on *his* break. Now we're on *mine!*")
5. That file's checked out. Can you come back next Wednesday?
6. The computer's down.
7. Are you ready to pay the $64 viewing fee?
8. You'll have to fill out this 30-page request form. Please take a seat.
9. It's locked up and we can't find the key.
10. Regresa usted cuando usted pueda entender mi lengua o cuando yo pueda entender la suya.

The last one, of course, may be spoken in any language whether or not the clerk actually speaks that particular language. You may even catch the same clerk switching languages in mid-excuse.

Remember, these government employees are not in any way bad people—they've simply learned how to cope with the astounding number of inconsiderate, demanding and impatient people who make it to their counter. If you approach them warmly and with human kindness, you'll see the other side of them—the side their nieces and nephews see on a good Saturday.

Fortunately, I almost never see the dark side of the people who watch over public records. In fact, most of them are happy to see me coming and are happy to help me find whatever I'm looking for. There are even a few who will call me up and alert me to a particularly interesting file or case that comes up. Many times they dig a little deeper and bring me more than I requested—or simply help me interpret the sometimes confusing documents. It's all because I try to be empathic and try to approach them as friends and allies—not enemies.

It's really not that difficult. Simply imagine that the person behind the counter is your mother's best friend. Look for something about that person you like—something you can comment on, such as "What an interesting watch you're wearing," or "I really like your hair," or "Great necktie!" or "I like your earrings!" Women have told me you can never go wrong by complimenting a woman's earrings—that is unless she's not wearing any (or, God forbid, she has no ears).

If you're out of practice complimenting people you may find it difficult at times. You'll find yourself at times grasping at straws. Be careful! Sometimes your attempted compliment may be taken wrong. Sensitivity is the watchword here. Avoid dangerous comments such as:

"Hey, Buddy, I love the way your bald spot glistens in the light." Or, "I just love your dress. Who says the '70s look is out of style?" Or, "You must never get cold with that extra layer of blubber." Or, "Hey, haven't I seen you on TV? Aren't you the one who played the fat drunk on Cheers?" Or, "I really admire you. How are you able to wear discount jewelry without getting green marks?"

There's a thin line between a compliment—even a slightly exaggerated compliment—and a boldface butt-smooching lie. I think I stretch things the most when I find myself in the position of being referred. Anyone else would hate being referred, but for me it's a chance to give an even bigger compliment with almost total impunity.

It works this way. The clerk in Room 102 tells you she doesn't have the *fictitious name statements* in her files—they're in Room 130. Don't just storm off to Room 130—angry that you're being "sent all over heck on a dang wild goose chase." Instead, gather two important pieces of information that will practically ensure you'll be treated as royalty at the other end. You need to learn the name of the clerk there in Room 102 as well as the name of someone you'll be seeing in Room 130.

I've learned that if you say to a bureaucrat, "What's your name?" there's a good chance he or she will get defensive. "What do you wanna know that for?" they might respond—as if you're about to report them to Edna the Evil Supervisor. It's better to draw their name out with a mild compliment or expression of gratitude. "Oh, the files are in Room 130? Great. Thanks so much, uh—I'm sorry, what's your first name?"

"Amanda. Amanda Baxter." She'll almost always identify herself. Now you have to say her name aloud—people love it when you use their name.

"Amanda. Thanks so much, Amanda."

Now at this point you must execute a *Columbo move*. Just as Lt. Columbo does it, you start to walk away. Then you put your forefinger and index finger to your temple—as if just remembering something—and turn back around to the clerk.

"Oh, uh, Amanda? I almost forgot. Who should I ask for over in Room 130?" The clerk will almost always give you a name.

"Just talk to Bill."

Now you're sizzling. First, do everything in your power to remember the names Amanda and Bill. Now step over to Room 130 with the body language and attitude of someone about to be pampered—because you are. Walk up to the person who most looks like a Bill and say, "Hi, I'm supposed to ask for Bill?" Either that person will be Bill or he'll point Bill out to you.

"I'm Bill," he'll say, slightly wondering how you know his name and wondering maybe if you're someone important or connected. Here's where you conduct magic.

You say something such as "Fantastic! I'm so glad you're here. Amanda over in Room 102 says you know everything there is to know about *fictitious name statements*." Put on your helpless, puppy dog face and look him in the eye. "Could you possibly help me?"

Even if Bill is the nastiest, least competent human on earth, he will not be able to resist accepting the *misinformation* you've been given.

"Well," he'll say modestly but proudly, "I'm not so sure I know *everything*—but tell me what you need and I'll give it a try." I promise you this guy will not rest until he finds the file you want, helps you interpret it and makes you copies. He'll feel so good about himself that he'll etch your image into his brain and forever keep an eye out for that one customer who thinks he knows everything. If you don't believe me, try it.

If it makes you cringe just thinking about doing it, try it on the telephone one time. When someone tries to transfer you, quickly interrupt and say, "Oh, in case I get cut off, what's the number you're sending me to?" And then ask, "And who should I ask for?" They'll have no problem telling you the name of the person at the other end.

Then you just say, "Thanks so much. I really appreciate your kindness, uh . . ." He or she will fill in at least a first or a last name. Then you greet the next person as if they've been described as God's right hand person.

"Is this Judy? Wonderful. I just got off the line with Fred there in your building and he said that if I was really nice to you you'd bend over backwards to help me solve my problem. Can you help me?"

Again, Judy will not be able to resist the chance to be a heroine. Even if everyone in her office knows her as the poster girl for *National Grump Week Magazine*, she'll do cartwheels for the one person dumb enough to think she's helpful.

In explaining this to a classroom of seasoned police investigators, one old-timer volunteered, "Hey everybody, this stuff works! I accidentally discovered it a few months ago at a restaurant where I had the world's worst waitress. She was slow, unresponsive and rude—and she screwed up practically every order she took. She was so bad that simply stiffing her wasn't enough. I even thought complaining to the manager would be useless—almost a cliché to him. All I had left was sarcasm. So when she finally checked back with us, I said, 'You know Mabel, I've been served by a lot of waitresses in my day, but no one compares to you. I've never encountered a waitress as polite, as responsive, as professional as you are. I just want to thank you!'

"I couldn't believe it," he said. "Instead of dumping coffee on me for my snide remark, her nasty old face brightened up, she smiled and said, 'Why thank you, sir. Finally, someone appreciates me!'

"Then, all of a sudden, she actually became the great waitress I had described. I tried it again on another server the next time I went out and it worked the same way. Now I compliment every waiter or waitress before we're too far into the meal. Nowadays, I'm treated like a king!"

Here's a rule of thumb. Put the uniform on someone you want them to wear—and they'll usually slip right into it. If you say, "Hey you lazy government bureaucrat, help me," you're going to see just how slowly an employee can move. On the other hand, you could say, "I'm in need of a miracle. I'm told you're the one person who does miracles here. Could you make one for me?" The person will dive into his desk for a magic wand. Again, try it.

Case Studies
The experts share their winning techniques

Even if you're so experienced that you've already learned the lessons in the case studies that follow, you might read on and possibly pick up a technique or two. You might also find some of the examples a bit interesting.

The Reagan Assassination Attempt

All of the other segment producers in the Arizona newsroom of the weekly news magazine were glued to the television when word hit that someone had shot newly elected President Ronald Reagan. One of the student interns came to me and said, "Don Ray, shouldn't we be looking for some kind of a local angle?" She was right. We sent one student to the courts just in case John Hinckley might have once been arrested or sued in Phoenix. Another student checked the then-open files of the Motor Vehicle Department in the event the young man had once lived in Arizona.

When the networks broadcasted a hometown for John Hinckley, one student immediately dialed for directory assistance in Colorado and quickly found one Hinckley family living there in Evergreen. A quick call to the local library in Colorado resulted in us learning the names and addresses of neighbors to the Hinckleys. This, of course, came from the reverse phone directory (the regular phone book sorted not by name, but by address). Neighbors quickly confirmed that John lived there and that federal officers were, at that moment, converging on the Hinckley home.

Another intern called the Chamber of Commerce and asked about gun shops in Evergreen. Armed with the names of the nearest stores, he called and was able to get confirmation from one gun dealer that Hinckley had, indeed, purchased a gun from that store. The networks were soon saying that Hinckley once attended an Ivy League college. We immediately called the school and, among other things, asked for the name of the school Hinckley transferred from. They confirmed he had come from a Texas university. We quickly called that school, confirmed he had been a student and then asked what his major was. We then called back and asked for the particular department that administered that major. The woman at that office willingly pulled Hinckley's three-by-five information card and read off to us the would-be assassin's Texas address when he was in school there. Again to the library for the reverse directory. One student telephoned the house to the left of Hinckley's old address while I called the house to the right. Another intern called the number now assigned to the house Hinckley once inhabited—you never know, maybe he left threats or something written on the wall.

Unfortunately, the intern reached the new inhabitant of Hinckley's old house a moment before I connected with a neighbor. As the intern was saying, "Hey, that guy who shot President Reagan once lived in the house you're in now," the neighbor was telling me that, yes, Hinckley once lived next door with his sister—his sister who *still lives* in the same house.

Oops! Had we timed it better we may have been able to approach Hinckley's sister with a little more care. She ended up hanging up on my intern. But at the very least, I'm convinced we were the first to find the gun sale information and the first to contact Hinckley's sister.

Tools, tips and techniques that worked: Reference librarians will help you look up addresses in their local reverse directories. Chamber of commerce staffers will help you find local businesses. College and university staffers will often provide personal information about a current or former student. Neighbors will usually provide important details.

Goof-ups: Don't assume the person you're calling is not very close to the person you're investigating.

The Reagans' Secret Mansion

Shortly before President Reagan was to leave office, rumors were darting throughout the news media that some of the Reagans' friends, possibly his inner circle of California friends known as the Kitchen Cabinet, were in the process of buying a Bel Air Estates mansion—a mansion they were going to give as a gift to the retired President and First Lady. This was significant because First Lady Nancy Reagan had been criticized for receiving gifts of expensive furnishings and personal items during the Reagan presidency.

Several news outlets called us with addresses of houses in the Bel Air section of Los Angeles that they believed might be earmarked as possible Reagan retirement homes.

We found that the quickest way to talk to someone who had been inside a particular house—someone likely to talk to us—was to go to City Hall and pull the building permits on the house in question. The building permits would name contractors who had surely worked inside. On two occasions, the contractors clearly knew who was paying for ongoing remodeling work and they also clearly knew who would be occupying the properties—certainly not the Reagans.

Then one day a bureau chief from Cable News Network in Los Angeles called with a vague rumor. According to a source—a source we couldn't question further—an adult man with the last name of Bennett (for privacy purposes, I've changed the name here) told a CNN journalist that his mother had recently sold her Bel Air Estates home to the people who were planning to give it to the Reagans.

We knew neither the first name of Mr. Bennett nor the address of his mother—in fact it was her address we were seeking. It would have been possible to spend days at the County Recorder's Grantor-Grantee section looking at every recent deed transferred by everyone with the name of Bennett. Or we could have knocked on every door in Bel Air Estates. Either approach would possibly have worked. We decided, though, to narrow the search.

Using the *voter registration index*, at that time still available to the public, we searched for everyone with the name of Bennett registered to vote in Bel Air. There were a couple dozen. Then we narrowed the search down to females with a Bennett surname. Now we had only about 18 to look through. Next, we checked the dates of birth and eliminated any of the woman under about 50 years of age—our thinking was that we were looking for someone old enough to have a full-grown son. Now we were down to about ten. Could we narrow it down more?

Remember, the rumor didn't say *Dad* was selling the house—or even *Mom and Dad.* It said *Mom.* Therefore we eliminated any of the ten women whose voting records showed she was living with a Mr. Bennett of similar or greater age, i.e. husbands who were still living in the same household. That left us with five candidates and, of course, their addresses.

With only five addresses, we used a database, in this case Dataquick, to see who the current assessees were for these five properties. We could have also made a trip to the County Assessor's office to accomplish the same thing. If our theory was correct, four of the five addresses were likely to be assessed to people with the name of Bennett. The fifth, we believed, would be newly assessed to someone else—maybe a Kitchen Cabinet Member?

Indeed, four of the five were under the name Bennett. The fifth property had recently changed hands. The new assessee (remember the assessee receives the property tax bill, but isn't necessarily the true owner) was Wall Management, Inc. Who the heck it that?

To find out, we called the California Secretary of State's Corporate Status line. At that time anyone could call in. Now you need an easy-to-obtain account. Over the phone we were authorized to learn the status of the corporation, its address, the president and the Agent for Service of Process (often either the president or an attorney). The president and agent were one in the same—a name we had never heard of. Now we needed to learn the names of the other officers. That information, however was not available over the phone.

We asked for a supervisor and told her that we were close to breaking an important story. Would she bend the rules this one time and manually pull the annual *Statement of Officers* on file there? We promised we wouldn't ask any favors for an entire year. She laughed, marked her next year calendar and pulled the *Statement of Officers.* Just as we had suspected, one of the officers was a prominent Southern California businessman—and well-known member of Reagan's Kitchen Cabinet.

At that point we were convinced. The bureau chief at CNN telephoned the White House press secretary and asked outright. "Is it true that President and Mrs. Reagen are planning to move into a house at 666 St. Cloud Road in the Bel Air Estates section of Los Angeles?" The President's spokesperson could not lie—and soon everyone knew. By the way, the entire search took less than an hour.

An interesting note, Mrs. Reagan reportedly didn't like the satanic connotation of "666" so she had the address changed to "668" instead. There have been several subsequent transferences of deeds regarding the property since the Reagans moved in. From Wall Management, the title was transferred to a trust in the name of an attorney and eventually the owner was listed as the Reagan Family Trust.

Tools, tips and techniques that worked: Planning a more efficient search strategy saved us valuable time. Voter records identified surnames, and addresses that helped us weed out bad leads. Assessor records identified recent sales. The Secretary of State Corporate Status Division helped us learn the names of the people running a corporation. A little groveling sped things up.

Goof-ups: Charging CNN by the hour instead of by the importance of the story. Then again, I never was very good with money.

The Michael Jackson Child Molestation Case

It was early on a Sunday Morning, August 22, 1993 when I received the anonymous call. It sounded as if it was coming from an outdoor pay phone.

"Hey, you might be interested in a couple of search warrants that just went down," the obviously disguised voice said. This type of call is not uncommon, but I wasn't about to get out of bed unless it was more than just a search for drugs or welfare fraud.

"Yeah," I said with as much enthusiasm I could muster up with limited sleep, "what got searched?"

"Neverland."

Forgive me, everyone, for not being more hip. Ask any of my friends and they'll tell you I only listen to Latin music. And I guess I don't read enough of the tabloids or entertainment rags to know or care about the estates of rich rock singers.

"Neverland? What? They searched Peter Pan's place?" Looking back, I was pretty close—but didn't know it.

"You idiot!," my source said in frustration. "Does the term *'moonwalk'* mean anything to you?" I could tell all this should be obvious to me, but I still drew a blank. If only Vanna were around to sell me a vowel.

"Uh, rap music?" I was trying. "Let's see, MTV? Michael Jackson?"

"That's it," the voice confirmed.

"Oh," I said, "Neverland must be that big amusement park or zoo or whatever it is up on the Santa Ynez Valley." All of a sudden this was turning out to be something worth getting out of bed for. "What were they looking for?"

"He's suspected of being a child molester, I think," the source said. He also said he heard someone had also searched Michael Jackson's Century City condominium. If you're a member of the news media, you'll understand this next part. If you're not, you probably won't believe we actually go so far to check things out before we print or broadcast it. You see, it was obvious my source didn't want to be identified. I now had to start looking for independent sources who would confirm or correct the story.

"Wait," I said. "Before you hang up—do you know of anyone else who would know about all this?"

"Well, I understand they had to use a locksmith to get into parts of the compound." With that, he hung up.

I was in Los Angeles County. The search took place in Santa Barbara County about a hundred miles to the northwest. It seemed to me that whoever searched the place probably called on a local locksmith. If the libraries would have been open I'd have called the reference desk and asked them to grab the yellow pages. The next best thing was to call my brother-in-law in Santa Barbara. He called a friend of his over the hill in the Santa Ynez Valley. I soon had the names and phone numbers of five locksmiths in the general area who advertised a 24-hour phone number.

The first one was disconnected. A woman answered the second number I called.

"Hi. I'd like to talk to the locksmith who was in Neverland this morning." I was fishing.

"That would have to be Duane," she said matter-of-factly. "I'll see if I can find him."

A moment or two later a man's voice came on the line.

"This is Duane. Can I help you?" I identified myself as a journalist.

"I understand you were in Neverland this morning."

"Nope," he said. I was about to thank him anyway and move on, but he continued, "It was yesterday. I was in there yesterday."

"Of course, yesterday." Keep in mind, if I would have said, "Were you there with the police?" a "yes" might mean he was confirming something he knew nothing about. I had to get him to say why he was there. "Tell me about it," I said instead.

"Sorry, I can't tell you anything. They told me not to talk about it."

"Who told you not to talk about it?"

"The police." Okay, I thought. We're getting warm here.

"Then who should I talk to about this?" I asked.

"Talk to the police."

"What police?"

"Los Angeles Police," he said. Hmm, I thought. They're not even from Santa Barbara County. Maybe they were part of a state or federal task force.

"Were there people from other departments there?"

"Listen," he said, "just talk with the LAPD, okay? I can't say any more." But I still hadn't gotten him to confirm why he was there.

"Duane, tell me how you feel about all this," I said.

"Look," he replied, "I like Michael Jackson—and so whatever it was they were looking for, I hope they didn't find it."

Looking for? As in *searching*? Like maybe a *search warrant*? That was enough for me. I then took my story to Kenny Boles, the then managing editor at KNBC-TV News in Burbank. He brought me on board to work the story with his news team. Eventually the Santa Barbara Sheriff's deputies confirmed the existence of the search warrant. The security people at Jackson's Century City condominium confirmed that a slew of police had entered Jackson's unit. And LAPD's spokesman confirmed they were involved in a criminal investigation regarding Michael Jackson. But they wouldn't confirm the searches or the nature of the investigation.

KNBC-TV broke the story the next day, Monday afternoon, saying only that we had confirmed two search warrants had been served on Jackson properties—nothing was said about child molestation. Apparently the spokesperson for Michael Jackson didn't see the broadcast and assumed KNBC reporters had divulged the nature of the investigation. He then appeared for an interview for a later newscast. He came forward saying the child molestation claims against his client were really nothing more than an extortion attempt.

Needless to say, when he divulged the child molestation allegations, the mass media worldwide dropped what they were doing and spent the next year or so demonstrating just how journalistically low they could go. It would take the O.J. Simpson murder case to divert their attention.

Tools, tips and techniques that worked: Carefully working sources is a skill that requires practice. Remember to always ask the question, "who would know?" It worked here. The same principle applies to finding someone, *anyone*, in another part of the country to help you. If I hadn't known someone in Santa Barbara, I might have dialed a number at random in the Santa Ynez Valley and asked whoever answered to open up their yellow pages. Questioning a reluctant source requires care. If you put words in their mouth, you may have lost the confirmation you were seeking. Asking too much could turn them off even more. Asking not enough can limit you. Then, armed with a little information, it's important to know how to use it to get more information.

Goof-ups: If I were to do it over, I'd demand that I be the segment producer or even the reporter who would break the story. It took a long time for my colleagues in the media to learn that I initially broke the story. I've since been told I could have asked for upwards of $50,000 for the story. In another life maybe. In this life I'm a journalist and not a story broker. I still stand by my policy that I don't sell story ideas—I only get paid to write or produce stories.

The Tale of the Traveling Salesman

Alicia worked in Los Angeles as a ticketing agent for a major airline. She had on several occasions chatted with a salesman we'll call Rudy who often commuted from the San Francisco Bay area. Although he had hinted about seeing Alicia socially, she avoided any kind of a commitment.

Then one day a bouquet of flowers arrived at her counter, along with card from Rudy. It said he was coming to Los Angeles the next day and that he would like very much to take her to dinner. But something about his demeanor bothered Alicia—she had a hunch he was otherwise attached. She skimmed through her copy of *A Public Records Primer and Investigator's Handbook*—a copy the adoptee had earlier purchased to help her locate and identify her birth parents—and decided she'd use her new skills to check out her salesman suitor.

Since she was already in Los Angeles, she checked the local records first and found that Rudy had been married in Los Angeles County some fifteen years earlier to a woman named Barbara. She was thorough enough to learn he had divorced Barbara after seven years of marriage.

Next, she used the telephone to check him out in the Bay area. At that time it was possible to verify voter registration over the phone. She first confirmed he was living and voting at a certain address. She then asked for the names of other voters in that household. The registrar told her there was a woman named Denise, with the same last name as Rudy, voting there—and Denise was two years younger than Rudy. Possible sister? Maybe not.

Alicia then called the County Recorder up there and found the marriage record between Rudy and Denise. She made note of the place of employment Rudy listed on the certificate. She was thorough enough to look for divorces, but there were none on record.

Next, Alicia called the County Assessor to learn that Rudy and Denise were both listed as assessees of the house at the address where they voted.

Still not convinced that maybe the two were separated, she called Rudy's place of employment and simply asked for an "employment verification."

"Yes, Rudy still works here," the person at the other end of the phone said. "And in fact," she volunteered, "his wife Denise works here also."

When Rudy arrived the next day, he came to Alicia's counter and asked if she'd made up her mind. Would she go out with him?

"It depends on your answer to one question," she told him. "Rudy, answer me honestly. Are you married?"

"Of course I'll be honest with you, Alicia," he said. "Yes, I am married, but you need to know that I haven't even talked to my wife Barbara for six years."

Rudy could have passed a polygraph exam with that *technically true* answer. And any other woman might have fallen for his deception.

"Well of course you haven't talked to Barbara for six years—you divorced her seven years ago. But what about your wife Denise?"

Rudy dined alone that evening.

Tools, tips and techniques that worked: Alicia was smart to look for nearby records—even though she knew Rudy was currently living far away. Her telephone demeanor enhanced her ability to gather vital information. She was thorough enough to have the County Recorder read to her *all* the information listed on the marriage certificate.

Goof-ups: Some would suggest that Alicia might have been a bit more creative in the way she revealed her knowledge of Rudy's marital status. Some have suggested she might have found a creative way to use the airport's public address system to communicate with Rudy—but that's not in Alicia's nature.

The Official in Possession

Sometimes, despite the best efforts of law enforcement and the news media, important people surface unscathed from an investigation, despite overwhelming evidence of improprieties. The following is a true story, although I've changed the names and some specific identifiable details. The principle and the lessons, however, remain the same.

A burglary victim discovered a custom-made ring that had been stolen from him in the possession of the brother of a prominent public official. When police confronted the official, he explained that he, himself, had purchased the ring and had given it as a gift to his brother. He insisted he hadn't known it was stolen. From whom did he buy the ring? From some guy named "Eddie"—a guy he was introduced to at a local donut shop, Klark's House 'O Donuts. The official told police he walked to Eddie's house a couple of blocks from the donut shop—but he couldn't remember the street or anything else.

After looking through his copy of *A Public Records Primer and Investigator's Handbook*, the police investigator went to the *fictitious names index* at the office of the County Clerk. He first ran the company name, Klark's House 'O Donuts through the index sorted by company (or fictitious) name. He pulled the original Fictitious Name Statement and discovered that Klark's House 'O Donuts was a sole proprietorship owned by Klark Kabutsksan (can you tell I'm carefully making up fictitious names of my own?). The home address listed for Klark Kabutsksan was nowhere near the house described by the public official who had gone there to purchase the property that turned out to be stolen.

The police investigator then ran the name Klark Kabutsksan through the fictitious names index sorted by the names of the true owners. By doing this, he found four other fictitious name companies owned by Klark Kabutsksan. All four were pawn shops. Hmm. Interesting.

Then the investigator pulled the hard copies of those four Fictitious Name Statements. While two of the pawn shops were sole proprietorships owned by Klark Kabutsksan, the other two were partnerships. And both of the partnerships consisted of Klark Kabutsksan and Eddie Kabutsksan. You guessed it! Eddie listed his home address and it was, coincidentally, a couple of blocks from the donut shop.

The investigator also noted that the four pawn shops were strategically situated far from each other—in the four corners of the county. Four pawn shops and a donut shop? The investigator immediately saw the possibility that the pawn shops were taking in stolen property and then laundering the profits through the donut shop—a perfect cash-oriented laundering outlet. Could it be the public official was being bribed with valuable stolen property?

Our investigator decided to compare the city taxes paid by Klark's House 'O Donuts with a similar donut shop on a nearby street—a donut shop that seemed to have about the same amount of foot traffic. If his theory was correct, he'd find Klark's House 'O Donuts was paying much more in city sales taxes—an indicator that Klark Kabutsksan was running a lot of non-donut cash through the donut shop. While the City Clerk's tax files are not public, the investigator had no trouble enlisting the assistance of the clerk. He turned out to be right.

Tools, tips and techniques that worked:. The *fictitious names index* is a great place to check if you suspect someone may be involved in some shady business practice. Often, a scamster will have a history of opening numerous fictitious name companies. Sometimes, the flakier the person, the more fictitious name companies the person has owned. Also, always remember to cross check any names you find in any file. Here, it resulted in identifying a suspect and uncovering a possible fencing and bribery operation.

Goof-ups: The public official is still firmly ensconced (I *knew* I'd get a chance to used that word) in his cushy public office—despite the good efforts of investigators and the news media. I'm not sure if it's a goof-up or a sad fact of life—a corrupt person with power can easily use that power to thwart almost any attempt to unseat him.

The Secret Witness

While investigating a major anti-trust case, we heard that an angry, former employee of one of the accused corporations had spilled the beans to federal authorities and then gone into hiding. We first looked for lawsuits against the corporation. We found another disgruntled former employee who didn't know the name of the secret witness, but who was happy to give us a copy of the corporation's internal phone directory. It didn't take long to call everyone listed in the department we assumed the witness had worked. We accounted for everyone except one—Barnett Whistleblower (I know it's subtle, but this, also, is not a real name). When we called his former office asking for him, the personnel there denied he'd ever worked there. Now we *knew* we were on the right track.

Our former employee friend was familiar with Mr. Whistleblower and told us the man had a brother on the Des Moines, Iowa Police Department. It took only two calls to zero in on Sgt. B. Randolf Whistleblower.

"My brother and I are not very close," he said when we reached him, but I have an address for him in Atlanta.

There was no phone number listed for Barnett Whistleblower in Atlanta, so we called the public library and asked the reference librarian to look up the address in the reverse telephone directory. Turns out it was a condominium complex with about 60 names listed—none of them Whistleblower. We didn't have time to send a telegram—we needed to reach him on the phone. We knew there would be an office or manager or association or something that would have a list all of the condominium owners and their phone numbers, but we also knew it would be against the association rules for anyone to give out a phone number—after all, we have to protect our members.

Now watch the logic here. We asked the reference librarian to give us at least a dozen names and numbers of people with listed phones in the condo complex. When the first person answered, we politely asked for the number of the association. She gave it to us with no problem. Then we kept dialing the other numbers. When anyone answered, we apologized and said we had dialed the wrong number. Finally, we found what we were looking for—a number that was disconnected "and there's no new number." The number had belonged to a Buster Boondogle.

Now we called the association—knowing they would go to any length to protect anyone we were looking for.

"Hi, I'm trying to get a new phone number for my old pal Buster Boondogle. Apparently he moved away."

"I'm sorry, but we can't give out any information about your friend. It's our policy," the woman said.

"But Buster always lists his phone number. It's clear he wants people to reach him. I just don't know what city he moved to."

"Sorry, sir," she repeated.

"Well, when I was there visiting him he introduced me to his friend, a neighbor. *He'd* give me Buster's phone number! Trouble is I can't find the business card he gave me."

"What's the neighbor's name?" she asked.

"Whistleblower, Barney Whistleblower."

"Barnett Whistleblower? Okay, here's *his* number. If *he* wants to give you Mr. Boondogle's number, that's *his* business!"

When we called Whistleblower he was astounded.

"How the hell did you find me? The FBI's been looking for me for two years. How did *you* do it?"

Tools, tips and techniques that worked:. To get information about what goes on inside any organization (or family), look for *victims and enemies*. In this case, court records led us to one such enemy who helped us in a couple of ways. Family members will often hand you information on a silver platter. People with the job of protecting information can sometimes be lulled into protecting the wrong information. In this case, the person with the information was bent on protecting Boondogle and inadvertently gave up Whistleblower's number.

Goof-ups: We did this story in 1980. I'm not sure I'd do the same thing today. Before I ever endorse even the slightest deception I hold all the elements up to a stringent balancing test. Does the importance of the information I need clearly outweigh the potential ramifications of the deception itself? In this case, I knew Whistleblower might be willing to talk—and he was. I also knew that the association employee would not suffer because she released the information. I certainly wasn't going to turn her in. And, of course, I would never tell Whistleblower how I got his number.

The Infant Snitch

Detective Frank Dickey of the East Bay Regional Park Police was investigating a burglary. Witnesses told of a man and a woman driving away from the scene. Detective Dickey distributed a flier that included the descriptions of the couple and the car. A citizen was able to provide Dickey with a license plate number.

The plate came back to a woman living outside the nearby town of Richmond. Dickey and his partner paid a visit to the registered owner—but she did not fit the description of his female suspect. The woman did, however, tell the detectives she had recently sold the vehicle in question to her sister. She identified her sister but could only say the woman was living with a boyfriend somewhere in Oakland and that the couple had recently had a baby.

The detectives ran the sister's name through law enforcement computers and discovered she had an extensive criminal record—including arrests for robbery, burglary, grand theft, prostitution, drugs and assault with a deadly weapon. She was on probation, but no one knew a good address for her and no one knew the name of her boyfriend.

"At this point," Dickey recalls, "my investigation leads on identifying the boyfriend had come to a stop. I then recalled a class I'd taken on public records sources and decided to try to get the boyfriend's name from the birth certificate of the child recently born to the female suspect."

Detective Dickey called upon the female suspect's sister once again and learned the approximate date the child was born, it's sex and the hospital in which the girl was born.

He then went to the office of the County Recorder and looked at the birth certificate. And, indeed, the mother had dutifully named the child's father—the man who turned out to be the male suspect.

Tools, tips and techniques that worked:. Detective Dickey was able to turn what could have been a hostile family member into an ally. His manner with her encouraged her to talk and thereby provide information that would ultimately lead to a solution to the mystery. By checking something as obscure as a birth certificate, he was able to identify his suspect.

Goof-ups: The detective's only mistake was not making note the first time of the information about the newborn. You never know when a vital record may be your only good lead.

The Secret Witness II

This one is similar to the earlier Secret Witness story, but a different technique. This time we were working with retired Postal Inspector Boyd Manes on a case he didn't get permission to complete while he was a federal investigator. ABC's 20/20 had hired us to find a link between some seemingly small-time crooks and another group suspected of raising money for Middle Eastern terrorists.

The one person who could connect the two was a former informant, I'll call him Harry Mole, who had allowed federal investigators to wire him for sound and send him undercover. Following his assignment, however, he had disappeared.

All we knew about the man was his name and the fact he had been in the San Bernardino area a few years back. It was 8 p.m. as we sat in Boyd's home contemplating how (not if) we'd find Mr. Mole. Of course there were few government offices open at that hour, but I had with me the microfiche indices of the voter registration records for San Bernardino as well as Riverside counties. At that time, anyone could purchase the indices. After calling the night desk of the Department of Motor Vehicles (available to law enforcement and journalists with paid accounts) and finding no record of Harry Mole, we looked him up in the San Bernardino County voter index and found an address and phone number for him. The number was disconnected. We could have eventually driven to his old address and chatted with former neighbors, but we decided to run his name through the Riverside County. Why? Because we had the index.

Bingo! We found an even more recent address and phone number for him in Riverside, but again, the number was disconnected. Again, before considering driving to the Riverside address to knock on doors, we decided to look for other people with the same last name. Sure enough, there was another Mole listed—a woman with the first name of Mary, same address, same phone, close to the same age. A wife maybe?

Now we decided to backtrack. We called DMV again, this time providing Mary's name and date of birth. We scored. Mary was living in a quiet neighborhood near Sacramento. We called the local library up there and asked the reference librarian to check the reverse directory. He gave us the name and phone number of the next-door neighbor. We called and asked the neighbor to deliver a message to Harry Mole.

Twenty minutes later Harry called us. When he found out why we were looking he said, "You guys are good. I've managed to elude both the Feds and the terrorists for over a year now. How'd you find me?"

Tools, tips and techniques that worked:. It turned out to be a wise investment to buy microfiche copies of public record indices. Checking even unlikely areas paid off in this case. An advantage of microfiche over databases is that it's easier to visually scan for nearby names that are different, but similar. If you ask a computer to find the name "Anderson", it will pay no more attention to "Andersen" that it will to "Ziglar". In this case, we found the wife. We were wise to retrace our foot steps using the new name we had discovered. Reference librarians, reverse directories and a non-threatening demeanor with strangers helped us zero in on our subject. The entire search took 25 minutes.

Goof-ups: The only mistake we made was not starting the investigation sooner. The correspondent with whom we were working quit working at 20/20 shortly thereafter and, as a result, the story was canceled.

The Family Photo Fiasco

On a stormy and rainy spring morning in the mid 1970s, a couple of years before I would become an investigative reporter, a friend talked me into helping him move an old piano from an estate sale in Highland Park to his house in South Pasadena. After struggling to load the old upright into the cheap trailer my friend had rented, I went back into the cluttered old house where the estate sale was being held to wash my hands.

While inside, I noticed the most beautiful family photograph album sitting on an old coffee table. When I opened the velvet-covered relic, I marveled at the collection of quality portraits of various family members. Some of the portraits certainly dated back to before the turn of the century. I was especially intrigued with one particular image of a young woman with long dark curls. She was holding a bouquet in her left hand and leaned with her right hand on a credenza. Her white cotton dress flowed down below her knees, exposing her fine, laced-up shoes. Her eyes and smile were playful yet confident—almost flirtatious.

"Twenty dollars!" The woman handling the sale startled me.

"Is this the woman who just passed away?" I asked.

"Probably," she said. "You can have it for twenty dollars."

"You're not actually selling this, are you?" It was more a statement than a question. "It's a shame to have these wonderful pictures leave the family."

"She's a distant relative. She was very old, she was blind and lived here by herself for years. She had no close family," she said. "No one even knows who most these faces are."

"But surely there's some family member who would treasure this album," I argued.

"No. No one wants it. Do you want to buy it?"

I decided it would be a sin for the family members to be separated—even in the form of photos. So I bought the album, took it home and put it in a box—not knowing exactly what I'd do with it. Before I left, I begged the woman to identify anyone in the album. She looked again at the young woman pictured in the Victorian dress and speculated more confidently that she was probably Leta Sherred, the woman who had just died. Then she concluded that a young man in many of the portraits must be the woman's brother, Rudell. As she guessed at the identities of a few others, I quickly scribbled on a piece of paper, tore out the names and tucked them behind the selected photographs. I took the album home and put away in a box.

Fast forward 10 years or so. Now I'm an investigative reporter with gobs of people-searching experience. One day I happened to be searching for something in an old box and I came across that old collection of photographs.

"I knew there was a reason I bought that old album," I said to myself. "Now I'll be able to find someone related to the people in the pictures—someone who'll treasure such an heirloom. But how do I find a family member?" In looking at the torn pieces of paper slipped behind some of the photographs, I was not sure of the spelling. I pulled some of the pictures from their pockets and found writing on the backs of some. On some were written the name Sherred. On others it was Shirrid and on others still is was Sherrid. But what I also noticed was that most of the portraits were made by photographers in Woodstock, Ontario, Canada and in Michigan. Maybe that Sherred family member I was seeking was in Canada.

I called around and finally found a most helpful person, Mrs. Susan V. Start. She worked in the local history department of the Woodstock Public Library and Art Gallery. She immediately dove in and checked her records for Sherreds, Sherrids and Shirrids in her area. I photocopied each portrait and transcribed any notes on the back sides and sent them to her. Unfortunately, she could find no one still living near Woodstock she could identify as being closely related.

However, she was able to find clippings from the local Woodstock newspaper from 1922 that made reference to the death in Highland Park, California, of former Woodstock resident J.A. Sherred. It indicated he was survived by his wife, a son named Rudell and a daughter, Leta O.I. And for an added bonus, it indicated the family's actual street address.

I drove there and instantly recognized the house I'd been to on that rainy day years ago. Neighbors still remembered Leta had lived there, alone and in solitude, for many years.

The County Assessor's office is only about five miles from Highland Park so I drove there and checked the old tax roles for that particular address. Indeed, Leta Sherred had been listed as the assessee until her death. I impatiently scurried over to the County Clerk's office to look up Leta Sherred in the *probate file index*.

Her full name showed up as Leta Olive Irene Sherred. In the file, the closest relatives listed were cousins living in various places on the West Coast. I went home and methodically called each cousin. I described for them the album I wanted to give away and asked who might be the best candidate in the family—someone who would surely treasure this fine collection of photographs. Nobody I talked with had any interest whatsoever in the album, but two of them mentioned the name of one woman who seemed to know more about the family than others.

Excitedly, I called her.

"Hello, my name is Don Ray. I have in my possession the most beautiful old family album filled with pictures of your relatives and I'm anxious to place it in the hands of a family member who'll treasure it, take care of it and ensure it stays in the family."

"I'm sorry, but we're not interested in buying any family album," she said, obviously mistaking me for some genealogical mercenary.

"Oh, no," I laughed out loud, "I'm not trying to sell it—I want to give it to you!"

"Nope," she insisted. "Not interested." Then she paused for a moment. "Say, are you that guy who came to the estate sale years ago and tried to convince me to not sell the family album? I told you then and I'm telling you again, we're not interested!"

Needless to say, I still have the album. Unless this story leads to me finding someone in the family who seems to care, I'll be donating it to the Woodstock Public Library and Art Gallery.

Tools, tips and techniques that worked: Enlisting the help of a reference librarian will often produce great results. Old newspaper clips led me to the address I needed. Assessor's records led me to the name of the former owner and eventually to her probate file. The probate file provided me with a map of the family.

Goof-ups: Had I been an investigative reporter at the time I purchased the album, I would have known to make note of the address of the woman who had died—along with more specific information about her. Obviously I erred in my belief that someone, *anyone*, in a family would want to preserve the images of family members and ancestors.

Pssst!

Got a great story that needs to be told?

You're in luck. There's an investigative reporter who'd love to hear from you. And he'll handle everything.

Even if you remain anonymous.

Don Ray
P.O. Box 4375
Burbank, CA 91503-4375
(818) THE-NEWS

Ps. I never give up my sources!

How to Use This Book

This book is separated into two general sections. One section provides you with information about the kinds of records available at various government offices and other semi-public outlets. The other section lists thousands of the addresses and telephone numbers of the offices in practically every city and large town in California.

"No more voice mail hell. With A Public Records Primer and Investigator's Handbook *at your fingertips, it will be the person you want who puts you on hold."* (This endorsement is courtesy of Michael G. Schott, private investigator and paralegal.)

Even if you're familiar with the functions of most government offices, you should keep this book handy at your desk or in your brief case, purse or car. It's when you're far from your office and have an unpredicted need for information that this book will save your day.

"You're in a strange land. Vern and Goob at the fillin' station can't steer you to the courthouse. You reach for A Public Records Primer and Investigator's Handbook *before the other extras from* Deliverance *show up."* (Another jewel submitted by Michael Schott. I couldn't decide which of the three he sent me I should put on the cover. I played it safe on the outside so you'd buy this book. I saved the outrageous stuff for the inside—*after* you've plunked down your $18.95. I'm learning.)

In general, if you need a specific piece of information—a person's date of birth, address assets, for example—you should first check the index. The listings there will point you toward the various government offices or other resources that may list the information you need. When you've determined which agency or level of government you need to call, write or visit, you can then look for that particular office in one of the sections that list the specific offices according to level of government—*i.e.* federal, state, county, municipal.

Most information is generally found at the county level. If you know the city of the person or company you're investigating, first look it up in the *Municipalities* section starting on page 131. There, you'll likely find the addresses and phone numbers of city hall, the police department, the library, the local chamber of commerce and the daily newspaper. The listing will also tell you the county in which the city is located. Switch now to the *County Records* section starting on page 223. Here you'll be able to learn the addresses and phone numbers of the county clerk, tax assessor, registrar of voters, recorder of deeds, sheriff, county library and every superior and municipal court.

If you've done a thorough enough job of gathering information from the city and county level, turn now to the *State Offices* section starting on page 89 to find where to call, write or visit for even more information.

The *Federal* section, starting on page 113, includes U.S. Government listings not only in California, but in other parts of the country that may have information relevant to your investigation.

And the always-popular *Other Resources* section, starting on page 73, will provide you with other valuable repositories of information as well as the names and phone numbers of living, breathing experts you can hire to do specific work for you.

Non-Governmental Resources

Telephone Directory/Reverse Directory—They're not really public records, but the first place you should look for personal information. Reverse (criss-cross) directories are phone listings sorted by address or telephone number. They generally include only listed phones. It's a great way to get in immediate touch with neighbors of people who have unlisted phones. It also allows you to learn the names of other people at a given address.

You'll be amazed to learn just how helpful neighbors can be, as long as you approach it with the proper attitude. Most neighbors are going to be more protective about their next door neighbor than about themselves. I make it a point to *never* ask anyone for a neighbor's phone number. Many times the neighbor will volunteer the information, but I never ask for it.

If I use the name of the person I'm calling and let them know I'm having trouble getting in touch with their neighbor they'll usually help out. I always apologize for bothering them and talk in a very chatty, open manner. I end up asking the person I call if they'll run next door and give my number to their neighbor. They almost always will.

An amazing thing—in the million years or so I've been using reverse directories *no one* has ever asked me how I learned their name, phone number or how I knew they lived next door to the person I needed to reach. I imagine they all scratched their heads a few hours later and said, "Wait a minute! How did he know?"

Reverse directories are generally for sale or lease. You can also find them at most local libraries, city newspaper offices, realty offices, chambers of commerce, television stations and police departments.

Many of the investigators and journalists I've trained make extensive use of reverse directories published by Haines and Company Inc. (see *Other Resources* section, page 73). For a long time I was incorrectly using one feature of the Haines directory. I've encountered a few others have also misinterpreted the "Age of Listing" code that may appear to the right of the phone number. It's a one-digit code that designates the last digit of the year that number was first listed in the directory. If you see a "9" following the phone number it *doesn't* mean the phone has been listed there for nine years—it actually means the phone was probably first listed in 1989. If you're looking for someone in an apartment building or neighbor who has been there a long time, look for a listing with no "Age of Listing" code. That means they've probably been there more than 10 years. Finally, if there's a plus sign preceding the "Age of Listing" code, it means the phone was first listed within the year prior to the publication of the directory. For example, "+4" means the phone was first listed in 1994

Remember that libraries also keep copies of telephone directories for their areas and sometimes other areas. Reference librarians (if treated nicely) will often go the extra mile for you and look up things in the yellow pages. Most telephone directory assistance operators will *not* look up yellow pages for you.

If all else fails, here's a great technique. Call up *anyone* in the city in which you need information. There's a phone book in almost *every* household. You'll be amazed how many people will look something up for you. I once needed to find a particular person with a common last name in a medium-sized city in Spain. The information operator would not help. I asked for three numbers of *anyone* with the last name in question. Then I called one of them and had *them* look through the long list of names in the phone book. Eventually, they led me to the person I was searching for.

News Media Resources—Why not check to see if someone has already done the work for you? There are several easy ways to gain access to newspaper or magazine articles and transcripts or tapes of

television and radio broadcasts that may contain vital information about your search subject. Most large libraries maintain indices of metropolitan newspapers such as *The Los Angeles Times Index*. Almost all libraries also maintain complete sets of *Reader's Guide to Periodic Literature*.

Many data bases offer on-line access to numerous newspaper and magazine stories from around the United States or the world. If all else fails, call the library or *morgue* at the daily newspaper nearest the area in which you have an interest. Many will search their files for stories about your subject. Also, consider others who may have had an interest in clipping stories on your subject. The late activist Abbie Hoffman told me how he tapped into the best news clipping service in the country—the FBI. He said he regularly filed Freedom Of Information Act requests for copies of any stories the FBI clipped regarding him.

More and more transcripts of television and radio broadcasts are being offered. Contact the producers of programs such as *60 Minutes* for information about transcripts and tapes. Many are published in bound form and are at larger libraries. Also, databases such a *Nexis* provide full text, on-line searches.

Libraries are listed in the municipalities section, Appendix A starting on page 131 and in the County Records section, Appendix B starting on page 223. Newspapers are listed in the municipalities section.

ANI Automated Name Index
Intelligence Information Services

Search & Access

- Real Property
- Public Filings
- Criminal
- Address Update
- Recorded Judgments
- Bankruptcies
- Notice of Default
- Recorder General Index
- U.C.C.
- Tax Liens
- Watercraft
- Criss Cross
- Board of Equalization
- Statewide Searches
- Multi-County Searches

- Corporations
- Civil Index
- DBAs
- SSN Trace
- LTD Partnerships
- Surname Scan
- Pilots License
- Sales Tax Lic.
- 10Ks
- Nat'l Death
- Business Info
- Aircraft Reg.
- Professional Licenses
- Custom Searches
- Full Text News

& More

You may not find it cost effective to research and learn which sources are the most suitable for your needs. Let Automated Name Index (ANI) be your intelligence network link.

Experienced Information Professionals

P.O. Box 813, Glendale CA 91209
(818) 637-8625   FAX (818) 637-8630

Public Resource Databases
On-line and CD ROM resources.

There are several ways to approach an investigation. If you have unlimited time, you can manually search for any public records files you might need. If you have unlimited money but limited time, you can subscribe to every public records database. For a smaller investment you can buy a CD-ROM reader for your computer and pick up a few key CD-ROM databases and search without the on-line fees. Or, if you have limited time and limited money, it might be better to pay someone else to do the search for you.

This chapter lists a few of the more popular commercial databases and CD-ROM databases. If you'd rather contract out your work, take a look in the Other Valuable Resources, Chapter 8, starting on page 73.

In case all this sounds like a foreign language to you, it's not all that difficult. A *commercial database* is a collection of data housed in someone else's computer—someone who is willing to let you tap into the information—for a price. The way you get into their computer is through your own personal computer and the use of a Modem. *Modem* is actually an acronym of sorts that stands for *mo*dulator/*dem*odulator. It turns computer data into sounds that can travel over phone lines and then turns the sounds back into computer data at the other end.

You pay for the data in a number of ways—a monthly subscription fee, a per-minute charge or a per-line charge. Sometimes it's a combination of all three. When you talk to the sales representatives for the commercial databases, make sure they explain all possible fees they charge. The advantage of using a commercial database is that the provider keeps the files up to date and you pay only for what you use (except monthly fees).

A *CD-ROM* (*C*ompact *D*isk-*R*ead-*O*nly *M*emory) database is one you buy and then put into your personal computer when you need the information. The information is stored on a compact disk (CD) that looks (and is) exactly like the ones you use for music. The difference is, instead of music sounds, this CD stores random data. You're computer sorts the data based upon the criteria you present it. The advantage is you can search to your heart's content and not have to pay any more than the original cost of the CD. The down side is the information cannot update itself—you have to buy a new CD every so often.

CDB Infotek has dozens of on-line databases for California including fictitious business name indices, criminal, civil and probate court indices and marriage indices. CDB also offers a number of nationwide services such as the individual Address Update, which provides an individual's most current address, Social Security number and year of birth based on credit profiles. Other nationwide services include Telephone Reverse Directory, DMV driving records, bankruptcy filings, FAA pilot and aircraft records OSHA violations and business profiles.

CDB Infotek
6 Hutton Centre
Santa Ana, 92707
(800) 427-3747, Fax (714) 708-1000

IRSC, Information Resource Service Company, likewise provides criminal, civil filings in California, as well as federal criminal, civil and bankruptcy filings. Need to check out property or marriage records, a fictitious business names or UCC filing? IRSC has a database for the job. Other IRSC services include individual and asset searches, business profiles and partial access to voter registration and DMV data.

    IRSC
    3777 North Harbor Blvd.
    Fullerton, CA 92635-1300
    (800) 640-4772

Info AmeriCall offers some basic services for California such as court and other records, but for only a few California counties. The firm also has access to aircraft and boat registration records.

    Info AmeriCall
    (800) 532-9876

Dataquick limits its information to real estate records—and it does the job quite well. It allows the investigator to search for information on property based on the name of the assessee (usually the owner), the street address or the assessor's file number. As I write this, the monthly subscription fee is still $50. The on-line charges are reasonable. It's especially good for California-related investigations because it covers the entire state. Dataquick now offers an extensive CD-ROM collection that includes countywide property data, statewide property records and the actual assessor's parcel maps. And if you're really old fashioned, Dataquick will sell you microfiche indices for the more-populous counties in California.

    Dataquick
    9171 Towne Centre Drive, Suite 600
    San Diego, CA 92122
    (619) 455-6900, Fax: (619) 455-6173

Standard & Poor's Register On-line is available on the DIALOG on-line service. The two DIALOG files, File 527 and File 526 offer information that can occasionally be just what the investigator needs. File 527 is S&P's Register—Corporate Database. It includes business information on more than 55,000 companies. That includes virtually all publicly held companies as well as privately owned companies with annual sales of $1 million or more or with 50 or more employees. This powerful tool can help you quickly identify a large business and get quick leads as to who's owning it and who's running it. File 526 contains vital biographical information on more than 70,000 top-level executives in the United States. This information is available in S&P's books, but if you don't want to buy all the books and the updates and don't want to trek off to the library, this could be the cat's meow.

> Standard & Poor's Corporation
> 25 Broadway
> New York, NY 10004
> (800) 237-8552
> On-line Customer Support (212) 208-8429

Lexis-Nexis, a division of Mead Data Central, is the legal and newspaper database of all databases. In the past few years it has jumped, feet first, into the world of public records. First a refresher on the newspapers. The Nexis database is the most powerful newspaper, magazine, wire service, broadcast script and newsletter resource anywhere. And although the searches can be expensive, an experienced researcher can get in and out fairly quickly and inexpensively. What makes Nexis so great is that most of the stories in its system can be searched in the full-text mode. That means it will find names of people even if the name never shows up in the body of the story. If the name shows up in headlines, sub-heads, bylines or even in charts or photograph captions, the computer will find it.

Its California public records capabilities enable you to search property records, recorder information (deeds, deeds of trust and more) for at least 27 counties, Secretary of State corporate information, limited partnerships, Board of Equalization resale permits, fictitious names statements in selected counties, bankruptcy filings, UCC filings, professional licenses, contractors licenses, federal tax liens and state tax liens.

Lexis-Nexis public records information is not limited to California. It can provide you access to indices from every state as well as information about various aspects of other countries.

> Lexis-Nexis
> Mead Data Central
> 9443 Springboro Pike
> P.O. Box 933
> Dayton, OH 45401
> (800) 543-6862, (513) 859-5398

Gale Research Inc. offers several CD-ROM databases that can be useful to investigators. *Companies International* offers information on nearly a quarter-million companies worldwide, other disks include biographies, associations and even directories of CD-ROM databases. Gale Research sells mostly to libraries and therefore charges a lot more than most investigators can afford. However, if you have an unlimited funding, go for it.

> Gale Research Inc.
> P.O. Box 33477
> Detroit, MI 48232-5477
> (800) 877-GALE, Fax: (313) 961-6083

ProPhone puts out The National Telephone Directory on CD-ROM. It includes six CDs that cover most cities in the United States and one CD that lists businesses nationwide. With a little practice you can turn it into a reverse directory. A great tool.

> ProCD, New Media Publishing
> 8 Doaks Lane
> Little Harbor
> Marblehead, MA 01945
> (617) 631-1712, Fax: (617) 631-9299

DATABASE RESOURCES

Merlin Information Services—Here's a great source for public records on CD-ROM. They offer for sale California Statewide Property listings, California Corporations and Limited Partnerships, California UCC Index, Southern California Superior Civil Indexes, Southern California Fictitious Names, California Professional Licenses, California Board of Equalization files, Business names listings, Southern California Criminal Indexes, Social Security Death Records (nationwide), Social Security verification and place of issue, Oregon Drivers Records, Federal Aviation Administration Pilots Licenses, Aircraft Registrations and Aircraft Engine Numbers, National and telephone listings.

Merlin Information Services
3450 Highway 93 South
Kalispell, MO 59901
(800) 367-6646

Other Valuable Resources
Other people or companies who may help you.

Some things are difficult to categorize. What follows are some of **Don Ray's Best Bets**. These are the people, places and services I either use regularly or know to be the best of the best.

Sherman Foundation Library—This is a gold mine of information about Southwest United States. In particular, it houses the most wonderful collection of city directories and telephone directories going back to beginning of such books in California as well as reverse directories for scores of communities going back to the 1950s. Unfortunately, the library is a non-profit foundation open only to its members or walk-in users. They'll do telephone searches for law enforcement, but just don't have the staff to take on genealogical requests. Please don't even ask them! I suggest you become an annual contributor by sending them $35. It will help them buy new directories and maintain the ones that are getting tattered. An easy way to get information without going there is to hire a qualified researcher. See the next listing for the one I use.

Sherman Foundation Library, 614 Dahlia Ave., Corona Del Mar, 92625-2101 (714) 673-1880

Victor Cook—Since the Sherman Foundation Library is not a public facility, your best bet is to contact Victor Cook. There are several good reasons—the most important being he's about the best there is in Orange County at getting information and getting it right and he lives

around the corner from the library and can trot over there in his sleep. He'll charge you $20 an hour for any Sherman Foundation work. Victor has also taken over all of the public records work formerly done by ENG News Service. He works mainly for news media clients at the bargain rate of $50 per hour. He is the best in California.
    Victor Cook, P.O. Box 5675, Balboa Island, CA 92662
    (714) 675-5407

Exclusive News Group—It's the people who put this book together. In the past **ENG News Service** provided public records assistance to news media clients. That work now goes to Victor Cook (see listing above). But **ENG Productions** still provides television production services to television stations and networks as well as to non-media clients. Its current videos are both three-tape VHS sets: *A Public Records Odyssey* and *How to Locate and Investigate People.* that will help you or your employees enhance investigative skills. Finally **Exclusive News Group** has provided public records and news media training to thousands of law enforcement personnel, private investigators, genealogists, news persons and corporate security specialists. Call me directly for information about any of ENG's services.
    Don Ray, ENG, P.O. Box 4375
    Burbank, CA 91503-4375 (818) THE-NEWS

Quint & Associates—Barbara Quint is a living legend. When she speaks to groups on the subject of computer database sources, stonecutters hang around in hopes of getting the contract to make her statue. Police block off the streets for the inevitable ticker tape. She's the "Master of the Printed Word." Those are *her* words. "If it's in a computerized database," she says, "I can find it. With my richly evocative software I can turn a rock into a diamond—depending on how I hold it up to the light." Barbara's training is in library science. She's the former head of reference for the Rand Corporation. Bottom line—there's no one better, faster or more knowledgeable than Barbara Quint when it comes to *complete* information gathering using the computer and modem. She's also the editor of *Searcher Magazine*. Important to note, Barbara doesn't do the public records search—she does the higher-level searches that require her unique expertise. Call on her to do the impossible or to work or as a consultant. It'll be the most you've ever gotten for $65 an hour.

 Quint and Associates, 932 11th St.,
 Santa Monica, CA 90403, (310) 451-0252

 Searcher Magazine
 Information Today, Inc.
 143 Old Marlton Pike
 Medford, NJ 08055, (609) 654-4888

GKL Corporate/Search, Inc.—When you find there are documents you need at the Secretary of State or other Sacramento offices, give GKL a call. They'll ship it, fax it, read it to you, mail it or even deliver it. They really know what they're doing.

 GKL Corporate/Search, Inc., P.O. Box 1913
 Sacramento, CA 95812-1913 (916) 442-7652

Jan Jennings—A genealogist and a wonderful person too. She stays busy all the time doing contract work for people from all over the world who need the best genealogy researcher this side of Salt Lake City (and probably beyond). Her biggest flaw she practically gives herself away. Call her just so you can hear how great her prices are.

 Jan Jennings, 3324 Crail Way,
 Glendale, CA 91206, (818) 790-2642

MUNICIPAL AGENCIES

Haines and Company, Inc.—These are the folks who provide most of the reverse (criss-cross) directories that cover the California area. You'll also find these directories in libraries, police stations, newspaper offices and television station. If you subscribe to their services (lease or buy), you will be issued a pass word and phone number that will enable you to make two calls per day to the Haines office.

    Haines and Co., Inc., Reverse Directories (714) 523-7420

Privacy Rights Clearing House—Here's how you can learn to protect yourself from the bad people who somehow got their hands this book. This non-profit group is on the cutting edge of privacy rights. It's funded partially by the Telecommunications Education Trust. And it truly is a clearinghouse. Call, fax them, modem them or write them and ask them to send you (at no charge) any or all of their 16 fact sheets—each one providing tips on how to handle delicate privacy situations—or their other publications.

    Privacy Rights Clearing House
    Center for Public Interest Law
    University of San Diego School of Law
    5998 Alcala Park
    San Diego, CA 92110-2492
    (619) 260-4806, Fax: (619) 260-4753
    Hotline: (800) 773-7748 (California only), (619) 298-3396
    Call them for computer access numbers.

Automated Name Index—Why spend all that money buying CD ROMs or subscribing to databases when you can call Ron Farmer's Automated Name Index (ANI). Ron is a veteran private investigator who has trained hundreds of P.I.s. He and his staff know exactly which database, CD ROM or microfiche to access to zero in on the information you need. For ANI's services, see its ad on page 66.

    Automated Name Index (ANI)
    P.O. Box 813
    Glendale, CA 91209
    (818) 637-8625   Fax 637-8630

Municipal Agencies
The most commonly used or most valuable resources at the city level.

Building Permits—Find them at the city level (County level for unincorporated areas in most counties). You can examine or buy copies of permits for demolition, grading, concrete, plumbing, electrical, carpentry, air conditioning, etc. You should look for contractors' names, fees paid, descriptions of work done, names of persons authorizing work, etc. Ask to see actual plans on file. Same office may also have information about abandoned property and *slumlord* properties. *See City Hall listings in the City Records Section.*

City Business Licenses—Three types of information are usually available—the company name, the address of the company and the name of the person or corporation who requested the license (owner of the business). Ask for any one of these items and get the other two. Business permits for companies in unincorporated areas of Los Angeles County are on file at the county level. *See City Hall listings in the City Records Section.*

City Elections Office (City Clerk)—Most city clerks handle documents similarly to those described on pages 79-80 for municipal (and some school board) elections. The clerk may also maintain a copy of the county-wide voter registration listing (remember, it's not as public as it used to be). It can save a trip to the county offices. *See the City Records Section.*

Animal Regulation Department—Yes, you can even check on someone's pets—*whether or not they're licensed.* Generally even unlicensed animals are often on file. A great resource! One technique good investigators use is to approach an interview or interrogation armed with a fat file that includes information about the person's pets. He or she will think the investigator knows absolutely everything. This often makes the subject quite reluctant to tell less than the whole truth. You can check with the Animal Regulation department or with the **Humane Society** under contract to learn which animals are residing at any particular address. Also, you can usually access the files by using the owner's name or the actual license number of the animal. Under state law, any veterinarian who vaccinates an animal for rabies must submit one copy of the vaccination certificate to the appropriate agency that Animal Regulation Department in his or her jurisdiction.

> *For incorporated cities, see the City Records section, for unincorporated cities, check with the County Clerk listed in the County Records section.*

County Agencies
The most commonly used or most valuable offices.

Registrar of Voters (County level in California, city level in some states)

    A. Voter Registration Affidavits—Bad news for researchers who aren't either journalists or government investigators—a new law has severely limited what you can see. About all the registrar can now do for you is confirm that someone is registered and tell you in what city the person is registered. If you're involved in a political campaign, political action committee or ballot measure, you can purchase the countywide index. If you're a government investigator or a full-time journalists, you may still view wat everyone could see before: The index usually includes a voter's name, address, prior addresses, date of birth, state of birth, date of registration, affiliation and affidavit number. The index also often includes the voter's occupation and telephone number. The actual affidavit will always include more than the index—including a copy of the voter's signature.

B. Precinct Listings and Maps—Also no longer open for inspection, the precinct listing is a complete list of everyone registered to vote in a certain area, usually at one particular polling place. The listings are sorted by address and include the voters' names and any phone numbers the voters may have provided when they filled out their affidavits. Again, government investigators and journalists can still get access.

C. Campaign Contributions—Federal, state and local laws require candidates and political action committees to file periodic financial statements that, in essence, disclose the sources of contributions and how the candidate or committee ended up spending the money. The good news is that these files are still available to anyone who wishes to view or copy them.

The documents most commonly used (in California) are the *Campaign Disclosure Statement Summary Page* (totals of all contributions received and expenditures made), *Schedule A* (itemized monetary contributions received), *Schedule B* (loans received), *Schedule C* (non-monetary contributions received—services, food, office space, etc.), *Schedule D* (pledges), *Schedule E* (payments and contributions made), *Schedule EE* (loans made) and *Schedule F* (accrued expenses—unpaid bills).

Registrars are listed in the County Records section.

Statement of Economic Interests

—The Political Reform Act of 1974 requires certain public officials (elected and appointed) to file an annual *Statement of Economic Interests*. The official is required to disclose any financial interests which could foreseeably cause conflicts. The areas include investments, interests in real property, income, loans received, gifts, honoraria, commission income and interests in real property and investments held by business entities or trusts.

Copies of completed statements are on file at the administrative office at the actual level of government of the official. Municipal court judges, for example, file their statements with the clerk of the municipal court. City council members file with the city clerk. Superior court judges file with the county clerk, etc. They are also available from the Secretary of State (see *State Offices* section).

Assessor—This office exists to determine how much property taxes should be paid for each piece of land in the county and to determine to whom the tax bill should be sent. You should keep in mind that the assessor is less concerned with ownership than with identifying someone who can be billed for the taxes. It's important that people looking at the records not make an assumption of ownership. Lawyers, accountants, relatives and other *straw parties* often receive and pay the tax bill even though they're not the owners.

A. Secured Property (land and buildings)—Real property is usually indexed by the situs address, the Assessor's Parcel Number (A.P.N.—map book, page and parcel), occasionally by the assessee's name and usually by the legal description (tract name or number, block, lot, etc.). The actual assessment rolls indicate assessed taxes, exemption and assessed value of the land and the improvements (buildings).

More recent entries in the map books in L.A. County provide the instrument number (document number assigned by the County Recorder—see below) of the deed. In some counties more information is available such as a property description, square footage, room count, year built, zoning, trust deeds, sale price and usage codes.

Assessor records can provide a rough history of the probable ownership of a piece of property—a good place to check before visiting the County Recorder.

Assessors are listed in the County Records section.

B. Unsecured Property—The assessor also determines the taxes that should be paid on expensive property that's not necessarily secured to the ground—such as airplanes, large boats and large equipment. This can be a bit more difficult to check out, but anyone can search a name index and come up with document numbers that relate to the tax collector's records of payment.

Unsecured Property files are handled by various county offices—most usually by the assessor or tax collector.

County Recorder—The County Recorder's purpose is to make and maintain true copies of various types of documents to ensure there is a permanent record for possible future reference.

    A. Vital Statistics—Birth, marriage and death certificates. In Los Angeles County you may view marriage and death indices and records. The only way to get information off the birth certificate is to actually order a copy and have it mailed to yourself (or Federal Expressed for an extra charge). The normal cost is $11 for the copy.

    The **birth certificate** will provide the child's name, date, time and place of birth as well as its sex and whether it was a single or multiple birth. It also provides the parents' birth names, ages, occupations and places of birth. It will occasionally include mention of any complications during birth, the number of the mother's previous deliveries—alive or stillborn—and almost always the doctor's signature.

    The **marriage certificate** shows the birth names of both parties, their ages, places of birth, occupations, addresses, highest education levels, signatures, number of previous marriages, how and when the last marriages ended, parents' names and places of birth, date and location of marriage, name and signature of person administering the vows and names, addresses and signatures of witnesses. Be aware that some marriage certificates are, by law, not public record. See *County Clerk* description for information about **Confidential Marriages**.

    The **death certificate** provides the name of decedent, date and time of death, sex, race/ethnicity, date of birth, age, birthplace, name and birthplace of father and mother, citizenship, dates of military service, social security number, marital status, name of surviving spouse, primary occupation, number of years in the occupation, employer, kind of industry or business, residence, name and address and relationship of informant, place of death, primary and contributing causes of death, indications of autopsy, name and address and license number of physician, dates of treatment, information concerning nature and location of accidents, suicide, etc., disposition of the body, date of cremation (interment, etc.), name and address of cemetery or crematory, embalmer's license number and signature, name and license of funeral director and recording date.

B. Grantor-Grantee—This is where other documents are recorded (copied onto microfilm) to serve as a permanent legal copy for future use. They're usually indexed only by the names of the parties giving away the documents (grantors) and by the receivers of the documents (grantees). Documents include deeds, grant deeds, quitclaim deeds, trust deeds, reconveyances, mechanics' liens, tax liens, powers of attorney, some contracts, abstracts of judgments, some UCC financing statements, notaries' bonds and various other documents filed as required by law or for the convenience of the person filing (military discharge papers, etc.).

For Grantor/Grantee, see "Recorder" listings in the County Records section starting on page 223.

County Clerk

A. Marriage Licenses—Different than the marriage certificate. Remember that not everyone who takes out a license gets married. Therefore, marriage licenses are often great places to find victims and enemies—people very likely to talk about the person under investigation. In Los Angeles County the indices are on file for a decade. The actual hard copies of the licenses are kept only for one year. Indices provide names of both parties, their ages at the time, date of issuance and the document number. The actual document contains most of the information that will eventually be on the marriage certificate.

In California it's possible to get married without generating public records. Under state law, any couple that has cohabited (for even one night) may obtain a marriage license without the normal requirements of blood tests, waiting periods *or* public availability of the records. The only information a recorder (not the clerk) may release about a **confidential marriage** is an actual confirmation that the couple was, indeed, married on a particular date. The person requesting the information must, however, provide both parties' names and the exact date of the marriage.

Marriage licenses are listed under County Clerk in the County Records section.

B. Fictitious Name Statements (DBAs)—If an individual, corporation or partnership chooses to do business under a name other than its legal name, it must file a fictitious name statement (Joe Jones does business as JJ Diaper Service, Pacific Bell does business as The Phone Shop, Joe Jones and Fred Smith do business as 5th Street Partnership—all must file statements). Usually indexed by the true, legal name of the filer (Joe Jones, Pacific Bell, etc.) and by the fictitious name (JJ Diaper Service, The Phone Shop, etc.). Both make reference to a case file number. The case file usually consists of the original form filed and a copy of the newspaper announcement that was filed in accordance with the law. The form includes the names, signatures, addresses and titles of owners, the type of business, and the fictitious name itself.

See "County Clerk" listings in the County Records section.

C. Superior Court Clerk—Curator of **civil, divorce, probate** and **criminal** as well as **Reciprocal Enforcement Support Law (RESL)** case files (all public record). **Civil** cases give identifying information regarding both parties, names of attorneys, other victims or enemies, addresses, some financial information and much more. **Divorce** files identify both parties, children, financial information, property owned and sometimes a great deal of dirt on either or both parties. **Probate** files include wills, financial and property information, lists of next of kin, lists of claims against the estate, personal information about the dead person and a breakdown of who ended up with what. **Criminal** cases provide identification of suspect, details of the alleged crime, occasional police reports, occasional criminal history records, probation reports (public record for the first 60 days after sentencing or after later charges are filed) and record of all proceedings and incarcerations. **RESL** files exist when one party of a domestic case (divorce, dissolution or child support) leaves the county of the court and either owes or is owed child support or alimony and the other party isn't paying. The district attorneys in the two counties get together and collect, transfer and disburse moneys owed. At each end, there's a fat file that contains information about both parties and the children. Look for addresses, financial information, employment information and vehicles owned by all parties.

Superior Court Clerks are listed in the County Records section.

Municipal Court Clerk—This is generally at the city level, but administered in California by county-level employees. Civil, criminal, small claims and traffic court information is available without question to anyone who asks. Municipal criminal courts are good places to look for **search warrants**. Law enforcement investigators usually present search warrants to a municipal court judge, along with a supporting affidavit, for his or her approval. If the judge agrees that whatever investigators believe is in someone's house (or car, brief case, office, bank account, phone bill, clothing, etc.) is more important than the person's right to privacy, he or she will sign it. The investigator who executes (serves) the search warrant must return these two documents with the Return (a list of what was confiscated) to the Municipal Court Clerk within 10 days of issuance. It's then public record unless a judge seals it. The affidavit includes more information about the investigators, suspects, witnesses and investigation than one could wish for. No one will know that anyone's looking.

Municipal Courts are listed in the County Records section.

Justice Court—Not! All of these lowest-level courts were either closed or promoted to the level of municipal court.

County Codes

California counties are designated by two-digit numbers. Various agencies, firms, data bases or directories refer to these numbers. For convenience the County Codes are listed below along with the page numbers in this book.

Number	County	Page	Number	County	Page
01 or 60	Alameda	165	32	Plumas	196
02	Alpine	166	33	Riverside	196
03	Amador	166	34	Sacramento	199
04	Butte	167	35	San Benito	199
05	Calaveras	167	36	San Bernardino	200
06	Colusa	168	37 or 80	San Diego	203
07	Contra Costa	168	38 or 90	San Francisco	205
08	Del Norte	169	39	San Joaquin	205
09	El Dorado	169	40	San Luis Obispo	207
10	Fresno	170	41	San Mateo	208
11	Glenn	171	42	Santa Barbara	209
12	Humboldt	172	43	Santa Clara	210
13	Imperial	172	44	Santa Cruz	211
14	Inyo	173	45	Shasta	211
15	Kern	174	46	Sierra	212
16	Kings	176	47	Siskiyou	213
17	Lake	176	48	Solano	214
18	Lassen	177	49	Sonoma	214
19 or 70	Los Angeles	178	50	Stanislaus	215
20	Madera	188	51	Sutter	216
21	Marin	188	52	Tehama	216
22	Mariposa	189	53	Trinity	217
23	Mendocino	189	54	Tulare	217
24	Merced	190	55	Tuolumne	218
25	Modoc	191	56	Ventura	218
26	Mono	191	57	Yolo	219
27	Monterey	192	58	Yuba	219
28	Napa	193	60	Alameda	165
29	Nevada	193	70	Los Angeles	178
30	Orange	194	80	San Diego	203
31	Placer	195	90	San Francisco	205

Don Ray in Person!
Bring the expert to you!

Things have changed!
New procedures
New Databases
New resources
New Laws
Tips
Strategies

Don Ray only wishes he were this skinny ⇨

Don Ray can train,
He can entertain!
Book 'em today.

Thousands of criminal investigatiors, journalists, private investigators, genealogists and librarians have improved their investigative skills while smiling through Don Ray's lively, humorous and energetic presentations.

To book him, Call (818) THE-NEWS.

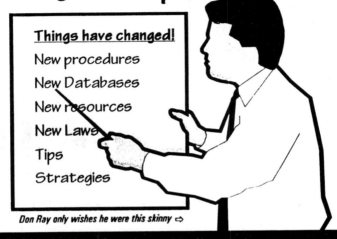

Don Ray in Person!
Bring the expert to you!

Things have changed!
New procedures
New Databases
New resources
New Laws
Tips
Strategies

Don Ray only wishes he were this skinny ⇨

Don Ray can train,
He can entertain!
Book 'em today.

Thousands of criminal investigatiors, journalists, private investigators, genealogists and librarians have improved their investigative skills while smiling through Don Ray's lively, humorous and energetic presentations.

To book him, Call (818) THE-NEWS.

Statewide Offices
Headquarters and selected regional offices.

Alcoholic Beverage Control—Restaurants, taverns, bars, liquor stores and grocery stores must have licenses to sell alcoholic beverages. The investigators for ABC do thorough checks on applicants. Quite a bit of information is available regarding establishments and individuals, including the *Application for Alcoholic Beverage License*, *Notice of Intended Transfer of Retail Alcoholic Beverage License*, the *Accusation* and other files relating to actions of and decisions made by the ABC and/or administrative law judges. There are numerous branch offices where complete files are maintained on area alcoholic beverage manufacturers and retailers. Check your local telephone directory.

>Department of Alcoholic Beverage Control
>3810 Rosin Ct., Suite 150
>Sacramento, 95834
>(916) 263-6898

Secretary of State Special Filings Division—Oversees auctioneers and auction operations.

>923 12th St., Suite 300
>Sacramento, 95814, (916) 653-3984

Banking Department—Oversees operation of state-chartered banks in California. Licenses various aspects of the banking business. While most records regarding banks are not open to public inspection, a bank's *Application Facing Page* will give some insight into who is operating the bank.

> California Banking Department
> 111 Pine St., Suite 1100
> San Francisco, 94111
> (415) 557-3232, Fax: (415) 989-5310

Boating and Waterways—Overseas licensing of yacht brokers, ship brokers and operators of vessels for hire.

> Department of Boating and Waterways
> 1629 "S" St.
> Sacramento, 95814-7291
> (916) 445-5684

State Department of Consumer Affairs—In California, you should open up the white pages of the telephone directory and look under the words "Consumer Affairs." You will find the phone numbers listed there for the regulating boards, commissions or committees for just about any type of professional, tradesman or technician who requires a license. That includes physicians, dentists, hair dressers, plumbers, electrical contractors, private investigators, security guards, automobile repair shops, etc. For lawyers, check with the state bar association for licensing and local associations for additional information.

> *Check the white pages of your local phone book first. If all else fails, here are some main numbers:*

Department of Consumer Affairs Offices
    Accountants, 2000 Evergreen St., Suite 250
        Sacramento, 95815-3832 (916) 263-3680
    Architects, 400 "R" St., Suite 4000
        Sacramento, 95814
        P.O. Box 944258, Sacramento, 94244-2580
        (916) 445-3393
    Athletic Commission, 1424 Howe Ave., Suite 33,
        Sacramento, 95825 (916) 263-2195
    Automotive Repair, 10240 Systems Parkway
        Sacramento, 95827 (916) 255-4300
        (800) 952-5210, Fax: (916) 255-1369
    Barbers, 400 "R" St, Suite 4080, Sacramento, 95814
        P.O. Box 944226, Sacramento, 94244-2260
        (916) 445-7061, Fax: (916) 445-8893
    Behavioral Scientists, 400 "R" St., Suite 3150
        Sacramento, 95814 (916) 324-1706
    Cemetery Board, 2535 Capital Oaks Dr., Suite 300B
        Sacramento, 95833 (916) 263-2660
    Chiropractic Examiners, 3401 Folsom Blvd., Suite B
        Sacramento, 95816-5354 (916) 227-2790
    Collection and Investigative Services, 400 "R" St., # 2001
        Sacramento, 95814-6234 (916) 445-7366
    Contractors, 9835 Goethe Rd., Sacramento, 95827
        (916) 255-3985, (800) 321-2752
        Fax: (916) 364-0130
    Cosmetologists -- See Barbers
    Dentists, 1432 Howe Ave., Suite 85B
        Sacramento, 95825-3241 (916) 263-2292
    Electronic and Appliance Repairs, 909 "S" St.
        Sacramento, 95814
        (916) 445-4751, Fax: (916) 327-5594
    Funeral Directors and Embalmers
        2535 Capital Oaks Dr., Suite 300A
        Sacramento, 95833 (916) 263-3180, (213) 897-1233
    Geologists and Geophysicists, 400 "R" St., Suite 4060
        Sacramento, 95814
        (916) 445-1920, Fax: (916) 445-8859

Department of Consumer Affairs Offices, Continued
  Guide Dogs for the Blind, 830 "K" St., Rm. 222
    Sacramento, 95814
    (916) 445-9041, Fax: (916) 323-0364
  Home Furnishings, 3485 Orange Grove Ave.
    North Highlands, 95660
    (916) 574-2040, Fax: (916) 574-2052
    Dry Cleaning Plants (916) 322-1394
    Thermal Insulation Program (916) 574-2046
  Landscape Architects, 400 "R" St. Suite 4020
    Sacramento, 95814
    (916) 445-4954, Fax: (916) 324-2333
  Medical Board, 1426 Howe Ave., Suite 54
    Sacramento, 95825 (916) 263-2388
  Allied Health Committees (916) 263-2669
      Allied Health Complaints (800) 633-2322
      Acupuncture (916) 263-2680
      Hearing Aid Dispensers (916) 263-2288
      Physical Therapy (916) 263-2550
      Physician's Assistant (916) 263-2670
      Podiatry (916) 263-2647
      Psychology (916) 263-2699
      Registered Dispensing Opticians/Contact Lens
        (916) 263-2634
      Respiratory Care (916) 263-2626
      Speech Pathology and Audiology (916) 263-2666
      Those not listed (916) 263-2393
  Nursing Homes, 1420 Howe Ave., Sacramento, 95825
      (916) 263-2685
      Los Angeles (213) 351-8200
  Optometrists, 400 "R" St., Suite 3130
      Sacramento, 95814 (916) 323-8720
  Personnel Services, 1426 Howe Ave., Suite 54, Sacramento,
      95825 (916) 263-2466
  Pharmacists, 400 "R" St., Suite 4070
      Sacramento, 95814
      (916) 445-5014, Fax: (916) 327-6308
      Los Angeles, 107 S. Broadway, 90012
        (213) 897-3125

Department of Consumer Affairs Offices, Continued
    Private Investigators -- See Collection Services
    Professional Engineers and Land Surveyors
        2535 Capital Oaks Dr., Suite 300
        Sacramento, 95833 (916) 263-2222
    Registered Nurses, 400 "R" St., Suite 4030, 95814
        P.O. Box 944210, Sacramento, 94244-2100
        (916) 322-3350
        Los Angeles, 107 S. Broadway, Rm. 8026
            Los Angeles, 90012 (213) 897-3590
    Shorthand Reporters, 2535 Capital Oaks Dr., Suite 140
        Sacramento, 95833 (916) 263-3660
    Structural Pest Control, 1432 Howe Ave.
        Sacramento, 95825
        (800) 737-8188, (916) 263-2540
        Los Angeles (213) 897-7838
        San Francisco (415) 800-8188
    Tax Preparers, 400 "R" St., Suite 3140
        Sacramento, 95814 (916) 324-4977
    Veterinary Medicine, 1420 Howe Ave., Suite 6
        Sacramento, 95825 (916) 263-2610
    Vocational Nurse and Psychiatric Technicians
        2535 Capital Oaks Dr., Suite 205
        Sacramento, 95833 (916) 263-7800
    Not listed above (800) 952-5210

Corporations Department—For the most part, the Department of Corporations regulates public corporations. Information can be helpful, but you should be checking first with the **California Secretary of State** and with the **Securities and Exchange Commission** on the federal level.

> Department of Corporations, 1115 11th St.
> Sacramento, 95814
> (916) 445-6273, Fax: (916) 322-5875
> Los Angeles, 3700 Wilshire Blvd., Suite 600, Los Angeles, 90010 (213) 736-2731,
> Fax: (213) 736-3593
> San Diego, 1350 Front St., Room 9034
> San Diego, 92101
> (619) 525-4233, Fax: (619) 525-4045
> San Francisco, 1390 Market St., Suite 810
> San Francisco, 94102
> (415) 557-3787, Fax: (415) 557-7166

Corrections Department—While someone's criminal history cannot legally be given out to the public, someone's record of detention in state prisons is available. Make sure you've done your homework first so that you can properly identify the person in whom you have an interest. The following information is available on current inmates or parolees: name, age, birthplace, place of previous residence, physical description, commitment information from the adult probation report (as excerpted in the Cumulative Case Summary), institutional assignments and behavior, general sense of health, cause of death, nature of injury (unless condition relates to AIDS) and actions regarding sentence and release.

> Department of Corrections, 1515 "S" St.
> Sacramento, 95814-0001 (916) 445-7682

Courts of Appeal—Civil and criminal cases at the Superior Court level (counties) appeal to the State Court of Appeals. Public records are available, but sometimes it's difficult to get copies. Often times the clerk will require you bring in your own photocopy machine. I usually look at the case file, take down the phone numbers of the attorney's representing both sides and then call one of them and ask for copies.

> First Appellate District, 303 Second St., San Francisco,
> 94107 (415) 396-9600, Fax: (415) 396-9668
> Second Appellate District, 300 S. Spring St., 2nd Floor,
> North Tower, Los Angeles, 90013 (213) 897-2307
> Division Six, 1280 S. Victoria Ave., Rm. 201,
> Ventura, 93003 (805) 651-4720
> Third Appellate District, 900 "N" St., Room 400, 4th Fl.
> Sacramento, 95814 (916) 654-0209
> Fourth Appellate District, Division One, 750 "B" St., #300
> San Diego, 92101
> (619) 645-2760, Fax: (619) 237-7098
> Division Two, 303 W. 5th St.
> San Bernardino, 92401
> (909) 383-4441, Fax: (909) 383-4660
> Division Three, 925 Spurgeon St.
> Santa Ana, 92701
> (714) 558-4312, Fax: (714) 543-1318
> Fifth Appellate District, 2525 Capitol St., Fresno, 93721
> (209) 445-5491, Fax: (209) 445-5769
> Sixth Appellate District, 333 W. Santa Clara St., #1060
> San Jose, 95113
> (408) 277-1004, Fax: (408) 277-9916

Equalization Board -- Any person or business who sells actual items on a retail basis must apply for a resale permit which permits them to buy the items without paying sales tax. Instead, they pay the sales tax when they sell the goods to the ultimate retail customers. The Board of Equalization will provide you with the correct owner of a business if it's an individual, the corporate name if it's a corporation, the location of the business, the mailing address, type of business, business name if shown, starting date of the business, the closing date if it's no longer in business and the permit number. It's a good place to start when you're trying to identify a business entity or simply want to know if a retail business operation is complying with fundamental regulations. Collection agencies, lawyers and consumers are the regular users of this information.

>State Board of Equalization
>450 "N" St., Sacramento, 95814
>P.O. Box 942879, 94279-0001
>(916) 445-6464, Fax: (916) 445-1990

Fair Political Practices Commission—These folks monitor which political candidates or political action committees are getting what money from what interest group. They'll send you extensive print-outs showing expenditures and receipts. They're the ones who sue candidates for not following the letter of the law when it comes to political fund raising and advertising.

>Fair Political Practices Commission
>428 "J" St., Suite 800, Sacramento, 95814
>P.O. Box 807, 95812
>(916) 322-5660, Fax: (916) 322-1932, (916) 327-2026

California Highway Patrol—As a state law enforcement agency, the CHP is required to provide certain information regarding calls for assistance and regarding circumstances surrounding arrests they make (see the California Public Records Act).

**Headquarters, 2555 First Ave., Sacramento, 95818,
P.O. Box 942898, 942898-0001 (916) 657-7261**

<u>Northern Division</u>
Northern Division, 2485 Sonoma St., Redding, 96001-3026
  (916) 225-2715, Fax: (916) 241-1590
Alturas, 905 W. "C" St., 96101 (916) 233-2919, Fax: (916) 233-5720
Clear Lake, 5700 Live Oak Dr., P.O. Box 340, Kelseyville, 95451
  (707) 279-0103, Fax: (707) 279-2863
Crescent City, 1444 Parkway Dr., 95531
  (707) 464-3117, Fax: (707) 465-6427
Garberville, 30 West Coast Rd., Redway, 95560, P.O. Box 515,
  Garberville, 95542 (707) 923-2155, Fax: (707) 923-2159
Humboldt, 255 E. Samoa Blvd, Arcata, 95521
  (707) 822-5981, Fax: (707) 822-8939
Mt. Shasta, 618 W. Jessie St., 96067
  (916) 926-2627, Fax: (916) 926-6935
Mt. Shasta (Dunsmuir Grade) Inspection Facility, So. Bound I-5 at
  Mott Rd., 96067 (916) 926-2425, Fax: (916) 926-2463
Quincy, 86 W. Main St., P.O. Box 656, 95971 (916) 283-1100
Red Bluff, 2550 Main St, 96080 (916) 527-2034, Fax: (916) 527-8432
Redding, 2503 Cascade Blvd., 96003
  (916) 225-2700, (916) 225-2703, Fax: (916) 225-2726
Susanville, 472-400 Diamond Crest Rd., 96130-5001
  (916) 257-2191, (916) 257-6061, Fax: (916) 257-0244
Trinity River, Hwy. 299, 1261 Main St., P.O. Box 1350, Weaverville,
  96093 (916) 623-3832
Ukiah, 540 Orchard Ave., 95482
  (707) 463-4717, (707) 463-4719, Fax: (707) 463-5557
Williams, 806 North St., P.O. Box 488, 95987
  (916) 473-2821, Fax: (916) 473-5183

California Highway Patrol Offices Continued
Willows, 464 N. Humboldt Ave., P.O. Box 883, 95988
  (916) 934-5424, Fax: (916) 934-3238
Yreka, 1687 S. Main St., P.O. Box 450, 96097 (916) 841-2505

Valley Division
Valley Division, 11336 Trade Center Dr., Rancho Cordova, 95742,
  P.O. Box 640, 95741-0640
  (916) 464-2090, Fax: (916) 464-2097
Sacramento Communications Center, 2555 First Ave.,
  P.O. Box 942898-0001, 95818
  (916) 445-1562, (916) 445-2211, Fax: (916) 323-4538
Traffic Operations Center, 2555 First Ave., Sacramento, 95818
  (916) 323-4232, Fax: (916) 227-4923
Amador, 301 Clinton Rd., Jackson, 95642
  (209) 223-4890, Fax: (209) 223-4894
Auburn, 9440 Indian Hill Rd., P.O. Box 709, Newcastle, 95658
  (916) 663-3344, Fax: (916) 663-2859
Chico, 995 Fir St., P.O. Box 1779, 95927
  (916) 895-4444, (916) 895-4453, Fax: (916) 895-4040
Gold Run, Interstate 80 (2 mi. east of Gold Run), P.O. Box 8, Gold
  Run, 95717 (916) 389-2205, Fax: (916) 389-2298
Grass Valley, 11900 Sutton Way, 95945
  (916) 273-4415, Fax: (916) 273-7143
North Sacramento, 5109 Tyler St., P.O. Box 41098, Sacramento,
  95841-0098 (916) 263-3550, Fax: (916) 349-9826
Oroville, 2072 Third St., P.O. Box 1471, 95965
  (916) 533-3822, Fax: (916) 533-2703
Placerville, 3031 LoHi Way, P.O. Box 1417, 95667-1417
  (916) 622-1110, Fax: (916) 621-0139
San Andreas, 749 Mountain Ranch Rd., Route 1, 95249
  (209) 754-3541, Fax: (209) 754-4842
South Lake Tahoe, 1050 Navahoe Dr. at Hwy 50, Meyers, South Lake
  Tahoe, 96105 (916) 577-1001, Fax: (916) 577-7625
South Sacramento, 6 Massie Ct., Sacramento, 95823
  (916) 445-2118, Fax: (916) 688-3109
Stockton, 3330 N. Ad Art Rd., P.O. Box 8466, 95208
  (209) 948-7225, Fax: (209) 931-4622

California Highway Patrol Offices Continued
Tracy, 385 W. Grantline Rd., 95376
    (209) 835-8920, Fax: (209) 835-7136
Truckee, 10077 State Route 89 South, 96161
    (916) 587-3518, Fax: (916) 587-7833
Truckee (Donner Pass) Inspection Facility, 12800 I. S. 80,
    P.O. Box 8786, 96162 (916) 587-1242, Fax: (916) 587-0484
Woodland, 41928 County Road 23, 95776
    (916) 662-4685, Fax: (916) 662-8549
Yuba-Sutter, 1619 Poole Blvd., Yuba City, 95993 (916) 674-5141

Golden Gate Division
Golden Gate Division, 1551 Benicia Rd., Vallejo, 94591
    (707) 648-4180, Fax: (707) 648-4055
Golden Gate Communications Center, 1551 Benicia Rd., Vallejo,
    94591 (707) 648-4144, Fax: (707) 648-5300
  Traffic Operations (707) 648-5550, Fax: (707) 648-4199
Contra Costa, 5001 Blum Rd., Martinez, 94553
    (510) 646-4980, Fax: (510) 646-4990
Cordelia Inspection Facility, Eastbound 3895 I-80, Westbound 3895
    I-80, Suisun, 94585 Eastbound (707) 428-2092
    Westbound (707) 428-2090, Fax: (707) 428-2026
Dublin, 4999 Gleason Dr., 94568 (510) 828-0466, Fax: (510) 828-1377
Hayward, 2434 Whipple Rd., 94544
    (510) 489-1500, Fax: (510) 489-8452
Marin, 53 San Clemente Dr., P.O. Box 6, Corte Madera, 94925
    (415) 924-1100, Fax: (415) 924-4074
Mission Grade Inspection Facility, 4751 Hwy. 680, P.O. Box 553,
    Sunol, 94586 (510) 862-2223, Fax: (510) 862-0100
Napa, 975 Golden Gate Dr., P.O. Box 208, 94559
    (707) 253-4906, Fax: (707) 253-4909
Nimitz Inspection Facility, 4416 I-880, Fremont, 94539
    (510) 794-3658, Fax: (510) 794-3663
Oakland, 3601 Telegraph Ave., 94609
    (510) 450-3821, (510) 464-3818, Fax: (510) 450-3829
Redwood City, 355 Convention Way, 94063
    (415) 369-6261, Fax: (415) 369-6268
San Francisco, 1748 Army St., 94124
    (415) 557-1094, Fax: (415) 557-1541

California Highway Patrol Offices Continued
San Jose, 2020 Junction Ave., 95131
    (408) 277-1800, Fax: (408) 277-1072
Santa Rosa, 6100 LaBath Ave., Rohnert Park, 94928
    (707) 576-2175, Fax: (707) 576-2179
Solano, 3050 Travis Blvd., Fairfield, 94533
    (707) 428-2100, Fax: (707) 428-2039

Central Division
Central Division, 5179 N. Gates Ave., Fresno, 93722
    (209) 488-4329, Fax: (209) 276-2949
Bakersfield, 4040 Pierce Rd., 93308
    (805) 327-1069, (805) 334-3913, Fax: (805) 327-0704
Buttonwillow, 29449 Stockdale Hwy., Bakersfield, 93312
    (805) 764-5580, Fax: (805) 764-5608
Coalinga, 125 S. 6th St., P.O. Box 866, 93210
    (209) 935-2093, Fax: (209) 935-2092
Fort Tejon, 1033 Lebec Rd., P.O. Box 792, Lebec, 93243
    (805) 248-6655, Fax: (805) 248-5107
Fresno, 1382 W. Olive Ave., 93728-2890
    (209) 488-4321, (209) 445-6681, Fax: (209) 488-4326
Grapevine Inspection Facility, Route 1 Box 34, Lebec, 93243
    (805) 858-2540, Fax: (805) 858-6506
Hanford, 1565 Glendale Ave., P.O. Box F 831, 93230
    (209) 582-0231, Fax: (209) 582-7336
Los Banos, 706 W. Pacheco Blvd., 93635
    (209) 826-3811, Fax: (209) 826-9548
Madera, 3051 Airport Dr., 93637 (209) 675-1025, Fax: (209) 675-1029
Mariposa, 5264 Hwy. 49 North, P.O. Box 217, 95338
    (209) 966-3656, Fax: (209) 966-6765
Merced, 1800 E. Childs Ave., 95340
    (209) 726-6520, (209) 726-6524, Fax: (209) 383-2230
Modesto, 4030 Kiernan Ave., 95356
    (209) 576-6300, Fax: (209) 545-2636
Porterville, 861 W. Morton Ave., 93257
    (209) 784-7444, Fax: (209) 784-2146
Sonora, 18437 5th Ave., P.O. Box 676, Jamestown, 95327
    (209) 984-3944, Fax: (209) 984-3660

California Highway Patrol Offices Continued
Visalia, 5025 W. Noble Ave., 93277
   (209) 734-6767, Fax: (209) 734-3007

Southern Division
Southern Div. Admin. Services, 411 N. Central Ave., Suite 410,
   Glendale, 91203 (818) 240-8200, Fax: (818) 240-5962
Southern Div. Investigative Services, 437 N. Vermont Ave.
   Los Angeles, 90004 (213) 664-0695, Fax: (213) 662-5647
Los Angeles Communications Center, 4016 Rosewood Ave
   Los Angeles, 90004
   (213) 736-2991, PIO (213) 953-7383 Fax: (213) 662-5647,
Antelope Valley, 2041 W. Avenue "I", Lancaster, 93536,
   P.O. Box 1570, Lancaster, 93539
   (805) 948-8541, Fax: (805) 948-8544
Baldwin Park, 14039 Francisquito Ave., P.O. Box 1010, 91706
   (818) 338-1164, (818) 575-6634, Fax: (818) 814-2783
Castaic Inspection Facility, 27858 Golden State Hwy, Valencia, 91354
   (818) 885-3908
Central Los Angeles, 777 W. Washington Blvd., P.O. Box 15660
   Los Angeles, 90015 (213) 744-2331, Fax: (213) 744-2856
East Los Angeles, 2201 W. Via Campo, P.O. Box 3060
   Montebello, 90640 (213) 724-5150, Fax: (818) 575-6813
Fort Tejon, 1033 Lebec Rd., P.O. Box 792, Lebec, 93243
   (805) 248-6655, Fax: (805) 248-5107
Newhall, 28648 N. The Old Road, Valencia, 91355
   (805) 257-6030, Fax: (805) 367-6178
Santa Fe Springs, 10051 Orr and Day Rd., 90670
   (310) 868-0503, Fax: (310) 864-4218
South Los Angeles, 19700 Hamilton Ave., Torrance, 90502
   (213) 323-5450, (310) 736-2990, Fax: (310) 323-5411
Verdugo Hills, 2130 Windsor Ave., Altadena, 91001
   Pasadena (818) 794-0304, Glendale (818) 244-8101
   (818) 575-6656, Fax: (818) 575-6668
West Los Angeles, 6300 Bristol Parkway, Culver City, 90230
   (310) 670-0938, Fax: (310) 670-0193
West Valley, 5825 De Soto Ave., Woodland Hills, 91367
   (818) 888-0980, Fax: (818) 888-1034

California Highway Patrol Offices Continued
Border Division
Border Communications Center, 9330 Farham St., San Diego, 92123
 (619) 637-7158, (619) 268-2276, Fax: (619) 268-2851
 Traffic Operations Center, 4120 Taylor St., San Diego, 92110
 (619) 220-5360, Fax: (619) 688-6098
Banning, 60 N. Highland Springs Ave., 92220
 (909) 845-4661, Fax: (909) 769-9049
Blythe, 430 S. Broadway, 92225 (619) 922-6141, Fax: (619) 922-2405
Capistrano, 32951 Camino Capistrano, San Juan Capistrano, 92675
 (714) 661-6215, Fax: (714) 661-0146
El Cajon, 1722 E. Main St., 92021
 (619) 440-4303, Fax: (619) 440-2524
El Centro, 2331 Hwy 86, Imperial, 92251 (619) 352-4111,
 Fax: (619) 352-0937
Indio, 79-650 Varner Rd., 92203 (619) 345-2544
 (619) 360-3104, Fax: (619) 360-4290
Oceanside, 1888 Oceanside Blvd., 92054 P.O. Box 2000, 92051-0359
 (619) 757-1675, Fax: (619) 757-0907
San Diego, 4902 Pacific Hwy, 92110
 (619) 296-6661, Fax: (619) 296-6667
San Onofre Inspection Facility, P.O. Box 2030, Oceanside,
 92051-2030 (619) 430-7026
Santa Ana, 2031 E. Santa Clara Ave., P.O. Box 11487, 92711
 (714) 547-8311, (714) 567-7187, Fax: (714) 547-8344
 Traffic Operations Center, 2501 Pullman St., Santa Ana, 92705
 (714) 474-0757, Fax: (714) 474-1471
Temecula, 27685-A Commerce Center Dr., 92590
 (909) 676-0112, Fax: (909) 699-0547
Rainbow Inspection Facility, 27685 Commerce Center Dr.
 Temecula, 92589 (619) 728-0512
Westminster, 13200 Golden West St., 92665
 (714) 892-4426, Fax: (714) 891-7615
Winterhaven Inspection Facility, 3524 W. Interstate 8, 92283
 (619) 572-0781
Winterhaven, 3524 W. Interstate 8, 92283
 (619) 572-0294, Fax: (619) 572-2510

California Highway Patrol Offices Continued
Coastal Division
Coastal Division, 4115 Broad St., Suite B-10, San Luis Obispo, 93401
    (805) 549-3261, Fax: (805) 546-9176
Buellton, 166 Industrial Way, 93427
    (805) 688-5551, Fax: (805) 668-7284
Conejo Inspection Facility, 4001 U.S. Hwy 101
    Thousand Oaks, 91360 (805) 498-3853, Fax: (805) 498-9975
Gilroy Inspection Facility, 9800 U.S. 101, Gilroy, 95020
    (408) 848-3078, Fax: (408) 848-2457
Hollister-Gilroy, 740 Renz Lane, Gilroy, 95020, P.O. Box 337
    Gilroy, 95021 (408) 848-2324, Fax: (408) 848-2438
King City, 2 Broadway Circle, 93930
    (408) 385-3216, Fax: (408) 385-3745
Monterey, 19055 Portola Dr., Salinas, 93908
    (408) 455-1822, (408) 372-8013
    (408) 455-1826, Fax: (408) 455-1846
San Luis Obispo, 675 California Blvd., 93401
    (805) 549-3092, (805) 549-3619, Fax: (805) 543-4130
Santa Barbara, 6465 Calle Real, Goleta, 93117
    (805) 967-1234, Fax: (805) 967-7095
Santa Cruz, 10395 Soquel Dr., Aptos, 95003
    (408) 662-0511, Fax: (408) 662-0116
Santa Maria, 1710 N. Carlotti, 93454
    (805) 349-8728, Fax: (805) 349-9567
Templeton, 101 Duncan Rd., P.O. Box 668, 93465
    (805) 434-1822, Fax: (805) 434-2197
Ventura, 4656 Valentine Rd., 93003, P.O. Box 3237, 93003
    (805) 654-4571 (805) 654-4570, Fax: (805) 642-5032

Inland Division
Inland Division, 847 E. Brier Dr., San Bernardino, 92408
    (909) 383-4811, Fax: (909) 888-4228
Inland Communications Center, 847 E. Brier Dr., San Bernardino,
    92408 (909) 383-4644, (909) 383-6959, Fax: (909) 383-4826
  Traffic Operations Center, (909) 383-4644, Fax: (909) 383-4826
Arrowhead, 31230 Hwy. 18, P.O. Box 997, Running Springs, 92382
    (909) 867-2791, Fax: (909) 867-2662

California Highway Patrol Offices Continued
Barstow, 300 E. Mt. View, 92311 (619) 256-1727
  (619) 256-1617, Fax: (619) 256-2321
Bishop, 469 S. Main St., 93514 (619) 873-3531
  (619) 873-5328, Fax: (619) 873-8956
Bridgeport, 125 Main St., P.O. Box 158, 93517
  (619) 932-7995, Fax: (619) 932-7352
Mojave, 1365 Hwy. 58, 93501 (805) 824-2408, Fax: (805) 824-4820
Morongo Basin, 63683-29 Palms Hwy, HCR 1, Box 61
  Joshua Tree, 92252 (619) 367-7517, Fax: (619) 366-3042
Needles, 1916 "J" St., 92363 (619) 326-2000, Fax: (619) 326-4542
Ontario, 9530 Pittsburg Ave., P.O. Box 608, Rancho Cucamonga,
  91730 (909) 980-3994, Fax: (909) 980-4354
Riverside, 8118 Lincoln Ave., 92504
  (909) 688-8000, Fax: (909) 688-8003
San Bernardino, 2211 Western Ave., 92411
  (909) 383-4247, Fax: (909) 383-6996
Victorville, 14210 Amargosa Rd., 92392
  (619) 241-1186, Fax: (619) 241-6409

Horse Racing Board— Oversees horse racing operations in California. Approves license applications for race meets.

> California Horse Racing Board
> 1010 Hurley Way #190, Sacramento, 95825
> (916) 263-6000, Fax: (916) 263-6042

Department of Insurance—Regulates practices of insurance companies, brokers and salespersons. Provides information from insurance companies' *License Files*.

> Department of Insurance, 770 "L" St., Sacramento, 95814
> (800) 927-4357

Justice Department—There are lots of things of interest in the Department of Justice, but to me, the absolute most important office is the **Registry of Charitable Trusts**. This is one of the rare places where you can look at copies of tax returns. Any non-profit corporation or organization (with the exception of churches) soliciting funds in California must file copies of its income tax return (CA-1 at the state level—IRS 990 at the federal) with this office. From these files you can see how much money an organization is taking in, who's operating the organization and how much of the money they're keeping for themselves. You may not want to "give at the office" anymore after you've seen how very little a charity has to pass on to the needy while the operators are living like kings. The kind folks at this office will send entire files to the state office nearest you so that you can examine the files before deciding which documents to copy.

      Registry of Charitable Trusts, 1718 3rd St., 95814
      P.O. Box 903447, Sacramento, 94203-4470
      (916) 445-2021

Department of Motor Vehicles—Recent changes in California law have caused drastic changes in the accessibility of certain types of information. At the time of this printing, the statute and the DMV's interpretation forbids DMV personnel from giving out or selling the actual addresses off drivers licenses or vehicle registration forms.

      Other information is available, but the DMV requires *all* requesters to open an account with them and post a $50,000 bond (no bond is required for news media accounts). People or firms with approved accounts must agree to not give out DMV information to anyone else who doesn't have an account and all requesters must maintain a record of all the information they received and what they did with it. The new law is obviously a setback to many, but there are still ways of legally obtaining information.

    A.   **Drivers License Information**—DMV personnel will provide account holders with a person's exact name, drivers license number, date of birth, previous name used, expiration date and the all-important abstracts that may lead you to an address. Always ask for abstracts. They include traffic citations (ask for violation date, conviction date, section violated, court number, docket number and vehicle license number), failures to appear and traffic accidents (usually only names the city, date of accident and a file number). Once you've identified the actual citation number (docket number) you can view the actual citation at the court that heard or processed the case. It's on that citation you will be able to see the address shown at the time of the citation.

B. Vehicle Registration—If you provide to DMV personnel a license plate number or a vehicle owner's name and address you can get the registered owner, legal owner, the vehicle's make, model and vehicle identification number, date of transfer, date first sold and even a complete vehicle history (if you're willing to wait longer and pay more). Also, motorcycles, trailers and small boats are registered here. Remember, if you don't have an account, you can't get information this way.

There is other information available to any member of the public. The DMV will provide any consumer with certain information in its Occupational Licensing Files. These relate to automobile manufacturers and their representatives, new and used automobile dealerships, salespersons, dismantling yards, traffic violator schools, driving instructors, driving schools, private vehicle registrations services, vehicle verifiers and lessor retailers. DMV will generally confirm that the person or firm has a license, their business address, any departmental actions and bonding information.

Department of Motor Vehicles, Press Relations
2415 First Ave., Sacramento, 95818
(916) 657-6437, Fax: (916) 657-8282

Osteopathic Board—Oversees licensing of doctors of osteopathy.

> Board of Osteopathic Examiners
> 444 N. 3rd St., Suite A200
> Sacramento, 95814
> (916) 322-4306, Fax: (916) 327-6119

Real Estate Department—Regulates the people and corporations who deal in real estate. Oversees licensing of real estate sales persons and brokers as well as brokers of minerals, oil and gas.

> Department of Real Estate
> 2201 Broadway, Sacramento, 95818
> (916) 227-0931, Fax: (916) 227-0925

Secretary of State

  A. **Corporation Information**—In most states you can phone directly for corporate information. If you know the corporate name or number you can get the exact name, address corporate status (good standing, suspended, dissolved, etc.), date of incorporation, state of incorporation, president or chief executive officer, agent for service of process (and their addresses) and statement of officers number.

  In the past, the California Secretary of State provided telephone information at no charge. But now, to obtain corporate status information over the phone, you must enroll in the new "Pre-pay priority telephone service." Subscribers (who place pre-payment funds in a special account) are given unlisted phone numbers for phone requests. Each request for status costs $4.00. Statement of Officers copies are $1.00. Staff members will fax Statements of Officers and status information to their customers for an additional $5.00.

  They're talking of providing a toll-free number for non-subscribers who are willing to pay with a major credit card. You might check to see if that's available yet.

  Regardless, though, you may write in for status information ($4.00) and/or Statements of Officers ($1.00). They've even made it harder to walk in to the office and make inquiries. There is limited self-service capabilities, but they'll charge you $4.00 if someone across the counter punches up a status inquiry.

Your best bet is to use one of the many commercial databases that allow full text searches of corporate information, UCC filings and limited partnerships. For example, with Nexis/Lexis, you can search the files by the name of an officer or by an address—searches you *can't* make using the state's computers.

>California Secretary of State
>Corporate Status and Records Information
>1500 11 St., 3rd Fl., Sacramento, 95814
>To subscribe: (916) 657-5448

B. Limited Partnerships—Prior to July 1, 1984, limited partners in California were often filed at the county level as a fictitious name filing. Since then the general partners are on file at the Secretary of State's office. Limited partners are no longer listed.

>California Secretary of State
>Limited Partnership Division
>1500 11 St., 3rd. Floor
>Sacramento, 95814
>P.O. Box 944225
>Sacramento, 94244-2250
>Status (916) 653-3365

C. Limited Liability Companies— Newly added. The Limited Liability Company a is sort of hybrid entity. Members of an LLC are afforded the limited liability enjoyed by corporate shareholders and the pass through tax advantages of a partnership—this without the restrictions imposed on limited partnerships and Subchapter S corporations. There needs to at least two members of an LLC. The lawyers at the Limited Liability Company Unit tell us that every document filed by an LLC is available for viewing and copying. Be sure to ask specifically for the Articles of Organization, form LLC-1, which will show you the organizer and the initial agent for service of process. Also, be sure to ask for a copy of the Form LLC-12,

Statement of Information. This form must be completed within 90 days following the LLC's formation. It will provide you with the names of the currently agent, the address of the principal executive office, the names and addresses of the managers (if none have been appointed or elected, the form will provide the name and address of each member), and the name and address of the chief executive officer, if any.

>Limited Liability Company Unit
>1500 11 St., #345
>Sacramento, 95814
>P.O. Box 944228
>Sacramento, 94244-2280
>(916) 653-3365, (916) 653-3795

D. Notary Public—Track down the notary public listed on any recorded document and the specific line items on his or her log are public record. These include name, address, driver's license number, type of document, date and time signed and, newly added, the signer's thumb print. Often you can find other transactions involving parties in whom you have an interest.

>California Notary Public Division
>1500 11 St., 5th Fl.
>Sacramento, 95814
>Records (916) 653-3595

E. Uniform Commercial Code—When someone borrows money and uses anything other than real property (land) for collateral, the lender may have to (or choose to) file a financing statement as required by the UCC. You generally must request information in person in Sacramento or through the mail. Listings here will indicate from whom someone is borrowing money and what is offered as collateral. Social Security numbers and Federal IDs are here.

>Secretary of State, UCC
>1500 11 St., 2nd Fl., Sacramento, 95814
>P.O. Box 942835, Sacramento, 95825-0001
>(916) 653-3516, (916) 653-3516

State Bar Association—Regulates and licenses attorneys. The folks there will tell you an attorney's standing and will provide the full name, undergraduate and law school, State Bar Number, address, phone number, admission date, birth date and birth place. If there has been certain disciplinary action, you may view or buy copies of the records. *Public Reprovals, Probation,* actual *Suspensions* and *Disbarrments* are a matter of public record.

> The State Bar of California, 555 Franklin St.,
> San Francisco, 94102 (415) 561-8200
> 1149 S. Hill, 4th Floor, Los Angeles, 90015 (213) 580-5040
> State Hotline (800) 843-9053, Membership (415) 346-6601
> State Bar Court Clerk (213) 765-1400

Statewide Office of Vital Statistics—Every state has some statewide system of keeping track of births, marriages, divorces and deaths. In California, it's part of the state Health Department. Access varies from state to state, but you can always chat with them on the phone for procedures. You can use a Visa or Mastercard with many states and they'll do research and send the copies. You'd be wise to purchase the microfiche indices of California statewide marriages going back to 1960, divorces back to the mid-60s and deaths going all the way back to 1940. The entire set will cost less than $200.

> Office of State Registrar of Vital Statistics
> 304 "S" St., Sacramento, 95814
> (916) 445-1719, Fax: (800) 858-5553

Workers' Compensation Appeals Board—This is where people go to fight for benefits following an on-the-job injury. The dispute is generally between an employee and his or her employer. As with other court records, much of the case file is public record. However, this agency has put in place procedures that are meant to keep track of the people viewing the files to make sure the person requesting the file isn't using the file for criminal or commercial purposes, or in a way that would violate other labor laws. But don't fret—almost anyone can view the file. Here's how: If you already somehow know the case file number, you'll probably get the file with no questions asked. If you don't know it, they'll ask you why you want it and probably give it to you for viewing. If you're going to be doing a lot of looking at files, they'll ask you to fill out a request form for a "DWC Authorization Number." If they agree you're not going to do anything that's taboo, you'll get your number and you'll be able to waltz into any WCAB office and view anything that's available to the public. If you're a law enforcement investigator, you should first go to the WCAB where you believe the case is being heard. The staff there will make a call or two and then probably let you see the complete file. If you're a journalist, consider getting a DWC Authorization Number so that you're always prepared. If not, you can walk into any office or first call the Communications Manager at (415) 703-3731, Ext. 150.

**Workers' Compensation Appeals Board
Headquarters, 455 Golden Gate Avenue, Room 5182
After August, 1995 the WCAB will be at 45 Fremont St.
P.O. Box 420603, San Francisco, 94102 (415) 703-3731**

District Offices
Agoura, 30125 W. Agoura Rd., 91301 (818) 879-2925
Anaheim, 1661 N. Raymond Ave., Suite 200, 92801 (714) 738-4038
Bakersfield, 1800 30th St., Room 100, (805) 395-2514
Eureka, 100 "H" St., Room 201, 95501 (707) 441-5723
Fresno, 2550 Mariposa St., Room 3014 (209) 445-5355
Grover Beach, 1562 Grand Ave., 93433-2261 (805) 481-4912
Long Beach, 245 W. Broadway, Room 230, 90802-4460
  (310) 590-5240
Los Angeles, 107 S. Broadway, Room 4107, 90012 (213) 897-1446
Norwalk, 12440 Firestone Blvd., Suite 3001, 90650 (310) 406-7107
Oakland, 2229 Webster St., Room 300, 94612 (510) 286-1358
Pasadena, 55 Eureka Street, Suite A, 91103 (818) 578-8664
Pomona, 971 Corporate Center Dr., 91768 (909) 623-8568
Redding, 2115 Akard, Room 21, 96001-2796 (916) 225-2047
Sacramento, 2424 Arden Way, Suite 230, 95825 (916) 263-2741,
  (916) 263-2718
Salinas, 1880 N. Main St., Suite 100, 93906-3287 (408) 443-3058
    San Bernardino, 303 W. Third St., Room 400, 92401-1888
    (909) 383-4522

Workers Compensation Appeals Board District Offices Continued
San Diego, 1350 Front St., Room 3050, 92101 (619) 525-4589,
(619) 525-4590
San Francisco, 30 Van Ness Ave., Room 3700, 94102 (415) 557-1954
San Jose, 100 Paseo de San Antonio, Room 240, 95113
(408) 277-1292
Santa Ana, 28 Civic Center Plaza, Room 451, (714) 558-4597,
(714) 558-4598
Santa Barbara, 1525 State St., Suite 102, 93101 (805) 966-9872
Santa Monica, 2701 Ocean Park Blvd., Suite 222, 90405
(310) 452-1188
Santa Rosa, 50 "D" St., Room 430, 95404 (707) 576-2452
Stockton, 31 E. Channel St., Room 450, 95202-2314 (209) 463-6201
Van Nuys, 6150 Van Nuys Blvd., Room 105, 91401-3373
(818) 901-5374
Ventura, 5810 Ralston St., Room 115, 93003-6085 (805) 654-4701
Walnut Creek, 175 Lennon Lane, Room 200, 94598 (510) 977-8343

U.S. Government Offices
Includes California and National Offices.

Armed Service Locators—If you're looking for someone who's on active military duty, at very least you'll need the correct name of the person and either the date of birth or his or her social security number. Unless you're a law enforcement person, you're probably not going to get much information over the telephone. New federal legislation allows the branches to charge $3.50 for locator assistance—and that's through the mail. Each branch seems to be unique in its procedure.

U.S. Army—State and federal investigators as well as members of the service person's immediate family don't have to pay the $3.50 fee. Everyone else must. Make the check payable to **Finance Officer** and mail it to:

>Finance Officer
>Army Worldwide Locator Service
>U.S. Army Enlisted Records & Evaluation Center
>Fort Benjamin Harrison, IN 46249-5301
>(317) 542-4211

U.S. Government Offices

U.S. Air Force—Similar to the Army, except they'll waive the $3.50 fee only if your request is on official government letterhead signed by someone important -- such as the boss. Otherwise throw in a check in the amount of $3.50 and make it out to **AFO Randolph AFB, TX** and send it to:

> AFMPC-RMIQL
> Attn: Worldwide Locator
> Randolph AFB, TX 78150-4752
> (210) 652-1110

U.S. Navy—The folks here remind us they will *not* give any phone assistance to creditors or debt collectors *and* they don't provide information about members of the Marine Corps. Hmph! But they didn't say they wouldn't help others over the phone. But if it doesn't work out, make out a check or money order payable to **U.S. Treasury** and mail it *today* to:

> Chief of Naval Personnel
> Bureau of Naval Personnel
> #2 Navy Annex
> Washington, DC 20370-5021 (20370-5312 if you're a gov't employee -- no charge)
> (703) 614-3155, (800) 535-2699 for reservists

U.S. Marine Corps—Call them first, or write to them at:

> CMC
> MMSB-10
> Building 2008
> Quantico, VA 22134
> (703) 640-3942, 614-2645 (24-hour)

U.S. Coast Guard—Things haven't seemed to change as much here. Call them for possible phone assistance or write to:

> Coast Guard Locator Service
> Room 4502 (for enlisted personnel)
> Room 420B (for officers)
> 2100 2nd Street, S.W.
> Washington, DC 20593
> (202) 267-6971

Other U. S. Coast Guard Records

All recreational boats in the United States bear a hull number that is traceable through the Coast Guard. The first three digits of the number are the *Manufaciurer's Identification Code* (MIC number). From this number you can learn manufacturer's name and address, whether it is still in business, the USCG district in which the manufacturer is located, its state of origin, the types of vessels it manufactures, the date that particular number was assigned and the manufacturer's telephone number. Usually the manufacturer can provide you with some ownership and maintenance information about the specific vessel.

> U.S. Coast Guard, Office of Navigation Safety & Waterway Services, 2100 2nd St., S.W., Washington, DC 20593-0001 (202) 267-1077, (800) 367-5647.

Federal Aviation Administration

The friendly folks in Oklahoma City will provide information about any pilot (name, address, rating, date of last exam, license number) or any plane (including owners, aircraft type, wing number, aircraft history, etc.). For rush orders, you can send them a check by overnight mail. Marked the check "Not to exceed $10.00". They'll provide hard copies or microfiche.

> F.A.A. Airman Certification Branch, Box 25082,
> Attn: AVN460, Oklahoma City, OK 73125
> (405) 954-3261
> **Aircraft Certification** (405) 954-3261
> **Medical Certification** (405) 954-4821
> **Accidents and violations** (405) 954-4173

Federal Election Commission—This is where to go for information about political candidates, campaigns and political action committees (PACs) at the federal level. The information is similar to that available at the county registrar of voters, but more automated. The FEC's reports enable you to learn the full names and addresses of candidates, how much money was spent on campaigns, how much money was loaned to a candidate or PAC, where the money is going and who's contributing. Clearly identify the candidate or PAC, the date of the report and the type of the report. Payment is required in advance (5 cents per page for copies from paper, 15 cents per page for copies from microfilm).

It's also possible to access the FEC's computers directly. It requires a pre-paid account deposit of at least $25.00. For information, contact Phyliss Thompson at (800) 424-9530.

> Public Records Office, 999 E St., N.W., Washington, DC 20463 (800) 424-9530

National Archives—You could spend a career looking through the mountains of material stored at the National Archives in the nation's capital. The people there store inactive material from hundreds of current and former government agencies. There are experts on duty there in just about every field available. Looking for German spies during World War II? There's an expert who will send you indices of all the German papers captured by U.S. forces.

There are also regional **Federal Records Centers** around the U.S. that store inactive and semi-inactive records for all federal agencies in California and some western states. It's important you always first contact the agency so that it can help you identify the files they may have sent there. This is also where U.S. District Courts send their inactive civil, criminal and bankruptcy files.

To review and/or copy case file information you must first obtain critical information from the U.S. District Court that issued the case. (See listings under **U.S. District Court**). You must obtain the case file number, case file name(s), FRC (Federal Records Center) accession number, FRC location number and the agency box number.

Then you must telephone the appropriate Federal Records Center and provide the staff member with the above information. After that person confirms your file is there, he or she will set up an appointment for you to view and/or copy the materials. Copies are $.50 per page—$2.00 per case file for certification. You may also order copies by mail, but be sure to chat with the people first.

The **Federal Records Centers** also house genealogical records including microfilm of U.S. Census records up to 1910.

>**National Archives and Records Administration, 7th and Pennsylvania Ave., NW, Washington, DC 20408 (202) 501-5402**
>
>**Federal Records Center -- Southern California, 24000 Avila Road, P.O. Box 6719, Laguna Niguel, CA 92677-6719 (714) 643-4241 (serves Arizona Clark County, Nevada and So. Calif. counties of Imperial, Inyo, Kern, Los Angeles, Orange, Riverside, San Bernardino, San Diego, San Luis Obispo, Santa Barbara and Ventura).**
>
>**Federal Records Center -- Northern California, 1000 Commodore Drive, San Bruno, CA 94066 (415) 876-9009 (serves Hawaii, Nevada -- except Clark County, and the California counties not listed in the Southern California branch listed above).**

National Personnel Records Center

This is where you can obtain military records for *most* persons retired or discharged from the military. Before you start, keep in mind that a fire on July 12, 1973 destroyed all Army records between 1912 and 1960 and all records of former Air Force personnel whose last names begin with H-Z for the years 1947-1963. A Freedom of Information Act Request is required for the release of information. You must know the person's name, age or date of birth, branch of service and, preferably, the date of entrance and/or discharge.

You can either use Standard Form 180, *Request for Military Information*, or submit a typed letter in the form of a Freedom of Information Act request. For normal requests there's a basic fee that ranges between $8 and $12. The folks there will acknowledge the request within 10 days and will provide the information within about three weeks. In the FOIA request you should specifically ask for all the following items:

> Marital status
> Dependents (name, sex, age)
> Rank or grade and date of salary
> Present and past duty assignments
> Future assignments
> Office phone numbers
> Source of commission
> Military and civilian education level
> Promotion sequence number
> Decorations and/or awards
> Education and schooling
> Duty status
> Photograph
> Records of court martial trials (unclassified)
> Serial number or service number
> Social Security number
> Home town (newly available)

They will *not* provide date of birth, home address or other personal information. For deceased persons, they'll also provide:

> Dates of service
> Date and place of birth
> Date and location of death
> Place of burial

National Personnel Records Center, 9700 Page Blvd., St. Louis, MO 63132. (314) 263-3901

Other Custodians of Military Records -- This is
going to seem confusing, but take a deep breath and read on. What follows comes from the back side of **Standard Form 180, Request Pertaining To Military Records**. The information listed in this chapter titled **Armed Service Locators** may be more up to date regarding active duty personnel, but the information that follows *is* the official stuff. Don't blame me, blame Uncle Sam. Information on the following pages relates to these custodians:

1. Air Force Manpower and Personnel Center
   Military Personnel Records Division
   Randolph AFB, TX 78150-6001

2. Air Reserve Personnel Center
   Denver, CO 80280-5000

3. Commandant
   U.S. Coast Guard
   Washington, DC 20593-0001

4. Commandant of the Marine Corps (Code MMRB-10)
   Headquarters, U.S. Marine Corps
   Washington, DC 20380-0001

5. Marine Corps Reserve Support Center
   10950 El Monte
   Overland Park, KS 66211-1408

6. Military Archives Division
   National Archives and Records Administration
   Washington, DC 20408

7. Commander
   U.S. Army Reserve Personnel Center
   ATTN: DARP-PAS
   9700 Page Boulevard
   St. Louis, MO 63132-5200

8. USA MILPERCEN
   ATTN: DAPC-MSR
   200 Stoval Street
   Alexandria, VA 22332-0400

U.S. GOVERNMENT OFFICES

9. Commander
   U.S. Army Enlisted Records & Evaluation Center
   Ft. Benjamin Harrison, IN 46249-5301

10. Commander
    Naval Military Personnel Command
    ATTN: NMPC-036
    Washington, DC 20370-5036

11. Naval Reserve Personnel Center
    New Orleans, LA 70146-5000

12. Army National Guard Personnel Center
    Columbia Pike Office Building
    5600 Columbia Pike
    Falls Church, VA 22041

13. The Adjutant General
    (of the appropriate state, DC, or Puerto Rico)

14. National Personnel Records Center
    (Military Personnel Records)
    9700 Page Boulevard
    St. Louis, MO 63132

Air Force: *Except for service persons on the Temporary Disability Retirement List (TDRL) and general officers retired with pay, Air Force records are transferred to #14 from #1, 90 days after separation and from #2, 150 days after separation.*

Active members (includes National Guard on active duty in the Air Force, TDRL, and general officers retired with pay). See #1.

Reserve, retired reservist in nonpay status, current National Guard officers not on active duty in Air Force, and National Guard released from active duty in Air force. See #2.

Current National Guard enlisted not on active duty in Air Force. See #13.

Discharged, deceased, and retired with pay. See #14 (and *National Personnel Records Center* listing on page 51 in this book).

Coast Guard: *Coast Guard officer and enlisted records are transferred to #14 7 months after separation.*
Active, reserve, and TDRL members. See #3.
Discharged, deceased and retired members (see next item). See #14 (And Page 51).
Officers separated before 1/1/29 and enlisted personnel separated before 1/1/14. See #6.

Marine Corps: *Marine Corps records are transferred to #14 between 6 and 9 months after separation.*
Active, TDRL, and Selected Marine Corps Reserve members. See #4.
Individual Ready Reserve and Fleet Marine Corps Reserve members. See #5.
Discharged, deceased, and retired members (see next item). See #14 (and page 51).
Members separated before 1/1/1905. See #6.

Army: *Army records are transferred to #14 as follows: Active Army and Individual Ready Reserve Control Groups: About 60 days after separation. U.S. Army Reserve Troop Unit personnel: About 120 to 180 days after separation.*
Reserve, living retired members, retired general officers, and active duty records of current National Guard members who performed service in the U.S. Army before 7/1/72. See #7.
Active officers (including National Guard on active duty in the U.S. Army). See #8.
Active enlisted (including National Guard on active duty in the U.S. Army) and enlisted TDRL. See #9.
Current National Guard officers not on active duty in the U.S. Army. See #12.
Current National Guard enlisted not on active duty in the U.S. Army. See #13.
Discharged and deceased members (see next item). See #14 (and page 51).
Officers separated before 7/1/17 and enlisted separated before 11/1/12. See #6.
Officers and warrant officers TDRL. See #8.

Navy: *Navy records are transferred to #14 six months after retirement or complete separation.*
Active members (including reservists on duty). For personnel and medical records see #10.

Discharged, deceased, retired (with and without pay) less than six months, TDRL, drilling and nondrilling reservists. For personnel records see #10. For medical records see #11.

Discharged, deceased, retired (with or without pay) more than six months (see next item). See #14 (and page 51).

Officers separated before 1/1/03 and enlisted separated before 1/1/1886. See #6.

Office of Personnel Management—Write to these folks to locate retired military or retired civil service members who receive a retirement check.

The Office of Personnel Management, 1900 E Street, N.W., Washington, DC 20415.

Securities and Exchange Commission—Any company that sells stock openly to the public or is a very large privately-owned firm must file various reports with the SEC. Sometimes volumes of information are available—including the compensation of top executives, what the corporation does, manufactures and owns, who's suing the firm and who owns large portions of the stock.

Disclosure Inc. is a commercial demand center on contract with the SEC to provide copies of all filings. The folks there will deliver, mail or overnight mail hard copies or microfiche copies for a fee. They'll also fax you hard copies for a fee. Information seekers with heavy demand for SEC information might consider some of Disclosure's other services.

Their "Laser D" provides image-based documents stored on laser disk. It provides actual computer images of 10Ks, 10Qs, 8Ks, perspecti, proxies, registrations and annual reports as well as many banking-related documents filed with other agencies. These images are also available for sale on microfiche. Since these are images of documents, they are not full-text searchable. For more information, contact Laddie Hunter at (213) 934-8531 or Karen Walshe at (415) 986-3780.

Disclosure also provides information abstracted from SEC filings on CD format. Since this is loaded in the ASCII computer language, you can do full-text searches.

They'll also sell you floppy computer disks that store in-depth information about the top 500 industrial firms and the top 500 service corporations.

Still not easy enough? Disclosure's ORDERLINE enables you to use your computer and modem to access indices of SEC filings available. Subscribers pay a minimum of $75.00 per month (which includes one hour of on-line time). Additional time is about $1.25 per minute.

Disclosure, Inc., 5757 Wilshire Blvd., Los Angeles, 90036 (213) 934-8313, Fax: (213) 934-1829
Downtown L.A., World Trade Center, 350 S. Figueroa St., #475, Los Angeles, 90071 (213) 621-2927, Fax: (213) 621-2927, (800) 843-7747
San Francisco, 425 California St., #410, San Francisco, 94104 (415) 986-1775, Fax: (415) 986-4159
Bethesda, MD, 5161 River Rd., Bethesda, MD 20816 (800) 638-8241, Fax: (301) 951-1302
U.S. Securities and Exchange Commission, 450 5th St. Northwest, Washington DC 20549 (202) 942-8090
Los Angeles Regional Office, 5770 Wilshire Blvd., Suite 268 East, Los Angeles 90036-3648 (213) 965-3998, Fax: (213) 965-3815 (serves Nevada, Arizona, California, Hawaii and Guam).
San Francisco Branch Office, 44 Montgomery St., #1100, San Francisco 94104 (415) 705-2500, Fax: (415) 705-2501

Social Security Administration—Not a great source of information for either the private citizen or law enforcement. However, the folks there will verify that the bearer of a particular Social Security number has died. They will also tell you when and where the death was reported. And, in the most urgent and extreme cases, the people there will forward a letter to another person on behalf of another person.

Office of Public Inquiries, 4100 Annex Building, Social Security Administration, 6401 Security Blvd., Baltimore, MD 21231 (800) 772-1213

Social Security Numbers by State

—The social security number can be helpful in identifying records as to belonging to a particular person. It often shows up on voter records, on credit applications, on marriage and divorce records, as an employee identification number or credit union account number or driver's license number (in some states) and, for the past two decades, as a military serial number. The first three digits of the number can help you determine where the card was issued.

001-003	New Hampshire	478-485	Iowa
004-007	Maine	486-500	Missouri
008-009	Vermont	501-502	North Dakota
010-034	Massachusetts	503-504	South Dakota
035-039	Rhode Island	505-508	Nebraska
040-049	Connecticut	509-515	Kansas
050-134	New York	516-517	Montana
135-158	New Jersey	518-519	Idaho
159-211*	Pennsylvania	520-520	Wyoming
212-220	Maryland	521-524	Colorado
221-222	Delaware	525-525	New Mexico
223-231	Virginia	526-527	Arizona
232	W. VA or NC	528-529	Utah
233-236	West Virginia	530	Nevada
237-246	North Carolina	531-539	Washington
247-251	South Carolina	540-544	Oregon
252-260	Georgia	545-573	California
261-267	Florida	574-574	Alaska
268-302	Ohio	575-576	Hawaii
303-317	Indiana	577-579	Washington DC
318-361	Illinois	580**	P.R./Virgin Isl.
362-386	Michigan	581-584	Puerto Rico
387-399	Wisconsin	585-585	New Mexico
400-407	Kentucky	586**	New Mexico
408-415	Tennessee	587	Mississippi
416-424	Alabama	589-595	Florida
425-428	Mississippi	600-601	Arizona
429-432	Arkansas	602-626	California
433-439	Louisiana	627-699	Unassigned
440-448	Oklahoma	700-728	RR Retirement
449-467	Texas	729-999	Unassigned
468-477	Minnesota		

* Some 200 series issued to aliens and Puerto Ricans during the war.
** Also assigned to South East Asian refugees from 4/75 to 11/79.

U.S. District Court—Civil, criminal, bankruptcy and naturalization cases are filed and heard here. Civil and criminal (including search warrants—usually sealed) are similar to those at the county level. Bankruptcy cases will provide lots of information about an individual or corporation. Look for extensive financial information and lists of debts and debtors.

> U.S. District Court, Northern District, 450 Golden Gate Ave., 16th Floor, Room 1111, San Francisco, 94102 (415) 556-4166
> Closed Files (415) 556-3030
> Naturalization (415) 556-1481
> Bankruptcy Clerk, 235 Pine St., 23rd Floor, San Francisco, 94104 (415) 705-3200
> U.S. District Court, Eastern District, 2546 U.S. Courthouse, 650 Capitol Mall, Sacramento, 95814
> Clerk (916) 551-2615, Bankruptcy (916) 551-2662
> U.S. District Court, Central District, 312 N. Spring Street, Los Angeles, 90012
> Criminal Section (213) 894-3646
> Civil (213) 894-2215, Records (213) 894-3649
> Los Angeles Area Bankruptcy (213) 894-4696, 894-5978, 894-3118
> Santa Ana Area Bankruptcy, 34 Civic Center Dr., #506, Santa Ana, 92701 (714) 836-2993
> San Bernardino Area Bankruptcy, 699 N. Arrowhead Ave., #105, San Bernardino, 92401 (909) 383-5717
> U.S. District Court, Southern District, 940 Front St., Room 1160, San Diego, 92189
> Clerk, Room (619) 557-5600
> San Diego Area Bankruptcy (619) 557-5620

U.S. Postal Service—Post office box applications are not public record unless the box holder is soliciting business though the mail. Show the postmaster or box section clerk that the box is used to solicit business and certain information is available off the application—such as name of box holder, address and phone number. One might also talk them into sharing the drivers license number of the box holder. It's worth a try. Another way of obtaining change of address information is to mail a letter to the old address marked **DO NOT FORWARD -- ADDRESS CORRECTION REQUESTED.** The Postal Service will note the new address on your envelope and return it to you postage due. And, there are records available on metered and permit mail. Jot down the numbers in the indicia and call the post office to find out who holds the permit or meter.

Veterans Administration -- A good source for tracing missing persons. Because of the Privacy Act, the V.A. cannot directly provide a person's address. But they'll forward a letter if the part they are to forward is in an unsealed envelope (they check it for threatening or insulting messages).

Veterans Administration, 536 S. Clark Street, Chicago, IL 60680

Genealogical Collections
Selected Government and Private Libraries.

Anaheim -- LDS Family History Library, 440 N. Loara, (714) 533-2772
Burbank -- Southern California Genealogical Society, 122 S. San Fernando Blvd., P.O. Box 4377, 91503 (818) 843-7247
Burbank -- Burbank Public Library, 110 N. Glenoaks Blvd., 91502 (818) 953-9737
Burbank -- The Immigrant Genealogical Society, 1310-B Magnolia Blvd., 91510 (818) 848-3122
Carlsbad -- Carlsbad City Library, 1250 Carlsbad Village Dr., 92008-1991 (619) 434-2870
Chino -- San Bernardino County Library, Chino Branch, 13180 Central Ave., 91710 (909) 590-5225
Claremont -- Honnold Library-Claremont Colleges, 800 N. Dartmouth Ave., 91711 (909) 621-8150, Fax: (909) 621-4733
Claremont -- Francis Bacon Library, 655 N. Dartmouth Ave., 91711-3979 (909) 624-6305
Claremont -- L.A. County Library, Claremont Branch, 208 N. Harvard, 91711 (909) 621-4902, Fax: (909) 621-2366
Claremont -- Claremont School of Theology Library, 1325 N. College, 91711-3199 (909) 626-3521
Coalinga -- Coalinga Unified School District Library, 305 N. 4th St., 93210 (209) 935-1676, Fax: (209) 935-1058
Corona -- Corona Public Library, 650 S. Main, 91720-3493 (909) 736-2381, 736-2387
Corona Del Mar -- Sherman Library and Gardens, 2647 E. Pacific Coast Hwy, 92625 (714) 673-2261
Covina -- LDS Family History Library, Covina Branch, 656 S. Grand Ave., 91723 (818) 331-7117

Diamond Bar -- L.A. County Library, Diamond Bar Branch, 1061 S. Grand Ave., 91765 (909) 861-4978
El Segundo -- El Segundo Library, 111 W. Mariposa Ave., 90245 (310) 322-4121, Fax: (310) 322-4323
Fullerton -- California State University, Fullerton, 800 N. State College Blvd., 92634 (714) 773-3455
Glendale -- Glendale Central Library, 222 E. Harvard St., 91205-1075 (818) 548-2020
Glendale -- Sons of the Revolution Library, 600 S. Central Ave., 91204 (818) 240-1775
Hemet -- California Family History Center, 425 N. Kirby St., 92343 (909) 658-8104
Huntington Beach -- Hungtington Beach Central Library, 7111 Talbert Ave., 92648 (714) 842-4481
Huntington Park -- Huntington Park Regional Library, 6518 Miles Ave., 90255 (213) 583-1461
Laguna Niguel -- National Archives Federal Record Center, 24000 Avila Rd., 92677-6719 (714) 643-4220
La Verne -- L.A. County Library, La Verne Branch, 3640 "D" St., 91750 (909) 596-1934
La Verne -- University of La Verne Wilson Library, 1950 3rd St., 91750 (909) 593-3511
La Verne -- German Genealogical Society of America, 2125 Wright Ave., 91750 (909) 593-0509
Long Beach -- Long Beach Public Library, 101 Pacific Ave., 90822 (310) 570-6291
Los Angeles -- California State University, Los Angeles Library, 5151 State University Dr., 90032 (213) 343-3980, 343-3995
Los Angeles -- L.A. Central Public Library, 630 W. 5th St., 90017 (213) 228-7000
Los Angeles -- LDS Family History Library, 10741 Santa Monica Blvd., 90025 (310) 474-9990
Los Angeles -- UCLA Research Library, 405 Hilgard Ave., 90024-1575 (310) 825-1323
Mission Viejo -- LDS Genealogical Library, 27976 Marguerite Pkwy, (714) 364-2742
Montclair -- San Bernardino County Library, Montclair Branch, 9955 Fremonts Street, 91763 (909) 624-4671
Oakland -- Oakland Public Library, 125 14th St., 94612 (510) 238-3281
Ontario -- Ontario Public Library, 215 E. "C" St., 91764-4198 (909) 988-8481
Orange -- LDS Family History Library, 674 S. Yorba St., 92613-6471 (714) 997-7710
Palm Springs -- Palm Springs Public Library, 300 S. Sunrise Way, 92262-7699 (619) 322-7323

Pasadena -- Pasadena Public Library, 285 E. Walnut St., 91101 (818) 405-4052
Pomona -- Pomona Public Library, 625 S. Garey Ave., P.O. Box 2271, 91766 (909) 620-2473
Rancho Cucamonga -- Chaffey College Library, 5885 Haven Ave., 91731 (909) 941-2400
Rancho Cucamonga -- San Bernardino County Law Library, 8303 Haven Ave., 91762 (909) 944-5106
Riverside -- LDS Family History Library, Riverside Branch, 4375 Jackson Ave., 92503 (909) 687-5542
Riverside -- Riverside City-County Library, 3581 7th St., P.O. Box 468, 92502 (909) 782-5201
Riverside -- University of California, Riverside, University Ave., 92517 (909) 787-4392
Roseville -- California State Archives, 201 N. Sunrise St., 95661 (916) 773-3000
Sacramento -- California State Library, 914 Capitol Mall, 95809 (916) 654-0183
San Bernardino -- San Bernardino County Law Library, 401 N. Arrowhead Ave., 92415 (909) 885-3020
San Diego -- San Diego Public Library, 820 "E" St., 92101-6478 (619) 236-5870
San Dimas -- L.A. County Library, San Dimas Branch, 145 N. Walnut, 91773 (909) 599-6738
San Francisco -- California Historical Society Library, 2099 Pacific Ave., 94019 (415) 567-1848
San Francisco -- San Francisco Public Library, 200 Larkin, 94102 (415) 557-4400
San Francisco -- California State Library, Sutro Branch, 480 Winston Dr., 94132 (415) 731-4477
San Jose -- Santa Clara County Free Library, 1095 N. 7th St., 95112-4434 (408) 293-2326
San Marino -- The Huntington Library, 1151 Oxford Rd., San Marino, CA 91108 (818) 405-2100
Santa Barbara -- Santa Barbara Historical Society, 136 E. De la Guerra, P.O. Box 578, 93102 (805) 966-1601
Santa Clara -- Santa Clara Public Library, 2635 Homestead Rd., 95051 (408) 984-3236
Santa Fe Springs -- Santa Fe Springs Library, 11700 E. Telegraph Rd., 90670 (310) 868-7738
Santa Rosa -- Sonoma County Library, 3rd and "E" Sts., 95404 (707) 545-0831
Stockton -- Stockton-San Joaquin Library, 605 N. El Dorado St., 95202 (209) 937-8221
Thousand Oaks --Thousand Oaks Public Library, 1401 E. Janss Rd., 91362-2199 (805) 497-6282

Torrance -- The Augustan Society, 1313 Sartori Ave., 90501
(310) 320-7766
Tulare -- Tulare Public Library, 113 N. "F" St., 93274 (209) 685-2341
Ukiah -- Mendocino County Library, 105 N. Main St., 95482-4482
(707) 463-4491
Upland -- LDS Family History Library, Upland Branch, 785 N. San
Antonio Ave., 91786 (909) 985-8821
Upland -- Upland Public Library, 450 N. Euclid Ave., 91786
(909) 981-1033
Walnut -- L.A. County Library, Walnut Branch, 21155 La Puente Rd.,
91789 (714) 595-0757
Whittier -- Whittier College Library, 7031 Founders Hill Rd.,
90608-9984 (310) 907-4247
Yreka -- Siskiyou County Library, 719 4th St., 96097
(916) 842-8175

California Municipalities
Including selected unincorporated cities, towns and neighborhoods.

What follows is a listing of every incorporated city in California as well as other towns, neighborhoods or districts. Listings here which show no address for a city hall, library or police department may actually be either unincorporated cities or cities that contract certain services with the county. If that's the case, simply turn to the *Counties* section for listings of the county clerk, county library, the county sheriff and other offices. Many outlying sheriff stations are also listed in the *Counties* section. You'll find all daily newspapers included here, usually listed in the city of publication. If no newspaper is listed, again, turn to the *Counties* section to determine the county seat and then look up that county seat in this *Municipalities* section.

Acton (Los Angeles Co.), 93510, Unincorporated
   Chamber of Commerce, P.O. Box 81, 93510 (805) 269-5785, Fax: (805) 269-4639
Adelanto (San Bernardino Co.), 11600 Air Base Road, P.O. Box 10, 92301 (619) 246-2300, Fax: (619) 246-8421
   Chamber of Commerce, 17451 Racoon Ave., #1, P.O. Box 700, 92301 (619) 246-5711
   Library, 11744 Bartlett St., 92301 (619) 246-5661
   Police, P.O. Box 10, 92301 (619) 246-8636

Agoura Hills (Los Angeles Co.), 30101 Agoura Court, Suite 102, 91301
(818) 597-7300, Fax: (818) 597-7341
Chamber of Commerce, 29054 Thousand Oaks Blvd., 91301
(818) 889-3150, Fax: (818) 889-3366
Library, 29130 W. Roadside Dr., 91301 (818) 889-2278
Sheriff Station, 27050 Agoura Rd., Calabasas, 91301 (818) 878-1808
Agua Dulce (Los Angeles Co.), Unincorporated
Chamber of Commerce, (see Santa Clarita)
Alameda (Alameda Co.), 2263 Santa Clara Ave., 94501 (510) 748-4500,
Fax: (510) 748-4504
Chamber of Commerce, 909 Marina Village Pkwy., P.O. Box 348,
94501 (510) 522-0414, Fax: (510) 522-7677
Library, 2264 Santa Clara Ave., 94501 (510) 748-4660
Newspaper, *The Alameda Times Star*, 1516 Oak St., 94501
(510) 523-1200, Fax: (510) 748-0437
Police, 1555 Oak St., 94501 (510) 748-4508
Albany (Alameda Co.), 1000 San Pablo Ave., 94706 (510) 528-5720,
Fax: (510) 528-5797
Chamber of Commerce, 1108 Solano Ave., 94706 (510) 525-1771,
(510) 525-1850
Library, 1216 Solano Ave., 94706 (510) 526-3720,
Fax: (510) 526-8754
Police, 1000 San Pablo Ave., 94706 (510) 525-7300
Alhambra (Los Angeles Co.), 111 S. First St., P.O. Box 351, 91802-2351,
(818) 570-5007, Fax: (818) 284-4905
Chamber of Commerce, 104 S. First St., 91801 (818) 282-8481,
Fax: (818) 282-5596
Library, 410 W. Main St., 91801 (818) 570-5079,
Fax: (818) 284-6251
Newspaper, *San Gabriel Valley Daily Tribune*, P.O. Box 1259,
Covina, 91722 (818) 962-8811, Fax: (818) 962-8849
Police, 211 S. First St., 91801 (818) 570-5151
Aliso Viejo (Orange County), Unincorporated
Chamber of Commerce, (see Laguna Hills)
Alpine (San Diego Co.), 90901, Unincorporated
Chamber of Commerce, 2157 Alpine Blvd., 90901, P.O. Box 69,
91903 (619) 445-2722, Fax: (619) 445-1421
Library, 2130 Arnold Way, 91901 (619) 445-4221
Newspaper, *Alpine Sun*, 2144-B Alpine Blvd., 91903 (619) 445-3288
Altadena (Los Angeles Co.), 91001, Unincorporated
Chamber of Commerce, 2246 N. Lake Ave., P.O. Box 336, 91001
(818) 794-3988
Library, 600 E. Mariposa St., 91001 (818) 798-0834
Alturas (Modoc Co.), 200 North St., 96101 (916) 233-2512,
Fax: (916) 233-3559
Chamber of Commerce, 522 S. Main St., 96101 (916) 233-4434
Library, 212 W. Third St., 96101-3913 (916) 233-6326,
Fax: (916) 233-3375
Newspaper, *Modoc County Record*, Box 531, 96101 (916) 233-2632,
Fax: (916) 233-5113
Police, 200 W. North St., 96101 (916) 233-2011

Alviso (Santa Clara Co.), 95103 Unincorporated,
   Police, 201 W. Mission St., San Jose, 95103 (408) 277-5300
   Sheriff, P.O. Box 270, San Jose, 95103 (818) 277-4212
Amador (Amador Co.), 14531 E. Schoolhouse Rd., 95601 (209) 267-0682
   Chamber of Commerce, (see Jackson)
   Sheriff, 700 Court St., Jackson, 95642 (209) 223-6500
American Canyon (Napa Co.), 2185 Elliott Dr., 94589 (707) 647-4360,
   Fax: (707) 642-1249
Anaheim (Orange Co.), 200 S. Anaheim Blvd., 92805, P.O. Box 3222, 92803
   (714) 254-5100, Fax: (714) 254-5164
   Chamber of Commerce, 100 S. Anaheim Blvd., #300, 92805
   (714) 758-0222, Fax: (714) 758-0468
   Library, 500 W. Broadway, 92805-3699 (714) 254-1880,
   Fax: (714) 254-1731
   Newspaper, *Anaheim Bulletin*, 17666 Fitch, Irvine, 92714
   (714) 634-1567, Fax: (714) 978-8062
   Newspaper, *The Orange County Register*, 625 N. Grand Ave., Santa
   Ana, 92701 (714) 835-1234, Fax: (714) 543-3904
   Police, P.O. Box 3369, 92803 (714) 254-1900
Anderson (Shasta Co.), 1887 Howard St., 96007 (916) 378-6626,
   Fax: (916) 378-6666
   Chamber of Commerce, 1856 Hwy. 273 & Deschutes Rd.,
   P.O. Box 1144, 96007 (916) 365-8095,
   Fax: (916) 365-4561
   Library, 3200 W. Center, 96007 (916) 365-7685
   Newspaper, *The Valley Post*, 2680 Gateway Dr., P.O. Box 1148,
   96007 (916) 365-2797
   Police, 2220 North St., 96007 (916) 378-6600
Angel's Camp (Calaveras Co.), 248 S. Main St., P.O. Box 667, 95222
   (209) 736-2181, Fax: (209) 736-0517
   Library, P.O. Box 456, 95222 (209) 736-2198
   Newspaper, *Calaveras Californian*, 1243 S. Main St., P.O. Box 9,
   95222-0009 (209) 736-2085
   Police, 753 S. Main St., 95222 (209) 736-2567
Angwin (Napa Co.), 94508, Unincorporated
   Chamber of Commerce, P.O. Box 747, 94508 (707) 965-2047
Antioch (Contra Costa Co.), 3rd & "H" Streets, P.O. Box 130, 94509-0504
   (510) 779-7000, Fax: (510) 778-8178
   Chamber of Commerce, 301 W. 10th St., 94509 (510) 757-1800,
   Fax: (510) 757-5286
   Library, 501 W. 18th St., 94509 (510) 427-8541
   Newspaper, *The Daily Ledger*, 1650 Cavallo Rd., 94509
   (510) 757-2525, Fax: (510) 754-9483
   Police, 301 "L" St., 94509 (510) 757-2236
Anza (Riverside Co.), 92539, Unincorporated
   Chamber of Commerce, P.O. Box 391460, 92539 (909) 763-0141
Apple Valley (San Bernardino Co.), 22521 Shawnee Rd., P.O. Box 429,
   92307 (619) 240-7000, Fax: (619) 247-3885
   Chamber of Commerce, 17928 Hwy. 18, P.O. Box 1073, 92307
   (619) 242-2753, Fax: (619) 242-0303
   Library, 15001 Wakita Rd., 92307 (619) 247-2022,
   Fax: (619) 247-9729

Apple Valley Newspapers, *Apple Valley News,* P.O. Box 1147,
    92307 (619) 247-6700
    Sheriff, 22521 Shawnee Rd., #B, 92308 (619) 240-7400
Aptos (Sacramento Co.), 95005, Unincorporated
    Chamber of Commerce, 9099 Soquel Dr., #12, 95003
        (408) 688-1467
Arcadia (Los Angeles Co.), 240 W. Huntington Dr., 91007, P.O. Box 60,
        91006-0060 (818) 574-5400, Fax: (818) 446-5729
    Chamber of Commerce, 388 W. Huntington Dr., 91007
        (818) 445-2159, (818) 445-1400, Fax: (818) 445-0273
    Library, 20 W. Duarte Rd., 91006 (818) 446-7112
    Police, 250 W. Huntington Dr., 91007 (818) 574-5150
Arcata (Humboldt Co.), 736 "F" St., 95521 (707) 822-5951,
        Fax: (707) 822-8018
    Chamber of Commerce, 1062 "G" St., 95521 (707) 822-3619,
        (707) 822-3515
    Library, 500 7th St., 95521 (707) 822-5954
    Humboldt State University Library, 95521 (707) 826-3441
    Newspaper, *The Union,* P.O. Box 1146, 95521-1146
        (707) 826-8550, Fax: (707) 826-8556
    Police, 736 "F" St., 95521 (707) 822-2428
Arleta (Los Angeles Co.), City of Los Angeles
Arroyo Grande (San Luis Obispo Co.), 214 E. Branch St., 93421,
        P.O. Box 550, 93420 (805) 489-1303, Fax: (805) 473-0386
    Chamber of Commerce, 800-A W. Branch St., 93420
        (805) 489-1488, Fax: (805) 489-2239
    Newspaper, *Five Cities Times Press Recorder,* P.O. Box 460, 93421
        (805) 489-4206, Fax: (805) 473-0571
    Police, 200 N. Halcyon Rd., 93420 (805) 489-2121
Artesia (Los Angeles Co.), 18747 Clarkdale Ave., 90701 (310) 865-6262,
        Fax: (310) 865-6240
    Chamber of Commerce, 11642 Artesia Blvd., 90701-3802
        (310) 924-6397, Fax: (310) 924-8545
    Library, 18722 S. Clarkdale Ave., 90701 (310) 865-6614,
        Fax: (310) 924-4644
    Sheriff, 5130 N. Clark Ave., Lakewood 90712 (310) 866-9061
Arvin (Kern Co.), 200 Campus Dr., P.O. Box 548, 93203 (805) 854-3134,
        Fax: (805) 854-0817
    Chamber of Commerce, P.O. Box 192, 93203 (805) 854-2265,
        (805) 854-3801
    Library, (see Bakersfield)
    Police, P.O. Box 548, 93203 (805) 854-5583
Atascadero (San Luis Obispo Co.), 6500 Palma Ave., 93422 (805) 461-5013,
        Fax: (805) 461-0606
    Chamber of Commerce, 6550 El Camino Real, 93422
        (805) 466-2044, Fax: (805) 466-9218
    Library, 6850 Morro Rd., 93422 (805) 466-0142
    Newspaper, *Atascadero News,* P.O. Box 6068, 93423
        (805) 466-2585, Fax: (805) 466-2714
    Police, P.O. Box 911, 93423 (805) 461-5051
Athens (Los Angeles Co.), Unincorporated

Atherton (San Mateo Co.), 91 Ashfield Rd., 94027 (415) 325-4457,
  Fax: (415) 688-6528
  Library, 2 Dinklespiel, 94027 (415) 328-2422, Fax: (415) 328-4138
  Police, 83 Ashfield Rd., 94025 (415) 323-8471
Atwater (Los Angeles Co.), City of Los Angeles
  Library, 3379 Glendale Blvd., 90039 (213) 664-1353,
    Fax: (213) 485-8159
Atwater (Merced Co.), 750 Bellevue Rd., 95301 (209) 357-6314,
    Fax: (209) 357-6333
  Chamber of Commerce, 1181 Third St., P.O. Box 388, 95301
    (209) 358-4251, Fax: (209) 358-0934
  Library, 1600 Third St., 95301 (209) 358-6651
  Newspaper, *The Signal*, 927 Atwater Blvd., 95301 (209) 358-6431,
    Fax: (209) 357-2968
  Police, 750 Bellevue Rd., 95301 (209) 357-6396
Auburn (Placer Co.), 1225 Lincoln Way, 95603 (916) 823-4211,
    Fax: (916) 885-5508
  Chamber of Commerce, 601 Lincoln Way, 95603 (916) 885-5616,
    (800) 427-6463, Fax: (916) 885-5854
  Library, 350 Nevada St., 95603-3789 (916) 889-4111,
    Fax: (916) 889-4111
  Newspaper, *The Auburn Journal*, 1030 High St., P.O. Box 5910,
    95604 (916) 885-5656, Fax: (916) 885-4902
  Police, 1215 Lincoln Way, 95603-5004 (916) 823-4235
Avalon (Los Angeles Co.), Catalina Island, 209 Metropole Ave.,
    P.O. Box 707, 90704-0707 (310) 510-0220,
    Fax: (310) 510-0901
  Chamber of Commerce, #1 Green Pier, P.O. Box 217, 90704
    (310) 510-1520, Fax: (310) 510-7606
  Library, 215 Sumner Ave., P.O. Box 585, 90704 (310) 510-1050,
    Fax: (310) 510-1645
  Newspaper, *The Catalina Islander*, P.O. Box 428, 90704
    (310) 510-0500, Fax: (310) 510-2882
  Sheriff, 215 Sumner Ave., P.O. Box 1551, 90704 (310) 510-0174
Avenal (Kings Co.), 919 Skyline Blvd., 93204 (209) 386-5766,
    Fax: (209) 386-0679
  Chamber of Commerce, 211 E. Kings St., 93204 (209) 386-0690,
    Fax: (209) 386-4208
  Library, 501 E. King St., 93204 (209) 386-5741
  Sheriff, P.O. Box 158, 93204 (209) 386-5361
Azusa (Los Angeles Co.), 213 E. Foothill Blvd., P.O. Box 1395, 91702
    (818) 334-5125, Fax: (818) 334-5464
  Chamber of Commerce, 240 W. Foothill Blvd., 91702
    (818) 334-1507, (818) 334-0507, Fax: (818) 334-5217
  Library, 729 N. Dalton Ave., 91702 (818) 334-0338,
    Fax: (818) 334-4868
  Police, 725 N. Alameda Ave., 91702 (818) 812-3252
Baker (San Bernardino Co.), Unincorporated
Bakersfield (Kern Co.), 1501 Truxtun Ave., 93301 (805) 326-3767,
    Fax: (805) 324-1850
  Chamber of Commerce, 1033 Truxtun Ave., P.O. Box 1947, 93303
    (805) 327-4421, Fax: (805) 327-8751

Bakersfield Library, 701 Truxtun Ave., 93301-4816 (805) 861-2130
Newspaper, *The Bakersfield Californian*, 1707 Eye St.,
P.O. Box BIN 440, 93302 (805) 395-7500,
Fax: (805) 395-7519
Police, P.O. Box 59, 93302 (805) 326-3800
Balboa Island (Orange Co.), City of Newport Beach
Baldwin Hills (Los Angeles Co.), City of Los Angeles
Library, 2906 S. La Brea Ave., 90016 (213) 733-1196,
Fax: (213) 612-0429
Baldwin Park (Los Angeles Co.), 14403 E. Pacific Ave., 91706
(818) 960-4011, Fax: (818) 962-2625
Chamber of Commerce, 4141 N. Maine Ave., 91706 (818) 960-4848,
Fax: (818) 960-2990
Library, 4181 Baldwin Park Blvd., 91706 (818) 962-6947,
Fax: (818) 337-6631
Newspaper, *San Gabriel Valley Daily Tribune*, P.O. Box 1259,
Covina, 91722 (818) 962-8811, Fax: (818) 962-8849
Police, 14403 E. Pacific Ave., 91706 (818) 960-1955
Banning (Riverside Co.), 99 E. Ramsey St., P.O. Box 998, 92220
(909) 922-1295, Fax: (909) 922-0445
Chamber of Commerce, 123 E. Ramsey St., P.O. Box 665, 92223
(909) 849-4695
Library, 21 W. Nicolet St., 92220-4699 (909) 849-3192
Newspaper,*The Record-Gazette*, 218 N. Murray, P.O. Box 727,
92220 (909) 849-4586, Fax: (909) 849-2437
Police, 125 E. Ramsey St., 92220 (909) 922-1290
Barstow (San Bernardino Co.), 220 E. Mountain View St., 92311
(619) 256-3531, Fax: (619) 256-1750
Chamber of Commerce, 222 E. Main St., #216, P.O. Box 698, 92311
(619) 256-8617, Fax: (619) 256-7675
Library, 304 E. Buena Vista, 92311 (619) 256-4850
Newspaper, *Desert Dispatch*, 130 Coolwater Lane, 92311
(619) 256-2257, Fax: (619) 256-0685
Police, 220 E. Mountain View St., 92311 (619) 256-3531
Bassett (Los Angeles Co.), Unincorporated
Bass Lake (Madera Co.), 93604, Unincorporated
Chamber of Commerce, P.O. Box 126, 93604 (209) 642-3676
Bay Area Rapid Transit District
Police, 800 Madison St., Oakland, 94607 (415) 464-7010
Baywood Park (San Luis Obispo Co.), Unincorporated
Chamber of Commerce, (see Los Osos)
Bear Valley Springs (Kern Co.), 93561, Unincorporated
Police, 25101 Bear Valley Rd., Tehachapi, 93561 (805) 821-3441
Beaumont (Riverside Co.), 550 E. 6th St., P.O. Box 158, 92223
(909) 845-1171, Fax: (909) 845-8483
Chamber of Commerce, 450 E. 4th St., P.O. Box 637, 92223
(909) 845-9541, Fax: (909) 769-9080
Library, 125 E. 8th St., 92223 (909) 845-1357, Fax: (714) 845-6217
Police, 660 Orange Ave., 92223 (909) 845-1161
Bel Air Estates (Los Angeles Co.), City of Los Angeles

Bell (Los Angeles Co.), 6330 Pine Ave., 90201 (213) 588-6211,
   Fax: (213) 771-9473
   Chamber of Commerce, 6526 Wilcox Ave., P.O. Box 294, 90201
      (213) 560-8755, Fax: (213) 560-0608
   Library, 4411 E. Gage Ave., 90201 (213) 560-2149,
      Fax: (213) 773-7557
   Police, 6326 Pine Ave., 90201-1290 (213) 588-6211
Bell Gardens (Los Angeles Co.), 7100 S. Garfield Ave., 90201
      (310) 806-7700, Fax: (310) 806-7709
   Chamber of Commerce, 6900 S. Garfield Ave., #C, 90201
      (310) 927-5418, (310) 927-5318
   Library, 7110 S. Garfield Ave., 90201 (310) 927-1309,
      Fax: (310) 928-4512
   Police, 7100 S. Garfield Ave., 90201 (310) 806-4573
Bellflower (Los Angeles Co.), 16600 Civic Center Dr., 90706 (310) 804-1424,
      Fax: 925-8660
   Chamber of Commerce, 9729 E. Flower St., 90706 (310) 867-1744,
      Fax: (310) 866-7545
   Library, 9945 E. Flower St., 90706 (310) 925-5543
   Sheriff, 5130 N. Clark Ave., Lakewood, 90712 (310) 866-9061
Belmont (San Mateo Co.), 1365 5th Ave., 94002 (415) 595-7408,
      Fax: (415) 595-5206
   Chamber of Commerce, 1365 5th Ave., P.O. Box 645, 94002
      (415) 595-8696
   Library, 1110 Alameda, 94002 (415) 591-8286, Fax: (415) 591-1195
   Police, 1215 Ralston Ave., 94002 (415) 595-7400
Belmont Shore (Los Angeles Co.), City of Long Beach
Belvedere (Marin Co.), 450 San Rafael Ave., 94920 (415) 435-3838,
      Fax: (415) 435-0430
   Library, P.O. Bldg., Beach Rd., Tiburon, 94920-2343
      (415) 435-1361, Fax: (415) 435-1786
   Police, 450 San Rafael Ave., 94920 (415) 435-2611
Benicia (Solano Co.), 250 E. "L" St., 94510 (707) 746-4201,
      Fax: (707) 747-8120
   Chamber of Commerce, 601 First St., P.O. Box 185, 94510
      (707) 745-2120, Fax: (707) 745-2275
   Library, 144 E. "L" St., 94510 (707) 745-2265
   Newspaper, *Benicia Herald*, 820 First Ben, 94510 (707) 745-0733
   Police, 200 E. "L" St., 94510 (707) 745-3412
Berkeley (Alameda Co.), 2180 Milvia St., 94704 (510) 644-6480,
      Fax: (510) 644-8801
   Chamber of Commerce, 1834 University Ave., 94703
      (510) 549-7000, Fax: (510) 549-1789
   Library, 2090 Kittredge St., 94704 (510) 644-6095
   Newspaper, *The Daily Californian*, 2150 Dwight Way. 94704
      (510) 849-2482, Fax: (510) 849-2803
   Police, 2171 McKinley Ave., 94703 (510) 644-6568
   U.C. Berkeley Police, Sproul Hall, Room 2, 94720 (510) 642-1133
   U.C. Lawrence Berkeley Lab, #1 Cyclotron Rd. 90-0014, 94720
      (510) 486-5472
Bethel Island (Contra Costa Co.), 94511, Unincorporated
   Chamber of Commerce, P.O. Box 263, 94511 (510) 684-3220

Beverly Glen (Los Angeles Co.), City of Los Angeles
Beverly Hills (Los Angeles Co.), 455 N. Rexford Dr., 90210 (310) 285-1000,
  Fax: (310) 274-3267
   Chamber of Commerce, 239 S. Beverly Dr., 90212 (310) 271-8126,
     (800) 345-2210, Fax: (310) 858-8032
   Library, 444 N. Rexford Dr., 90210-4877 (310) 288-2244,
     Fax: (310) 278-3387
   Newspaper, *Beverly Hills Post,* 1433 S. Robertson Blvd., L.A.,
     90035 (310) 552-5200, Fax: (310) 552-5212
   Police, 464 N. Rexford Dr., 90210 (310) 550-4951
Big Bear Lake (San Bernardino Co.), 39707 Big Bear Blvd., 92315,
   P.O. Box 10000, 92315-8900 (909) 866-5831,
   Fax: (909) 866-6766
   Chamber of Commerce, 630 Bartlett Rd., P.O. Box 2860, 92315
     (909) 866-4608, (909) 866-7008, Fax: (909) 866-5412
   Library, 41930 Garstin Dr., 92315 (909) 866-0162,
     Fax: (909) 866-6766
   Newspaper, *Big Bear Life & The Grrizly,* P.O. Box 1789, 92315
     (714) 866-3456, Fax: (714) 866-2302
   Sheriff, 477 Summit Blvd., P.O. Box 2803, 92315 (909) 866-0100
Big Sur (Monterey Co.), 93920, Unincorporated
   Library, Ripplewood Resort, P.O. Box 217, 93920 (408) 667-2537
Biggs (Butte Co.), 464-B "B" St., P.O. Box 307, 95917 (916) 868-5493
   Library, 464-A "B" St., P.O. Box 516, 95917 (916) 868-5724
   Police, P.O. Box 307, 95917 (916) 868-5590
Bishop (Inyo Co.), 377 W. Line St., 93514, P.O. Box 1236, 93515
     (619) 873-5863, Fax: (619) 873-4873
   Chamber of Commerce, 690 N. Main St., 93514 (619) 873-8405,
     Fax: (619) 873-6999
   Newspaper, *Review Herald,* 450 E. Line St., P.O. Box 787, 93515
     (619) 873-3535
   Police, 207 W. Line St., 93514 (619) 873-5866
Bloomington (San Bernardino Co.), 92316, Unincorporated
   Chamber of Commerce, 18461 11th St., P.O. Box 445, 92316
     (909) 877-5558, Fax: (909) 877-8569
   Library, 10145 Orchard St., 92316 (909) 877-1453
Blue Lake (Humboldt Co.), 111 Greenwood Ave., P.O. Box 458, 95525
     (707) 668-5655
   Chamber of Commerce, P.O. Box 476, 95525 (707) 668-4112
   Library, City Hall, 95525 (707) 668-5965
   Police, P.O. Box 458, 95525 (707) 668-5655
Blythe (Riverside Co.), 220 N. Spring St., 92225 (619) 922-6161,
     Fax: (619) 922-4938
   Chamber of Commerce, 201 S. Broadway, 92225 (619) 922-8166,
     (800) 445-0541, CA: (800) 443-5513
   Library, 125 W. Chanslorway, 92225-1293 (619) 922-5371,
     Fax: (619) 922-5371
   Newspaper, *Palo Verde Valley Times,* 231 N. Spring St.,
     P.O. Box 1159, 92226 (619) 922-3181,
     Fax: (619) 922-3184
   Police, 240 N. Spring St., 92225 (619) 922-6111

Bodega Bay (Sonoma Co.), 94923, Unincorporated
  Chamber of Commerce, 850 Hwy. 1, P.O. Box 146, 94923
    (707) 875-3422, (707) 875-2868
Boonville (Mendocino Co.), 95415, Unincorporated
  Chamber of Commerce, P.O. Box 275, 95415
Boron (Kern Co.), 93516, Unincorporated
  Chamber of Commerce, 26962-20 Mule Team Rd., 93516
    (619) 762-5810
  Library, (see Bakersfield)
Borrego Springs (San Diego Co.), 92004, Unincorporated
  Chamber of Commerce, 622 Palm Canyon Dr., P.O. Box 66, 92004
    (619) 767-5555
  Library, 652 Palm Canyon Dr., 92004-0297 (619) 767-5761
  Newspaper, *The Borrego Sun,* P.O. Box 249, 92004-0249
    (619) 767-5338, Fax: (619) 767-4971
Boyle Heights (Los Angeles Co.), City of Los Angeles
Bradbury (Los Angeles Co.), 600 Winston Ave., 91010 (818) 358-3218,
    Fax: (818) 303-5154
  Sheriff, 8838 E. Las Tunas Dr., Temple City, 91780 (818) 285-7171
Brawley (Imperial Co.), 400 Main St., 92227 (619) 344-9222,
    Fax: (619) 344-0907
  Chamber of Commerce, 204 S. Imperial Ave., P.O. Box 218, 92227
    (619) 344-3160, Fax: (619) 344-7611
  Library, 400 Main, 92227-2491 (619) 344-1891,
    Fax: (619) 344-0212
  Newspaper, *The Brawley News*, P.O. Box 2770, El Centro, 92244
    (619) 344-1220, Fax: (619) 344-1383
  Police, 351 Main St., 92227 (619) 344-2111
Brea (Orange Co.), #1 Civic Center Cir., 92621 (714) 990-7600,
    Fax: (714) 990-2258
  Chamber of Commerce, #1 Civic Center Cir., 92621 (714) 529-4938,
    Fax: (714) 529-6103
  Library, #1 Civic Center Dr., 92621 (714) 671-1722,
    Fax: (714) 990-0581
  Police, #1 Civic Center Cir., 92621 (714) 990-7633
Brentwood (Contra Costa Co.), 708 Third St., 94513 (510) 634-6900,
    Fax: (510) 634-6930
  Chamber of Commerce, 240 Oak St., P.O. Box 773, 94513
    (510) 634-3344
  Library, 751 Third St., 94513 (510) 634-4101, Fax: (510) 427-8540
  Police, 500 Chestnut St., 94513 (510) 634-6911
Brentwood (Los Angeles Co.), City of Los Angeles
  Library, 11820 San Vincente Blvd., 90049 (310) 826-6579,
    Fax: (818) 904-3281
Brents Junction (Los Angeles Co.), Unincorporated
Bridgeport (Mono Co.), 93517, Unincorporated
  Chamber of Commerce, 85 Main St., P.O. Box 541, 93517
    (619) 932-7500
  Library, 94 School St., P.O. Box 398, 93517-0398 (619) 932-7482

Brisbane (San Mateo Co.), 150 N. Hill Dr., Suite 40, 94005 (415) 467-1515,
Fax: (415) 467-4989
Chamber of Commerce, 345 Visitacion Ave., 94005 (415) 467-7283,
(415) 467-8099
Library, 250 Visitacion Ave., 94005 (415) 467-2060,
Fax: (415) 467-4824
Police, 150 N. Hill, #3, 94005 (415) 467-1123
Broadmoor (San Mateo Co.), 94015, Unincorporated
Police, 388 88th St., 94015-1717 (415) 755-3838
Buellton (Santa Barbara Co.), 107 W. Hwy. 247, P.O. Box 1819, 93427
(805) 686-0137, Fax: (805) 686-0086
Chamber of Commerce, 376 Avenue of Flags, P.O. Box 231, 93427
(805) 688-7829, Fax: (805) 688-5399
Library, P.O. Box 187, 93427 (805) 688-3115
Sheriff, P.O. Box 156, 93427-0156 (805) 686-8150
Buena Park (Orange Co.), 6650 Beach Blvd., 90620, P.O. Box 5009, 90622
(714) 562-3500, Fax: (714) 562-3599
Chamber of Commerce, 6280 Manchester Blvd., #102, 90621
(714) 521-0261, Fax: (714) 521-1851
Library, 7150 La Palma Ave., P.O. Box 6270, 90622-6270
(714) 826-4100, Fax: (714) 826-5052
Police, 6650 Beach Blvd., 90622 (714) 521-9352
Burbank (Los Angeles Co.), 275 E. Olive Ave., 91502, P.O. Box 6459, 91510
(818) 953-9701, Fax: (818) 953-8729
Chamber of Commerce, 200 W. Magnolia Blvd., 91502
(818) 846-3111, (213) 849-1828, Fax: (818) 846-0109
Library, 110 N. Glenoaks Blvd., 91502 (818) 953-9737
Southern California Genealogical Society Library, 122 S. San
Fernando Blvd., P.O. Box 4377, 91503 (818) 843-7247
Police, 272 E. Olive Ave., P.O. Box 6459, 91510-6459
(818) 953-8731
Burlingame (San Mateo Co.), 501 Primrose Rd., 94010-3997 (415) 696-7200,
Fax: (415) 342-8386
Chamber of Commerce, 290 California Dr., 94010 (415) 344-1735,
Fax: (415) 344-1763
Library, 480 Primrose Rd., 94010-4083 (415) 342-1038
Police, P.O. Box 551, 94011-0551 (415) 692-8440
Burney (Shasta Co.), 96013, Unincorporated
Chamber of Commerce, 37477 Main St., 96013 (916) 335-2111
Library, 1080 Siskiyou St., 96013 (916) 335-4317
Newspaper, *Intermountain News*, P.O. Box 1030, 96013
(916) 335-4533, Fax: (916) 335-5335
Buttonwillow (Kern Co.), 93206, Unincorporated
Chamber of Commerce, 104 W. Second St., P.O. Box 251, 93206
(805) 764-5406
Library, (see Bakersfield)
Cabazon (Riverside Co), 92230, Unincorporated
Chamber of Commerce, P.O. Box 268, 92230
Library, 50175 Ramona, 92230 (909) 849-4082
Calabasas (Los Angeles Co.), 26135 Mureau Rd., 91302-3172
(818) 878-4225, Fax: (818) 878-4215

Calabasas Chamber of Commerce, 23564 Calabasas Rd., , 91302
 (818) 222-5680, Fax: (818) 222-5690
 Police, 27050 Agoura Rd., 91301 (818) 878-1808
Calabasas Highlands (Los Angeles Co.), City of Calabasas
Calexico (Imperial Co.), 408 Heber Ave., 92231 (619) 768-2110,
 Fax: (619) 357-5864
 Chamber of Commerce, 1100 Imperial Ave., P.O. Box 948, 92232
 (619) 357-1166, Fax: (619) 357-9043
 Library, 850 Encinas Ave., 92231 (619) 768-2170,
 Fax: (619) 357-0404
 Police, 420 E. 5th St., 92231 (619) 768-2140
California City (Kern Co.), 21000 Hacienda Blvd., 93505 (619) 373-8661,
 Fax: (619) 373-2674
 Chamber of Commerce, 8001 California City Blvd., P.O. Box 2008,
 93504 (619) 373-8676, Fax: (619) 373-1414
 Library, (see Bakersfield)
 Police, 8190 Aspen Mall, 93505 (619) 373-8606
Calimesa (Riverside Co.), 908 Park Ave., P.O. Box 1190, 92320
 (909) 795-9801, Fax: (909) 795-4399
Calipatria (Imperial Co.), 125 N. Park Ave., P.O. Box 167, 92233
 (619) 348-4141, Fax: (619) 348-7035
 Library, 225 W. Main St., P.O. Box 707, 92233 (619) 348-2630
 Police, P.O. Box 668, Calipatria, 92233-0668 (619) 348-2211
Calistoga (Napa Co.), 1232 Washington St., 94515 (707) 942-2800,
 Fax: (707) 942-0732
 Chamber of Commerce, 1458 Lincoln, #4, 94515 (707) 942-6333
 Library, 1108 Myrtle, 94515 (707) 942-4833, Fax: (707) 942-0941
 Newspaper, *The Weekly Calistogan,* P.O. Box 385, 94515
 (707) 942-6242, Fax: (707) 942-4617
 Police, 1234 Washington St., 94515 (707) 942-6262
Camarillo (Ventura Co.), 601 Carmen Dr., 93010, P.O. Box 248, 93011-0248
 (805) 388-5316, Fax: (805) 388-5318
 Chamber of Commerce, 632 Las Posas Rd., 93010 (805) 484-4383,
 Fax: (805) 484-1395
 Library, 3100 Ponderosa Dr., 93010 (805) 482-1952
 Newspaper, *The Camarillo Daily News,* 1000 Avenida Acaso, 93012
 (805) 987-5001, Fax: (805) 987-5655
 Sheriff, 800 So. Victoria Ave., Ventura, 93009 (805) 648-3311
Cambria (San Luis Obispo Co.), 93428, Unincoporated
 Chamber of Commerce, 767 Main St., 93428 (805) 927-3624
 Library, 900 Main St., 93428 (805) 927-4336
 Newspaper, *The Cambrian,* 2442 Main St., P.O. Drawer 67, 93428
 (805) 927-8652
Cameron Park (El Dorado Co.), Unincorporated
 Chamber of Commerce, (see Shingle Springs)
Camino (El Dorado Co.), Unincorporated
 Chamber of Commerce, (see Pollock Pines)
Campbell (Santa Clara Co.), 70 N. First St., 95008 (408) 866-2100,
 Fax: (408) 374-6889
 Chamber of Commerce, 1628 W. Campbell Ave., 95008
 (408) 378-6252, Fax: (408) 378-0192

CALIFORNIA MUNICIPALITIES, CITIES AND TOWNS

Campbell Library, 77 Harrison Ave., 95008-1499 (408) 866-1991,
Fax: (408) 866-1433
Newspaper, *Campbell Express*, 267 E. Campbell Ave., 95008
(408) 374-9700, Fax: (408) 374-0813
Police, 70 N. First St., 95008 (408) 866-2121
Canoga Park (Los Angeles Co.), City of Los Angeles
Chamber of Commerce, 7248 Owensmouth Ave., 91303
(818) 884-4222, (818) 884-4263
Library, 7260 Owensmouth Ave., 91303 (818) 887-0320,
Fax: (818) 904-3284
Canyon Country (Los Angeles Co.), City of Santa Clarita
Chamber of Commerce, 27225 Camp Plenty Rd., #8, 91351
(805) 252-4131, (805) 252-4402, Fax: (805) 252-7839
Library, 18536 Soledad Canyon Rd., 91350 (805) 251-2720,
Fax: (805) 298-7137
Newspaper, *Santa Clarita Signal*, 24000 Creekside Rd.,
P.O. Box 801870, Santa Clarita, 91380-1870
(805) 259-1234, Fax: (805) 254-8068
Sheriff, 23740 Magic Mountain Pkwy., Valencia, 91355
(805) 255-1121
Canyon Lake (Riverside Co.), 31532 Railroad Canyon Rd., Suites 101 & 103,
92587 (909) 244-2955, Fax: (909) 246-2022
Sheriff, 100 N. Perris Blvd., Perris, 92370 (714) 657-7391
Capistrano Beach (Orange Co.), 92624, Unincorporated
Capitola (Santa Cruz Co.), 420 Capitola Ave., 95010 (408) 475-6522,
Fax: (408) 475-6530
Chamber of Commerce, 621-B Capitola Ave., 95010
(408) 475-6522, Fax: (408) 475-6530
Police, 422 Capitola Ave., 95010 (408) 475-4242
Cardif-By-The-Sea (San Diego Co.), 92007, Unincorporated
Chamber of Commerce, 125 Chesterfield St., P.O. Box 552, 92007
(619) 436-0431, (619) 944-6841
Library, 2027 San Elijo Ave., 92007 (619) 753-4027
Carlsbad (San Diego Co.), 1200 Carlsbad Village Dr., 92008 (619) 434-2820,
Fax: (619) 720-9461
Chamber of Commerce, 5411 Avenida Encinas, #100,
P.O. Box 1605, 92008 (619) 931-8400,
Fax: (619) 931-9153
Library, 1250 Carlsbad Village Dr., 92008-1991 (619) 434-2870,
Fax: (619) 729-2050
Newspaper, *Carlsbad Journal*, 2841 Loker Ave. E., 92008
(619) 431-4850, (619) 431-4888, Fax: (619) 431-4888
Police, 2560 Orion Way, 92008 (619) 931-2197
Carmel (Monterey Co.), Monte Verde between Ocean & 7th, P.O. Box CC,
93921 (408) 624-2781, Fax: (408) 624-4057
Chamber of Commerce, P.O. Box 4444, 93923 (408) 624-2522,
Fax: (408) 624-1329
Library, Ocean & Lincoln, P.O. Box 800, 93921 (408) 624-4629
Newspaper, *Carmel Pine Cone,* P.O. Box G-1, 93921
(408) 624-0162, Fax: (408) 624-8076
Police, P.O. Box 600, 93921-0600 (408) 624-6403

Carmel Valley Village (Monterey Co.), 93924, Unincorporated
    Chamber of Commerce, 71 W. Carmel Valley Rd., #206,
        P.O. Box 288, 93924 (408) 659-4000
    Library, 65 W. Carmel Valley Rd., 93924 (408) 659-2377
Carmichael (Sacramento Co.), 95608, Unincorporated
    Chamber of Commerce, 6825 Fair Oaks Blvd., #100, 95608
        (916) 481-1002
    Library, 5605 Marconi Ave., 95608 (916) 483-6058,
        Fax: (916) 483-6382
Carpinteria (Santa Barbara Co.), 5775 Carpinteria Ave., 93013-2698
    (805) 684-5405, Fax: (805) 684-5304
    Chamber of Commerce, 5320 Carpinteria Ave., P.O. Box 956, 93013
        (805) 684-5479, Fax: (805) 684-3477
    Library, 5141 Carpinteria Ave., 93013 (805) 684-4314
    Sheriff, 5775 Carpinteria Ave., 93013 (805) 684-4561
Carson (Los Angeles Co.), 701 E. Carson St., 90745, P.O. Box 6234, 90749
    (310) 830-7600, Fax: (310) 513-6243
    Chamber of Commerce, 22010 S. Avalon Blvd., P.O. Box 4626,
        90749 (310) 522-5595, Fax: (310) 522-5597
    Library, 151 E. Carson St., 90745 (310) 830-0901,
        Fax: (310) 830-6181
    Sheriff, 21356 Avalon Blvd., 90745 (310) 830-1123
Castellammare (Los Angeles Co.), City of Los Angeles
Castaic (Los Angeles, Co.), City of Santa Clarita
    Chamber of Commerce, (see Santa Clarita)
Castro Valley (Alameda Co.), 94546, Unincorporated
    Chamber of Commerce, 21096 Redwood Rd., P.O. Box 2312, 94546
        (510) 537-5300
    Library, 20055 Redwood Rd., 94546-4382 (510) 670-6280,
        Fax: (510) 537-5991
Castroville (Monterey Co.), 95012, Unincorporated
    Chamber of Commerce, P.O. Box 744, 95012 (408) 633-6545
    Library, 11266 Merritt, 95012 (408) 633-2829, Fax: (408) 633-6315
Cathedral City (Riverside Co.), 35-325 Date Palm Dr., Suite 136, 92234,
    P.O. Box 5001, 92235-5001 (619) 770-0340,
    Fax: (619) 324-4816
    Chamber of Commerce, 68845 Perez Rd., #6, 92234 (619) 328-1213,
        Fax: (619) 321-0659
    Library, 68-707 Hwy. 111, 92234 (619) 328-4262,
        Fax: (619) 770-9828
    Police, 68-625 Perez Rd., 92234 (619) 321-0111
Cayucos (San Luis Obispo Co.), 93430, Unincorporated
    Chamber of Commerce, 80 N. Ocean Ave., P.O. Box 141, 93430
        (805) 995-1200
    Library, 201 Ocean Front, 93430 (805) 995-3312
Central Valley (Shasta Co.), 96019, Unincorporated
    Chamber of Commerce, 5232-C Shasta Dam Blvd., P.O. Box 1368,
        96019 (916) 275-8862
Century City (Los Angeles Co.), City of Los Angeles
    Chamber of Commerce, (see Los Angeles)
    Sheriff, 11703 S. Alameda St., Lynwood, 90262 (213) 567-8121

Ceres (Stanislaus Co.), 2720 Second St., P.O. Box 217, 95307-0217
  (209) 537-5700, Fax: (209) 538-5780
  Chamber of Commerce, 2760-B Third St., P.O. Box 545, 95307
  (209) 537-2601, Fax: (209) 537-2699
  Library, 2250 Magnolia, 95307 (209) 537-8938
  Newspaper, *The Ceres Courier*, P.O. Box 7, 95307 (209) 537-5032,
  Fax: (209) 537-0543
  Police, 2727 Third St., 95307 (209) 538-5712
Cerritos (Los Angeles Co.), 18125 Bloomfield Ave. at 183 St., 90701,
  P.O. Box 3130, 90703-3130 (310) 860-0311,
  Fax: (310) 809-8411
  Chamber of Commerce, 17785 Center Court Dr., #150, 90701
  (310) 809-2262, Fax: (310) 809-8025
  Library, 18025 Bloomfield Ave., 90701 (310) 924-5776,
  Fax: (310) 865-5087
  Sheriff, 5130 N. Carson Ave., Lakewood, 90712 (310) 866-9061
Charter Oak (Los Angeles Co.), City of Covina, Unincorporated
  Library, 20562 Arrow Hwy., 91724 (818) 339-2151,
  Fax: (818) 339-2799
Chatsworth (Los Angeles Co.), City of Los Angeles
  Chamber of Commerce, 21943 Plummer St., 91311 (818) 341-2428,
  Fax: (818) 341-4930
  Library, Homestead Acre Historical Society, 10385 Shadow Oak Dr.,
  91311 (818) 882-5614
  Library, 21052 Devonshire St., 91311 (818) 341-4276,
  Fax: (818) 902-2177
Cherry Valley (Riverside Co.), 92223, Unincorporated
  Chamber of Commerce, P.O. Box 790, 92223-0790 (909) 845-8466
Chester (Plumas Co.), 96020, Unincorporated
  Chamber of Commerce, 529 Main St., P.O. Box 1198, 96020
  (916) 258-2426
Chico (Butte Co.), 196 E. 5th St., 95928, P.O. Box 3420, 95927
  (916) 895-4800, Fax: (916) 895-4825
  Chamber of Commerce, 500 Main St., P.O. Box 3038, 95927
  (916) 891-5556, Fax: (916) 891-3613
  Library, 1108 Sherman Ave., 95926-3575 (916) 891-2762
  Newspaper, *Enterprise-Record*, 400 E. Park Ave., P.O. Box 9,
  95927-0009 (916) 891-1234, Fax: (916) 342-3617
  CSU Chico Police, First and Normal St., 95929-0133
  (916) 898-5372
  Police, P.O. Box 3420, 95927 (916) 895-4905
China Lake (Kern Co.), 93555, Unincorporated
  Police, Naval Weapons Center, 93555 (619) 939-3226
Chino (San Bernardino Co.), 13220 Central Ave., 91710, P.O. Box 667, 91708
  (909) 627-7577, Fax: (909) 591-6829
  Chamber of Commerce, 13134 Central Ave., 91710 (909) 627-6177,
  (909) 627-2232, Fax: (909) 627-4180
  Library, 13180 Central Ave., 91710 (909) 590-5225
  Newspaper, *Chino Champion*, 13179 9th St., P.O. Box 607,
  91708-0607 (714) 628-5501, Fax: (714) 590-1217
  Police, 13250 Central Ave., 91710 (909) 591-9851

Chino Hills (San Bernardino Co.), 2001 Grand Ave., 91709 (909) 590-1511,
   Fax: (909) 590-5646
   Library, 2003 Grand Ave., 91709 (909) 590-5380,
      Fax: (909) 590-5383
Chowchilla (Madera Co.), 145 Robertson Blvd., 93610 (209) 665-8615,
   Fax: (209) 665-7418
   Chamber of Commerce, 115 S. Second St., 93610 (209) 665-5603
   Library, 621 Robertson Blvd., 93610 (209) 665-2630
   Police, 122 Trinity Ave., 93610 (209) 665-8600
Chula Vista (San Diego Co.), 276 Fourth Ave., 91910, P.O. Box 1087, 91912
   (619) 691-5031, Fax: (619) 691-6184
   Chamber of Commerce, 233 4th Ave., 91910 (619) 420-6602,
      Fax: (619) 420-1269
   Library, 365 "F" St., 91910-2697 (619) 691-5168
   Police, P.O. Box 1087, 92012 (619) 691-5185
Citrus Heights (Sacramento Co.), 95610, Unincorporated
   Chamber of Commerce, 7233 Sunrise Blvd., P.O. Box 191, 95611
      (916) 722-4545, Fax: (916) 722-4546
City Terrace (Los Angeles Co.), City of Los Angeles
   Library, 4025 City Terrace Dr., Los Angeles, 90063 (213) 261-0295,
      fax: (213) 261-1790
Claremont (Los Angeles Co.), 207 Harvard Ave., P.O. Box 880, 91711
   (909) 399-5460, Fax: (909) 399-5492
   Chamber of Commerce, 205 Yale Ave., 91711 (909) 624-1681,
      Fax: (909) 624-6629
   Library, 208 N. Harvard Ave., 91711 (909) 621-4902,
      Fax: (909) 621-2366
   Newspaper, *Claremont Courier,* 111 S. College Ave., 91711-0820
      (714) 621-4761
   Police, 570 W. Bonita Ave., 91711 (909) 399-5411
Clayton (Contra Costa Co.), 1007 Oak St., P.O. Box 280, 94517
   (510) 672-3622, Fax: (510) 672-4917
   Police, 1005 Oak St., 94517 (510) 672-4455
Clearlake (Lake Co.), 14360 Lakeshore Drive, P.O. Box 2440, 95422
   (707) 994-8201, Fax: (707) 995-2653
   Chamber of Commerce, 14335 Lakeshore Dr., P.O. Box 629, 95422
      (707) 994-3600
   Newspaper, *Clear Lake Observer American,* P.O. Box 6328, 95422
      (707) 994-6444, Fax: (707) 994-5335
   Police, 14360 Lakeshore Dr., 95422 (707) 994-8251
Cloverdale (Sonoma Co.), 124 N. Cloverdale Blvd., P.O. Box 217, 95425
   (707) 894-2521, Fax: (707) 894-3451
   Chamber of Commerce, 132 S. Cloverdale Blvd., P.O. Box 356,
      95425 (707) 894-4470, (707) 894-2508,
      Fax: (707) 894-4470
   Newspaper, *Cloverdale Reveille,* 207 N. Cloverdale Blvd.,
      P.O. Box 157, 95425 (707) 894-3339, Fax: (707) 894-3343
   Police, 112 Broad St., 95425 (707) 894-2150
Clovis (Fresno Co.), 1033 5th St., 93612 (209) 297-2300, Fax: (209) 297-2587
   Chamber of Commerce, 325 Pollasky Ave., 93612 (209) 299-7273,
      Fax: (209) 299-2969

Clovis Library, 1155 5th St., 93612 (209) 299-9531
Newspaper, *The Clovis Independent,* P.O. Box 189, 93613
(209) 298-8081, Fax: (209) 298-0459
Police, 1033 5th St., 93612 (209) 297-2400
Coachella (Riverside Co.), 1515 6th St., 92236 (619) 398-3502,
Fax: (619) 398-8117
Chamber of Commerce, 1258 6th St., P.O. Box, 126, 92236
(619) 398-5111, Fax: (619) 398-5622
Library, 1538 7th St., 92236 (619) 398-5148
Police, 1515 6th St., 92236 (619) 398-0101
Coalinga (Fresno Co.), 155 W. Durian, 93210 (209) 935-1533,
Fax: (209) 935-5912
Chamber of Commerce, 380 Coalinga Plaza, 93210 (209) 935-2948,
(800) 854-3885, Fax: (209) 935-9044
Library, 305 N. 4th St., 93210 (209) 935-1676, Fax: (209) 935-1058
Police, 240 N. 6th St., 93210 (209) 935-1525
Coleville (Mono Co.), 96107, Unincorporated
Colfax (Placer Co.), 33 S. Main St., P.O. Box 702, 95713 (916) 346-2313,
Fax: (916) 346-6214
Chamber of Commerce, 2 S. Railroad St., P.O. Box 86, 95713
(916) 346-8888
Library, P.O. Box 153, 95713 (916) 346-8211
Newspaper, *Colfax Record,* 25 Church, P.O. Box 755, 95713
(916) 346-2232, Fax: (916) 885-4902
Police, P.O. Box 691, 95713 (916) 346-2220
Colma (San Mateo Co.), 1198 El Camino Real, 94014 (415) 997-8300,
Fax: (415) 997-8308
Chamber of Commerce, (see Daly City)
Police, 1198 El Camino Real, 94014-3295 (415) 997-8321
Colton (San Bernardino Co.), 650 N. La Cadena Dr., 92324-2893
(909) 370-5099, Fax: (909) 370-5154
Chamber of Commerce, 620 N. La Cadena Dr., 92324
(909) 825-2222, Fax: (909) 824-1650
Library, 656 N. 9th St., 92324 (909) 370-5084, Fax: (909) 422-0873
Police, 650 N. LaCadena Dr., 92324 (909) 370-5000
Colusa (Colusa), 425 Webster St., P.O. Box 1063, 95932 (916) 458-4740,
Fax: (916) 458-8674
Newspaper, *Colusa Sun-Herald,* P.O. Box 809, 95932
(916) 458-2121, Fax: (916) 458-5711
Police, 260 6th St., 95932 (916) 458-5091
Commerce (Los Angeles Co.), 2535 Commerce Way, 90040 (213) 722-4805,
(213) 685-7363, Fax: (213) 726-6231
Chamber of Commerce, 5900 S. Eastern Ave., #150,
P.O. Box 91-1039, 90091 (213) 728-7222,
Fax: (213) 728-7565
Library, 5655 Jillson St., 90040-1485 (213) 722-6660
Sheriff, 5019 E. Third St., Los Angeles, 90022 (213) 264-4151
Compton (Los Angeles Co.), 205 S. Willowbrook Ave., P.O. Box 5118,
90220 (310) 605-5500, Fax: (310) 631-0322
Chamber of Commerce, 307 N. Tamarind Ave., #5C, 90220-2422
(310) 631-8611, Fax: (310) 631-2066

Compton Library, 240 W. Compton Blvd., 90220 (310) 637-0202,
   Fax: (310) 537-1141
East Compton Library, 4205 E. Compton Blvd., 90221
   (310)632-6193
Police, 301 S. Willowbrook Ave., 90220-3189 (310) 605-5660
Concord (Contra Costa Co.), 1950 Parkside Dr., 94519 (510) 671-3417,
   Fax: (510) 671-3375
Chamber of Commerce, 2151-A Salvio St., 94521 (510) 685-1181,
   Fax: (510) 685-5623
Costa County Hispanic Chamber of Commerce, P.O. Box 5396,
   94524 (510) 806-8040, (510) 235-4779,
   Fax: (510) 229-0309
Library, 2900 Salvio St., 94520-2597 (510) 646-5455,
   Fax: (510) 646-5453
Police, Willow Pass Rd. & Parkside Dr., 94519 (510) 671-3232
Corcoran (Kings Co.), 1033 Chittenden Ave., 93212 (209) 992-2151,
   Fax: (209) 992-2348
Chamber of Commerce, 800 Dairy Ave., P.O. Box 459, 93212
   (209) 992-4514, Fax: (209) 992-2341
Library, 1001-A Chittenden Ave., 93212 (209) 992-3314
Newspaper, *The Corcoran Journal*, P.O. Box 487, 93212
   (209) 992-3115
Police, 1031 Chittenden Ave., 93212 (209) 992-5151
Cornell (Los Angeles Co.), Unincorporated
Corning (Tehama Co.), 794 Third St., 96021 (916) 824-7020,
   Fax: (916) 824-2489
Chamber of Commerce, 1401 Solano St., P.O. Box 871, 96021
   (916) 824-5550
Library, 740 Third St., 96021 (916) 824-7050
Newspaper, *Corning Daily Observer*, 710 5th St., P.O. Box 558,
   96021 (916) 824-5464
Police, 774 Third St., 96021 (916) 824-7000
Corona (Riverside Co.), 815 W. 6th St., 91720, P.O. Box 940, 91718-0090
   (909) 736-2201, Fax: (909) 736-2399
Chamber of Commerce, 904 E. 6th St., 91719 (909) 737-3350,
   Fax: (909) 737-3531
Library, 650 S. Main St., 91720-0090 (909) 736-2381
Police, P.O. Box 940, 91718-0090 (909) 736-2330
Corona Del Mar (Orange Co.), City of Newport Beach
Chamber of Commerce, 2843 E. Coast Hwy., P.O. Box 72, 92625
   (714) 673-4050
Library, 420 Marigold Ave., 92625 (714) 644-3135,
   Fax: (714) 673-4917
Coronado (San Diego Co.), 1825 Strand Way, 92118 (619) 522-7300,
   Fax: (619) 437-0371
Chamber of Commerce, 1009 "C" Ave., 92118 (619) 435-9260,
   Fax: (619) 522-6577
Library, 640 Orange Ave., 92118 (619) 522-7393
Newspaper, *The Coronado Journal*, 1224 10th St., Suite 102, 92118
   (619) 435-3141, Fax: (619) 435-3051
Police, 578 Orange Ave., 92118 (619) 522-7355

Corte Madera (Marin Co.), 300 Tamalpais Dr., 94925, P.O. Box 159,
94976-0159 (415) 927-5050, Fax: (415) 927-5087
Chamber of Commerce, 121 Corte Matera Town Center, 94925
(415) 924-0441, Fax: (415) 924-1839
Library, 707 Meadowsweet, 94925-1717 (415) 924-4844,
Fax: (415) 924-8227
Costa Mesa (Orange Co.), 77 Fair Dr., 92626, P.O. Box 1200, 92628-1200
(714) 754-5223, Fax: (714) 556-7508
Chamber of Commerce, 1835 Newport Blvd., E-270, 92627
(714) 574-8780, Fax: (714) 574-8784
Library, 1855 Park Ave., 92627 (714) 646-8845,
Fax: (714) 631-3112
Newspaper, *Daily Pilot,* 330 W. Bay St., 92627 (714) 642-4321,
Fax: (714) 646-4170
Newspaper, *The Orange County Register,* 625 N. Grand Ave., Santa
Ana, 92701 (714) 835-1234, Fax: (714) 543-3904
Police, P.O. Box 1200, 92626 (714) 754-5256
Cotati (Sonoma Co.), 201 W. Sierra Ave., 94931-4217 (707) 792-4600,
Fax: (707) 795-7067
Chamber of Commerce, 8000 Old Redwood Hwy., P.O. Box 592,
94931 (707) 795-5508
Police, 201 W. Sierra Ave., 94931 (707) 792-4611
Cottonwood (Shasta Co.), 96022, Unincorporated
Chamber of Commerce, P.O. Box 584, 96022 (916) 347-6800
Coulterville (Mariposa Co.), 95311, Unincorporated
Chamber of Commerce, 5007 Main St., P.O. Box 333, 95311
(209) 878-3074
Covelo (Mendocino Co.), 95428, Unincorporated
Chamber of Commerce, P.O. Box 458, 95428 (707) 983-6906,
(707) 983-6488
Covina (Los Angeles Co.), 125 E. College St., 91723-2199 (818) 858-7212,
Fax: (818) 332-5427
Chamber of Commerce, 935 W. Badillo, #100, 91722
(818) 967-4191, Fax: (818) 966-9660
Library, 234 N. Second Ave., 91723-2198 (818) 858-7297,
Fax: (818) 915-8915
Newspaper, *San Gabriel Valley Daily Tribune,* P.O. Box 1259,
91722 (818) 962-8811, Fax: (818) 962-8849
Police, 444 N. Citrus Ave., 91723 (818) 331-3391
Crenshaw (Los Angeles Co.), City of Los Angeles
Chamber of Commerce, (see Los Angeles)
Crescent City (Del Norte Co.), 377 "J" St., 95531 (707) 464-7483,
Fax: (707) 465-4405
Chamber of Commerce, 1001 Front St., 95531 (707) 464-3174,
(800) 343-8300, Fax: (707) 464-9676
Library, 190 Price Mall, 95531 (707) 464-9793, Fax: (707) 464-6726
Newspaper, *The Triplicate,* P.O. Box 277, 95531 (707) 464-2141,
Fax: (707) 464-5102
Police, 686 "G" St., 95531 (707) 464-2133
Crestline (San Bernardino Co.), 92325, Unincorporated
Chamber of Commerce, P.O. Box 926, 92325 (909) 338-2706,
Fax: (909) 338-2368

Crestline Library, 23555 Knapp's Cut Off, 92325 (909) 338-3294
Newspaper, *Crestline Courier News,* 24028 Lake Dr.,
P.O. Box 3307, 92325 (714) 338-1893,
Fax: (714) 338-4449
Crowley Lake (Mono Co.), 93546, Unincorporated
Chamber of Commerce, Route 1, Box 1111, 93546 (619) 935-4666
Cudahy (Los Angeles Co.), 5220 Santa Ana St., P.O. Box 1007, 90201
(213) 773-5143, Fax: (213) 771-2072
Chamber of Commerce, 4708 Elizabeth St., 90201 (213) 771-0219
Library, 5218 Santa Ana St., 90201 (213) 771-1345,
Fax: (213) 771-6973
Sheriff, 5019 E. Third St., Los Angeles, 90022 (213) 264-4151
Culver City (Los Angeles Co.), 4095 Overland Ave., P.O. Box 507,
90232-0507 (310) 202-5851, Fax: (310) 839-5895
Chamber of Commerce, 3882 Midway Ave., P.O. Box 707, 90232
(310) 287-3850, Fax: (310) 287-1350
Library, 4975 Overland Ave., 90230 (310) 559-1676,
Fax: (310) 559-2994
Newspaper, *Culver City News,* 4043 Irving Plaza, 90232
(213) 839-5271, Fax: (213) 839-9372
Police, 4040 Duquesne Ave., 90232 (310) 202-5600, 837-1221
Cupertino (Santa Clara Co.), 10300 Torre Ave., 95014-3202, (408) 777-3200,
Fax: (408) 777-3333
Chamber of Commerce, 20455 Silverado Ave., 95050
(408) 252-7054, Fax: (408) 252-0638
Library, 10400 Torre Ave., 95014-3254 (408) 446-1677,
Fax: (408) 252-8749
Sheriff, 14374 Saratoga Ave., Saratoga, 95070 (408) 867-9719
Cypress (Orange Co.), 5275 Orange Ave., P.O. Box 609, 90630
(714) 229-6700, Fax: (714) 229-0154
Chamber of Commerce, 9471 Walker St., 90630 (714) 827-2430,
Fax: (714) 827-1229
Library, 5331 Orange Ave., 90630 (714) 826-0530,
Fax: (714) 828-1103
Police, 5275 Orange Ave., 90630 (714) 229-6620
Daggett (San Bernardino Co.), 92327, Unincorporated
Chamber of Commerce, P.O. Box 327, 92327 (619) 254-2427
Daly City (San Mateo Co.), 333 90th St., 94015 (415) 991-8000,
Fax: (415) 991-9459
Chamber of Commerce, 244 92nd St., P.O. Box CC, 94015
(415) 755-8526, Fax: (415) 755-7620
Library, 40 Wembly Dr., 94015-4399 (415) 991-8025,
Fax: (415) 878-5079
Police, 333 90th St., 94015 (415) 991-8142
Dana Point (Orange Co.), 33282 Golden Lantern, 92629 (714) 248-9890,
Fax: (714) 248-9920
Chamber of Commerce, 24681 La Plaza, #120, P.O. Box 12, 92629
(714) 496-1555, Fax: (714) 496-5321
Sheriff, 33282 Golden Lantern, 92629 (714) 248-3550

Danville (Contra Costa Co.), 510 La Gonda Way, 94526 (510) 820-6337,
   Fax: (510) 838-0360
   Chamber of Commerce, 380 Diablo Rd., #103, 94526
      (510) 837-4400, Fax: (510) 837-5709
   Library, 555 S. Hartz Ave., 94526-3465 (510) 837-4889
   Newspaper, *San Ramon Valley Times*, 524 Hartz Ave., P.O. Box 68,
      94526 (510) 837-4267, Fax: (510) 837-4334
   Sheriff, 510 La Gonda Way, 94526 (510) 820-4481
Davis (Yolo Co.), 23 Russell Blvd., 95616 (916) 757-5602,
   Fax: (916) 758-0204
   Chamber of Commerce, 228 "B" St., 95616 (916) 756-5160,
      Fax: (916) 756-5190
   Library, 315 E. 14th St., 95616 (916) 757-5593,
      Fax: (916) 756-2332
   Newspaper, *Davis Enterprise*, 315 "G" St., P.O. Box 1470, 95617
      (916) 756-0800, Fax: (916) 756-6707
   Police, 226 "F" St., 95616 (916) 756-3740
   U.C. Davis Police, U.C. Davis, Fire/Police Building, 95616
      (916) 752-1727
Del Mar (San Diego), 1050 Camino Del Mar, 92014 (619) 755-9313,
   Fax: (619) 755-2794
   Chamber of Commerce, 1442 Camino Del Mar, #214, 92014
      (619) 755-4844, Fax: (619) 755-0056
   Library, 235 11th St., 92014-2693 (619) 755-1666
   Sheriff, 175 N. El Camino Real, Encinitas, 92024 (619) 966-3500
Del Rey Oaks (Monterey Co.), 650 Canyon Del Rey Rd., 93940
   (408) 394-8511, Fax: (408) 394-6421
   Police, 650 Canyon Del Rey Rd., 93940 (408) 394-9333
Delano (Kern Co.), 1015 11th Ave., 93215, P.O. Box 939, 93216-0939
   (805) 721-3303, Fax: (805) 721-2135
   Chamber of Commerce, 931 High St., 93215 (805) 725-2518
   Library, (see Bakersfield)
   Newspaper, *Delano Record*, P.O. Box 938, 93216 (805) 725-0600,
      Fax: (805) 725-4373
   Police, P.O. Box 218, 93216-0218 (805) 721-3377
Desert Hot Springs (Riverside Co.), 65950 Pierson Blvd., 92240
   (619) 329-6411, Fax: (619) 251-3523
   Chamber of Commerce, 11711 West Dr., P.O. Box 848, 92240
      (619) 329-6403, (800) 346-3347, Fax: (619) 329-2833
   Library, 11691 West Dr., 92240 (619) 329-5926,
      Fax: (619) 329-3593
   Newspaper, *Desert Sentinel*, P.O. Box 338, 92240 (619) 329-1411,
      Fax: (619) 329-3860
   Sheriff, 65950 Pierson Blvd., 92240 (619) 329-2904
Diamond Bar (Los Angeles Co.), 21660 E. Copley Dr., Suite 100, 91765
   (909) 860-2489, Fax: (909) 861-3117
   Chamber of Commerce, 22640 Golden Springs Dr., 91765
      (909) 861-2121, Fax: (909) 861-1753
   Library, 1061 S. Grand Ave., 91765 (909) 861-4978,
      Fax: (909) 860-3054
   Sheriff, 21695 E. Valley Blvd., Walnut, 91789 (818) 913-1715

Dinuba (Tulare Co.), 405 E. El Monte, 93618 (209) 591-5900,
　　Fax: (209) 591-5902
　　Chamber of Commerce, 210 N. "L" St., 93618 (209) 591-2707,
　　　　Fax: (209) 591-2712
　　Library, 150 S. "I" St., 93618 (209) 591-5828
　　Newspaper, *Dinuba Sentinel,* 145 South L, P.O. Box 247, 93618
　　　　(209) 591-4632
　　Police, 420 E. Tulare St., 93618 (209) 591-6130
Dixon (Solano Co.), 600 E. "A" St., 95620 (916) 678-7000,
　　Fax: (916) 678-0960
　　Chamber of Commerce, 201 S. First St., 95620 (916) 678-2650,
　　　　Fax: (916) 678-8930
　　Library, 230 N. First St., 95620 (916) 678-2934,
　　　　Fax: (916) 678-3515
　　Newspaper, *The Dixon Tribune,* 145 E. "A" St., 95620
　　　　(916) 678-5594
　　Police, 201 W. "A" St., 95620 (916) 678-7070
Dominguez (Los Angeles Co.), City of Carson
　　CSU Dominguez Hills Police, 1000 E. Victoria St., 90747
　　　　(213) 516-3639
Dorris (Siskiyou Co.), 307 S. Main St., P.O. Box 768, 96023 (916) 397-3511,
　　Fax: (916) 397-8831
　　Library, P.O. Box 649, 96023-0288 (916) 397-4932
　　Newspaper, *Butte Valley Star,* 111 W. Third St., 96023
　　　　(916) 397-2601
　　Police, P.O. Box 768, 96023 (916) 397-5251
Dos Palos (Merced Co.), 1546 Golden Gate Ave., 93620 (209) 392-2174,
　　Fax: (209) 392-2801
　　Chamber of Commerce, P.O. Box 92, 93620
　　Library, 2002 Almond, 93620 (209) 392-2155
　　Newspaper, *Dos Palos Star,* 3033 N. "G" St., 95340 (209) 722-1511
　　Police, 1546 Golden Gate Ave., 93620 (209) 392-2176
Downey (Los Angeles Co.), 11111 Brookshire Blvd., P.O. Box 607,
　　　　90241-0607 (310) 904-7284, Fax: (310) 923-6388
　　Chamber of Commerce, 11131 Brookshire Ave., 90241
　　　　(310) 923-2191, Fax: (310) 869-0461
　　Library, 11121 Brookshire, 90241-7015 (310) 904-7364,
　　　　Fax: (310) 904-3763
　　Police, 10911 Brookshire Ave., 90241-3847 (310) 861-0771
Downieville (Sierra Co.), 95936, Unincorporated
Duarte (Los Angeles Co.), 1600 Huntington Dr., 91010 (818) 357-7931,
　　Fax: (818) 358-0018
　　Chamber of Commerce, 1026 Huntington Dr., 91010 (818) 357-3333
　　Library, 1301 Buena Vista Ave., 91010 (818) 358-1865,
　　　　Fax: (818) 303-4917
　　Newspaper, *The Mountain Messenger,* Drawer A, 95936-0395
　　　　(916) 289-3262
　　Sheriff, 8838 E. Las Tunas Dr., Temple City, 91780 (818) 285-7171
Dublin (Alameda Co.), 100 Civic Plaza, P.O. Box 2340, 94568
　　　　(510) 833-6600, Fax: (510) 833-6651
　　Chamber of Commerce, 7080 Donlon Way, #110, 94568
　　　　(510) 828-6200, Fax: (510) 828-4247

Dublin Library, 7606 Amador Valley Blvd., 94568-2383
(510) 828-1315, Fax: (510) 828-9296
Police, 100 Civic Plaza, 94568 (510) 833-6670
Sheriff, 100 Civic Plaza, 94568 (510) 833-6670
Dunsmuir (Siskiyou Co.), 5915 Dunsmuir Ave., 96025 (916) 235-4822,
Fax: (916) 235-4824
Chamber of Commerce, P.O. Box 17, 96025 (916) 235-2177
Library, 5714 Dunsmuir Ave., 96025 (916) 235-2035
Newspaper, *Dunsmuir News*, 5711 Dunsmuir, 96025
(916) 235-4808, Fax: (916) 926-4166
Police, 5902 Dunsmuir Ave., Suite 201, 96025 (916) 235-4333
Eagle Rock (Los Angeles Co.), City of Los Angeles
Library, 5027 Caspar Ave., 90041 (213) 258-8078,
Fax: (213) 485-8154
East Bay Regional Park District (Alameda Co.), 94619
Police, 17930 Lake Chabot Rd., Castro Valley, 94546
(510) 881-1833
East Los Angeles (Los Angeles Co.), City of Los Angeles, Unincorporated
Chamber of Commerce, 3590 First St., 90063 (213) 266-6774
Library, 4801 E. Third St., 90022 (213) 264-0155,
Fax: (213) 264-5465
East Palo Alto (San Mateo Co.), 2415 University Ave., 94303
(415) 853-3100, Fax: (415) 853-3115
Chamber of Commerce, P.O. Box 51358, 94303
Library, 2415 University Ave., 94303 (415) 321-7712,
Fax: (415) 326-8961
Police, 2415 University Ave., 94303 (415) 853-3100
East San Pedro (Los Angeles Co.), City of Los Angeles
Echo Park (Los Angeles Co.), City of Los Angeles
Library, 515 N. Laveta Terrace, 90026 (213) 250-7808,
Fax: (213) 612-0421
El Cajon (San Diego Co.), 200 E. Main St., 92020 (619) 441-1776,
Fax: (619) 588-1190
Chamber of Commerce, 109 Rea Ave., 92020 (619) 440-6161,
Fax: (619) 440-6164
Library, 200 E. Lexington, 92020 (619) 579-4454,
Fax: (619) 697-3751
Police, 100 Fletcher Pkwy., 92020 (619) 579-3311
El Centro (Imperial Co.), 1275 Main St., P.O. Box 4450, 92244-4450
(619) 337-4540, Fax: (619) 352-6177
Chamber of Commerce, 1100 Main St., P.O. Box 3006, 92244
(619) 352-3681
Library, 539 State St., 92243-2973 (619) 337-4565,
Fax: (619) 352-1384
Newspaper, *Imperial Valley Press*, 205 N. 8th St., P.O. Box 2770,
92244 (619) 337-3400, Fax: (619) 353-3003
Police, 150 N. 11th St., 92243 (619) 352-2111
El Cerrito (Contra Costa Co.), 10890 San Pablo Ave., 94530-2392
(510) 215-4300, Fax: (510) 233-5401
Chamber of Commerce, 10848 San Pablo Ave., P.O. Box 538, 94530
(510) 233-7040, Fax: (510) 232-0796
Library, 6510 Stockton Ave., 94530-3189 (510) 526-7512

El Cerrito Police, 10900 San Pablo Ave., 94530 (510) 215-4400
El Dorado Hills (El Dorado Co.), 95630, Unincorporated
    Chamber of Commerce, 889 Embarcadero Dr., #102, 95761
        (916) 933-1335
    Library, 1120 Harvard Way, 95630 (916) 933-6982
El Monte (Los Angeles Co.), 11333 Valley Blvd., 91731, P.O. Box 6008,
        91734-2008 (818) 580-2001, Fax: (818) 580-2068
    Chamber of Commerce, 10822 Valley Mall, P.O. Box 5866, 91734
        (818) 443-0180, Fax: (818) 443-0463
    Library, 3224 N. Tyler Ave., 91731 (818) 444-9506,
        Fax: (818) 443-5864
    Newspaper, *San Gabriel Valley Daily Tribune*, P.O. Box 1259,
        Covina, 91722 (818) 962-8811, Fax: (818) 962-8849
    Police, 11333 Valley Blvd., P.O. Box 6008, 91734 (818) 580-2100
El Nido (Los Angeles Co.), Unincorporated
El Nido (Los Angeles Co.), City of Torrance
El Paso de Robles (San Luis Obispo Co.), 93446, Unincorporated
El Porto (Los Angeles Co.), City of Manhattan Beach
El Segundo (Los Angeles Co.), 350 Main St., 90245 (310) 322-4670,
        Fax: (310) 322-7137
    Chamber of Commerce, 427 Main St., 90245 (310) 322-1220,
        Fax: (310) 322-6880
    Library, 111 W. Mariposa Ave., 90245-2299 (310) 322-4121
    Newspaper, *El Segundo Herald*, P.O. Box 188, 90245
        (310) 322-1830, Fax: (310) 322-2787
    Police, 348 Main St., 90245-3885 (310) 322-9114
El Sereno (Los Angeles Co.), City of Los Angeles
    Library, 4990 Huntington Dr. S., 90032 (213) 225-9201
El Sobrante (Contra Costa Co.), 94803, Unincorporated
    Chamber of Commerce, 3817 San Pablo Dam Rd., #330, 94803
        (510) 223-0757
    Library, 4191 Appian Way, 94803 (510) 374-3043
El Toro (Orange Co.), 92630, Unincorporated
    Chamber of Commerce, (see Laguna Hills)
    Library, 24672 Raymond Way, 92630 (714) 855-8173,
        Fax: (714) 586-7412
Elk Grove (Sacramento Co.), 95624, Unincorporated
    Chamber of Commerce, 8970 Elk Grove Blvd., 95624
        (916) 685-3911, Fax: (916) 686-5814
    Library, 8962 Elk Grove Blvd., 95624 (916)685-5270,
        Fax: (916) 685-5266
    Newspaper, *Elk Grove Citizen*, P.O. Box 1777, 95759
        (916) 685-3945, Fax: (209) 745-4492
Emerald Lake (San Mateo Co.), 94063, Unincorporated
    Sheriff, 401 Marshall St., Redwood City, 94063 (415) 364-1811
Emeryville (Alameda Co.), 2200 Powell St., #207, 94608 (510) 652-5223,
        Fax: (510) 652-4223
    Chamber of Commerce, 2200 Powell St., 94608 (510) 652-5223,
        Fax: (510) 652-4223
    Police, 2449 Powell St., 94608 (510) 596-3707

Encinitas (San Diego Co.), 505 S. Vulcan Ave., 92024-3633 (619) 633-2600,
Fax: (619) 633-2627
Chamber of Commerce, 345 First St., 92024 (619) 753-6041,
Fax: (619) 753-6270
Library, 540 Cornish Dr., 92024-4599 (619) 753-7376
Encino (Los Angeles Co.), City of Los Angeles
Chamber of Commerce, 4933 Balboa Blvd., 91316 (818) 789-4711,
Fax: (818) 789-2485
Library, 18231 Ventura Blvd., Tarzana, 91356 (818) 343-1983,
Fax: (818) 904-3285
Escalon (San Joaquin Co.), 1854 Main St., P.O Box 248, 95320
(209) 838-3556, Fax: (209) 838-8045
Chamber of Commerce, 1537 Second St., P.O. Box 115, 95320
(209) 838-2793
Library, 1540 Second St., 95320 (209) 838-2478,
Fax: (209) 838-2032
Police, 1855 Coley Ave., 95320 (209) 838-7093
Escondido (San Diego Co.), Civic Center Plaza, 201 N. Broadway, 92025
(619) 641-4880, Fax: (619) 741-7541
Chamber of Commerce, 720 N. Broadway, 92025 (619) 745-2125,
Fax: (619) 745-1183
Library, 239 S. Kalmia St., 92025 (619) 741-4601
Newspaper, *Times-Advocate,* 207 E. Pennsylvania Ave., 92025
(619) 745-6611
Police, 700 W. Grand Ave., 92025 (619) 741-4722
Esparto (Yolo Co.), 95627, Unincorporated
Chamber of Commerce, P.O. Box 194, 95627 (916) 787-3242
Library, At Esparto Union High School,17155 Yolo Ave., 95627
(916) 787-3426
Etna (Siskiyou Co.), 440 Main St., P.O. Box 460, 96027 (916) 467-5256
Library, 520 N. Main, P.O. Box 130, 96027-0130 (916) 467-3400
Police, P.O. Box 460, 96027 (916) 467-3400
Eureka (Humboldt Co.), 531 "K" St., 95501 (707) 443-7929,
Fax: (707) 442-3989
Chamber of Commerce, 2112 Broadway, 95501-2189
(707) 442-3738, Fax: (707) 442-0079
Library, 421 "I" St., 95501 (707) 445-7284
Newspaper, *Times-Standard,* P.O. Box 3580, 95502 (707) 442-1711,
Fax: (707) 445-3117
Police, 604 "C" St., 95501 (707) 441-4060
Exeter (Tulare Co.), 137 N. "F" St., P.O. Box 237, 93221 (209) 592-9244,
Fax: (209) 592-3556
Chamber of Commerce, 101 W. Pine St., P.O. Box 215, 93221
(209) 592-2919
Library, 230 E. Chestnut, 93221 (209) 592-5361
Newspaper, *Exteter Sun,* 120 N. "E" St., P.O. Box 7, 93221
(209) 592-3171, Fax: (209) 592-4308
Police, 115 S. "B" St., 93221 (209) 592-3103

Fair Oaks (Sacramento Co.), 95628, Unincorporated
    Chamber of Commerce, 10224 Fair Oaks Blvd., P.O. Box 352,
        95628 (916) 967-2903
    Library, 11601 Fair Oaks Blvd., 95628 (916) 966-5742,
        Fax: (916) 966-5612
Fairfax (Marin Co.), 142 Bolinas Rd., 94930 (415) 453-1584,
        Fax: (415) 453-1618
    Library, 2097 Sir Francis Drake Blvd., 94930-1198 (415) 453-8092,
        Fax: (415) 453-7154
    Police, 144 Bolinas Rd., 94930 (415) 453-5330
Fairfield (Solano Co.), 1000 Webster St., 94533 (707) 428-7400,
        Fax: (707) 428-7631
    Chamber of Commerce, 1111 Webster St., 94533 (707) 425-4625,
        Fax: (707) 425-0826
    Library, 1150 Kentucky St., 94533-5799 (707) 421-6510,
        Fax: (707) 421-7474
    Newspaper, *Daily Republic,* 1250 Texas St., P.O. Box 47, 94533
        (707) 425-4646, Fax: (707) 425-5924
    Police, 1000 Webster St., 94533 (707) 428-7300
Fall River Mills (Shasta Co.), 96028
    Chamber of Commerce, P.O. Box 475, 96028 (916) 336-5840
    Newspaper, *Mountain Echo,* P.O. Box 224, 96028 (916) 336-6262,
        Fax: Voice act.
Fallbrook (San Diego Co.), 92028, Unincorporated
    Chamber of Commerce, 233-A E. Mission Rd., 92028
        (619) 728-5845, Fax: (619) 728-4031
    Library, 124 S. Mission Rd., 92028-2896 (619) 728-2373
    Newspaper, *The Enterprise,* P.O. Box 2800, 92088 (619) 728-5511,
        Fax: (619) 723-4967
Farmersville (Tulare Co.), 147 E. Front St., 93223 (209) 747-0458,
        Fax: (209) 747-3963
    Chamber of Commerce, P.O. Box 452, 93223 (209) 747-0822,
        Fax: (209) 594-5996
    Library, 457 W. Visalia Rd., P.O. Box 336, 93223 (209) 747-0178
    Police, 147 E. Front St., 93223 (209) 747-0321
Felton (Santa Cruz Co.), 95018, Unincorporated
    Chamber of Commerce, 6396 Hwy. 9, P.O. Box 67, 95018-0067
        (408) 335-2764, Fax: (408) 335-0222
    Library, 6299 Gushee St., P.O. Box 56, 95018 (408) 335-4052
    Newspaper, *The Valley Press,* P.O. Box V-1, 95018 (408) 335-5321,
        Fax: (408) 438-4141
Ferndale (Humboldt Co.), 834 Main St., P.O. Box 236, 95536
        (707) 786-4224, Fax: (707) 786-9314
    Chamber of Commerce, P.O. Box 325, 95536 (707) 786-4477
    Library, Main St., 95536 (707) 786-9559
    Newspaper, *The Ferndale Enterprise,* P.O. Box 268, 95536
        (707) 786-4611
    Police, P.O. Box 1096, 95536 (707) 786-4225
Fernwood (Los Angeles Co.), Unincorporated

Fillmore (Ventura Co.), 524 Sespe Ave., 93015, P.O. Box 487, 93016
  (805) 524-3701, Fax: (805) 524-5707
  Chamber of Commerce, 344 Central Ave., 93015 (805) 524-0351,
    Fax: (805) 524-2551
  Library, 502 Second St., 93015 (805) 524-3355
  Newspaper, *The Fillmore Herald,* P.O. Box 727, 93016
    (805) 524-0153
  Sheriff, 800 S. Victoria Ave., Ventura, 93009 (805) 524-2233
Firebaugh (Fresno Co.), 1575 11th St., 93622 (209) 659-2043,
    Fax: (209) 659-3412
  Chamber of Commerce, P.O. Box 606, 93622 (209) 659-3701
  Police, 1575 11th St., 93622 (209) 659-3051
Five Points (Los Angeles Co.), City of El Monte
Flintridge (Los Angeles Co.), City of La Canada/Flintridge
Florence (Los Angeles Co.), Unincorporated
Folsom (Sacramento Co.), 50 Natoma St., 95630 (916) 355-7200,
    Fax: (916) 355-7227
  Chamber of Commerce, 200 Wool St., 95630 (916) 985-2698,
    Fax: (916) 985-4117
  Library, 638 E. Bidwell St., 95630 (916) 983-9753,
    Fax: (916) 983-4267
  Newspaper, *Folsom Telegraph,* 825 Sutter St., 95630
    (916) 985-2581, Fax: (916) 985-0720
  Police, 46 Natoma St., 95630 (916) 355-7230, Fax: (916) 355-7227
Fontana (San Bernardino Co.), 8353 Sierra Ave., 92335, P.O. Box 518, 92334
    (909) 350-7600, Fax: (909) 350-7691
  Chamber of Commerce, 8575 Sierra Ave., #A, 92335
    (909) 822-4433, Fax: (909) 822-6238
  Library, 8334 Emerald St., 92335 (909) 822-2321,
    Fax: (909) 350-4211
  Newspaper, *Fontana Herald-News,* P.O. Box 549, 92335
    (909) 822-2231, Fax: (909) 355-9358
  Police, 17005 Upland Ave., 92335 (909) 350-7740
Foresthill (Placer Co.), 95631, Unincorporated
  Chamber of Commerce, P.O. Box 274, 95631 (916) 367-2474
  Library, P.O. Box 393, 95631 (916) 367-2785
Forestville (Sonoma Co.), 95436, Unincorporated
  Chamber of Commerce, 6701 Front St., P.O. Box 546, 95436
    (707) 887-1111, Fax: (707) 887-3311
Fort Bragg (Mendocino Co.), 416 N. Franklin St., 95437 (707) 961-2825,
    Fax: (707) 961-2802
  Chamber of Commerce, 332 N. Main St., P.O. Box 1141, 95437
    (707) 961-6300, Fax: (707) 964-2056
  Library, 499 Laurel St., 95437 (707) 964-2020, Fax: (707) 961-2623
  Newspaper, *Fort Bragg Advocate-News,* P.O. Box *1188,* 95437
    (707) 964-5642, Fax: (707) 964-0424
  Police, 153 N. Main St., 95437-3693 (707) 961-2800

Fort Jones (Siskiyou Co.), 11960 East St., P.O. Box 40, 96032
(916) 468-2281
Library, 119 Sixty E., P.O. Box 446, 96032-0446 (916) 468-2383
Newspaper, *Pioneer Press,* P.O. Box 400, 96032 (916) 468-5355,
Fax: (916) 468-5356
Sheriff, Courthouse, 311 Lane St., Yreka, 96097 (916) 842-8300
Fortuna (Humboldt Co.), 621 11th St., P.O. Box 545, 95540 (707) 725-6125,
Fax: (707) 725-4601
Chamber of Commerce, 735 14th St., P.O. Box 797, 95540
(707) 725-3959
Library, 14th & "N" Sts., 95540 (707) 725-3460
Newspaper, *Humboldt Beacon & Advance,* P.O. Box 310, 95540
(707) 725-6166, Fax: (707) 725-4981
Police, 621 11th St., 95540 (707) 725-1161
Foster City (San Mateo Co.), 610 Foster City Blvd., 94404 (415) 349-1200,
Fax: (415) 574-3483
Chamber of Commerce, 1125 E. Hillsdale Blvd., #114, 94404
(415) 573-7600, Fax: (415) 573-5201
Library, 600 Foster City Blvd., 94404 (415) 574-4842,
Fax: (415) 572-1875
Newspaper, *Foster City Islander,* 1185 Chess Dr., Suite B, 94404
(415) 574-5952, Fax: (415) 341-9977
Police, 1030 E. Hillsdale Blvd., 94404 (415) 574-5555
Fountain Valley (Orange Co.), 10200 Slater Ave., 92708 (714) 963-8321,
Fax: (714) 965-4498
Chamber of Commerce, 11100 Warner Ave., #204, 92708
(714) 668-0542, Fax: (714) 668-9164
Library, 17635 Los Alamos, 92708 (714) 962-1324,
Fax: (714) 964-8164
Police, 10200 Slater Ave., 92708-8030 (714) 965-4450
Fox Hills (Los Angeles Co.), City of Culver City
Fowler (Fresno Co.), 128 S. 5th St., P.O. Box 99, 93625 (209) 834-3113,
Fax: (209) 834-0185
Chamber of Commerce, P.O. Box 412, 93625 (209) 834-3869
Newspaper, *The Fowler Ensign,* 207 E. Merced St., 93625
(209) 834-2535
Police, P.O. Box 99, 93625 (209) 834-2112
Frazier Park (Kern Co.), 93225, Unincorporated
Chamber of Commerce, P.O. Box 763, 93225 (805) 245-1212,
Fax: (805) 245-1923
Library, (see Bakersfield)
Fremont (Alameda Co.), 39700 Civic Center Dr., 94538, P.O. Box 5006,
94537 (510) 791-4300, Fax: (510) 745-2888
Chamber of Commerce, 2201 Walnut Ave., #110, 94538
(510) 795-2240, Fax: (510) 795-2240
Library, 2450 Stevenson Blvd., 94538-2326 (510) 745-1500,
Fax: (510) 793-2987
Newspaper, *The Argus,* 3850 Decoto Rd., 94555 (510) 794-0111,
Fax: (510) 794-9605
Police, 39710 Civic Center Dr., 94537 (510) 790-6849
French Camp (San Joaquin Co.), 95231, Unincorporated

Fresno (Fresno Co.), 2600 Fresno St., 93721-3601 (209) 498-1563,
  Fax: (209) 488-1015
  Chamber of Commerce, 2331 Fresno St., P.O. Box 1469, 93721
    (209) 233-4651, Fax: (209) 233-6631
  Central California Hispanic Chamber of Commerce, 1900 Mariposa
    Mall, #100, 93721 (209) 485-6640, Fax: (209) 233-3709
  Library, 2420 Mariposa St., 93721-2285 (209) 488-3185
  Newspaper, *The Fresno Bee,* 1626 "E" St., 93786 (209) 441-6111,
    Fax: (209) 441-6436
  Police, P.O. Box 1271, 93715 (209) 498-1202
Fullerton (Orange Co.), 303 W. Commonwealth Ave., 92632 (714) 738-6300,
  Fax: (714) 738-6758
  Chamber of Commerce, 219 E. Commonwealth Ave., P.O. Box 529,
    92632 (714) 871-3100, Fax: (714) 871-2871
  Library, 353 W. Commonwealth Ave., 92632 (714) 738-6380
  CSU Fullerton Police, 800 North State College Blvd., 92634
    (714) 773-2515
  Police, 237 W. Commonwealth Ave., 92632 (714) 738-6800
Galt (Sacramento Co.), 380 Civic Dr., P.O. Box 97, 95632 (209) 745-2961,
  Fax: (209) 745-9794
  Chamber of Commerce, 425 Pine St., #5, 95632 (209) 745-2529
  Library, 380 Civic Dr., 95632 (209) 745-2066, Fax: (209) 745-6981
  Newspaper, *The Galt Herald,* 604 N. Lincoln Way, P.O. Box 307,
    95632 (209) 745-1552, Fax: (209) 745-4492
  Police, P.O. Box 97, 95632 (209) 745-1535
Garberville (Humboldt Co.), 95440, Unincorporated
  Chamber of Commerce, 773 Redwood Dr., #E, P.O. Box 445, 95442
    (707) 923-2613, Fax: (707) 923-4789
  Library, 715 Cedar St., 95440 (707) 923-2230
Garden Grove (Orange), 11391 Acacia Pkwy., 92640, P.O. Box 3070, 92642
  (714) 741-5000, Fax: (714) 741-5205
  Chamber of Commerce, 11400 Stanford Ave., P.O. Box 464, 92642
    (714) 638-7950, Fax: (714) 636-6672
  Library, 11200 Stanford, 92640 (714) 530-0711,
    Fax: (714) 530-9405
  Newspaper, *Orange County News,* 9872 Chapman, Suite 108, 92641
    (714) 530-7622, Fax: (714) 530-7142
  Police, P.O. Box 3070, 92642 (714) 741-5900
Gardena (Los Angeles Co.), 1700 W. 162nd St., 90247-3778,
  P.O. Box 47003, 90247-6803 (310) 217-9500,
  Fax: (310) 217-9694
  Chamber of Commerce, 1204 W. Gardena Blvd., #E, 90247
    (310) 532-9905, Fax: (310) 515-4893
  Library, 1731 W. Gardena Blvd., 90247 (310) 323-6363,
    Fax: (310) 327-0922
  Library, 14433 S. Crenshaw Blvd., 90249 (310) 679-0638
  Newspaper, *Gardena Valley News,* P.O. Box 219, 90247
    (310) 329-6351, Fax: (310) 329-7501
  Police, 1718 W. 162nd St., 90247 (310) 217-9601

Geyserville (Sonoma Co.), 95441, Unincorporated
  Chamber of Commerce, P.O. Box 276, 95441 (707) 857-3745
Gilroy (Santa Clara), 7351 Rosanna St., 95020 (408) 848-0400,
  Fax: (408) 842-2409
  Chamber of Commerce, 7471 Monterey Rd., 95020 (408) 842-6437,
  Fax: (408) 842-6010
  Library, 7387 Rosanna St., 95020-6193 (408) 842-8207,
  Fax: (408) 842-0489
  Newspaper, *The Dispatch,* 6400 Monterey, P.O. Box 22365,
    95021-2365 (408) 842-6400, Fax: (408) 842-7105
  Police, 7370 Rosanna St., 95020 (408) 848-0300
Glassell Park (Los Angeles Co.), City of Los Angeles
Glendale (Los Angeles Co.), 613 E. Broadway, 91206-4393 (818) 548-4000,
  Fax: (818) 547-6740
  Chamber of Commerce, P.O. Box 112, 91209 (818) 240-7870,
  Fax: (818) 240-2872
  Library, 222 E. Harvard St., 91205-1075 (818) 548-2027
  Newspaper, *Glendale News-Press,* 111 N. Isabel St., 91206
    (818) 241-4141, Fax: (818) 241-1975
  Police, 140 N. Isabel St., 91206-4382 (818) 548-3142
Glendora (Los Angeles Co.), 131 W. Foothill Blvd., 91741-3355
    (818) 963-4128, Fax: (818) 914-4822
  Chamber of Commerce, 224 N. Glendora Ave., 91740
    (818) 963-4128
  Library, 140 S. Glendora Ave., 91740-1899 (818) 914-8640
  Police, 150 S. Glendora Ave., 91741 (818) 914-8250
Glenview (Los Angeles Co.), Unincorporated
Goleta (Santa Barbara Co.), 93111, Unincorporated
  Chamber of Commerce, 5730 Hollister Ave., #1, P.O. Box 781,
    93116 (805) 967-4618, Fax: (805) 967-4615
  Library, 500 N. Fairview Ave., 93117 (805) 964-7878
  Newspaper, *Carpinteria Herald,* P.O. Box 1670, Goleta, 93116
    (805) 683-1955, Fax: (805) 684-6961
Gonzales (Monterey Co.), 109 4th St., P.O. Box 647, 93926 (408) 675-5000,
  Fax: (408) 675-2644
  Chamber of Commerce, 347 Belden St., P.O. Box 216, 93926
    (408) 675-3961
  Library, 851 5th St., P.O. Box 1397, 93926 (408) 675-2209
  Police, P.O. Box 647, 93926 (408) 675-2321
Granada Hills (Los Angeles Co.), City of Los Angeles
  Chamber of Commerce, 10727 White Oak Ave., #101, 91344
    (818) 368-3235, Fax: (818) 366-7425
  Library, 10640 Petit Ave., 91344 (818) 368-5687,
    Fax: (818) 904-3286
Grand Terrace (San Bernardino Co.), 22795 Barton Rd., 92324
    (909) 824-6621, Fax: (909) 783-7629
  Chamber of Commerce, 22795 Barton Rd., #2, 92324
    (909) 783-3581
  Library, 22795 Barton Rd., 92324 (909) 783-0147
  Sheriff, 655 E. Third St., San Bernardino, 92410 (909) 387-3500

Granite Bay (Placer Co.), 95661, Unincorporated
  Chamber of Commerce, 8605 Auburn-Folsom Rd., P.O. Box 2054, 95746 (916) 791-7187
  Lirary, 8715 Auburn-Folsom Rd., P.O. Box 2605, 95661 (916) 791-5590
Grass Valley (Nevada Co.), 125 E. Main St., 95945 (916) 273-2203, Fax: (916) 477-6943
  Chamber of Commerce, 248 Mill St., 95945 (916) 273-4667, Fax: (916) 272-5440
  Library, 207 Mill St., 95945-6789 (916) 273-4117, Fax: (916) 273-5619
  Newspaper, *The Union,* 11464 Sutton Way, P.O. Box 1025, 95945 (916) 273-9561, Fax: (916) 273-1854
  Police, City Hall, 125 E. Main, 95945 (916) 273-3321
Greenfield (Monterey Co.), 213-215 El Camino Real, P.O. Box 127, 93927 (408) 674-5591, Fax: (408) 674-3149
  Chamber of Commerce, P.O. Box 333, 93927 (408) 674-3222
  Library, 131 El Camino Real, P.O. Box 158, 93930 (408) 674-2614
  Newspaper, *Greenfield News,* P.O. Box 187, King City, 93930 (408) 674-5907, Fax: (408) 385-4799
  Police, 215 El Camino Real, 93927 (408) 674-5111
Greenview (Siskiyou Co.), 96037, Unincorporated
  Chamber of Commerce, P.O. Box 111, 96037 (916) 468-2161
Greenville (Plumas Co.), 95947, Unincorporated
  Chamber of Commerce, 208 Main St., P.O. Box 516, 95947 (916) 284-6633
Gridley (Butte Co.), 685 Kentucky St., 95948 (916) 846-5695, Fax: (916) 846-3229
  Chamber of Commerce, 14 E. Gridley Rd., P.O. Box 332, 95948 (916) 846-3142
  Library, 299 Spruce St., 95948-0397 (916) 846-3323
  Newspaper, *The Gridley Herald,* 630 Washington St., P.O. Box 68, 95948 (916) 846-3661, Fax: (916) 846-4519
  Police, 685 Kentucky St., 95948 (916) 846-5670
Grover Beach (San Luis Obispo Co.), 154 S. 8th St., P.O. Box 365, 93433 (805) 473-4567, Fax: (805) 489-9657
  Chamber of Commerce, 177 S. 8th St., 93433 (805) 489-9091
  Police, P.O. Box 365, 93433 (805) 489-1313
Guadelupe (Santa Barbara Co.), 918 Obispo St., 93434 (805) 343-1340, Fax: (805) 343-5512
  Chamber of Commerce, P.O. Box 417, 93434 (805) 343-2236
  Police, 4490 10th St., Room 5, 93434-1420 (805) 343-2112
Guerneville (Sonoma Co.), 95446, Unincorporated
  Chamber of Commerce, 16200 First St., P.O. Box 331, 95446 (707) 869-9000, Fax: (707) 869-9009
Gustine (Merced Co.), 682 Third Ave., P.O. Drawer A, 95322 (209) 854-6471, Fax: (209) 854-2840
  Chamber of Commerce, P.O. Box 306, 95322 (209) 854-6975
  Library, 205 6th St., 95322 (209) 854-3013
  Newspaper, *The Gustine Standard,* 3033 N. "G" St., Merced, 95340 (209) 722-1511
  Police, P.O. Box A, 95322-0016 (209) 854-3737

Hacienda Heights (Los Angeles Co.), 91745, Unincorporated
  Library, 16010 La Monde St., 91745 (818) 968-9356,
    Fax: (818) 336-3126
Half Moon Bay (San Mateo Co.), 501 Main St., P.O. Box 338, 94019
    (415) 726-8270, Fax: (415) 726-9389
  Chamber of Commerce, 520 Kelly Ave., 94019 (415) 726-8380,
    (415) 726-5202, Fax: (415) 726-8389
  Library, 620 Correas St.; 94019 (415) 726-2316,
    Fax: (415) 726-9282
  Police, 537 Kelly Ave., 94019 (415) 726-8288
Hancock Park (Los Angeles Co.), City of Los Angeles
Hanford (Kings Co.), 400 N. Douty St., 93230 (209) 585-2500,
    Fax: (209) 583-1529
  Chamber of Commerce, 200 Santa Fe Ave., #D, 93230
    (209) 582-0483, (800) 722-1114, Fax: (209) 582-0960
  Library, 401 N. Douty St., 93230 (209) 582-0261,
    Fax: (209) 583-6163
  Newspaper, *The Hanford Sentinel,* 300 W. 6th, P.O. Box 9, 93232
    (209) 582-0471, Fax: (209) 582-8631
  Police, 425 N. Irwin St., 93230 (209) 584-5511
Harbor City (Los Angeles Co.), City of Los Angeles
  Chamber of Commerce, 1319 1/2 Carson St., 90501, P.O. Box 523,
    Torrance, 90710 (310) 212-6300, Fax: (310) 548-1982
Hawaiian Gardens (Los Angeles Co.), 21815 Pioneer Blvd., 90716-1299
    (310) 420-2641, Fax: (310) 496-3708
  Chamber of Commerce, P.O. Box 1801, 90716 (310) 421-1632
  Library, 12100 N.E. Carson St., 90716 (310) 496-1212,
    Fax: (310) 425-0410
  Sheriff, 5130 N. Clark Ave., Lakewood, 90712 (310) 866-9061
Hawthorne (Los Angeles Co.), 4455 W. 126th St., 90250 (310) 970-7902,
    Fax: (310) 970-7058
  Chamber of Commerce, 12427 Hawthorne Blvd., 90250
    (310) 676-1163, Fax: (310) 676-7661
  Library, 12700 S. Grevillea Ave., 90250 (310) 679-8193,
    Fax: (310) 679-4846
  Newspaper, *Daily Breeze,* 5215 Torrance Blvd., Torrance, 90509
    (310) 540-5511, Fax: 310) 540-6272
  Police, 4440 W. 126th St., 90250 (310) 970-7975
Hayfork (Trinity Co.), 96041, Unincorporated
  Chamber of Commerce, (see Weaverville)
  Library, P.O. Box 700, Hayfork, 96041 (916) 628-5427
  Fax: (510) 293-2341
Hayward (Alameda Co.), 25151 Clawiter Rd., #600, 94545-2731
    (510) 293-5000, Fax: (510) 293-1580
  Chamber of Commerce, 22300 Foothill Blvd., #600, 94541
    (510) 537-2424, Fax: (510) 537-2630
  Library, 835 "C" St., 94541-5120 (510) 293-8688,
    Fax: (510) 733-6669
  Newspaper, *The Daily Review,* 116 W. Winton Ave., P.O. Box 5050,
    94540 (510) 783-6111, Fax: (510) 293-2341
  CSU Hayward Police, 25800 Carlos BEc Blvd., 94542-3053
    (415) 881-3791

Hayward Police, 300 W. Winton Ave., 94544 (510) 293-7272
Healdsburg (Sonoma Co.), 126 Matheson St., P.O. Box 578, 95448
(707) 431-3316, Fax: (707) 431-2852
Chamber of Commerce, 217 Healdsburg Ave., 95448
(707) 433-6935, (800) 648-9922 (CA only)
Newspaper, *The Healdsburg Tribune*, P.O. Box 518, 95448
(707) 433-4451, Fax: (707) 431-2693
Police, 126 Matheson St., 95448 (707) 431-3377
Hemet (Riverside Co.), 450 E. Latham Ave., 92543 (909) 765-2300,
Fax: (909) 765-2337
Chamber of Commerce, 395 E. Latham Ave., 92543 (909) 658-3211,
Fax: (909) 766-5013
Library, 510 E. Florida Ave., 92543 (909) 658-7294,
Fax: (909) 765-2446
Newspaper, *The Hemet News*, 474 W. Esplanade, P.O. Box 12003,
92546 (909) 487-2200, Fax: (714) 487-2250
Police, 210 N. Juanita, 92543 (909) 765-2400
Hercules (Contra Costa Co.), 111 Civic Dr., 94547 (510) 799-8200,
Fax: (510) 799-2521
Chamber of Commerce, P.O. Box 5283, 94547 (510) 799-0282
Police, 111 Civic Dr., 94547 (510) 799-8260
Herlong (Lassen Co.), 96113, Unincorporated
Police, Sierra Army Depot, 96113-5191 (916) 827-4215
Hermosa Beach (Los Angeles Co.), 1315 Valley Dr., 90254 (310) 318-0239,
Fax: (310) 372-6186
Chamber of Commerce, 323 Pier Ave., P.O. Box 404, 90254
(310) 376-0951, Fax: (310) 798-2594
Library, 550 Pier Ave., 90254 (310) 379-8475, Fax: (310) 374-0746
Newspaper, *Daily Breeze*, 5215 Torrance Blvd., Torrance, 90509
(310) 540-5511, Fax: (310) 540-6272
Police, 540 Pier Ave., 90254 (310) 318-0360
Hesperia (San Bernardino Co.), 15776 Main St., #213, 92345 (619) 947-1000,
Fax: (619) 949-7013
Chamber of Commerce, P.O. Box 403656, 92340 (619) 244-2135
Library, 9565 7th St., 92345 (619) 244-4898
Newspaper, *Hesperia Reporter*, 16925 Main St., P.O. Box 400937,
92340 (619) 244-0021, Fax: (619) 244-6609
Sheriff, 9393 E. Santa Fe Ave., 92345 (619) 947-1500
Hidden Hills (Los Angeles Co.), 24549 Long Valley Rd., 91302
(818) 888-9281, Fax: (818) 719-0083
Sheriff, 27050 Agoura Rd., Calabasas, 91301 (310) 456-6652
Highland (San Bernardino Co.), 26985 E. Baseline Ave., 92346
(909) 864-6861, Fax: (909) 862-3180
Chamber of Commerce, 7223 N. Church P.O. Box 455, 92346
(909) 864-4073, Fax: (909) 864-4583
Library, 27167 Baseline, 92346 (909) 862-8549
Sheriff, 655 E. Third St., San Bernardino, 92410 (909) 387-3531
Highland Park (Los Angeles Co.), City of Los Angeles
Highway Highlands (Los Angeles Co.), City of Glendale
Hilmar (Merced Co.), 95324, Unincorporated
Chamber of Commerce, P.O. Box 385, 95324 (209) 667-5701
Library, 20041 W. Falke St., 95324 (209) 632-0746

Hillsborough (San Mateo Co.), 1600 Floribunda Ave., 94010 (415) 579-3800,
Fax: (415) 340-1555
Police, 1600 Floribunda Ave., 94010 (415) 579-3818
Hollister (San Benito Co.), 375 5th St., 95023 (408) 636-4300,
Fax: (408) 637-7662
Chamber of Commerce, 649C San Benito St., 95023 (408) 637-5315,
Fax: (408) 637-1008
Library, 470 5th St., 95023-3885 (408) 637-2013,
Fax: (408) 636-1712
Newspaper, *The Free Lance*, 350 6th St., P.O. Box 1417, 95023
(408) 637-5566, Fax: (408) 637-4104
Police, 395 Apollo Court, 95023 (408) 636-3711
Hollydale (Los Angeles Co.), City of South Gate
Library, 12000 S. Garfield Ave., South Gate, 90280 (310) 634-0156,
Fax: (310) 531-9530
Hollywood (Los Angeles Co.), City of Los Angeles
Chamber of Commerce, 7000 Hollywood Blvd., #1, 90028
(213) 469-8311, Fax: (213) 469-2805
Library, 1623 Ivar Ave., 90028 (213) 467-1821,
Fax: (213) 467-5707
Hollywood Riviera (Los Angeles Co.), City of Torrance
Holtville (Imperial Co.), 121 W. 5th St., 92250 (619) 356-2912,
Fax: (619) 356-1863
Chamber of Commerce, 101 W. 5th St., P.O. Box 185, 92250
(619) 356-2923, (619) 356-2925
Newspaper, *Holtville Tribune*, 523 Pine Ave., P.O. Box 118, 92250
(619) 356-2995, Fax: (619) 356-5728
Police, P.O. Box 427, 92250-0427 (619) 356-2991
Hughson (Stanislaus Co.), 7018 Pine St., P.O. Box 9, 95326 (209) 883-4055,
Fax: (209) 883-2638
Chamber of Commerce, P.O. Box 1031, 95326 (209) 883-4995
Library, 6935 Hughson Ave., 95326 (209) 883-2293
Newspaper, *Hughson Chronicle*, P.O. Box 65, 95388
(209) 358-5311, Fax: (209) 358-7108
Police, P.O. Box 9, 95326 (209) 883-4052
Huntington Beach (Orange Co.), 2000 Main St., P.O. Box 190, 92648
(714) 536-5511, Fax: (714) 374-1557
Chamber of Commerce, 2100 Main St., #200, 92648
(714) 536-8888, Fax: (714) 960-7654
Library, Information & Cultural Resource Center, 7111 Talbert Ave.,
92648 (714) 842-4481
Police, P.O. Box 70, 92648 (714) 536-5903
Huntington Park (Los Angeles Co.), 6550 Miles Ave., 90255
(213) 582-6161, Fax: (213) 588-4577
Chamber of Commerce, 6330 Pacific Blvd., #208, P.O. Box 456,
90255 (213) 585-1155, Fax: (213) 585-2176
Library, 6518 Miles Ave., 90255 (213) 583-1461,
Fax: (213) 587-2061
Police, 6542 Miles Ave., 90255 (213) 587-5211

Huron (Fresno Co.), 36311 Lassen Ave., P.O. Box 339, 93234
(209) 945-2241, Fax: (209) 945-2609
Library, 305 N. 4th St., Huron, 93210 (209) 935-1676,
Fax: (209) 935-1058
Police, P.O. Box 275, 93234 (209) 945-2348
Hyde Park (Los Angeles Co.), City of Los Angeles
Library, 6527 Crenshaw Blvd., 90043 (213) 750-7241,
Fax: (213) 612-0436
Idyllwild (Riverside Co.), 92549, Unincorporated
Chamber of Commerce, 54274 N. Circle Dr., P.O. Box 304, 92349 (909) 659-3259
Library, 54926 Pinecrest Rd., 92549 (909) 659-2300
Imperial (Imperial Co.), 420 S. Imperial Ave., 92251 (619) 355-4371,
Fax: 355-2013
Chamber of Commerce, 101 E. 4th St., 92251 (619) 355-1609,
Fax: (619) 355-3920
Library, 200 W. 9th St., P.O. Box 38, 92251-0038 (619) 355-1332,
Fax: (619) 355-4857
Police, 424 S. Imperial Ave., 92251 (619) 355-1158
Imperial Beach (San Diego Co.), 825 Imperial Beach Blvd., 91932
(619) 423-8300, Fax: (619) 429-9770
Chamber of Commerce, 600 Palm Ave., #221, 91932
(619) 424-3151
Library, 810 Imperial Beach Blvd., 91932-2798 (619) 424-6981
Sheriff, 845 Imperial Beach Blvd., 91932 (619) 498-2400
Independence (Inyo Co.), 93526, Unincorporated
Library, 168 N. Edwards, P.O. Drawer K, 93526 (619) 878-0260
Indian Wells (Riverside Co.), 44-950 ElDorado Dr., 92210 (619) 346-2489,
Fax: (619) 346-0407
Indio (Riverside Co.), 100 Civic Center Mall, 92201, P.O. Box 1788, 92202
(619) 342-6570, Fax: (619) 342-6556
Chamber of Commerce, 82-503 Hwy. 111, P.O. Box TTT, 92201
(619) 347-0676, Fax: (619) 347-6069
Library, 200 Civic Center Mall, 92201 (619) 347-2383
Police, 46-800 Jackson St., 92201 (619) 347-8522
Industry (Los Angeles Co.), 15651 E. Stafford St., P.O. Box 3366, 91744
(818) 333-2211, Fax: (818) 961-6795
Chamber of Commerce, 255 N. Hacienda Blvd., #100, 91744
(818) 968-3737, Fax: (818) 330-5060
Sheriff, 150 N. Hudson Ave., (818) 330-3322, (909) 595-3649
Inglewood (Los Angeles Co.), One Manchester Blvd., 90301, P.O. Box 6500,
90306 (310) 412-5301, Fax: (310) 412-8788
Chamber of Commerce, 330 E. Queen St., 90301 (310) 677-1121,
Fax: (310) 677-0748
Los Angeles County Black Chamber of Commerce, 3860 Amberly
Dr., #H, 90305 (310) 412-1991, Fax: (310) 412-1868
Library, 101 W. Manchester Blvd., 90301-1771 (310) 412-5397
Police, One Manchester Blvd., P.O. Box 6500, 90301
(310) 412-5210

Inyokern (Kern Co.), 93527, Unincorporated
    Chamber of Commerce, P.O. Box 232, 93527 (619) 377-4712
Ione (Amador Co.), #1 Main St., P.O. Box 398, 95640 (209) 274-2412,
    Fax: (209) 274-2830
    Police, #1 Main St., 95640 (209) 274-2456
Irvine (Orange Co.), #1 Civic Center Plaza, 92714, P.O. Box 19575, 92713
    (714) 724-6001, Fax: (714) 724-6045
    Chamber of Commerce, 17200 Jamboree Rd., #A, 92714
    (714) 660-9112, Fax: (714) 660-0829
    Library, 14361 Yale, 92714 (714) 551-7151
    Police, #1 Civic Center Plaza, 92714 (714) 724-7101
    U.C. Irvine Police, 150 Public Services Bldg., 92717 (714) 856-5223
Irwindale (Los Angeles Co.), 5050 N. Irwindale Ave., 91706 (818) 962-3381,
    Fax: (818) 962-4209
    Chamber of Commerce, 16102 Arrow Hwy., P.O. Box 2307, 91706
    (818) 960-6606, Fax: (818) 960-3868
    Library, 5050 N. Irwindale Ave., 91706 (818) 962-5255
    Newspaper, *San Gabriel Valley Daily Tribune*, P.O. Box 1259,
    Covina, 91722 (818) 962-8811, Fax: (818) 962-8849
    Police, 5050 N. Irwindale Ave., 91706 (818) 962-3601
Isleton (Sacramento Co.), 210 Jackson Blvd., P.O. Box 716, 95641
    (916) 777-7770, Fax: (916) 777-7775
    Chamber of Commerce, P.O. Box 758, 95641 (916) 777-5880
    Library, 412 Union St., P.O. Box 517, 95641 (916) 777-6638
    Police, P.O. Box 716, 95641 (916) 777-7774
Jackson (Amador Co.), 33 Broadway, 95642 (209) 223-1646,
    Fax: (209) 223-3141
    Chamber of Commerce, 125 Peek St., P.O. Box 596, 95642
    (209) 223-0350, (800) 649-4988 (CA only),
    Fax: (209) 223-4425
    Library, 530 Sutter St., 95642 (209) 223-6400
    Police, 33-D Broadway, 95642 (209) 223-1771
Julian (San Diego Co.), 92036, Unincorporated
    Chamber of Commerce, 2133 Main St., P.O. Box 413, 92036
    (619) 765-1857
    Library, 2133 4th St., 92036-0326 (619) 765-0370
June Lake (Mono Co.), 93529, Unincorporated
    Chamber of Commerce, P.O. Box 2, 93529 (619) 648-7584
Kagel Canyon (Los Angeles Co.), City of Los Angeles, Unincorporated
Kensington (Contra Costa Co.), 94708, Unincorporated
    Police, 217 Arlington Ave., 94707 (510) 526-4141
    Library, 61 Arlington Ave., 94707-1098 (510) 524-3043
Kerman (Fresno Co.), 850 S. Madera Ave., 93630-1799 (209) 846-9384,
    Fax: (209) 846-9435
    Chamber of Commerce, 681 S. Madera Ave., #106, 93630
    (209) 846-6343
    Newspaper, *The Kerman News*, P.O. Box 336, 93630
    (209) 846-6689
    Police, 850 S. Madera Ave., 93630 (209) 846-6633

Kernville (Kern Co.), 93238, Unincorporated
    Chamber of Commerce, 11447 Kernville Rd., P.O. Box 397, 93238
        (619) 376-2629, Fax: (619) 376-4371
    Library, (see Bakersfield)
Kettleman City (Kings Co.), 93239, Unincorporated
    Chamber of Commerce, 101 4th St., P.O. Box 66, 93239
        (209) 386-5850
    Library, 104 Becky Pease St., 93239 (209) 386-9804
King City (Monterey Co.), 212 S. Vanderhurst Ave., 93930 (408) 385-3281,
        Fax: (408) 385-6887
    Chamber of Commerce, 203 Broadway, 93930 (408) 385-3814
    Library, 212 S. Vanderhurst Ave., 93930 (408) 385-3677
    Newspaper, *Gonzales Tribune*, P.O. Box 187, 93930
        (408) 674-5907, Fax: (408) 385-4799
    Police, 415 Bassett St., 93930 (408) 385-4848
Kingsburg (Fresno Co.), 1401 Draper St., P.O. Box 397, 93631
        (209) 897-5821, Fax: (209) 897-5568
    Chamber of Commerce, 1401 California St., P.O. Box 515, 93631
        (209) 897-2925
    Newspaper, *Recorder*, 1467 Marison St., P.O. Box 126, 93631
        (209) 897-2993, Fax: (209) 897-4868
    Police, 1440 Marion St., 93631 (209) 897-2931
Klamath River (Siskiyou Co.), 96050, Unincorporated
    Chamber of Commerce, P.O. Box 25, 96050 (916) 465-3325
La Canada Flintridge (Los Angeles Co.), 1327 Foothill Blvd., 91011
        (818) 790-8880, Fax: (818) 790-7536
    Chamber of Commerce, 4529 Angeles Crest Hwy., #102, 91011
        (818) 790-4289, Fax: (818) 790-8930
    Library, 4545 N. Oakwood Ave., 91011 (818) 790-3330,
        Fax: (818) 952-1754
    Newspaper, *La Canada Valley Sun*, 1 Valley Sun Lane, 91011
        (818) 790-8774, Fax: (818) 790-5690
    Sheriff, 4554 N. Briggs Ave., La Crescenta, 91214 (818) 248-3464
La Crescenta (Los Angeles Co.), 91214, Unincorporated
    Chamber of Commerce, 3131 Foothill Blvd., #M, 91214
        (818) 248-4957, Fax: (818) 957-1391
    Library, 4521 La Crescenta Ave., 91214 (818) 248-5313,
        Fax: (818) 248-1289
    Sheriff, 4554 N. Briggs Ave., 91214 (818) 248-3464
La Habra (Orange Co.), 201 E. La Habra Blvd., 906331-0337, P.O. Box 337,
        90633-0337 (310) 905-9700, Fax: (310) 905-9719
    Chamber of Commerce, 321 E. La Habra Blvd., 90631
        (310) 697-1704, (714) 992-4702
    Library, 221 E. La Habra Blvd., 90631 (714) 526-7728,
        (310) 694-0078, Fax: (213) 691-8043
    Police, 150 N. Euclid St., 90631 (310) 905-9751
La Habra Heights (Los Angeles Co.), 1245 N. Hacienda Blvd., 90631
        (310) 694-6302, Fax: (310) 694-4410
    Sheriff, 150 N. Hudson Ave., City of Industry, 91744
        (818) 330-3322, (909) 595-3649

La Jolla (San Diego Co.), 92037, Unincorporated
    Chamber of Commerce, 1055 Wall St., #110, P.O. Box 1101, 92038
        (619) 454-1444, Fax: (619) 454-1314
    Library, 7555 Draper Ave., 92037 (619) 552-1657
    Newspaper, *La Jolla Light,* 850 Pearl St., P.O. Box 1927, 92038
        (619) 459-4201, Fax: (619) 459-0971
La Mesa (San Diego Co.), 8130 Allison Ave., 91941-5096, P.O. Box 937,
        91944-0937 (619) 463-6611, Fax: (619) 462-7528
    Chamber of Commerce, 8155 University Ave., P.O. Box 235, 91944
        (619) 465-7700
    Library, 8055 University Ave., 92041-5097 (619) 469-2151
    Newspaper, *La Mesa Forum,* 3434 Grove St., P.O. Box 127, Lemon
        Grove, 91946 (619) 469-0101
    Police, 8181 Allison Ave., 92041-5099 (619) 469-6111
La Mirada (Los Angeles Co.), 13700 La Mirada Blvd., 90638, P.O. Box 828,
        90637-0828 (310) 943-0131, Fax: (310) 943-1464
    Chamber of Commerce, 16700 Valley View Ave., #240, 90638
        (714) 521-1700, (310) 946-6485, Fax: (714) 522-8611
    Library, 13800 La Mirada Blvd., 90638 (310) 943-0277,
        Fax: (310) 943-3920
    Sheriff, 12335 Civic Center Dr., Norwalk, 90650 (310) 863-8711
La Palma (Orange Co.), 7822 Walker St., 90623 (714) 523-7700,
        Fax: (714) 523-7351
    Chamber of Commerce, 1 Centerpoint Dr., #210, 90623
        (714) 228-2218, Fax: (714) 228-2208
    Library, 7842 Walker St., 90623 (714) 523-8585,
        Fax: (213) 431-4143
    Police, 7792 Walker St., 90623 (714) 523-4552
La Puente (Los Angeles Co.), 15900 E. Main St., 91744 (818) 330-4511,
        Fax: (818) 961-4626
    Chamber of Commerce, 15917 E. Main St., P.O. Box 327, 91747
        (818) 330-3216, Fax: (818) 330-9524
    Library, 15920 E. Central Ave., 91744 (818) 968-4613,
        Fax: (818) 369-0294
    Sheriff, 150 N. Hudson Ave., City of Industry, 91744
        (818) 330-3322, (909) 595-3649
La Quinta (Riverside Co.), 48795 Calle Tampico, P.O. Box 1504, 92253
        (619) 777-7000, Fax: (619) 564-5617
    Chamber of Commerce, 51-351 Avenida Bermudas, P.O. Box 255,
        92253 (619) 564-3199, Fax: (619) 564-3111
    Library, 78080 Calle Estado, 92253 (619) 564-4767
    Sheriff, P.O. Box 1504, 92253 (619) 564-2246
La Verne (Los Angeles Co.), 3660 "D" St., 91750 (909) 596-8726,
        Fax: (909) 596-8737
    Chamber of Commerce, 2078 Bonita Ave., 91750 (909) 593-5265,1
        Fax: (909) 596-0579
    Library, 3640 "D" St., 91750 (909) 596-1934
    Police, 2061 Third St., 91750 (909) 596-1913
Ladera Heights (Los Angeles Co.), Unincorporated

Lafayette (Contra Costa Co.), 3675 Mt. Diablo Blvd., Suite 210,
P.O. Box 1968, 94549 (510) 284-1968,
Fax: (510) 284-3169
Chamber of Commerce, 100 Lafayette Cir., #103, 94549
(510) 284-7404, Fax: (510) 284-3109
Library, 952 Moraga Rd., 94549-4594 (510) 283-3872
Newspaper, *Contra Cosa Sun,* P.O. Box 599, 94549 (510) 284-4444,
Fax: (510) 284-1039
Sheriff, 3675 Mt. Diablo Blvd., Suite 130, 94549 (510) 284-5010
Laguna Beach (Orange Co.), 505 Forest Ave., 92651 (714) 497-3311,
Fax: (714) 497-0771
Chamber of Commerce, 357 Glenneyre Ave., 92652 (714) 494-1018,
Fax: (714) 497-0105
Library, 363 Glenneyre, 92651 (714) 497-1733, Fax: (714) 497-2876
Police, 505 Forest Ave., 92651 (714) 497-0385
Laguna Hills (Orange Co.), 25201 Paseo De Alicia, Suite 150, 92653
(714) 707-2600, Fax: (714) 707-2614
Chamber of Commerce, 25431 Cabot Rd., #205, 92653
(714) 837-3000, Fax: (714) 837-1452
Leisure World Hill Library, 24262 Calle Aragon, P.O. Box 2220,
92654 (714) 951-2274
Laguna Niguel (Orange Co.), 27801 La Paz Rd., 92656 (714) 362-4300,
Fax: (714) 362-4340
Chamber of Commerce, 30110 Crown Valley Pkwy., #201, 92677
(714) 363-0136, Fax: (714) 363-9026
Library, 30341 Crown Valley Pkwy., 92677 (714) 249-5252
Newspaper, *Laguna Niguel News,* P.O. Box 3629, Mission Viejo,
92691 (714) 768-3631, Fax: (714) 830-9504
Sheriff, 27821 La Paz Rd., 92656 (714) 643-1610
Lake Arrowhead (San Bernardino Co.), 92352, Unincorporated
Chamber of Commerce, 28200 Hwy. 189, Bldg."J", P.O. Box 219,
92352 (909) 337-3715, (909) 336-1547,
Fax: (909) 336-1548
Library, 27235 Hwy. 189, Blue Jay, 92317 (909) 337-3118
Newspaper, *Mountain News and Mountaineer,* Box 2410, 92352
(714) 336-3555, Fax: (714) 337-5275
Lake Elsinore (Riverside Co.), 130 S. Main St., 92330 (909) 674-3124,
Fax: (909) 674-2392
Chamber of Commerce, 132 W. Graham Ave., 92530
(909) 674-2577, Fax: (909) 245-9127
Library, 400 W. Graham, 92330 (909) 674-4517,
Fax: (909) 245-7715
Newspaper, *Lake Elsinore Valley Sun-Tribune,* P.O. Box 2108,
92531 (909) 674-1535, Fax: (909) 674-0280
Sheriff, 117 S. Langstaff St., 92330 (909) 674-3131
Lake Forest (Orange Co.), 23778 Mercury Rd., 92630 (714) 707-5583,
Fax: (714) 707-5723
Chamber of Commerce, (see Laguna Hills)

Lake Isabella (Kern Co.), 93240, Unincorporated
    Chamber of Commerce, 6617 Isabella Blvd., P.O. Box 567, 93240
        (619) 379-5236, (619) 379-4379, Fax: (619) 379-8885
    Newspaper, *Kern Valley Sun*, P.O. Box 3074, 93240 (619) 379-3667,
        Fax: (619) 379-4343
Lake Los Angeles (Los Angeles Co.), Unincorporated
    Chamber of Commerce, P.O. Box 500071, 93550-0017
        (805) 264-2786
Lake Shastina (Siskiyou Co.), 96094, Unincorporated
    Police, 16309 Everhart Dr., Weed, 96094 (916) 938-2226
Lake Tahoe, (see South Lake Tahoe)
    Chamber of Commerce, 245 N. Lake Blvd., P.O. Box 884, Tahoe
        City, 95730 (916) 581-6900, Fax: (916) 581-6904
Lakeport (Lake Co.), 225 Park St., 95453 (707) 263-5615,
    Fax: (707) 263-8584
    Chamber of Commerce, 290 S. Main St., 95453 (707) 263-5092,
        Fax: (707) 263-5104
    Library, 1425 N. High St., 95453 (707) 263-8816,
        Fax: (707) 263-6796
    Newspaper, *Lake County Record-Bee*, 2150 S. Main, P.O. Box 849,
        95453 (707) 263-5636, Fax: (707) 263-0600
    Police, 445 N. Main St., 95453 (707) 263-5491
Lakeside (San Diego Co.), 92040, Unincorporated
    Chamber of Commerce, 9760 Winter Gardens Blvd., #C,
        P.O. Box 515, 92040 (619) 561-1031
    Library, 9839 Vine St., 92040-3199 (619) 443-1811
Lakeside Park (Los Angeles Co.), City of Los Angeles
Lakewood (Los Angeles Co.), 5050 Clark Ave., 90712, P.O. Box 158, 90714
        (310) 866-9771, Fax: (310) 866-0505
    Chamber of Commerce, 5445 E. Delamo Blvd., #101, P.O. Box 160,
        90714 (310) 920-7737, Fax: (310) 920-3762
    Library, 4990 Clark Ave., 90712 (310) 866-1777
    Sheriff, 5130 N. Clark Ave., 90712 (310) 866-9061
Lamont (Kern Co.), 93241, Unincorporated
    Chamber of Commerce, P.O. Box 593, 93241 (805) 845-1992
    Library, (see Bakersfield)
    Newspaper, *Lamont Reporter*, Box 548, 93241 (805) 845-3704,
        Fax: (805) 832-0841
Lancaster (Los Angeles Co.), 44933 N. Fern Ave., 93534 (805) 723-6000,
        Fax: (805) 723-6141
    Chamber of Commerce, 44335 Lowtree Ave., 93534
        (805) 948-4518, Fax: (805) 949-1212
    Library, 1150 W. Ave. "J", 93534 (805) 948-5029,
        Fax: (805) 945-0480
    Newspaper, *Desert Mailer News*, 741 "E" Ave. I, 93535
        (805) 945-8671, Fax: (805) 942-6418
    Sheriff, 1010 W. Ave. "J", 93534 (805) 948-8466
Larkspur (Marin Co.), 400 Magnolia Ave., 94939 (415) 927-5110,
    Fax: (415) 927-5022
    Chamber of Commerce, P.O. Box 315, 94977 (415) 927-4360

Larkspur Library, P.O. Box 525, 400 Magnolia Ave., 94939
(415) 927-5005, Fax: (415) 927-5022
Sheriff, 250 Doherty Dr., 94939 (415) 927-5150
Lathrop (San Joaquin Co.), 16775 S. Howland Rd., Suite 1, 95330
(209) 858-2860, Fax: (209) 858-5259
Chamber of Commerce, 15557 5th St., P.O. Box 313, 95330
(209) 858-2700
Sheriff, 4331 Lennox Blvd., Inglewood, 90304 (310) 671-7531
Lawndale (Los Angeles Co.), 14717 Burin Ave., P.O. Box 98, 90260
(310) 973-4321, (310) 772-4191, Fax: (310) 644-4556
Chamber of Commerce, 14704 Hawthorne Blvd., 90260
(310) 679-3306
Library, 14615 Burin Ave., 90260 (310) 676-0177,
Fax: (310) 973-0498
Sheriff, 4331 Lennox Blvd., Inglewood, 90304 (310) 671-7531
Laytonville (Mendocino Co.), 95454, Unincorporated
Chamber of Commerce, P.O. Box 457, 95454
Lee Vining (Mono Co.), 93541, Unincorporated
Chamber of Commerce, P.O. Box 130, 93541 (619) 647-6303
Leggett (Mendocino Co.), 95455, Unincorporated
Chamber of Commerce, Drive Thru Tree Rd., P.O. Box 105, 95585
(707) 925-6385
Leisure World (Orange County), Unincorporated
Lemon Grove (San Diego Co.), 3232 Main St., 91945 (619) 464-6934,
Fax: (619) 460-3716
Chamber of Commerce, 3443 Main St., 91945 (619) 469-9621
Library, 8073 Broadway, 91945-2599 (619) 463-9819,
Fax: (619) 463-8069
Newspaper, *Lemon Grove Review*, 3434 Grove St., P.O. Box 127,
91946 (619) 469-0101
Lemoore (Kings Co.), 119 Fox St., 93245 (209) 924-6700,
Fax: (209) 924-9003
Chamber of Commerce, 218 W. "D" St., 93245 (209) 924-6401,
Fax: (209) 924-4520
Library, 457 "C" St., 93245 (209) 924-2188
Newspaper, *The Lemore Advance*, P.O. Box 547, 93245
(209) 924-5361, Fax: (209) 924-6220
Police, 210 Fox St., 93245 (209) 924-9574
Lennox (Los Angeles Co.), 90304, Unincorporated
Library, 4359 Lennox Blvd., 90304 (310) 674-0385,
Fax: (310) 673-6508
Leucadia (San Diego Co.), 92024, Unincorporated
Chamber of Commerce, (see Encinitas)
Lewiston (Trinity Co.), 96052, Unincorporated
Chamber of Commerce, (see Weaverville)
Lincoln (Placer Co.), 1530 Third St., Suite 111, 95648 (916) 645-3314,
Fax: (916) 645-9502
Chamber of Commerce, 511 5th St., P.O. Box 608, 95648
(916) 645-2035, Fax: (916) 945-9455
Library, 590 5th St., 95648 (916) 645-3607, Fax: (916) 645-7924
Newspaper, *Lincoln News-Messenger*, Box 368, 95648
(916) 654-7733, Fax: (916) 645-2776

Lincoln Police, 472 "E" St., 95648 (916) 645-3391
Lincoln Heights (Los Angeles Co.), City of Los Angeles
    Library, 2217-19 N. Broadway, 90031 (213) 225-3977,
        Fax: (213) 612-0423
Linden (San Joaquin Co.), 95236, Unincorporated
    Chamber of Commerce, P.O. Box 557, 95236
    Library, 19012 E. Main St., 95236 (209) 887-3370
    Newspaper, *The Linden Herald,* 4959 N. Bonham, P.O. Box 929,
        95236 (209) 887-3112, Fax: (209) 887-3112
Lindsay (Tulare Co.), 251 E. Honolulu St., P.O. Box 369, 93247
    (209) 562-5928, Fax: (209) 562-5748
    Chamber of Commerce, 147 N. Gale Hill Ave., P.O. Box 989, 93247
        (209) 562-4929, Fax: (209) 562-5219
    Library, 165 N. Gale Hill St., 93247 (209) 562-3021
    Newspaper, *The Lindsay Gazette,* 136 E. Honolulu St.,
        P.O. Box 308, 93247 (209) 562-2585, Fax: (205) 562-2214
    Police, 185 N. Gale Hill St., 93247 (209) 562-2511
Littlerock (Los Angeles Co.), 93543, Unincorporated
    Chamber of Commerce, P.O. Box 326, 93543 (805) 944-6990
    Library, 8135 Pearblossom Hwy., P.O. Box 218, 93543
        (805) 944-4138, Fax: (805) 944-4150
    Newspaper, *Antelope Valley Press,* 37404 N. Sierra Hwy.,
        P.O. Box 880, Palmdale, 93590 (805) 273-2700,
        Fax: (805) 947-4870
Live Oak (Sutter Co.), 9955 Live Oak Blvd., 95953 (916) 695-2112
    Chamber of Commerce, P.O. Box 338, 95923 (916) 695-1519
    Sheriff, 9867 "O" St., 95953 (916) 695-2122
Livermore (Alameda Co.), 1052 S. Livermore Ave., 94550-4899
    (510) 447-1606, Fax: (510) 447-1641
    Chamber of Commerce, 2157 First St., 94550-4543 (510) 447-1606,
        Fax: (510) 447-1641
    Library, 1000 S. Livermore Ave., 94550 (510) 373-5500
    Newspaper, *The Livermoore Herald,* 4770 Willow Rd., Pleasonton,
        94588 (510) 734-8600, Fax: (510) 734-8043
    Police, 1050 S. Livermore Ave., 94550 (510) 373-5303
Livingston (Merced Co.), 1416 "C" St., P.O. Box 308, 95334 (209) 394-8041,
    Fax: (209) 394-4190
    Chamber of Commerce, P.O. Box 308, 95334 (209) 394-8041
    Library, 1212 Main St., 95334 (209) 394-7330
    Newspaper, *The Chronicle,* 424 Main St., 95334 (209) 394-7939,
        Fax: (209) 394-7930
    Police, P.O. Box 308, 95334 (209) 394-7916
Lockeford (San Joaquin Co.), 95237, Unincorporated
    Chamber of Commerce, P.O. Box 524, 95237 (209) 727-3142
Lodi (San Joaquin Co.), 221 W. Pine St., 95240, P.O. Box 3006, 95241-1910
    (209) 334-5634, Fax: (209) 333-6807
    Chamber of Commerce, 1330 S. Ham Lane, #102, P.O. Box 386,
        95241 (209) 367-7840, (209) 367-5634,
        Fax: (209) 334-0528
    Library, 201 W. Locust, 95240-2099 (209) 333-8507
    Newspaper, *Lodi News-Sentinel,* P.O. Box 1360, 95241
        (209) 369-2761, Fax: (209) 369-1084

Lodo¡Police, 230 W. Elm St., 95240 (209) 333-6725
Loleta (Humboldt Co.), 95551, Unincorporated
   Chamber of Commerce, P.O. Box 327, 95551 (707) 733-5470
Loma Linda (San Bernardino Co.), 25541 Barton Rd., 92354-3901
   (909) 799-2800, Fax: (909) 799-2890
   Chamber of Commerce, 25541 Barton Rd., #4, P.O. Box 343, 92354
   (909) 799-2828, Fax: (909) 799-2825
   Library, 25581 Barton Rd., 92354 (909) 796-8621
   Sheriff, 655 E. Third St., San Bernardino, 92410 (909) 387-3500
Lomita (Los Angeles Co.), 24300 Narbonne Ave., P.O. Box 339, 90717
   (310) 325-7110, Fax: (310) 325-4024
   Chamber of Commerce, 24300 Narbonne Ave., P.O. Box 425, 90717
   (310) 326-6378, Fax: (310) 325-4024
   Library, 24200 Narbonne Ave., 90717 (310) 539-4515,
   Fax: (310) 534-8649
   Sheriff, 26123 Narbonne Ave., 90717 (310) 539-1661
Lompoc (Santa Barbara Co.), 100 Civic Center Plaza, P.O. Box 8001,
   93438-8001 (805) 736-1261, Fax: (805) 736-5347
   Chamber of Commerce, 111 S. "I" St., P.O. Box 626, 93438-0626
   (805) 736-4567, Fax: (805) 737-0453
   Library, 501 E. North Ave., 93436-3477 (805) 736-3477
   Newspaper, *Lompoc Record,* 115 N. "H" St., 93436 (805) 736-2313,
   Fax: (805) 736-5654
   Police, 107 Civic Center Plaza, 93436 (805) 736-2341
Lone Pine (Inyo Co.), 93545, Unincorporated
   Chamber of Commerce, 126 S. Main St., P.O. Box 749, 93545
   (619) 876-4444
Long Beach (Los Angeles Co.), 333 W. Ocean Blvd, 90802 (310) 570-6555,
   Fax: (310) 570-6583
   Chamber of Commerce, One World Trade Center, #350, 90805
   (310) 436-1251, Fax: (310) 436-7099
   Library, 101 Pacific Ave., 90822-1097 (310) 570-6291
   Newspaper, *Long Beach Community News,* P.O. Box 92825, 90809
   (310) 987-4058, Fax: (310) 987-0729
   CSU Long Beach Police, 1331 Palo Verde Ave., 90840
   (310) 985-4101
   Police, 400 W. Broadway, 90802 (310) 570-7301
Loomis (Placer Co.), 6140 Horseshoe Bar Rd., P.O. Box 1327, 95650
   (916) 652-1840, Fax: (916) 652-1847
   Chamber of Commerce, P.O. Box 1212, 95650 (916) 652-7252
   Library, P.O. Box 610, 95650 (916) 652-7061
   Newspaper, *Loomis News,* P.O. Box 125, 95650 (916) 652-7939
Los Alamitos (Orange Co.), 3191 Katella Ave, P.O. Box 3147, 90720
   (310) 431-3538, Fax: (310) 493-1255
   Chamber of Commerce, 3243 Katella Ave., P.O. Box 111, 90720
   (310) 598-6659, Fax: (213) 598-6650
   Library, 12700 Montecito Rd., Seal Beach, 90740 (310) 430-1048,
   (714) 846-3240, Fax: (213) 431-2913
   Newspaper, *News-Enterprise,* 3622 Florista, P.O. Box 1010, 90720
   (714) 527-8210, Fax: (310) 493-2310
   Police, 3201 Katella Ave., 90720 (714) 431-1344

Los Altos (Los Angeles Co.), City of Long Beach
  Library, 5614 Britton Dr., 90815 (310) 596-7370
Los Altos (Santa Clara Co.), One N. San Antonio Rd., 94022 (415) 948-1491,
  Fax: (415) 941-7419
  Chamber of Commerce, 321 University Ave., 94022 (415) 948-1455,
  Fax: (415) 948-6238
  Library, 13 S. San Antonio Rd., 94022-3099 (415) 948-7412,
  Fax: (415) 941-6308
  Newspaper, *Los Altos Town Crier*, 138 Main St., P.O. Drawer F,
  94023 (415) 948-4489, Fax: (415) 948-6647
Los Altos Hills (Santa Clara Co.), 26379 Fremont Rd., 94022 (415) 941-7222,
  Fax: (415) 941-3160
  Police, #1 N. San Antonio Rd., 94022-3088 (415) 948-8223
  Sheriff, 14374 Saratoga Ave., Saratoga, 95070 (408) 867-9719
Los Angeles (Los Angeles Co.), 200 N. Spring St., 90012 (213) 485-2121,
  Fax: (213) 680-0085
  Administrative Officer (213) 485-2885
  City Attorney
    Civil (213) 485-6370
    Criminal (213) 485-5470
  Building and Safety, Rm. 403 (213) 485-2327
  Chamber of Commerce, 404 S. Bixel St., P.O. Box 3696,
    90051-1696 (213) 629-0602, Fax: (213) 629-0708
  Black Business Assn. of L.A., 3683 Crenshaw Blvd., 4th Floor,
    90016 (213) 292-0274, Fax: (213) 292-0548
  Century City Chamber of Commerce, 49 Century Park.E., #460,
    90067 (310) 553-2222, Fax: (310) 553-4623
  Crenshaw Chamber of Commerce, 4716 Crenshaw Blvd., 90043
    (213) 292-7000, Fax: (213) 291-5302
  Eagle Rock Chamber of Commerce, P.O. Box 41354, 90041
  East Los Angeles Chamber of (818) 796-0156, Fax: (818) 796-6037
  Commerce, 4716 E. Brooklyn Ave., P.O. Box 63220, 90063-0220
    (213) 266-6774, Fax: (213) 780-7986
  Highland Park Chamber of Commerce, 131 S. Ave. 57,
    P.O. Box 42949, 90050-0949 (213) 256-0920
  Japanese Chamber of Commerce of Southern California, 244 S. San
    Pedro, #504, 90017 (213) 626-3067, Fax: (213) 626-3070
  Lincoln Heights Chamber of Commerce, 2722 N. Broadway, 90031
    (213) 221-6571, Fax: (213) 222-1038
  L.A. Business Council, 10880 Wilshire Blvd., #1109, 90024
    (310) 475-4574, Fax: (310) 475-1427
  Mexican Chamber of Commerce, 125 Paseo de Plaza, #404, 90012
    (213) 688-7330, Fax: (213) 688-7562
  Mid-City Chamber of Commerce, 4729 Venice Blvd., 90019
    (213) 937-3532
  Westside Chamber of Commerce, 10779 W. Pico Blvd., Second
    Floor, P.O. Box 64512, 90064 (310) 475-8806
  Wilshire Chamber of Commerce, 3460 Wilshire Blvd., #411, 90010
    (213) 386-8224, (800) 288-3068, Fax: (213) 386-1655

Los Angeles Continued
  City Clerk, City Hall, Rm. 101 (213) 485-5708
    Business Permits (213) 485-3960
    Election Division (213) 485-3581
    Police and Fire Permits (213) 485-3936
    Property Ownership (213) 485-5741
  Fire Dept. Records (213) 485-5982
  Libraries, Main, 630 W. 5th St., 90071 (213) 228-7000
    Periodicals (213) 612-3200
    Braille Institute Library, 741 N. Vermont Ave., 90029
      (213) 663-1111
    City Hall Library, 200 N. Main St., Room 530, 90012
      (213) 485-3791
    Water & Power Library, 111 N. Hope St., 90012
      (213) 481-4611
    Angeles Mesa, 2400 52nd St., L.A., 90043 (213) 292-4328
    North Hollywood, 5211 Tujunga Ave., N.H., 91601
      (818) 766-7185
    Arroyo Seco, 6145 N. Figueroa, L.A., 90042
      (213) 237-1181
    San Pedro, 931 S. Gaffey St., San Pedro, 90731
      (310) 548-7785
    West Valley, 19036 Vanowen St., Reseda 91335
      (818) 345-4394
    West Los Angeles, 11360 Santa Monica Blvd., L.A.,
      90025 (310) 575-8323
  Newspaper, *Daily Commerce,* 915 E. First St., 90012
    (213) 229-5300, Fax: (213) 680-3682
  Newspaper, *Daily News,* 21221 Oxnard St., Woodland Hills, 91367
    (818) 713-3000, Fax: (818) 713-0058
  Newspaper, *Investor's Business Daily,* 12655 Beatrice Ave., 90025
    (310) 448-6000, Fax: (310) 577-7350
  Newspaper, *La Opinion* (Spanish), 411 W. 5th St., 90013
    (213) 896-2020, Fax: (213) 896-2144
  Newspaper, *Los Angeles Times,* Times Mirror Square, 90053
    (213) 237-5000, (800) LA-TIMES, Fax: (213) 237-4712
  Police, 150 N. Los Angeles St., 90012, P.O. Box 30158, 90030
      (213) 485-3202
      Auto Theft (213) 485-2507
      Bunco (213) 485-3795
      Burglary (213) 485-2524
      Forgery (213) 485-4131
      Missing Persons (213) 485-5381
      Pawnshop Detail (213) 485-2525
    Central Area, 251 E. 6th St., L.A., 90014 (213) 485-3294
      Central Traffic Div. (213) 485-3122
      Narcotics Div., Rm. 316 (213) 485-4504
      Organized Crime Intelligence Div. (213) 485-5201
      Press Relations Div., Rm. 626 (213) 485-4064
      Records & Identification Div., Rm. 210 (213) 485-2603
      Robbery-Homocide Div., Rm. 321 (213) 485-485-2511
      Scientific Investigation Div., Rm. 435 (213) 485-2535

Los Angeles Police Continued
  Devonshire Area Desk, 10250 Etiwanda Ave., Northridge, 91325 (818) 756-8285
  Foothill Area Desk, 12760 Osborne St., Pacoima, 91331 (818) 756-8861
  Harbor Area Desk, 2175 John S. Gibson Blvd., San Pedro, 90731 (310) 548-7603
  Hollenbeck Area Desk, 2111 E. First St., L.A., 90033 (213) 485-2942
  Hollywood Area Desk, 1358 N. Wilcox Ave., L.A., 90028 (213) 485-4302
  Newton Area Desk, 1354 Newton St., L.A., 90021 (213) 485-5265
  North Hollywood Area Desk, 11480 Tiara St., North Hollywood, 91601 (818) 756-8824
  Northeast Area Desk, 3353 San Fernando Rd., L.A., 90065 (213) 485-2563
  Pacific Area Desk, 12312 Culver Blvd., L.A., 90066 (310) 202-4502
  Rampart Area Desk, 2710 W. Temple St., 90026 (213) 485-4063
  77th Street Area Desk, 235 W. 77th St., 90003 (213) 485-4164
  Southeast Area Desk, 145 W. 108th St., 90061 (213) 485-6914
  Southwest Area Desk, 1546 W. Martin Luther King Blvd., L.A., 90062 (213) 485-2582
  Van Nuys Area Desk, 6240 Sylmar Ave., Van Nuys, 91401 (818) 756-8343
  West Los Angeles Area Desk, 1663 Butler Ave., L.A., 90025 (310) 575-8401
  West Valley Area Desk, 19020 Vanowen St., Reseda, 91335 (818) 756-8543
  Wilshire Area Desk, 4861 Venice Blvd., L.A., 90019 (213) 485-4022
CSU Los Angeles Police, 5151 State University Dr., 90032 (213) 343-3700
U.C.L.A. Police, 601 Westwood Plaza, 90024 (213) 825-1633
Los Banos (Merced Co.), 520 "J" St., P.O. Box 31, 93635 (209) 826-5119, Fax: (209) 827-7006
  Chamber of Commerce, 503 "J" St., P.O. Box 2117, 93635 (209) 824-2495, (800) 336-6354, Fax: (209) 826-9689
  Library, 1312 7th St., 93635 (209) 826-5254
  Newspaper, *Los Banos Enterprise,* 1253 W. "I" St., 93635 (209) 826-3831
  Police, P.O. Box 31, 93635 (209) 827-7070
Los Feliz (Los Angeles Co.), City of Los Angeles
  Library, 1939 1/2 Hillhurst Ave., 90027 (213) 664-2903, Fax: (213) 612-0402

Los Gatos (Santa Clara Co.), 110 E. Main St., 95032, P.O. Box 949, 95031 (408) 354-6834, Fax: (408) 354-8431
 Chamber of Commerce, 50 University Ave., #5, P.O. Box 1820, 95031 (408) 354-9300, Fax: (408) 395-6593
 Library, 110 E. Main St., 95032 (408) 354-6891, Fax: (408) 351-8431
 Newspaper, *Los Gatos Weekly-Times,* 245 Almendra Ave., 95030 (408) 298-8000, Fax: (408) 298-0602
 Police, P.O. Box 973, 95031 (408) 354-5257
Los Molinos (Tehama Co.), 96055, Unincorporated
 Chamber of Commerce, 7904 Hwy. 99E, P.O. Box 334, 96055 (916) 384-2251
 Library, 7804 Hwy. 99, P.O. Box 334, 96055 (916) 384-2772
Los Nietos (Los Angeles Co.), City of Santa Fe Springs
 Library, 11644 E. Slauson Ave., Whittier, 90606 (310) 695-0708, Fax: (310) 699-3876
Los Osos (San Luis Obispo Co.), 93402, Unincorporated
 Chamber of Commerce, 781 Los Osos Valley Rd., P.O. Box 6282, 93412 (805) 528-4884
Loyalton (Sierra Co.), 115 Front St., P.O. Box 128, 96118 (916) 993-6750, Fax: (916) 993-4752
 Newspaper, *Sierra Booster,* P.O. Box 9, 96118 (916) 993-4379
 Sheriff, P.O. Box 1109, 96118 (916) 993-4479
Lucerne Valley (San Bernardino Co.), 92356, Unincorporated
 Chamber of Commerce, 32750 Old Woman Springs Rd., P.O. Box 491, 92356 (619) 248-7215
 Library, 33103 Old Woman Springs Rd., 92356 (619) 248-7521
 Newspaper, *The Leader,* Box 299, 92356 (619) 248-7878, Fax: (619) 248-2042
Lynwood (Los Angeles Co.), 11330 Bullis Rd., 90262 (310) 603-0220, Fax: (310) 764-4908
 Chamber of Commerce, 3651 E. Imperial Hwy., P.O. Box 763, 90262 (310) 537-6484, Fax: (310) 537-8143
 Library, 11320 Bullis Rd., 90262 (310) 635-7121, Fax: (310) 635-4967
 Newspaper, *Lynwood Press & Tribune,* 2621 W. 54th St., 90043 (213) 290-3000, Fax: (213) 291-0219
 Sheriff, 11703 S. Alameda St., 90262 (310) 567-8121
Madera (Madera Co.), 205 W. 4th St., 93637 (209) 661-5400, Fax: (209) 674-2972
 Chamber of Commerce, 131 W. Yosemite Ave., 93639 (209) 673-3563
 Library, 121 N. "G" St., 93637-3592 (209) 675-7871, Fax: (209) 675-7998
 Newspaper, *Madera Tribune,* P.O. Box 269, 93639 (209) 674-2424, Fax: (209) 673-6526
 Police, 203 W. 4th St., 93637 (209) 674-5611
Malibu (Los Angeles Co.), 23555 Civic Center Way, 90265 (310) 456-2489, Fax: (310) 456-3356
 Chamber of Commerce, 23805 Stuart Ranch Rd., #100, 90265 (310) 456-9025, Fax: (310) 456-0195

Malibu Library, 23519 Civic Center Way, 90265 (310) 456-6438,
    Fax: (310) 456-8681
Newspaper, *The Malibu Times*, P.O. Box 1127, 90265
    (310) 456-5507, Fax: (310) 456-8986
Sheriff, 27050 Agoura Rd., Calabasas, 91301 (818) 878-1808
Malibu Beach (Los Angeles Co.), City of Malibu
Malibu Bowl (Los Angeles Co.), Unincorporated
Malibu Junction (Los Angeles Co.), City of Agoura Hills
Malibu Lake (Los Angeles Co.), Unincorporated
Malibu Riviera (Los Angeles Co.), City of Malibu
Malibu Vista (Los Angeles Co.), Unincorporated
Mammoth Lakes (Mono Co.), Minaret Mall, Old Mammoth Road,
    P.O. Box 1609, 93546 (619) 934-8983,
    Fax: (619) 934-8608
Chamber of Commerce, P.O. Box 123, 93546 (619) 934-3064,
    (800) 367-6572
Newspaper, *Mammoth Times*, P.O. Box 3929, 93546
    (619) 934-3929, Fax: (619) 934-3916
Police, P.O. Box 2799, 93546 (619) 934-2011

Manhattan Beach (Los Angeles Co.), 1400 Highland Ave., 90266
    (310) 545-5621, Fax: (310) 545-5234
  Chamber of Commerce, 425 15th St., P.O. Box 3007, 90266
    (310) 545-5313, Fax: (310) 545-7203
  Library, 1320 Highland Ave., 90266 (310) 545-8595,
    Fax: (310) 545-5394
  Police, 420 15th St., 90266 (310) 545-5621
Manteca (San Joaquin Co.), 1001 W. Center, 95336 (209) 239-8400,
    Fax: (209) 825-2333
  Chamber of Commerce, 141 N. Maple Ave., 95336 (209) 823-6121,
    Fax: (209) 823-9959
  Library, 320 W. Center, 95336 (209) 825-2380, Fax: (209) 825-2394
  Newspaper, *Manteca Bulletin,* 531 E. Yosemite Ave., P.O. Box 912,
    95336 (209) 239-3531, Fax: (209) 239-1801
  Police, 1001 W. Center St., 95336 (209) 239-8401
Mar Vista (Los Angeles Co.), City of Los Angeles
  Library, 12006 Venice Blvd., 90066 (213) 390-3454,
    Fax: (818) 904-3282
Maricopa (Kern Co.), 400 California St., P.O. Box 548, 93252-0548
    (805) 769-8279, Fax: (805) 769-8130
  Sheriff, 209 E. Kern St., Taft, 93268 (805) 763-3101
Marina (Monterey Co.), 211 Hillcrest Ave., 93933 (408) 384-3715,
    Fax: (408) 384-0425
  Chamber of Commerce, P.O. Box 425, 93933 (408) 384-9155
  Library, 266 Reservation Rd., 93933 (408) 384-6971
  Police, 211 Hillcrest Ave., 93933 (408) 384-5225
Marina Del Rey (Los Angeles Co.), Unincorporated
  Chamber of Commerce, 4519 Admiralty Way, #206, 90292
    (310) 821-0555, (800) 919-0555, Fax: (310) 823-0461
  Library, 4533 Admiralty Way, 90292 (310) 821-3415,
    Fax: (310) 306-3372
  Newspaper, *The Argonaut,* P.O. Box 9995, 90295 (310) 822-1629,
    Fax: (310) 821-8029
  Police, 13851 Fiji Way, 90292 (310) 823-7762
Mariposa (Mariposa Co.), 95338, Unincorporated
  Chamber of Commerce, 5158 N. Hwy. 140, P.O. Box 425, 95338
    (209) 966-2456, (800) 208-2434, Fax: (209) 742-5409
  Newspaper, *Mariposa Gazette & Miner,* P.O. Box 38, 95338
    (209) 966-2500, Fax: (209) 966-3384
Markleeville (Alpine Co.), 96120, Unincorporated
  Chamber of Commerce, P.O. Box 265, 96120 (916) 694-2475,
    Fax: (916) 694-2478
  Library, 270 Laramie St., P.O. Box 187, 96120-0187
    (916) 694-2120, Fax: (916) 694-2408
Martinez (Contra Costa Co.), 525 Henrietta St., 94553 (510) 372-3500,
    Fax: (510) 372-0257
  Chamber of Commerce, 620 Las Juntas St., 94553 (510) 228-2345,
    Fax: (510) 228-2356
  Library, 740 Court St., 94553 (510) 646-2898
  Newspaper, *Martinez News-Gazette,* 615 Estudillo St., P.O. Box 151,
    94553 (707) 228-6400, Fax: (707) 557-6380
  Police, 1111 Ward St., 94553 (510) 372-3444

Marysville (Yuba Co.), 526 "C" St., P.O. Box 150, 95901 (916) 741-6633,
 Fax: (916) 742-7160
  Chamber of Commerce, 429 10th St., P.O. Box 1429, 95901
   (916) 743-6501, Fax: (916) 741-8645
  Library, 303 Second St., 95901 (916) 741-6241,
   Fax: (916) 741-3098
  Newspaper, *Appeal-Democrat*, 1530 Ellis Lake Dr., 95901
   (916) 741-2345, Fax: (916) 741-1195
  Police, P.O. Box 670, 95901 (916) 741-6611
Mayfair (Los Angeles Co.), City of Lakewood
Maywood (Los Angeles Co.), 4319 E. Slauson Ave., 90270 (213) 562-5000,
 Fax: (213) 773-2806
  Chamber of Commerce, 4747 E. 56th St., 90270 (213) 562-3373
  Library, 4323 E. Slauson Ave., 90270 (213) 771-8600,
   Fax: (213) 560-0515
  Police, 4319 E. Slauson Ave., 90270 (213) 562-5005
McCloud (Siskiyou Co.), 96057, Unincorporated
  Chamber of Commerce, P.O. Box 504, 96057 (916) 964-3105
  Library, 300 E. Colombero Dr., P.O. Box 425, 96057-0425
   (916) 964-2169
McFarland (Kern Co.), 401 Kern Ave., P.O. Box 1488, 93250
   (805) 792-3091, Fax: (805) 792-3093
  Police, 401 W. Kern Ave., 93250-1352 (805) 792-2121
McKinleyville (Humboldt Co.), 95521, Unincorporated
  Chamber of Commerce, P.O. Box 2144, 95521 (707) 839-2449
  Library, Murray Rd., 95521 (707) 839-1510
Mendota (Fresno Co.), 643 Quince St., 93640 (209) 655-3291,
   Fax: (209) 655-4064
  Chamber of Commerce, P.O. Box 682, 93640 (209) 655-2530
  Sheriff, 2200 Fresno St., 93717 (209) 655-4294
Menlo Park (San Mateo Co.), 701 Laurel St., 94025 (415) 858-3380,
   Fax: (415) 328-7935
  Chamber of Commerce, 1100 Merrill St., 94025 (415) 325-2818,
   Fax: (415) 325-0920
  Library, 800 Alma St., 94025-3460 (415) 858-3460,
   Fax: (415) 858-3466
  Newspaper, *Country Almanac*, P.O. Box 98, 94026 (415) 328-1600,
   Fax: (415) 328-9760
  Police, 801 Laurel St., 94025 (415) 858-3300
Merced (Merced Co.), 678 W. 18th St., 95340 (209) 385-6834,
   Fax: (209) 384-5805
  City Chamber of Commerce, 690 W. 16th St., 95340
   (209) 384-3333, (800) 446-5353, Fax: (209) 384-8472
  County Chamber of Commerce, 1636 Canal, P.O. Box 1112, 95340
   (209) 722-3864, Fax: (209) 722-2406
  Library, 2100 "O" St., 95340-3790 (209) 385-7485,
   Fax: (209) 726-7912
  Newspaper, *Merced Sun-Star*, 3033 N. "G" St., 95430
   (209) 722-1511, Fax: (209) 384-2226
  Police, 611 W. 22nd St., 95340 (209) 385-6912

Mill Valley (Marin Co.), 26 Corte Madera Ave., 94941, P.O. Box 1029, 94942
  (415) 388-4033, Fax: (415) 381-1736
  Chamber of Commerce, 85 Throckmorton Ave., P.O. Box 5123,
    94942 (415) 388-9700, Fax: (415) 383-9469
  Library, 375 Throckmorton Ave., 94941-2698 (415) 388-2190,
    Fax: (415) 388-8929
  Newspaper, *Pacific Sun,* Box 5553, 94942 (415) 383-4500
  Police, P.O. Box 1029, 94942 (415) 388-4142
Millbrae (San Mateo Co.), 621 Magnolia Ave., 94030 (415) 259-2334,
    Fax: (415) 259-2415
  Chamber of Commerce, 50 Victoria Ave., #103, 94030
    (415) 697-7324, Fax: (415) 259-7918
  Library, One Library Ave., 94030 (415) 697-7607,
    Fax: (415) 692-4747
  Police, P.O. Box 850, 94030 (415) 259-2300
Milpitas (Santa Clara Co.), 455 E. Calavaras Blvd., 95035 (408) 942-2310,
    Fax: (408) 263-6541
  Chamber of Commerce, 75 S. Milpitas Blvd., #205,
    95035 (408) 262-2613, Fax: (408) 262-2823
  Library, 40 N. Milpitas Blvd., 95035-4495 (408) 262-1171,
    Fax: (408) 262-5806
  Police, 1275 N.Milpitas Blvd., 95035 (408) 942-2400
Mira Loma (Riverside Co.), Unincorporated
  Chamber of Commerce, P.O. Box 257, 91752 (909) 685-0801,
    Fax: (909) 685-9146
Mira Mesa (San Diego Co.), City of San Diego
  Library, 8450 Mira Mesa Blvd., 92126 (619) 538-8165
Miraleste (Los Angeles Co.), City of Rancho Palos Verdes
Mission Hills (Los Angeles Co.), City of Los Angeles
  Chamber of Commerce, 11150 Sepulveda Blvd., #A, 91345
    (818) 361-8888
Mission Viejo (Orange Co.), 26522 La Alameda, Suite 190, 92691
    (714) 582-2489, Fax: (714) 582-7530
  Chamber of Commerce, (see Laguna Hills)
  Library, 24851 Chrisanta Dr., 92691 (714) 830-7100,
    Fax: (714) 586-8447
  Newspaper, *Saddleback Valley News,* P.O. Box 3629, 92690
    (714) 768-3681, Fax: (714) 830-9504
  Sheriff, 25622 La Alameto, #190, 92691 (714) 582-2489
Modesto (Stanislaus Co.), 801 11th St., 95354, P.O. Box 642, 95353
    (209) 577-5200, Fax: (209) 571-5128
  Chamber of Commerce, 1114 "J" St., P.O. Box 844, 95353
    (209) 577-5757, Fax: (209) 577-2673
  Stanislaus County Chamber of Commerce, 605 "H" St., 95354
    (209) 575-2597, Fax: (209) 527-7839
  Library, 1500 "I" St., 95354 (209) 525-7814, Fax: (209) 529-4779
  Newspaper, *The Modesto Bee, 1325 "H"* St., Fresno 93786
    (209) 441-6111
  Police, P.O. Box 3313, 95353 (209) 572-9500

Mojave (Kern Co.), 93501, Unincorporated
    Chamber of Commerce, 15836 Sierra Hwy., 93501 (805) 824-2481,
        Fax: (805) 824-9626
    Library, (see Bakersfield)
    Newspaper, *The Mojave Desert News*, 8046C California City Blvd.,
        P.O. Box 937, 93502 (619) 373-4812, Fax: (619) 373-2941
Moneta (Los Angeles Co.), City of Gardena
Monrovia (Los Angeles Co.), 415 S. Ivy Ave., 91016 (818) 359-3231,
        Fax: (818) 359-8507
    Chamber of Commerce, 620 S. Myrtle Ave., 91016 (818) 358-1159
    Library, 321 S. Myrtle St., 91016-2848, (818) 358-0175,
        Fax: (818) 358-3782
    Police, 140 E. Lime Ave., 91016 (818) 359-1152
Montague (Siskiyou Co.), 230 S. 13th St., P.O. Box 428, 96064
        (916) 459-3030, Fax: (916) 459-3523
    Library, City Hall, 1030 13th St., 96064 (916) 459-5473
    Sheriff, Courthouse, 311 Lane St., Yreka, 96097 (916) 842-4141
Montclair (San Bernardino Co.), 5111 Benito St., P.O. Box 2308, 91763
        (909) 626-8571, Fax: (909) 621-1584
    Chamber of Commerce, 5220 Benito St., 91763 (909) 624-4569,
        Fax: (909) 625-2009
    Library, Civic Center, 9955 Femont, 91763 (909) 624-4671
    Police, P.O. Box 2308, 91763 (909) 621-5873
Monte Nido (Los Angeles Co.), Unincorporated
Monte Rio (Sonoma Co.), 95462, Unincorporated
    Chamber of Commerce, P.O. Box 220, 95462 (707) 865-1533
Monte Sereno (Santa Clara Co.), 18041 Saratoga-Los Gatos Rd., 95030
        (408) 354-7635, Fax: (408) 395-7653
    Sheriff, 14374 Saratoga Ave., Saratoga, 95070 (408) 867-9719
Montebello (Los Angeles Co.), 1600 W. Beverly Blvd., 90640
        (213) 887-1200, Fax: (213) 887-1410
    Chamber of Commerce, 1304 W. Beverly Blvd., 90640
        (213) 721-1153
    Library, 1550 W. Beverly Blvd., 90640 (213) 722-6551,
        Fax: (213) 722-3018
    Newspaper, *Montebello Messenger*, 108 W. Beverly Blvd.,
        P.O. Box 578, 90640 (213) 721-1735, Fax: (213) 721-2266
    Police, 1600 W. Beverly Blvd., 90640 (213) 887-1212
Montecito Heights (Los Angeles Co.), City of Los Angeles
Monterey (Monterey Co.), Corner of Madison & Pacific Sts., 93940
        (408) 646-3935, Fax: (408) 646-3702
    Chamber of Commerce, 380 Alvarado St., P.O. Box 1770, 93942
        (408) 649-1770, Fax: (408) 649-3502
    Library, 625 Pacific St., 93940-2866 (408) 646-3932,
        Fax: (408) 646-5618
    Newspaper, *The Monterey County Herald*, P.O. Box 271, 93942
        (408) 372-3311, Fax: (408) 646-4394
    Police, 351 Madison St., 93940 (408) 646-3830
Monterey Hills (Los Angeles Co.), City of Los Angeles

Monterey Park (Los Angeles Co.), 320 W. Newmark Ave., 91754
(818) 307-1359, Fax: (818) 280-4537
Chamber of Commerce, 231 W. Garvey Ave., P.O. Box 387, 91754
(818) 280-3864, (818) 280-3867, Fax: (818) 280-3868
Library, 318 S. Ramona Ave., 91754-3312 (818) 307-1333,
Fax: (818) 288-4251
Police, 320 W. Newmark Ave., 91754 (818) 573-1311
Montrose (Los Angeles Co.), 91020, Unincorporated
Chamber of Commerce, 3786 La Crescenta, #104, 91208
(818) 249-7171, (818) 249-3414, Fax: (818) 249-8919
Library, 2465 Honolulu Ave., 91020 (818) 548-2048,
Fax: (818) 548-2048
Moorpark (Ventura Co.), 799 Moorpark Ave., 93021 (805) 529-6864,
Fax: (805) 529-8270
Chamber of Commerce, 530 Moorpark Ave., #160, 93021
(805) 529-0322, Fax: (805) 529-5304
Library, 699 Moorpark Ave., 93021 (805) 529-0440
Newspaper, *Moorpark News-Mirror,* P.O. Box 775, 93020
(805) 523-7440, Fax: (805) 523-7816
Moraga (Contra Costa Co.), 2100 Donald Dr., P.O. Box 188, 94556
(510) 376-2590, Fax: (510) 376-2034
Chamber of Commerce, 440 Center St., P.O. Box 512, 94556
(510) 376-0150
Library, 1500 St. Mary's Rd., 94556-2099 (510) 376-6852
Police, 350 Rheem Blvd., 94556 (510) 376-2515
Moreno Valley (Riverside Co.), 23119 Cottonwood Ave., 92553,
P.O. Box 88005, 92552-0805 (909) 243-3000,
Fax: (909) 243-3009
Chamber of Commerce, 22620 Golden Crest Dr., #110, 92553
(909) 697-4404, Fax: (909) 697-4767
Library, 25480 Alessandro Blvd., 92553 (909) 247-0806,
Fax: (909) 247-8346
Newspaper, *The Valley Newspaper,* P.O. Box 9700, 92553
(714) 242-7614, Fax: (714) 247-1920
Sheriff, 23618 Sunnymead Blvd., 92388 (909) 924-3221
Morgan Hill (Santa Clara Co.), 17555 Peak Ave., 95037 (408) 779-7259,
Fax: (408) 779-3117
Chamber of Commerce, 25 W. First St., P.O. Box 786, 95037
(408) 779-9444, Fax: (408) 779-6798
Library, 17575 Peak Ave., 95037-4128 (408) 779-3196,
Fax: (408) 779-0883
Newspaper, *Morgan Hill Times,* 30 E. Third St., P.O. Box 757,
95038 (408) 779-4106, Fax: (408) 779-3886
Police, 17605 Monterey Rd., 95037 (408) 776-7300
Morningside (Los Angeles Co.), City of Inglewood
Morongo Valley (San Bernardino Co.), 92256, Unincorporated
Chamber of Commerce, 11207 Ocotillo, 92256 (619) 363-6454
Morro Bay (San Luis Obispo Co.), 595 Harbor St., 93442-1900
(805) 772-6200, Fax: (805) 772-7329
Chamber of Commerce, 895 Napa Ave., #A-1, 93442 (805) 772-4467
Library, 625 Harbor St., 93442 (805) 772-8754
Police, 850 Morro Bay Blvd., 93442 (805) 772-6225

Moss Landing (Monterey Co.), 95039, Unincorporated
  Chamber of Commerce, P.O. Box 41, 95039 (408) 633-4301
Mount Shasta (Siskiyou Co.), 305 N. Mt. Shasta Blvd., 96067
    (916) 926-3464, Fax: (916) 926-0339
  Chamber of Commerce, 310 N. Mount Shasta Blvd., P.O. Box 273,
    96067 (916) 926-6212, (800) 926-4865,
    Fax: (916) 926-0976
  Library, 515 E. Alma St., 96067 (916) 926-2031
  Newspaper, *Herald*, P.O. Box 127, 96067 (916) 926-5214,
    Fax: (916) 926-4166
  Police, 303 N. Mount Shasta Blvd., 96067 (916) 926-2345
Mountain View (Santa Clara Co.), 500 Castro, 94041, P.O. Box 7540, 94039
    (415) 903-6300, Fax: (415) 962-0384
  Chamber of Commerce, 580 Castro St., 94041 (415) 968-8378,
    Fax: (415) 968-5668
  Library, 585 Franklin St., 94041 (415) 903-6887
  Police, 1000 Villa St., 94041 (415) 903-6335
Murrieta (Riverside Co.), 26442 Beckman Court, 92562, (909) 698-1040,
    Fax: (909) 698-4509
  Chamber of Commerce, P.O. Box 124, 92564 (909) 677-7916,
    Fax: (909) 677-9976
  Police, 40080 California Oaks Rd., 92562 (909) 696-3600
Mt. Washington (Los Angeles Co.), City of Los Angeles
Napa (Napa Co.), 955 School St., P.O. Box 660, 94559 (707) 257-9501,
    Fax: (707) 257-9534
  Chamber of Commerce, 6590 Knoxville Rd., P.O. Box 9164, 94558
    (707) 966-2188, (800) 726-1256, Fax: (707) 963-2440
  Napa Valley Chamber of Commerce, 1556 First St., P.O. Box 636,
    94559-0636 (707) 226-7455, Fax: (707) 226-1171
  Library, 1150 Division St., 94559-3396 (707) 253-4241
  Newspaper, *The Napa Register*, 1615 Second St., P.O. Box 150,
    94558 (707) 226-3711, Fax: (707) 224-3963
  Police, 1539 First St., 94559 (707) 257-9573
Naples (Los Angeles Co.), City of Long Beach
National City (San Diego Co.), 1243 National City Blvd., 91950
    (619) 336-4200, Fax: (619) 336-4376
  Chamber of Commerce, 711 "A" Ave., P.O. Box 1055, 91950
    (619) 477-9339, Fax: (619) 477-5018
  Library, 200 E. 12th St., 91950-3399 (619) 336-4280,
    Fax: (619) 477-0724
  Police, 1200 "A" Ave., 91950 (619) 336-4400
Needles (San Bernardino Co..), 1111 Bailey Ave., P.O. Box 887, 92363
    (619) 326-2113, Fax: (619) 326-4349
  Chamber of Commerce, 100 "G" St., P.O. Box 705, 92363
    (619) 326-2050
  Library, 1111 Bailey, 92363 (619) 326-2623
  Newspaper, *Needles Desert Star*, P.O. Box 427, 92363
    (619) 326-2222, Fax: (619) 326-3480
  Sheriff, 1111 Bailey, 92363 (619) 326-9200, (619) 326-2111

Nevada City (Nevada Co.), 317 Broad St., 95959 (916) 265-2496,
  Fax: (916) 265-0187
  Chamber of Commerce, 132 Main St., 95959 (916) 265-2692
  Library, 211 N. Pine St., 95959-2592 (916) 265-4606
  Police, 317 Broad St., 95959 (916) 265-2626
Newark (Alameda Co.), 37101 Newark Blvd., 94560 (510) 793-1400,
  Fax: (510) 745-9972
  Chamber of Commerce, 6066 Civic Terrace 94560 (510) 657-9700,
  Fax: (510) 657-9555
  Library, 6300 Civic Terrace Ave., 94560 (510) 795-2627,
  Fax: (510) 797-3019
  Police, 37101 Newark Blvd., 94560 (510) 793-1400
Newhall (Los Angeles Co.), 91321, City of Santa Clarita
  Chamber of Commerce, (see Santa Clarita)
  Library, 22704 W. 9th St., 91321 (805) 259-0750,
  Fax: (805) 254-5760
  Newspaper, *The Signal,* P.O. Box 877, 91322 (805) 259-1234,
  Fax: (805) 254-8068
  Sheriff, 23740 Magic Mountain Pkwy., Valencia, 91355
  (805) 255-1121
Newman (Stanislaus Co.), 1162 "O" St., P.O. Box 787, 95360 (209) 862-3725,
  Fax: (209) 862-3199
  Chamber of Commerce, P.O. Box 753, 95360 (209) 862-3776
  Library, 1305 Kern, 95360 (209) 862-2010
  Newspaper, *The West Side Index,* 1021 Fresno St., P.O. Box 878,
  95360 (209) 862-2222, Fax: (209) 862-4133
  Police, 1200 "O" St., 95360 (209) 862-2902
Newport Beach (Orange Co.), 3300 Newport Blvd., 92663-3884,
  P.O. Box 1768, 92659-1768 (714) 644-3000,
  Fax: (714) 644-3339
  Chamber of Commerce, 1470 Jamboree Rd., 92660 (714) 729-4400,
  Fax: (714) 729-4417
  Library, 856 San Clemente Dr., 92660 (714) 644-3177
  Newspaper, *New Port Beach/Costa Mesa Daily Pilot,* 330 W. Bay
  St., P.O. Box 1560, Costa Mesa, 92627 (714) 642-4321,
  Fax: (714) 631-5902
  Police, P.O. Box 7000, 92658-7000 (714) 644-3701
Niland (Imperial Co.), 92257, Unincorporated
  Chamber of Commerce, 8031 Hwy. 111, P.O. Box 97, 92257
  (619) 359-0826
Nipomo (San Luis Obispo Co.), 93444, Unincorporated
  Chamber of Commerce, P.O. Box 386, 93444 (805) 929-1583
  Library, P.O. Box 38, 93444 (805) 929-3994
Norco (Riverside Co.), 2870 Clark Ave., P.O. Box 428, 91760
  (909) 270-5623, Fax: (909) 270-5622
  Chamber of Commerce, 632 6th St., #A, P.O. Box 27, 91760
  (909) 737-2531, Fax: (909) 737-2574
  Library, 3954 Old Hamner Ave., 91760 (909) 735-5329,
  Fax: (909) 735-0263
  Sheriff, P.O. Box 428, 91760 (909) 735-3900

North Fork (Madera Co.), 93643, Unincorporated
  Chamber of Commerce, P.O. Box 426, 93643 (209) 877-2410
  Library, P.O. Box 428, 93643 (209) 877-2387
North Highlands (Sacramento Co.), 95660, Unincorporated
  Chamber of Commerce, 3651 Elkhorn Blvd., 95660 (916) 334-2214,
    Fax: (916) 334-2214
  Library, 3601 Plymouth Dr., 95660 (916) 331-4367,
    Fax: (916) 332-0754
North Hollywood (Los Angeles Co.), City of Los Angeles
  Chamber of Commerce, 5019 Lankershim Blvd., 91601
    (818) 508-5155
  Library, 5211 Tujunga Ave., 91601 (818) 766-7185,
    Fax: (818) 902-2135
North Long Beach (Los Angeles Co.), City of Long Beach
Northridge (Los Angeles Co.), City of Los Angeles
  Library, 9051 Darby Ave., 91324 (818) 886-3640,
    Fax: (818) 902-2178
  Chamber of Commerce, 8801 Reseda Blvd., 91324 (818) 349-5676,
    349-4343
  CSU Northridge Police, P.O. Box 280759, 91328-0759
    (818) 885-2154
Norwalk (Los Angeles Co.), 12700 Norwalk Blvd., P.O. Box 1030, 90650
    (310) 929-2677, Fax: (310) 929-3880
  Chamber of Commerce, 12040 Foster Rd., 90650 (310) 864-7785,
    Fax: (310) 864-8539
  Library, 12350 Imperial Hwy., 90650 (310) 868-0775,
    Fax: (310) 929-1130
  Library, 11949 Alondra Blvd., 90650 (310) 868-7771
  Newspaper, *Norwalk Herald American*, 8800 National Ave., South
    Gate, 90280 (310) 927-8681, Fax: (310) 928-9092
  Sheriff, 12335 Civic Center Dr., 90650 (310) 863-8711
Norwood Village (Los Angeles Co.), City of El Monte
  Library, 4550 N. Peck Rd., El Monte, 91732 (818) 443-3147,
    Fax: (818) 350-6099
Novato (Marin Co.), 900 Sherman Ave., 94945 (415) 897-4311,
    Fax: (415) 897-4354
  Chamber of Commerce, 807 DeLong Ave., P.O. Box 824, 94945
    (415) 897-1164, Fax: (415) 898-9097
  Library, 1720 Novato Blvd., 94947-3084 (415) 897-1141,
    Fax: (415) 898-3454
  Police, 909 Machin Ave., 94945 (415) 897-4361
Oak Hills (San Bernardino Co.), Unincorporated
  Chamber of Commerce, 7927 Oak Hill Rd., 92371 (619) 949-0520,
    (619) 949-2991
Oakdale (Stanislaus Co.), 280 N. Third Ave., 95361 (209) 847-2244,
    Fax: (209) 847-0826
  Chamber of Commerce, 590 N. Yosemite Ave., 95361
    (209) 847-2244
  Library, 151 S. First St., 95361 (209) 847-4204
  Newspaper, *Oakdale Leader*, 122 S. Third Ave., P.O. Box 278,
    95361 (209) 847-3021
  Police, 245 N. Second St., 95361 (209) 847-2231

Oakhurst (Madera Co.), 93644, Unincorporated
    Chamber of Commerce, 49074 Civic Cir. 93644 (209) 683-7766,
        Fax: (209) 683-0784
    Library, P.O. Box 484, 93644 (209) 683-4838
Oakland (Alameda Co.), One City Hall Plaza, 94612 (510) 238-3301,
        Fax: (510) 238-4731
    Chamber of Commerce, 475 14th St., 94612 (510) 874-4800,
        Fax: (510) 839-8817
    Chinatown Chamber of Commerce, 320 8th St., #2B, 94607
        (510) 893-8979, Fax: (510) 893-8988
    US African American Chamber of Commerce, 117 Broadway, Jack
        London Square, 94607-3715 (510) 444-5741,
        Fax: (510) 444-5866
    Library, 125 14th St., 94612 (510) 238-3281, Fax: (510) 238-2232
    Newspaper, *The Oakland Tribune,* 409 13th St., P.O. Box 24304,
        94623 (510) 645-2000, Fax: (415) 645-2715
    Police, 455 7th St., 94607 (510) 238-3481
    Bay Area Rapid Transit District Police, 800 Madison St., Oakland,
        94607 (510) 464-7010
    East Bay Regional Park District Police, 11500 Skyline Blvd.,
        Oakland, 94619-2443 (510) 881-1833
Oakley (Contra Costa Co.), 94561, Unincorporated
    Chamber of Commerce, P.O. Box 1340, 94561 (510) 625-1035
    Library, 118 E. Ruby St., 94561 (510) 625-2400
Occidental (Sonoma Co.), 95465, Unincorporated
    Chamber of Commerce, P.O. Box 159, 95465 (707) 874-2183
Ocean Park (Los Angeles Co.), City of Santa Monica
    Library, 2601 Main St., 90405 (310) 392-3804
Oceanside (San Diego Co.), 300 N. Hill St., 92054 (619) 966-4410,
        Fax: (619) 966-4436
    Chamber of Commerce, 928 N. Hill St., P.O. Box 1578, 92054
        (619) 722-1534, Fax: (619) 722-8336
    Library, 330 N. Hill St., 92054 (619) 966-4690
    Newspaper, *Blade-Citizen,* 1722 S. Hill St., P.O. Box 90, 92049
        (619) 433-7333, Fax: (619) 439-8659
    Police, 1617 Mission Ave., 92054 (619) 966-4943
Ojai (Ventura Co.), 401 S. Ventura St., 93023, P.O. Box 1570, 93024
        (805) 646-5581, Fax: (805) 646-1980
    Chamber of Commerce, 338 E. Ojai Ave., P.O. Box 1134, 93024
        (805) 646-8126, Fax: (805) 646-9762
    Library, 111 E. Ojai Ave., 93023 (805) 646-1639
    Newspaper, *Ojai Valley News,* P.O. Box 277, 93024 (805) 646-1476,
        Fax: (805) 656-6399
    Sheriff, 800 S. Victoria Ave., Ventura, 93009 (805) 646-1414
Olive View (Los Angeles Co.), City of Los Angeles
Ontario (San Bernardino Co.), 303 E. "B" St., Civic Center, 91764-4196
        (909) 986-1151, Fax: (909) 391-2567
    Chamber of Commerce, 121 W. "B" St., #F, 91762 (909) 984-2458,
        Fax: (909) 984-6439
    Library, 215 E. "C" St., 91764-4198 (909) 988-8481
    Newspaper, *Inland Valley Daily Bulletin,* 2041 E. 4th St., 91764
        (909) 987-6397, Fax: (909) 948-0596

Ontario Police, 200 N. Cherry Ave., 91764 (909) 988-6481
Orange (Orange Co.), 300 E. Chapman Ave., P.O. Box 449, 92666
    (714) 744-5500, Fax: (714) 744-5515
    Chamber of Commerce, 80 Plaza Square, 92666 (714) 538-3581,
        Fax: (714) 532-1675
    Orange County Chamber of Commerce, One City Blvd. W., #401,
        92668 (714) 634-2900, Fax: (714) 978-0742
    Library, 101 N. Center St., 92666 (714) 288-2400,
        Fax: (714) 771-6126
    Newspaper, *The Orange County Register*, 625 N. Grand Ave., Santa
        Ana, 92701 (714) 835-1234, Fax: (714) 543-3904
    Police, 1107 Batavia St., 92667-5584 (714) 744-7300,
        Fax: (714) 532-0437
Orange Cove (Fresno Co.), 633 6th St., 93646-0056 (209) 626-4488,
    Fax: (209) 626-4653
    Chamber of Commerce, 570 Center St., 93646 (209) 626-7934
    Sheriff, P.O. Box 1788, Fresno, 93717 (209) 488-3939
Orangevale (Sacramento Co.), 95662 Unincorporated
    Chamber of Commerce, 8836 Greenback Lane, 95662
        (916) 988-0175
    Library, 8820 Greenback Lane, 95662 (916) 989-2192
Orick (Humboldt Co.), 95555, Unincorporated
    Chamber of Commerce, 121153 Hwy. 101, P.O. Box 234, 95555
        (707) 488-6755, (707) 441-4975, (707) 488-2885
Orinda (Contra Costa Co.), 26 Orinda Way, 94563 (510) 254-3900,
    Fax: (510) 254-9158
    Chamber of Commerce, 2 Theater Square, #137, 94563
        (510) 254-3909
    Library, 2 Irwin Way, 94563-2555 (510) 254-2184
    Sheriff, 26 Orinda Way, 94563 (510) 254-6820
Orland (Glenn Co.), 815 4th St., 95963 (916) 865-4741
    Chamber of Commerce, 401 Walker St., 95963 (916) 865-2311
    Library, 333 Mill St., 95963 (916) 865-3465, Fax: (916) 865-2124
    Newspaper, *Orland Press-Register*, P.O. Box 847, 95963
        (916) 865-4433, Fax: (916) 865-3110
    Police, 817 4th St., 95963 (916) 865-4747
Orosi (Tulare Co.), 93647, Unincorporated
    Chamber of Commerce, P.O. Box 237, 93647 (209) 528-6015,
        Fax: (209) 528-2384
    Library, 12646 Ave. 416, 93647 (209) 591-5830
Oroville (Butte Co.), 1735 Montgomery St., 95965 (916) 538-2401,
    Fax: (916) 538-2426
    Chamber of Commerce, 1789 Montgomery St., 95965
        (916) 533-2542, (800) 655-4653, Fax: (916) 533-5990
    Library, 1820 Mitchell Ave., 95966-5378 (916) 538-7525
    Newspaper, *Oroville Mercury Register*, 2081 Second St.,
        P.O. Box 651, 95965 (916) 533-3131, Fax: (916) 533-3127
    Police, 2055 Lincoln St., 95966-5385 (916) 538-2451
Otay Mesa (San Diego Co), 92073, Unincorporated
    Chamber of Commerce, 2320 Paseo de Las Americas, #112, 92173
        (619) 661-6111, Fax: (619) 661-6178
    Library, 3003 Coronado Ave., 92154 (619) 690-8374

Oxnard (Ventura Co.), 305 W. Third St., 93030-5790 (805) 486-4311,
Fax: (805) 486-9462
Chamber of Commerce, 711 S. "A" St., P.O. Box 867, 93032
(805) 385-8860, Fax: (805) 487-1763
Library, 251 S. "A" St., 93030 (805) 385-7500, Fax: (805) 487-5960
Newspaper, *The Press-Courier*, 300 W. 9th St., 93030
(805) 483-1101, Fax: (805) 483-1126
Police, 251 S. "C" St., 93030 (805) 385-7600
Pacific Grove (Monterey Co.), 300 Forest Ave., 93950 (408) 648-3100,
Fax: (408) 375-9863
Chamber of Commerce, P.O. Box 167, 93950 (408) 373-3304,
Fax: (408) 373-3317
Library, 550 Central Ave., 93950-2789 (408) 648-3160,
(408) 648-3162
Police, 580 Pine Ave., 93950 (408) 648-3143
Pacific Palisades (Los Angeles Co.), City of Los Angeles
Chamber of Commerce, 15330 Antioch St., 90272 (310) 459-7963,
Fax: (310) 459-9534
Library, 861 Alma Real Dr., 90272 (310) 459-2754
Pacifica (San Mateo Co.), 170 Santa Maria Ave., 94044 (415) 738-7300,
Fax: (415)359-6038
Chamber of Commerce, 450 Dondee Way, #2, 94044
(415) 355-4122, Fax: (415) 355-6949
Library, 104 Hilton, 94044 (415) 355-5196, Fax: (415) 355-6658
Newspaper, *Pacifica Tribune*, 59 Aura Yista, P.O. Box 1188, 94044
(415) 359-6666, Fax: (415) 359-3821
Police, 1850 Francisco Blvd., 94044 (415) 738-7314
Pacoima (Los Angeles Co.), City of Los Angeles
Chamber of Commerce, 11243 Glenoaks Blvd., #6, 91331
(818) 899-7401
Library, 13605 Van Nuys Blvd., 91331 (818) 899-5203,
Fax: (818) 902-2178
Palisades Highlands (Los Angeles Co.), City of Los Angeles
Palm Desert (Riverside Co.), 73-510 Fred Waring Dr., 92260 (619) 346-0611,
Fax: (619) 340-0574
Chamber of Commerce, 72-990 Hwy. 111, 92260 (619) 346-6111,
(800) 873-2428, Fax: (619) 346-3263
Library, 45-480 Portola, 92260 (619) 346-6552,
Fax: (619) 341-7862
Sheriff, 46-057 Oasis, Indio, 92201 (619) 342-8800
Palm Springs (Riverside Co.), 3200 Tahquitz-McCallum Way, 92262,
P.O. Box 2743, 92263-2743 (619) 323-8201,
Fax: (619) 323-7701
Chamber of Commerce, 190 W. Amado Rd., 92262 (619) 325-1577,
Fax: (619) 325-8549
Library, 300 S. Sunrise Way, 92262-7699 (619) 322-7323
Newspaper, *The Coachella Sun*, P.O. Box 27034, 92263
(619) 347-3313, Fax: (619) 778-4654
Police, 200 S. Civic Dr., 92262 (619) 323-8126

Palmdale (Los Angeles Co.), 38300 N. Sierra Hwy., 93550 (805) 267-5100,
    Fax: (805) 267-5122
    Chamber of Commerce, 38260 10th St. E., #A, 93550
        (805) 273-3232, Fax: (805) 273-8508
    Library, 700 E. Palmdale Blvd., 93550 (805) 267-5603,
        Fax: (805) 267-5606
    Newspaper, *Antelope Valley Press*, P.O. Box 880, 93590
        (805) 273-2700, Fax: (805) 947-4870
    Sheriff, 1020 E. Palmdale Blvd., 93550 (805) 267-4320
Palms (Los Angeles Co.), City of Los Angeles
    Library, 2920 Overland Ave., Los Angeles, 90064 (213) 838-2157,
        Fax: (213) 612-0427
Palo Alto (Santa Clara Co.), 250 Hamilton Ave., 94301, P.O. Box 10250,
    94303 (415) 329-2571, Fax: (415) 328-3631
    Chamber of Commerce, 325 Forest Ave., 94301 (415) 324-3121,
        Fax: (415) 324-1215
    Library, 1213 Newell Rd., 94303 (415) 329-2437
    Newspaper, *Palo Alto Weekly*, 703 High St., 94301 (415) 326-8210,
        Fax: (415) 326-3928
    Police, 275 Forest Ave., 94301 (415) 329-2406
Palos Verdes Estates (Los Angeles Co.), 340 Palos Verdes Drive W.,
    90274-1299, P.O. Box 1086, 90274-0283 (310) 378-0383,
    Fax: (310) 378-7820
    Chamber of Commerce, P.O. Box 2484, 90274 (310) 377-8111
    Library, 650 Deep Valley Dr., 90274-3662 (310) 377-9584,
        Fax: (310) 377-6403
    Police, 340 Palos Verdes Drive W., 90274 (310) 378-4211
Panorama City (Los Angeles Co.), City of Los Angeles
    Chamber of Commerce, (see Van Nuys)
    Library, 14345 Roscoe Blvd., 91402 (818) 894-4071,
        Fax: (818) 891-5960
Paradise (Butte Co.), 5555 Skyway, 95969 (916) 872-6291,
    Fax: (916) 877-5059
    Chamber of Commerce, 5587 Scottwood, 95969 (916) 877-9356
    Library, 5922 Clark Rd., 95969-4896 (916) 872-6320
    Newspaper, *The Paradise Post*, 5399 Clark Rd., P.O. Drawer 70,
        95967 (916) 877-4413, Fax: (916) 877-5213
    Police, 5595 Black Olive Dr., 95969 (916) 872-6241
Paramount (Los Angeles Co.), 16400 Colorado Ave., 90723-5091
    (310) 220-2000, Fax: (310) 630-6731
    Chamber of Commerce, 15357 Paramount Blvd., 90723
        (310) 634-3980, Fax: (310) 634-0891
    Library, 16254 Colorado Ave., 90723 (310) 630-3171,
        Fax: (310) 630-3968
    Newspaper, *The Paramount Journal*, 16460 Paramount Blvd.,
        Box 2055, 90723 (310) 633-1234, Fax: (310) 630-8141
    Sheriff, 5130 N. Clark Ave., Lakewood, 90712 (310) 866-9061
Park La Brea (Los Angeles Co.), City of Los Angeles
Parlier (Fresno Co.), 1100 E. Parlier Ave., 93648 (209) 646-3545,
    Fax: (209) 646-0416
    Chamber of Commerce, P.O. Box 453, 93648 (209) 646-6618
    Police, 1100 E. Parlier, 93648 (209) 646-3545

Pasadena (Los Angeles Co.), 100 N. Garfield Ave., 91109 (818) 405-4124,
   Fax: (818) 405-3921
   Chamber of Commerce, 117 E. Colorado Blvd., #100, 91105-1993
      (818) 795-3355, Fax: (818) 795-5603
   Library, 285 E. Walnut St., 91101 (818) 405-4052
   Newspaper, *Pasadena Star-News,* 525 E. Colorado Blvd., 91109
      (818) 578-6300, Fax: (818) 578-6460
   Police, 207 N. Garfield Ave., 91101-1791 (818) 405-4501
Paso Robles (San Luis Obispo Co.), 910 Park St., 93446 (805) 237-3888,
   Fax: (805) 238-4704
   Chamber of Commerce, 1225 Park St., 93446 (805) 238-0506,
      Fax: (805) 238-0527
   Library, 800 12th St., 93446 (805) 237-3870, Fax: (805) 238-3665
   Newspaper, *The Daily Press,* 1050 Park St., P.O. Box 427, 93447
      (805) 238-0330, Fax: (805) 238-6504
   Police, 840 10th St., 93446 (805) 238-3131
Patterson (Stanislaus Co.), 33 S. Del Puerto Ave., P.O. Box 667, 95363
      (209) 892-2041, Fax: (209) 892-6119
   Chamber of Commerce,2 Plaza, P.O. Box 365, 95363
      (209) 892-2821
   Library, 46 N. Salado, 95363 (209) 892-6473
   Newspaper, *Patterson Irrigator,* P.O. Box 157, 95363
      (209) 892-6187, Fax: (209) 892-3761
   Police, 344 W. Lamas, 95363-0667 (209) 892-5071
Pearblossom (Los Angeles Co.), 93553, Unincorporated
   Chamber of Commerce, P.O. Box 591, 93553 (805) 944-5224
Perris (Riverside Co.), 101 N. "D" St., 92570-1998 (909) 943-6100,
   Fax: (909) 657-7971
   Chamber of Commerce, 422 S. "D" St., P.O. Box 177, 92570
      (909) 657-3555
   Library, 424 "D" St., 92370 (909) 657-2358
   Newspaper, *The Perris Progress,* 240 W. 4th St., P.O. Box 128,
      92572 (714) 657-2181
   Police, 100 N. Perris Blvd., 92370 (909) 657-7391
Petaluma (Sonoma Co.), 11 English St., 94952, P.O. Box 61, 94953-0061
      (707) 778-4345, Fax: (707) 778-4419
   Chamber of Commerce, 799 Baywood Dr., #3, 94952
      (707) 762-2785, Fax: (707) 762-4721
   Newspaper, *Peraluma Argus-Courier,* 830 N. Petaluma Blvd. N.,
      P.O. Box 1091, 94953 (707) 762-4541,
      Fax: (707) 765-1707
   Police, 969 Petaluma Blvd. N., 94952-6320 (707) 778-4372
Phelan (San Bernardino Co.), 92371, Unincorporated
   Chamber of Commerce, P.O. Box 290010, 92329-0010
      (619) 868-3291
   Newspaper, *Mountaineer Progress,* 3936 Phelan Rd., Ste. A,
      P.O. Box 148, 92371 (619) 868-5757, Fax: (619) 868-2700
Phillips Ranch (Los Angeles Co.), City of Pomona

Pico Rivera (Los Angeles Co.), 6615 Passons Blvd., P.O. Box 1016, 90660
(310) 942-2000, Fax: (310) 801-4765
  Chamber of Commerce, 9122 E. Washington Blvd., P.O. Box 985,
90660 (310) 949-2473, Fax: (310) 949-8320
  Library, 9001 Mines Ave., 90660 (310) 942-7394,
Fax: (310) 942-7779
  Sheriff, 6631 S. Passons Blvd., 90660 (310) 949-2421
Piedmont (Alameda Co.), 120 Vista Ave., 94611 (510) 420-3040,
Fax: (510) 653-8272
  Police, 403 Highland Ave., 94611 (510) 420-3000
Pinole (Contra Costa Co.), 2131 Pear St., 94564 (510) 724-9000,
Fax: (510) 724-9061
  Chamber of Commerce, P.O. Box 1, 94564 (510) 724-4484
  Library, 2935 Pinole Valley Rd., 94564 (510) 758-2741,
Fax: (510) 258-2745
  Newspaper, *West County Times*, 4301 Lakeside Dr., P.O. Box 128,
94806 (510) 758-8400, Fax: (510) 262-2719
  Police, 880 Tennent Ave., 94564 (510) 724-8950
Pinon Hills (San Bernardino Co.), 92373, Unincorporated
  Chamber of Commerce, P.O. Box 720095, 92372
Piru (Ventura Co.), 93040, Unicorporated
  Library, 3811 Center St., 93040 (805) 521-1753
Pismo Beach (San Luis Obispo Co.), 1000 Bello St., P.O. Box 3, 93448
(805) 773-4657, Fax: (805) 773-7006
  Chamber of Commerce, 581 Dolliver St., 93449 (805) 773-4382,
(800) 443-7778
  Police, P.O. Box 3, 93449 (805) 773-2208
Pittsburg (San Juis Obispo Co.), 65 Civic Ave., P.O. Box 1518, 94565
(510) 439-4850, Fax: (510) 439-4851
  Chamber of Commerce, 2010 Railroad Ave., 94565 (510) 432-7301,
Fax: (510) 427-5555
  Library, 80 Power Ave., 94565 (510) 427-8390
  Newspaper, *Pittsburg Post Dispatch,* 1650 Cavallo Rd., Antioch,
94509 (510) 757-2525, Fax: (510) 754-9483
  Police, 55 Civic Ave., 94565 (510) 439-4987
Placentia (Orange Co.), 401 E. Chapman Ave., 92670 (714) 993-8117,
Fax: (714) 961-0283
  Chamber of Commerce, 201 E. Yorba Linda Blvd., #C, 92670
(714) 528-1873
  Library, 411 E. Chapman Ave., 92670-6198 (714) 528-1906,
Fax: (714) 528-8236
  Police, 401 E. Chapman, 92670 (714) 993-8154
Placerville (El Dorado Co.), 487 Main St., 95667 (916) 642-5220,
Fax: (916) 642-5228
  Chamber of Commerce, 542 Main St., 95667 (916) 621-5885,
(800) 457-6279, Fax: (916) 642-1624
  Library, 345 Fair Lane, 95667-4196, (916) 621-5540,
Fax: (916) 622-3911
  Newspaper, *Mountain Democrat,* P.O. Box 1088, 95667
(916) 622-1255, Fax: (916) 622-7894
  Police, 730 Main St., 95667 (916) 622-0111
Playa Del Rey (Los Angeles Co.), City of Los Angeles

Pleasant Hill (Contra Costa Co.), 100 Gregory Lane, 94523-3323
  (510) 671-5270, Fax: (510) 256-8190
    Chamber of Commerce, 91 Gregory Lane, #11, 94523
      (510) 687-0700, Fax: (510) 676-7422
    Library, 1750 Oak Park Blvd., 94523-4497 (510) 646-6423
    Police, 330 Civic Dr., 94523 (510) 671-4600
Pleasanton (Alameda Co.), 200 Old Bernal Ave., P.O. Box 520, 94566
  (510) 484-8000, Fax: (510) 484-8236
    Chamber of Commerce, 777 Peters Ave., 94566 (510) 846-5858,
      Fax: (510) 846-9697
    Library, 400 Old Bernal Ave., 94566-7012 (510) 462-3535,
      Fax: (510) 846-8517
    Newspaper, *Tri-Valley Herald*, 4770 Willow Rd., P.O. Box 697,
      94566 (510) 734-8600, Fax: (510) 734-8520
    Newspaper, *Valley Times*, 127 Spring St., P.O. Box 607, 94566
      (510) 462-4160, Fax: (510) 847-2177
    Police, P.O. Box 909, 4833 Bernal Ave., 94566-0802
      (510) 484-8128
Plymouth (Amador Co.), 9426 Main St., P.O. Box 429, 95669
    (209) 245-6941, Fax: (209) 245-6953
    Sheriff, 108 Court St., Jackon, 95642 (209) 223-6500
Point Arena (Mendocino Co.), 451 School St., P.O. Box 67, 95468
    (707) 882-2122
    Sheriff, 951 Low Gap Rd., Ukiah, 95482 (707) 463-4411
Point Reyes Station (Marin Co.), 94956, Unincorporated
    Chamber of Commerce, P.O. Box 1045, 94956 (415) 663-9232
    Library, W. Marin Shops, Fourth & "A" Sts.,Point Reyes Station,
      94956 (415) 663-8375
    Newspaper, *Point Reyes Light*, P.O. Box 210, 94956 (415) 663-8404
Pollock Pines (El Dorado Co.), 95726, Unincorporated
    Chamber of Commerce, 6532-C Pony Express Trail, P.O. Box 95,
      95726 (916) 644-3970
    Library, P.O. Box 757, 95726 (916) 644-2498
Pomona (Los Angeles Co.), 505 S. Garey Ave., 91766, P.O. Box 660, 91769
    (909) 620-2341, Fax: (909) 622-8382
    Chamber of Commerce, 485 N. Garey, P.O. Box 1457, 91767
      (909) 622-1256, Fax: (909) 620-5986
    Library, 625 S. Garey Ave., P.O. Box 2271, 91766-2271
      (909) 620-2473
    CPU Pomona Police, 3801 W. Temple Ave., 91768 (909) 869-3065
    Police, 490 W. Mission Blvd., 91766 (909) 620-2155
Poplar (Tulare Co.), 93257, Unincorporated
    Chamber of Commerce, P.O. Box 3386, 93257 (209) 784-7079
Port Hueneme (Ventura Co.), 250 N. Ventura Rd., 93041 (805) 986-6501,
      Fax: (805) 488-2633
    Chamber of Commerce, 220 N. Market St., 93041 (805) 488-2023,
      Fax: (805) 488-6993
    Library, 510 Park Ave., 93041 (805) 486-5460
    Police, 250 N. Ventura Rd., 93041 (805) 986-6531
Porter Ranch (Los Angeles Co.), City of Los Angeles

Porterville (Tulare Co.), 291 N. Main St., 93257, P.O. Box 432, 93258
(209) 782-7466, Fax: (209) 781-6437
Chamber of Commerce, 36 W. Cleveland St., 93257 (209) 784-7502,
Fax: (209) 784-0770
Library, 41 W. Thurman, 93257 (209) 784-0177,
Fax: (209) 781-4396
Newspaper, *Porterville Recorder,* 115 E. Oak Ave., P.O. Box 151,
93257 (209) 784-5000, Fax: (209) 784-1689
Police, 350 N. "D" St., 93257 (209) 782-7400
Portola (Plumas Co.), 47 Third Ave., P.O. Box 1225, 96122 (916) 832-4216,
Fax: (916) 832-5418
Chamber of Commerce, P.O. Box 1379, 96122 (916) 832-5444,
(800) 995-6057, Fax: (916) 832-5837
Sheriff, P.O. Box 1106, Quincy, 95971 (916) 832-4242
Portola Valley (San Mateo Co.), 765 Portola Rd., 94028 (415) 851-1700,
Fax: (415) 851-4677
Library, 765 Portola Rd., 94028 (415) 851-0560,
Fax: (415) 851-8365
Sheriff, 401 Marshall St., Redwood City, 94063 (415) 364-1811
Portuguese Bend (Los Angeles Co.), City of Rancho Palos Verdes
Poway (San Diego Co.), 13325 Civic Center Dr.,92064, P.O. Box 789,
92074-0789 (619) 748-6600, Fax: (619) 748-1455
Chamber of Commerce, 12709 Poway Rd., #101, P.O. Box 868,
92074-0868 (619) 748-0016, (619) 748-0082,
Fax: (619) 748-1710
Library, 13264 Poway Rd., 92064-4687 (619) 748-2411,
Fax: (619) 748-0671
Newspaper, *Penasquitos News,* 13247 Poway Rd., 92064
(619) 748-2311, Fax: (619) 748-0413
Quartz Hill (Los Angeles Co.), 93534, Unincorporated
Chamber of Commerce, P.O. Box 3023, 93586 (805) 943-6860
Library, 42018 N. 50th St. W., 93536 (805) 943-2454,
Fax: (805) 943-6337
Quincy (Plumas Co.), 95971, Unincorporated
County Chamber of Commerce, 91 N. Church, P.O. Box 4120,
95971 (916) 283-6345, (800) 326-2247,
Fax: (916) 283-5465
Chamber of Commerce, 372 W. Main St., #4, P.O. Box 3829, 95971
(916) 283-0188
Library, 445 Jackson St., P.O. Box 10270, 95971 (916) 283-6310,
Fax: (916) 283-3242
Newspaper, *Feather River Bulletin,* P.O. Box B, 95971
(916) 283-0800
Sheriff, P.O. Box 1106, 95971 (916) 832-4242
Ramona (San Diego Co.), 92065, Unincorporated
Chamber of Commerce, 1306 Main St., #106, P.O. Box 368, 92065
(619) 789-1311, Fax: (619) 789-1317
Library, 1406 Montecito Rd., 92065-2296 (619) 738-2434
Newspaper, *Ramona Sentinel,* 611 Main St., P.O. Box 367, 92065
(619) 789-1350, Fax: (619) 789-4057

Rancho Bernardo (San Diego Co.), 92128, Unincorporated
Chamber of Commerce, (see San Diego)
Library, 16840 Bernardo Center Dr., 92128 (619) 538-8163
Rancho Cordova (Sacramento Co.), 95670, Unincorporated
Chamber of Commerce, 11070 White Rock Rd., #170, 95670-5425
(916) 638-8700, Fax: (916) 638-6846
Library, 9845 Folsom Blvd., Sacramento, 95827 (916) 362-0643,
Fax: (916) 362-1758
Rancho Cucamonga (San Bernardino Co.), 10500 Civic Center, 91730,
P.O. Box 807, 91729 (909) 989-1851, Fax: (909) 948-1648
Chamber of Commerce, 8280 Utica Ave., #160, 91730
(909) 987-1012, Fax: (909) 987-5917
Library, 9191 Base Line, 91730 (909) 987-3107,
Fax: (909) 980-8945
Sheriff, 10510 Civic Center Dr., 91730 (909) 989-6611
Rancho Dominguez (Los Angeles Co.), Unincorporated
Rancho Mirage (Riverside Co.), 69-825 Hwy., 111, 92270 (619) 324-4511,
Fax: (619) 324-8830
Chamber of Commerce, 42-464 Rancho Mirage Lane, 92270
(619) 568-9351, Fax: (619) 779-9684
Sheriff, 46-057 Oasis, Indio, 92201 (619) 342-8800
Rancho Palos Verdes (Los Angeles Co.), 30940 Hawthorne Blvd., 90274
(310) 377-0360, Fax: (310) 377-9868
Library, 650 Deep Valley Dr. E., 90274 (310) 377-9584
Sheriff, 26123 Narbonne Ave., Lomita, 90717 (310) 539-1661
Rancho Park (Los Angeles Co.), City of Los Angeles
Library 2920 Overland Ave., Los Angeles, 90064 (213) 838-2157,
Fax: (213) 612-0427
Rancho Penasquitos (San Diego Co.), 92129, Unincorporated
Library, 13330 Salmon River Rd., 92129 (619) 538-8159
Rancho Santa Fe (San Diego Co.), 92067, Unincorporated
Library, 17040 Avenida de Acacias, 92067-0115 (619) 756-2512
Rancho Santa Margarita (Orange Co.), 92688, Unincorporated
Chamber of Commerce, (see Laguna Hills)
Red Bluff (Tehama Co.), 555 Washington, P.O. Box 400, 96080
(916) 527-2605
Chamber of Commerce, 100 Main St., P.O. Box 850, 96080
(916) 527-6220
Library, 645 Madison St., 96080-3383 (916) 527-0604,
Fax: (916) 527-1562
Newspaper, *Daily News,* 545 Diamond Ave., P.O. Box 220, 96080
(916) 527-2151, Fax: (916) 527-3719
Police, 555 Washington St., 96080 (916) 527-3131
Redding (Shasta Co.), 760 Parkview Ave., 96001, P.O. Box 496071,
96049-6071 (916) 225-4055, Fax: (916) 225-4434
Chamber of Commerce, 747 Auditorium Dr., 96001 (916) 225-4433,
Fax: (916) 225-4398
Library, 1855 Shasta St., 96001 (916) 225-5769
Newspaper, *Record Searchlight,* 1101 Twin View Blvd.,
P.O. Box 492397, 96049 (916) 243-2424,
Fax: (916) 225-8212

Redding Police, 1313 California St., 96001 (916) 225-4200
Convention Center, 700 Auditorium Dr., 96002 (916) 225-4130
Visitors Bureau, 777 Auditorium Dr., 96002 (916) 225-4100
Redlands (San Bernardino Co.), 30 Cajon St., P.O. Box 3005, 92373-0629
(909) 798-7500, Fax: (909) 798-7503
Chamber of Commerce, 1 E. Redlands Blvd., 92373 (909) 793-2546, Fax: (909) 335-6388
Library, 125 W. Vine St., 92373-4761 (909) 798-7565, Fax: (909) 798-7566
Newspaper, *Redlands Daily Facts,* 700 Brookside Ave., 92373 (909) 793-3221, Fax: (909) 793-9588
Police, P.O. Box 1025, 92373 (909) 798-7621
Redondo Beach (Los Angeles Co.), 415 Diamond St., P.O. Box 270, 90277 (310) 372-1171, Fax: (310) 379-9268
Chamber of Commerce, 200 N. Pacific Coast Hwy., 90277 (310) 376-6911, Fax: (310) 374-7373
Library, 415 N. Pacific Coast Hwy., 90277 (310) 318-0675, Fax: (310) 318-3809
Police, 401 Diamond St., 90277 (310) 379-2477
Redwood City (San Mateo Co.), 1017 Middlefield Rd., 94063-0478, P.O. Box 391, 94064-0478 (415) 780-7000, Fax: (415) 780-7225
Chamber of Commerce, 1675 Broadway, 94063 (415) 364-1722, Fax: (415) 364-1729
Library, 1044 Middlefield Rd., 94063 (415) 780-7018, (415) 780-7061, Fax: (415) 780-7069
Newspaper, *Redwood City Almanac,* P.O. Box 5347, 94063 (415) 364-9500, Fax: (415) 364-9502
Police, 1301 Maple St., 94063 (415) 780-7100
Reedley (Fresno Co.), 845 "G" St., 93654 (209) 637-4200, Fax: (209) 638-7218
Chamber of Commerce, 1613 12th St., 93654 (209) 638-3548, Fax: (209) 638-8479
Library, 1027 "E" St., 93654 (209) 638-2818
Newspaper, *Reedley Exponent,* 1130 "G" St., 93654 (209) 638-2244, Fax: (209) 638-5021
Police, 843 "G" St., 93654-2697 (209) 637-4246
Reseda (Los Angeles Co.), City of Los Angeles
Chamber of Commerce, 18645 Sherman Way, #105, 91335 (818) 345-1920, Fax: (818) 345-1925
Newspaper, *The Valley Vantage,* 7443 Reseda Blvd., 91335 (818) 881-9460, Fax: (818) 881-0572
Rialto (San Bernardino Co.), 150 S. Palm Ave., 92376 (909) 820-2525, Fax: (909) 820-2527
Chamber of Commerce, 120 N. Riverside Ave., 92376 (909) 875-5364, Fax: (909) 875-6790
Library, 251 W. First St., 92376 (909) 875-0144
Police, 128 N. Willow, 92376 (909) 820-2555

Richmond (Contra Costa Co.), 2600 Barrett Ave., P.O. Box 4046, 94804
  (510) 620-6513, Fax: (510) 620-6716
  Chamber of Commerce, 3925 MacDonald Ave., 94805
    (510) 234-3512, Fax: (510) 234-3540
  Contra Costa Black Chamber of Commerce, 3101 MacDonald Ave., 94804 (510) 235-9350
  Library, 325 Civic Center Plaza, 94804-3081 (510) 620-6561
  Police, 401 27th St., 94804 (510) 620-6655
Ridgecrest (Kern Co.), 100 W. California Ave., 93555 (619) 371-3700,
  Fax: (619) 371-1654
  Chamber of Commerce, 400 N. China Lake Blvd., 93555
    (619) 375-8331, Fax: (619) 375-0365
  Library, (see Bakersfield)
  Newspaper, *The Daily Independent*, 224 E. Ridgecrest Blvd., 93555
    (619) 375-4481, Fax: (619) 375-4480
  Police, 100 W. California Ave., 93555 (619) 371-3711
Rio Dell (Humboldt Co.), 675 Wildwood Ave., 95562 (707) 764-3532,
  Fax: (707) 764-5480
  Chamber of Commerce, 715 Wildwood Ave., 95562 (707) 764-3436,
    (707) 764-3310
  Library, 165 Wildwood Ave., 95562 (707) 764-3436
  Police, 715 Wildwood Ave., 95562 (707) 764-5642
Rio Linda (Sacramento Co.), 95673, Unincorporated
  Chamber of Commerce, 740 "M" St., P.O. Box 75, 95673
    (916) 991-9344
  Library, 902 Oak Lane, 95673 (916) 991-3910
Rio Vista (Solano Co.), #1 Main St., P.O. Box 745, 94571 (707) 374-6451,
  Fax: (707) 374-5063
  Chamber of Commerce, 187 Main St., 94571 (707) 374-2700
  Library, 44 Second St., 94571 (707) 374-2664, Fax: (707) 553-5656
  Newspaper, *River News Herald & Isleton Journal*, P.O. Box 786,
    94571 (707) 374-6431
  Police, P.O. Box 745, 94571 (707) 374-6367
Ripon (San Joaquin Co.), 259 N. Wilma Ave., 95366 (209) 599-2108,
  Fax: (209) 599-2685
  Chamber of Commerce, 311 W. First St., P.O. Box 327, 95366
    (209) 599-7519, Fax: (209) 599-2286
  Library, 430 W. Main St., 95366 (209) 599-3326,
    Fax: (209) 599-5530
  Newspaper, *The Ripon Record*, 130 W. Main St., 95366
    (209) 599-2194, Fax: (209) 823-7099
  Police, 259 N. Wilma Ave., 95366 (209) 599-2102
Riverbank (Stanislaus Co.), 6707 Third St., 95367 (209) 869-3671,
  Fax: (209) 869-1177
  Chamber of Commerce, 3237 Santa Fe St., 95367 (209) 869-4541,
    Fax: (209) 869-4639
  Library, 3442 Santa Fe, 95367 (209) 869-1001
  Police, 6701 Third St., 95367 (209) 869-2562

Riverside (Riverside Co.), 3900 Main St., 92522 (909) 782-5312,
    Fax: (909) 782-5470
    Chamber of Commerce, 3685 Main St., 92501 (909) 683-7100,
        Fax: (909) 683-2670
    Jurupa Chamber of Commerce, P.O. Box 3231, Riverside, 95219
        (909) 686-2860
    Library, 3581 7th St., P.O. Box 468, 92502-0468 (909) 782-5201,
        Fax: (909) 788-1528
    Newspaper, *The Press-Enterprise*, 3512 14th St., P.O. Box 792,
        92501 (909) 684-1200, Fax: (909) 782-7630
    Police, 4102 Orange St., 92501 (909) 782-5314
    U.C. Riverside Police, P.O. Box 12, 92507 (909) 787-5222
Rocklin (Placer Co.), 3980 Rocklin Rd., P.O. Box 1138, 95677
        (916) 632-4050, Fax: (916) 624-8018
    Chamber of Commerce, 4240 Rocklin Rd., #4B, P.O. Box 52, 95677
        (916) 624-2548, Fax: (916) 624-5743
    Library, 5460 5th St., 95677 (916) 624-3133
    Newspaper, *Placer Herald*, 5903 Sunset Blvd., Ste. B, 95677
        (916) 624-9713, Fax: (916) 624-7469
    Police, P.O. Box 1138, 95677 (916) 632-4060
Rodeo (Contra Costa Co.), 94572, Unincorporated
    Chamber of Commerce, P.O. Box 548, 94572 (510) 799-7351
    Library, 220 Pacific Ave., 94572 (510) 799-2606
Rohnert Park (Sonoma Co.), 6750 Commerce Blvd., 94928 (707) 795-2411,
    Fax: (707) 664-8474
    Chamber of Commerce, 6020 Commerce Blvd., #121, 94928
        (707) 584-1415, Fax: (707) 584-2945
    Police, 500 City Hall Dr., 94928 (707) 584-2600
Rolling Hills (Los Angeles Co.), #2 Portuguese Bend Rd., 90274
        (310) 377-1521, Fax: (310) 377-7288
    Chamber of Commerce, (see Palos Verdes Estates)
    Sheriff, 26123 Narbonne Ave., Lomita, 90717 (310) 539-1661
Rolling Hills Estates (Los Angeles Co.), 4045 Palos Verdes Drive N., 90274
        (310) 377-1577, Fax: (310) 377-4468
    Chamber of Commerce, (see Palos Verdes Estates)
    Sheriff, 26123 Narbonne Ave., Lomita, 90717 (310) 539-1661
Rosamond (Kern Co.), 93560, Unincorporated
    Chamber of Commerce, 2861 Diamond St., P.O. Box 365, 93560
        (805) 256-3248, Fax: (805) 256-3249
    Library, (see Bakersfield)
Rosemead (Los Angeles Co.), 8838 E. Valley Blvd., P.O. Box 399, 91770
        (818) 288-6671, Fax: (818) 307-9218
    Chamber of Commerce, 3953 Muscatel Ave., P.O. Box 425, 91770
        (818) 288-0811, Fax: (818) 288-2514
    Library, 8800 Valley Blvd., 91770 (818) 573-5220,
        Fax: (818) 280-8523
    Library, 3132 N. Del Mar Ave., 91770 (818) 280-4422
    Newspaper, *San Gabriel Valley Daily Tribune*, P.O. Box 1259,
        Covina, 91722 (818) 962-8811, Fax: (818) 962-8849
    Sheriff, 8838 E. Las Tunas Dr., Temple City, 91780 (818) 285-7171

Roseville (Placer Co.), 311 Vernon St., 95678 (916) 774-5200,
　　　Fax: (916) 786-9175
　　Chamber of Commerce, 650 Douglas Blvd., 95678 (916) 783-8136,
　　　Fax: (916) 783-5261
　　Library, 225 Taylor St., 95678-2681 (916) 774-5221,
　　　Fax: (916) 773-5594
　　Newspaper, *The Press-Tribune*, 188 Cirby Way, 95678
　　　(916) 786-8742
　　Police, 401 Oak St., 95678 (916) 781-0100
Ross (Marin Co.), Lagunitas Rd. & Sir Francis Drake Blvd., P.O. Box 320,
　　　94957 (415) 453-1453, Fax: (415) 453-1950
　　Police, P.O. Box 320, 94957 (415) 453-2727
Rough and Ready (Nevada Co.), 95975, Unincorporated
　　Chamber of Commerce, P.O. Box 801, 95975 (916) 432-4186,
　　　(916) 273-8897
Rowland Heights (Los Angeles Co.), Unincorporated
　　Library, 1850 Nogales, 91748 (818) 912-5348
Rubidoux (Riverside Co.), 92509, Unincorporated
　　Jurupa Chamber of Commerce, 6000 Camino Real, P.O. Box 3231,
　　　92519 (909) 681-9242, Fax: (909) 360-2080
　　Library, 5763 Tilton, Riverside, 92509 (909) 682-5485
Running Springs (San Bernardino Co.), 92382, Unincorporated
　　Chamber of Commerce, P.O. Box 2656, 92382 (909) 867-2411
　　Library, 31976 Hilltop Blvd., 92383 (909) 867-2554
Sacramento (Sacramento Co.), 915 "I" St., 95814 (916) 264-5426,
　　　Fax: (916) 264-7672
　　Black Chamber of Commerce, 2251 Florin Rd., #B3, 95822
　　　(916) 392-7222
　　County Chamber of Commerce, 6110 Mateo Court, Rio Linda,
　　　95673 (916) 991-5505
　　Hispanic Chamber of Commerce, P.O. Box 161933, 95816
　　　(916) 925-1925, (916) 925-5270
　　Metro Chamber of Commerce, 917 7th St., P.O. Box 1017, 95814
　　　(916) 552-6800, Fax: (916) 443-2672
　　North Sacramento Chamber of Commerce, P.O. Box 13322, 95813
　　　(916) 925-6773
　　Library, 914 Capitol Mall, Library & Courts Bldg., 95814,
　　　P.O. Box 942837, 94237-0001 (916) 654-0183
　　Library, 828 "I" St., 95814 (916) 440-5926
　　Newspaper, *The Sacramento Bee*, 2100 "Q" St., P.O. Box 15779,
　　　95852 (916) 321-1475, Fax: (916) 321-1306
　　CSU Sacramento Police, 6000 "J" St., 95819-6092 (916) 278-7321
　　Police, 813 6th St., 95814 (916) 264-5121
Saint Helena (Napa Co.), 1480 Main St., 94574 (707) 963-2741,
　　　Fax: (707) 963-7748
　　Chamber of Commerce, 1080 Main St., P.O. Box 124, 94574
　　　(707) 963-4456, (800) 767-8528, Fax: (707) 963-5396
　　Library, 1492 Library Lane, 94574 (707) 963-5244
　　Newspaper, *St. Helena Star*, 1328 Main St., P.O. Box 346, 94574
　　　(707) 963-2731, Fax: (707) 963-8957
　　Police, 1480 Main St., 94574 (707) 967-2850

Salida (Stanislaus Co.), 95368, Unincorporated
   Library, 4554 Broadway St., 95368 (209) 545-7353
Salinas (Monterey Co.), 200 Lincoln Ave., 93901 (408) 758-7201,
   Fax: (408) 758-7368
   Chamber of Commerce, 119 E. Alisal St., P.O. Box 1170, 93902
      (408) 424-7611, (408) 372-3214, Fax: (408) 424-8639
   Library, 26 Central Ave., 93901 (408) 755-5838,
      Fax: (408) 755-5839
   Newspaper, *The Californian*, 123 W. Alisal St., P.O. Box 81091,
      93912 (408) 424-2221, Fax: (408) 754-4293
   Library, 110 W. San Luis St., 93901 (408) 758-7311
   Police, 222 Lincoln Ave., 93901 (408) 758-7236
Salton Sea (Imperial Co.), 92274, Unincorporated
   Chamber of Commerce, P.O. Box 5185, 92275 (619) 394-4112
San Andreas (Calavaras Co.), 95249, Unincorporated
   Chamber of Commerce, 3 N. Main St., P.O. Box 115, 95249
      (209) 754-4009, Fax: (209) 754-4107
   Library, 46 N. Main St., P.O. Box 338, 95249 (209) 754-6510
   Newspaper, *Calaveras Prospect, Weekly Citizen & Chronicle*, 109 E.
      Saint Charles St., P.O. Box 605, 95249 (209) 754-4222
San Anselmo (Marin Co.), 525 San Anselmo Ave., 94960 (415) 258-4600,
   Fax: (415) 454-4683
   Chamber of Commerce, P.O. Box 2844, 94979 (415) 454-2510
   Library, 110 Tunstead Ave., 94960 (415) 258-4656,
      Fax: (415) 258-4666
   Police, P.O. Box 247, 94960 (415) 258-4610
San Bernardino (San Bernardino Co.), 300 N. "D" St., 92418 (909) 384-5122,
   Fax: (909) 384-5468
   Chamber of Commerce, 546 W. 6th St., P.O. Box 658, 92402
      (909) 885-7515, Fax: (909) 384-9979
   Library, 555 W. 6th St., 92410 (909) 381-8201, Fax: (714) 888-3171
   Newspaper, *The Sun*, 399 N. "D" St., 92401 (909) 889-9666
   CSU San Bernardino Police, 5500 State College Pkwy., 92407
      (909) 880-5165
   Police, P.O. Box 1559, 92402-1559 (909) 383-5011
San Bruno (San Mateo Co.), 567 El Camino Real, 94066 (415) 877-8897,
   Fax: (415) 742-6515
   Chamber of Commerce, 618 San Mateo Ave., P.O. Box 713, 94066
      (415) 588-0180, Fax: (415) 588-6473
   Library, 701 Angus Ave. W., 94066 (415) 877-8878,
      Fax: (415) 876-0848
   Police, 567 El Camino Real, 94066 (415) 877-8965
San Buenaventura (Ventura Co.), (see city of Ventura)
San Carlos (San Mateo Co.), 666 Elm St., 94070 (415) 593-8011,
   Fax: (415) 595-2044
   Chamber of Commerce, 1560 Laurel St, P.O. Box 1086, 94070
      (415) 593-1068, Fax: (415) 593-9108
   Library, 655 Chestnut St., 94070 (415) 591-0341,
      Fax: (415) 591-1585
   Police, 666 Elm St., 94070 (415) 593-8014

San Clemente (Orange Co.), 100 Avenida Presidio, 92672 (714) 361-8200,
Fax: (714) 361-8285
Chamber of Commerce, 1100 N. El Camino Real, 92672
(714) 492-1131, Fax: (714) 492-3764
Library, 242 Avenida Del Mar, 92672 (714) 492-3493,
Fax: (714) 498-5749
Newspaper, *Daily Sun-Post*, 1542 N. El Camino Real, P.O. Box 367,
92672 (714) 492-5121, Fax: (714) 492-0401
Police, 100 Avenido Presidio, 92672 (714) 361-8201
San Diego (San Diego Co.), 202 "C" St., 92101 (619) 236-5555,
Fax: (619) 236-6067
Chamber of Commerce, 402 W. Broadway, #1000, 92101
(619) 232-0124, Fax: (619) 234-0571
Diamond Gateway Chamber of Commerce, P.O. Box 720082, 92172
(619) 672-7722
Golden Triangle Chamber of Commerce, 4350 Executive Dr., #200,
92121 (619) 558-1744, Fax: (619) 552-0261
Hispanic Chamber of Commerce, P.O. Box 85152, MB 5120, 92186
(619) 492-1380
Mid City Chamber of Commerce, P.O. Box 5044, 92165
(619) 584-4638
Mira Mesa-Scripps Ranch Chamber of Commerce, P.O. Box 26174,
92126 (619) 693-1090, Fax: (619) 578-0637
Old Town Chamber of Commerce, 2461 San Diego Ave., 92110
(619) 291-4903
Peninsula Chamber of Commerce, P.O. Box 7018, 92167
(619) 223-9767
Rancho Bernardo Chamber of Commerce, 11650 Iberia Plaza, #220,
P.O. Box 28517, 92128 (619) 487-1767,
Fax: (619) 487-8051
Library, 820 "E" St., 92101-6478 (619) 236-5870
County Library, Bldg. 15, 5555 Oveland Ave., 92123
(619) 694-2414
Newspaper, *San Diego Daily Transcript*, 2131 Third Ave.,
P.O. Box 85469, 92101 (619) 232-4381,
Fax: (619) 239-5716
Newspaper, *San Diego Union Tribune*, 350 Camino de la Reina,
P.O. Box 191, 92112 (619) 299-3131, Fax: (619) 293-1896
Police, 1401 Broadway, 92101-5729 (619) 531-2777
U.C. San Diego Police, Building 500 MAAC, Q-017, La Jolla,
92093 (619) 534-4360
San Dimas (Los Angeles Co.), 246 E. Bonita Ave., 91773 (909) 394-6200,
Fax: (909) 394-6209
Chamber of Commerce, 246 E. Bonita Ave., P.O. Box 175, 91773
(909) 592-3818, Fax: (909) 592-8178
Library, 145 N. Walnut Ave., 91773 (909) 599-6738,
Fax: (909) 592-4490
Sheriff, 122 N. San Dimas Ave., 91773 (818) 332-1184,
(909) 599-1261

San Fernando (Los Angeles Co.), 117 Macneil St., 91340-2993
  (818) 898-1200, Fax: (818) 361-7631
  Chamber of Commerce, 519 S. Brand Blvd., 91340 (818) 361-1184,
    Fax: (818) 898-1986
  Library, 1050 Library St., 91340 (818) 365-6928,
    Fax: (818) 365-3820
  Police, 910 First St., 91340 (818) 898-1267
San Fernando Valley (Los Angeles Co.), Mostly City of Los Angeles, also
    Burbank, San Fernando, Glendale.
San Francisco (San Francisco Co. -- combined city/county), 400 Van Ness
    Ave., 94102 (415) 554-4000, Fax: (415) 554-6160
  Chamber of Commerce, 465 California St., #900, 94104
    (415) 392-4511, Fax: (415) 392-0485
  Black Chamber of Commerce, 1426 Fillmore St., #205, 94115
    (415) 923-0105, Fax: (415) 923-1704
  Chinese Chamber of Commerce, 730 Sacramento St., 94108
    (415) 982-3000, Fax: (415) 982-4720
  Hispanic Chamber of Commerce, 2601 Mission St, #900, 94110
    (415) 647-0224, Fax: (415) 282-3320
  Library, Civic Center, 94102 (415) 557-4277
  Library, 3359 24th St., 94110 (415) 695-5090
  Newspaper, *San Francisco Chronicle,* 901 Mission St., 94103
    (415) 777-1111, Fax: (415) 512-8196
  Newspaper, San Francisco Examiner, 110 5th, 94103
    (415) 777-5700, Fax: (415) 243-8058
  CSU San Francisco Police, 1600 Holloway Ave., 94132
    (415) 338-2747
  Police, 850 Bryant St., 94103 (415) 553-0123
  U.C. San Francisco Police, 500 Parnassus Ave., 94143
    (415) 476-1414
San Gabriel (Los Angeles Co.), 532 W. Mission Dr., P.O. Box 130,
    91778-0130 (818) 308-2800, Fax: (818) 458-2830
  Chamber of Commerce, 534 W. Mission Dr., 91776 (818) 576-2525,
    Fax: (818) 289-2901
  Library, 500 S. Del Mar Ave., 91776 (818) 287-0761, Newspaper,
    San Gabriel Valley Daily Tribune, P.O. Box 1259, Covina,
    91722 (818) 962-8811, Fax: (818) 962-8849
  Police, 625 S. Del Mar Ave., P.O. Box 130, 91778 (818) 308-2828
San Jacinto (Riverside Co.), 312 E. Main St., 92583 (909) 654-7337,
    Fax: (909) 654-3728
  Chamber of Commerce, 188 E. Main St., 92583 (909) 654-9246,
    Fax: (909) 654-5007
  Library, 165 W. 7th St., 92583 (909) 654-7450
  Police, 160 W. 6th St., 92383 (909) 654-2702
San Joaquin (Fresno Co.), 21900 Colorado Ave., P.O. Box 758, 93660
    (209) 693-4311, Fax: (209) 693-2193
San Jose (Santa Clara Co.), 801 N. First St., 95110 (408) 277-4000,
    Fax: (408) 277-3131
  Chamber of Commerce, 180 S. Market St., 95113 (408) 291-5250,
    Fax: (408) 286-5019
  County Library, 1095 N. 7th St., 95112-4434 (408) 293-2326
  Library, 180 W. San Carlos St., 95113-2096 (408) 277-4822

San Jose Library, 1230 Blaney Ave., 95129 (408) 996-1535
Newspaper, *San Jose Mercury News,* 750 Ridder Park Dr., 95190 (408) 920-5000
CSU San Jose Police, Washington Square, 95192 (408)924-2174
Police, P.O. Box 270, 95103 (408) 277-4212
San Juan Bautista (San Benito Co.), 311 Second St., P.O. Box 1086, 95045 (408) 623-4661, Fax: (408) 623-4093
Chamber of Commerce, 402A Third St., P.O. Box 1037, 95045 (408) 623-2454, Fax: (408) 623-0674
Library, 801 Second St., P.O. Box 1086, 95045 (408) 623-4687
Sheriff, P.O. Box 700, Holister, 95025-700 (408) 636-4080
San Juan Capistrano (Orange Co.), 32400 Paseo Adelanto, 92675 (714) 493-1171, Fax: (714) 493-1053
Chamber of Commerce, 26832 Ortega Hwy., 92675 (714) 493-4700
Library, El Paseo Real Plaza, 31495 El Camino Real, 92675 (714) 493-3948, Fax: (714) 240-7680
Sheriff, 32400 Paseo Adelanto, 92675 (714) 493-1171
San Leandro (Alameda Co.), 835 E. 14th St., 94577 (510) 577-3200, Fax: (510) 577-3340
Chamber of Commerce, 262 Davis St., P.O. Box 607, 94577 (510) 351-1481, Fax: (510) 351-6740
Library, 300 Estudillo Ave., 94577 (510) 577-3480
Newspaper, *San Leandro Observer,* P.O. Box 817, 94577 (510) 483-7119
Police, 901 E. 14th St., 94577 (510) 577-3200
San Lorenzo (Alameda Co.), 94580, Unincorporated
Library, 395 Paseo Grande, 94580-2491 (510) 670-6283, Fax: (510) 317-8497
San Luis Obispo (San Luis Obispo Co.), 990 Palm St., 93401, P.O. Box 8100, 93403-8100 (805) 781-7100, Fax: (805) 781-7109
Chamber of Commerce, 1039 Chorro St., 93401 (805) 781-2777, Fax: (805) 543-1255
Library, 995 Palm St., 93401 (805) 781-5784, Fax: (805) 543-9105
Newspaper, *Telegram-Tribune,* 1321 Johnson Ave., P.O. Box 112, 93406 (805) 595-1111, Fax: (805) 595-1184
CPU San Luis Obispo Police, Public Safety Service, 93407 (805) 756-2281
Police, P.O. Box 1328, 93406-1328 (805) 781-7337
San Marcos (San Diego Co.), 105 W. Richmar Ave., 92069 (619) 744-4020, Fax: (619) 744-7543
Chamber of Commerce, 144 W. Mission Rd., 92069 (619) 744-1270, Fax: (619) 744-5230
Library, 847 W. San Marcos Blvd., 92069-1698 (619) 744-0707
Newspaper, *San Marcos Courier,* 321 S. Rancho Santa Fe Rd., 92069 (619) 724-7161, Fax: (619) 726-3064
Sheriff, 325 S. Melrose, #210, Vista, 92083 (619) 940-4551
San Marino (Los Angeles Co.), 2200 Huntington Dr., 91108 (818) 300-0700, Fax: (818) 300-0709
Chamber of Commerce, 2304 Huntington Dr., 91108 (818) 286-1022

San Marino Library, 1890 Huntington Dr., 91108 (818) 282-8484,
   Fax: (818) 284-0766
Newspaper, *Tribune*, 2260 Huntington Dr., 91108 (818) 282-0556,
   Fax: (818) 457-6436
Police, 2200 Huntington Dr., 91108 (818) 300-0720

San Mateo (San Mateo Co.), 330 W. 20th Ave., 94403 (415) 377-3300,
   Fax: (415) 377-3494
Chamber of Commerce, 1730 S. El Camino Real, #200, 94402
   (415) 341-5679, Fax: (415) 341-0679
Library, 55 W. Third Ave., 94402 (415) 377-4680
Newspaper, *The Times*, 1080 S. Amphlett Blvd., 94402
   (415) 348-4321, Fax: (415) 348-4446
Police, 2000 S. Delaware St., 94403 (415) 377-4530

San Pablo (Contra Costa Co.), #1 Alvarado Square, 94806 (510) 215-3000,
   Fax: (510) 235-7059
Chamber of Commerce, P.O. Box 204, 94806 (510) 234-2067
Library, 2101 Market Ave., 94806 (510) 374-3998
Police, #5 Alvarado Square, 94806 (510) 215-3130

San Pedro (Los Angeles Co.), City of Los Angeles
Chamber of Commerce, 390 W. 7th St., P.O. Box 167, 90731
   (310) 832-7272, Fax: (310) 832-0685
Library, 931 S. Gaffey St., 90731 (310) 548-7779,
   Fax: (310) 548-7453
Newspaper, *News-Pilot*, P.O. Box 191, 90733 (310) 832-0221,
   Fax: (310) 833-1540

San Rafael (Marin Co.), 1400 5th Ave., 94901, P.O. Box 151560, 94915-1560
   (415) 485-3074, Fax: (415) 459-2242
Chamber of Commerce, 817 Mission Ave., 94901 (415) 454-4163,
   Fax: (415) 454-7039
Library, 1100 "E" St., 94901 (415) 485-3323, Fax: (415) 485-3112
Library, Civic Center Admin. Bldg., 4th Floor, 94903-4177
   (415) 499-6056
Newspaper, *Marin Independent Journal*, 150 Alameda del Pardo,
   Novato, 94949 (415) 883-8600, Fax: (415) 382-0549
Police, 1400 5th Ave., 94915 (415) 485-3004

San Ramon (Contra Costa Co.), 2222 Camino Ramon, 94583 (510) 275-2200,
   866-1400, Fax: (510) 866-1436
Chamber of Commerce, 2355 San Ramon Valley Blvd., #101, 94583
   (510) 831-9500, Fax: (510) 831-8840
Library, 100 Montgomery St., 94806 (510) 866-8467
Sheriff, 2222 Camino Ramon, 94583 (415) 275-2270

San Simeon (San Luis Obispo Co.), 93452, Unincorporated
Chamber of Commerce, 9511 Hearst Dr., P.O. Box 1, 93452
   (805) 927-3500, (800) 342-5613, Fax: (805) 927-8358

San Ysidro (San Diego Co.), 92073, Unincorporated
Chamber of Commerce, P.O. Box 433100, 92143-3100
   (619) 428-1281, Fax: (619) 662-1478
Library, 101 W. San Ysidro Blvd., 92073 (619) 690-8375

Sand City (Monterey Co.), #1 Sylvan Park, 93955 (408) 394-3054,
   Fax: (408) 394-2472
Police, #1 Sylvan Park Rd., 93955 (408) 394-1451

Sanger (Fresno Co.), 1700 7th St., 93657 (209) 875-2587,
  Fax: (209) 875-8956
  Chamber of Commerce, 1348 Church Ave., 93657 (209) 875-4575
  Library, 1812 7th St., 93657 (209) 875-2435
  Newspaper, *Sanger Herald,* 740 "N" St., 93657 (209) 875-2511,
  Fax: (209) 875-2521
  Police, 1700 7th St., 93657 (209) 875-8521
Santa Ana (Orange Co.), 20 Civic Center Plaza, P.O. Box 1988, 92702
  (714) 647-6900, Fax: (714) 647-6954
  Chamber of Commerce, 801 Civic Center, 92701 (714) 541-5353,
  (714) 541-2238
  Orange Co. Chamber of Commerce, One City Blvd. W., No. 401,
  92668 (714) 634-2900
  Library, 26 Civic Center Plaza, 92701 (714) 647-5250
  Newspaper, *The Orange County Register,* 625 N. Grand Ave., 92711
  (714) 835-1234, Fax: (714) 542-5037
  Police, P.O. Box 1981, 92701 (714) 647-5070
Santa Barbara (Santa Barbara Co.), 735 Anacapa St., 93101, P.O. Box 1990,
  93102-1990 (805) 963-0611, Fax: (805) 564-5556
  Chamber of Commerce, 504 State St., P.O. Box 299, 93101
  (805) 965-3023, Fax: (805) 966-5954
  Library, 40 E. Anapamu St., 93101, P.O. Box 1019, 93102
  (805) 962-7653, Fax: (805) 962-8972
  Newspaper, *Santa Barbara News-Press,* 722 De La Guerra Plaza,
  P.O. Drawer 1359, 93102 (805) 564-5200,
  Fax: (805) 966-6258
  Police, 215 E. Figueroa, 93102 (805) 897-2396
  U.C. Santa Barbara Police, Santa Barbara Campus, 93106
  (805) 893-3260
Santa Clara (Santa Clara Co.), 1500 Warburton Ave., 95050 (408) 984-3000,
  Fax: (408) 241-6771
  Chamber of Commerce, 2200 Laurelwood Rd., Second Floor,
  P.O. Box 387, 95054 (408) 970-9825, (408) 296-7111
  Fax: (408) 970-8864
  Library, 2635 Homestead Rd., 95051 (408) 984-3178,
  Fax: (408) 247-9657
  Police, 1541 Civic Center Dr., 95050 (408) 261-5300
Santa Clarita (Los Angeles Co.), 23920 Valencia Blvd., Suite 300, 91355
  (805) 259-2489, Fax: (805) 259-8125
  Chamber of Commerce, 23920 Valencia Blvd., #125, 91355
  (805) 259-4787, Fax: (805) 259-8628
  Newspaper, *Santa Clarita Signal,* 24000 Creekside Rd.,
  P.O. Box 801870, 91355 (805) 259-1234,
  Fax: (805) 254-8068
  Sheriff, 23740 Magic Mountain Pkwy., Valencia, 91355
  (805) 255-1121, (818) 984-0630

Santa Cruz (Santa Cruz Co.), 809 Center St., 95060 (408) 429-3540,
  Fax: (408) 459-9359
  Chamber of Commerce, 725 Front St., #108, P.O. Box 921, 95061
    (408) 423-1111, Fax: (408) 423-1847
  City-County Library, 224 Church St., 95060-3873 (408) 429-3533,
    Fax: (408) 425-4927
  Newspaper, *Santa Cruz Sentinel,* 207 Church St., P.O. Box 638,
    95061 (408) 423-4242, Fax: (408) 423-1154
  Police, 212 Locus St., 95060-3865 (408) 429-3714
  U.C. Santa Cruz Police, 1156 High St., 95064 (408) 459-2231
Santa Fe Springs (Los Angeles Co.), 11710 E. Telegraph Rd., P.O. Box 2120,
    90670 (310) 868-0511, Fax: (310) 868-7112
  Chamber of Commerce, 12016 Telegraph Rd., #100, 90670
    (310) 944-1616, Fax: (310) 946-2006
  Library, 11700 E. Telegraph Rd., 90670 (310) 868-7738,
    Fax: (310) 929-3680
  Sheriff, 12335 Civic Center Dr., Norwalk, 90650 (310) 863-8711
Santa Maria (Santa Barbara Co.), 110 E. Cook St., 93454-5190
    (805) 925-0951, Fax: (805) 349-0657
  Chamber of Commerce, 614 S. Broadway, 93454 (805) 925-2403,
    Fax: (805) 928-7559
  Library, 420 S. Broadway, 93454-5111 (805) 925-0994
  Newspaper, *Santa Maria Times,* 3200 Skyway Dr., P.O. Box 400,
    93456 (805) 925-2691, Fax: (805) 928-5657
  Police, 222 E. Cook St., 93454 (805) 928-3781
Santa Monica (Los Angeles Co.), 1685 Main St., P.O. Box 2200, 90407-2200
    (310) 393-9975, Fax: (310) 394-2692
  Chamber of Commerce, 501 Colorado Ave., 90401 (310) 393-9825,
    Fax: (310) 394-1868
  Library, 1343 6th St., P.O. Box 1610, 90406-1610 (310) 451-8859,
    (310) 458-8600, Fax: (310) 458-6980
  Newspaper, *The Daily Breeze,* 1920 Colorado Ave., 90404
    (310) 829-6811, Fax: (310) 453-3085
  Police, 1685 Main St., 90401 (310) 395-9931
Santa Paula (Ventura Co.), 970 Ventura St., P.O. Box 569, 93060
    (805) 525-4478, Fax: (805) 525-6278
  Chamber of Commerce, 200 N. 10th St., P.O. Box 1, 93061
    (805) 525-5561, Fax: (805) 525-8950
  Library, 119 N. 8th St., 93060-2784 (805) 525-3615,
    Fax: (805) 933-2324
  Newspaper, *The Santa Paula Chronicle,* 116 10th St., P.O. Box 30,
    93060 (805) 525-5555, Fax: (805) 525-7735
  Police, 214 S. 10th St., 93060 (805) 525-4474
Santa Rosa (Sonoma Co.), 100 Santa Rosa Ave., 95404, P.O. Box 1678,
    95402 (707) 524-5361, Fax: (707) 524-5017
  Chamber of Commerce, 637 First St., 95404 (707) 545-1414,
    Fax: (707) 545-6914
  Hispanic Chamber of Commerce, P.O. Box 11392, 95406
    (707) 526-7744, Fax: (707) 576-1976
  Library, 3rd & "E" Sts., 95404 (707) 545-0831
  Newspaper, *The Press Democrat,* 427 Mendocino Ave.,
    P.O. Box 569, 95402 (707) 546-2020, Fax: (707) 546-2473

Santa Rosa Police, P.O. Box 1678, 95402 (707) 524-5342
Santee (San Diego Co.), 10765 Woodside Ave., 92071 (619) 258-4100,
    Fax: (619) 258-9113
  Chamber of Commerce, 10315 Mission Gorge Rd., 92071
    (619) 449-6572
  Library, 9225 Carlton Hills Blvd., #17, 92071-3192 (619) 448-1863
Saratoga (Santa Clara Co.), 13777 Fruitvale Ave., 95070 (408) 867-3438,
    Fax: (408) 741-1132
  Chamber of Commerce, 20460 Saratoga-Los Gatos Rd., 95070
    (408) 867-0753, Fax: (408) 867-5213
  Library, 13650 Saratoga Ave., 95070-5099 (408) 867-6126,
    Fax: (408) 867-9806
  Newspaper, *Saratoga News,* 14375 Saratoga Ave., Suite E2, 95070
    (408) 867-6397, Fax: (408) 867-6397,
    Fax: (408) 867-1010
  Sheriff, 14374 Saratoga Ave., 95070 (408) 867-9719
Satacoy (Ventura Co.), 93004, Unincorporated
  Library, 11168 Violeta St., 93004 (805) 652-6295
Saugus (Los Angeles Co.), City of Santa Clarita
  Chamber of Commerce, (see Santa Clarita)
  Newspaper, *Santa Clarita Signal,* 24000 Creekside Rd.,
    P.O. Box 801870, Santa Clarita, 91380-1870
    (805) 259-1234, Fax: (805) 254-8068
  Sheriff, 23740 Magic Mountain Pkwy., Valencia, 91355
    (805) 255-1121
Sausalito (Marin Co.), 420 Litho St., 94965, P.O. Box 1279, 94966
    (415) 289-4100, Fax: (415) 289-4167
  Chamber of Commerce, 333 Caledonia St., P.O. Box 566, 94966
    (415) 332-0505, Fax: (415) 332-0323
  Library, 420 Litho St., 94965-1933 (415) 289-4120,
    Fax: (415) 289-4167
  Newspaper, *Ross Valley Reporter,* P.O. Drawer 1689, 94966
    (415) 332-3778, Fax: (415) 332-8714
  Police, P.O. Box 35, 94966 (415) 289-4170
Scotts Valley (Sacramento Co.), One Civic Center Dr., 95066 (408) 438-2324,
    Fax: (408) 438-2793
  Chamber of Commerce, 4 Camp Ever's Lane, P.O. Box 66928,
    95067-6928 (408) 438-1010, Fax: (408) 438-6544
  Police, One Civic Center Dr., 95066 (408) 438-2323
Seal Beach (Orange County), 211 8th St., 90740 (310) 431-2527,
    Fax: (310) 431-4067
  Chamber of Commerce, 13820 Seal Beach Blvd., #10, 90740
    (310) 799-0179
  Library, 12700 Montecito Rd., 90740 (310) 430-1048
  Police, 911 Seal Beach Blvd., 90740 (310) 431-2541
Seaside (Monterey Co.), 440 Harcourt Ave., P.O. Box 810, 93955-0810
    (408) 899-6200, Fax: (408) 899-6227
  Chamber of Commerce, 505 Broadway Ave., 93955 (408) 394-6501
  Library, 550 Harcourt Ave., 93955 (408) 899-2055,
    Fax: (408) 899-8133
  Police, P.O. Box 810, 93955 (408) 899-6290

Sebastopol (Sonoma Co.), 7120 Bodega Ave., 95472, P.O. Box 1776, 95473-1776 (707) 823-1153, (707) 823-3018
    Chamber of Commerce, 265 S. Main St., P.O. Box 178, 95473 (707) 823-3032
    Newspaper, *Russian River News,* P.O. Box 521, 95473 (707) 823-7845, Fax: (707) 823-7508
    Police, 6850 Laguna Pkwy., 95472 (707) 823-6446
Selma (Fresno Co.), 1814 Tucker St., 93662 (209) 896-1064, Fax: (209) 896-1068
    Chamber of Commerce, 1802 Tucker St., 93662 (209) 896-3315, Fax: (209) 896-1068
    Library, 2200 Selma St., 93662 (209) 896-3393
    Newspaper, *The Selma Enterprise,* 2045 Grant St., P.O. Box 100, 93662 (209) 896-1976, Fax: (209) 896-9160
    Police, 1935 E. Front St., 93662-3561 (209) 896-2525
Seminole Hot Springs (Los Angeles Co.), Unincorporated
Sepulveda (Los Angeles Co.), City of Los Angeles
    Chamber of Commerce, (see Van Nuys)
Shafter (Kern Co.), 336 Pacifica Ave., 93263 (805) 746-6361, Fax: (805) 746-0607
    Chamber of Commerce, 150 Central Valley Hwy., P.O. Box 1088, 93263 (805) 746-2600
    Library, (see Bakersfield)
    Newspaper, *Shafter Press,* 107 E. Ledro Hwy., 93263 (805) 746-4942, Fax: (805) 746-5571
    Police, 333 Sunset St., 93263 (805) 746-6341
Shasta Lake (Shasta Co.), 1650 Stanton Dr., P.O. Box 777, 96019 (916) 275-7400
Sherman Oaks (Los Angeles Co.), City of Los Angeles
    Chamber of Commerce, 14241 Ventura Blvd., #210, 91423 (818) 906-1951, Fax: (818) 783-3100
    Library, 14245 Moorpark St., 91403 (818) 981-7850, Fax: (818) 904-3288
Shingle Springs (El Dorado Co.), 95682, Unincorporated
    Chamber of Commerce, 4065 Mother Lode Dr., P.O. Box 341, 95682 (916) 677-8000, Fax: (916) 676-8313
Sierra Madre (Los Angeles Co.), 232 W. Sierra Madre Blvd., P.O. Box 0457, 91024 (818) 355-7135, Fax: (818) 355-2251
    Chamber of Commerce, 49 S. Baldwin Ave., #K, 91024 (818) 355-5111, Fax: (818) 306-1150
    Library, 440 W. Sierra Madre Blvd., 91024 (818) 355-7186, Fax: (818) 355-6218
    Newspaper, *Sierra Madre News,* 9 Kersting Court, 91024 (818) 355-3324, Fax: (818) 355-2341
    Police, 242 W. Sierra Madre, 91024 (818) 355-1414
Signal Hill (Los Angeles Co.), 2175 Cherry Ave., 90806 (310) 989-7300, Fax: (310) 989-7393
    Chamber of Commerce, 1919 E. Hill St., 90806 (310) 424-6489, Fax: (310) 989-0833

Signal Hill Library, 1770 E. Hill St., 90806 (310) 989-7323,
    Fax: (310) 989-7392
  Newspaper, *The Signal,* 2107 Cherry Ave., Suite B, 90806
    (310) 498-0707, Fax: (310) 498-7847
  Police, 1800 E. Hill St., 90806 (310) 426-7311
Silver Lake (Los Angeles Co.), City of Los Angeles
Simi Valley (Ventura Co.), 2929 Tapo Canyon Rd., 93063 (805) 583-6700,
    Fax: (805) 526-2489
  Chamber of Commerce, 40 W. Cochran St., #100, 93065
    (805) 526-3900, Fax: (805) 526-6234
  Library, 2969 Tapo Canyon Rd., 93063 (805) 526-1735
  Newspaper, *The Enterprise,* 888 Easy St., 93065 (805) 526-6211,
    Fax: (805) 526-0479/527-7009
  Police, 3200 Cochran St., 93065 (805) 583-6950
Solano Beach (San Diego Co.), 380 Stevens Ave., Suite 120, 92075
    (619) 755-2998, Fax: (619) 792-6513
  Chamber of Commerce, 210 W. Plaza St., P.O. Box 623, 92075
    (619) 755-4775, Fax: (619) 755-2998
  Library, 981 Lomas Santa Fe Dr., 92075-1873 (619) 755-1404,
    Fax: (619) 448-1497
  Newspaper, *Blade Citizen,* P.O. Box 7006, 92075 (619) 755-1127,
    Fax: (619) 755-5107
Soledad (Monterey Co.), 248 Main St., P.O. Box 156, 93960 (408) 678-3963,
    Fax: (408) 678-3965
  Chamber of Commerce, P.O. Box 156, 93960 (408) 678-2278
  Library, 179 Main St., 93960 (408) 678-2430, Fax: (408) 678-3087
  Newspaper, *Soledad Bee,* 635 Front St., P.O. Box 95, 93901
    (408) 678-2660, Fax: (408) 385-4799
  Police, 236 Main St., 93960 (408) 678-2411
Solemint (Los Angeles Co.), City of Santa Clarita
Solvang (Santa Barbara Co.), 1644 Oak St., 93463, P.O. Box 107, 93464
    (805) 688-5575, Fax: (805) 686-2049
  Chamber of Commerce, 1593 Mission Dr., P.O. Box 465, 93464
    (805) 688-0701, (800) 468-6765, Fax: (805) 688-8620
  Library, 1745 Mission Dr., 93463 (805) 688-4214
  Newspaper, *Santa Ynez Valley News,* 423 Second St., P.O. Box 647,
    93463 (805) 688-5522, Fax: (805) 688-7685
  Sheriff, 1745 Mission Dr., 93463 (805) 686-5000
Sonoma (Sonoma Co.), #1 The Plaza, 95476 (707) 938-3681,
    Fax: (707) 938-8775
  Chamber of Commerce, 645 Broadway, 95476 (707) 996-1033.
    Fax: (707) 996-9402
  Newspaper, *The Sonoma Index-Tribune,* P.O. Box C, 95476
    (707) 938-2111, Fax: (707) 938-1600
  CSU Sonoma Police, 1801 E. Cotati Ave., 94928 (707) 664-2143
  Police, 175 First St. W., 95476 (707) 996-3602
Sonora (Tuolumne Co.), 94 N. Washington St., 95370 (209) 532-4541,
    Fax: (209) 532-2738
  Chamber of Commerce, 55 Stockton St., 95370 (209) 532-4212

Sonora Library, 480 Greenley Rd., 95370 (209) 533-5507,
   Fax: (209) 533-0936
Newspaper, *The Union Democrat*, 84 S. Washington St., 95370
   (209) 532-7151, Fax: (209) 532-5139
Police, 542 W. Stockton Rd., 95370 (209) 532-8143
Soquel (Santa Cruz Co.), 95073, Unincorporated
   Chamber of Commerce, P.O. Box 333, 95073 (408) 475-1702
South El Monte (Los Angeles Co.), 1415 Santa Anita Ave., 91733
   (818) 579-6540, (818) 686-0460, Fax: (818) 579-2107
Library, 1430 N. Central Ave., 91733 (818) 443-4158,
   Fax: (818) 575-7450
Sheriff, 8838 E. Las Tunas Dr., Temple City, 91780 (818) 285-7171
South Gate (Los Angeles Co.), 8650 California Ave., 90280 (213) 563-9500,
   Fax: (213) 569-2678
Chamber of Commerce, 3350 Tweedy Blvd., 90280 (213) 567-1203
Library, 4035 Tweedy Blvd., 90280 (213) 567-8853
Police, 8620 California Ave., 90280 (213) 563-5400,
   Fax: (213) 569-2678
South Lake Tahoe (El Dorado Co.), 1052 Tata Lane, 96150-6324
   (916) 542-6000, Fax: (916) 544-8657
Chamber of Commerce, 3066 Lake Tahoe Blvd., 96150
   (916) 541-5255, Fax: (916) 541-7121
Library, 1000 Rufus Allen Blvd., 96150 (916) 573-3185
Newspaper, *Tahoe Daily Tribune*, 3079 Harrison Ave.,
   P.O. Box 1358, 95705 (916) 541-3880,
   Fax: (916) 541-0373
Police, 1352 Johnson Blvd., 96150-8217 (916) 542-6100
South Pasadena (Los Angeles Co.), 1414 Mission St., 91030 (818) 799-9101,
   Fax: (818) 799-1109
Chamber of Commerce, 1610 Mission St., 91030 (818) 799-7161,
   Fax: (818) 799-3008
Library, 1100 Oxley St., 91030 (818) 441-7833
Police, 1422 Mission St., 91030 (818) 799-1121
South San Francisco (San Mateo Co.), 400 Grand Ave., 94080, P.O. Box 711,
   94083 (415) 877-8500, Fax: (415) 871-7318
Chamber of Commerce, 213 Linden Ave., P.O. Box 469,
   94083-0469 (415) 588-1911
Library, 840 W. Orange Ave., 94080-3197 (415) 877-8521
Police, 33 Arroyo Dr., Suite C, 94080 (415) 877-8900
South San Gabriel (Los Angeles Co.), Unincorporated
Spring Valley (San Diego Co.), 92077, Unincorporated
   Chamber of Commerce, P.O. Box 1211, 91979 (619) 697-2500
   Library, 1043 Elkelton Blvd., 91977-4796 (619) 462-3006
Springville (Tulare Co.), 93265, Unincorporated
   Chamber of Commerce, 35680 State Hwy. 190, P.O. Box 104, 93265
      (209) 539-2312
   Library, 35800 Hwy. 190, P.O. Box 257, 93265 (209) 539-2624
   Newspaper, *Tule River Times*, P.O. Box 692, 93265 (209) 539-3166
Stallion Springs (Kern Co.), Unincorporated
   Police, Star Route Box 800-11, Tehachapi, 93561 (805) 822-7596
Stanton (Orange Co.), 7800 Katella Ave., 90680 (714) 379-9222,
   Fax: (714) 826-8730

Stanton Chamber of Commerce, 8381 Katella Ave., #B-1,
P.O. Box 353, 90680 (714) 995-1485
Library, 7850 Katella Ave., 90680 (714) 898-3302,
Fax: (714) 898-0040
Sheriff, 1110 Cedar, 92680 (714) 891-2481
Stockton (San Joaquin Co.), 425 N. El Dorado St., 95202 (209) 937-8212,
Fax: (209) 463-1550
Chamber of Commerce, 445 W. Weber Ave., #220, 95203
(209) 547-2770, Fax: (209) 466-5271
Library, 605 N. El Dorado St., 95202 (209) 937-8415,
Fax: (209) 944-8683
Newspaper, *The Stockton Record,* 530 E. Market St., 95202
(209) 943-6397
Police, 22 E. Market St., 95202 (209) 944-8377
Studebaker (Los Angeles Co.), City of Norwalk
Studio City (Los Angeles Co.), City of Los Angeles
Chamber of Commerce, 12153 Ventura Blvd., #100, 91604
(818) 769-3213, (818) 980-3811, Fax: (818) 769-7135
Library, 4400 Babcock Ave., 91604 (818) 769-5212,
Fax: (213) 612-0403
Suisun City (Solano Co.), 701 Civic Center Blvd., 94585 (707) 421-7300,
Fax: (707) 421-7366
Chamber of Commerce, (see Fairfield)
Library, 1150 Kentucky St., Fairfield, 94533 (707) 429-6500,
Fax: (707) 421-7207
Police, 701 Civic Center Blvd., 94585-2693 (707) 421-7353
Sulpher Springs (Los Angeles Co.), Unincorporated
Sun City (Riverside Co.), 92381, Unincorporated
Chamber of Commerce, 26936 Cherry Hills Blvd., P.O. Box 656,
92586 (909) 672-1991
Sun Valley (Los Angeles Co.), City of Los Angeles
Chamber of Commerce, 8128-A Sunland Blvd., 91352
(818) 768-2014, Fax: (818) 767-1947
Library, 7935 Vineland Ave., 91352 (818) 764-7907,
Fax: (818) 904-3289
Sunland (Los Angeles Co.), City of Los Angeles
Chamber of Commerce, (see Tujunga)
Library, 7771 Foothill Blvd., Tujunga, 91042 (818) 352-4481,
Fax: (818) 352-2501
Sunnyvale (Santa Clara Co.), 456 W. Olive Ave., 94086, P.O. Box 3707,
94088-3707 (408) 730-7500,
Fax: (408) 730-7655
Chamber of Commerce, 499 S. Murphy Ave., 94086
(408) 736-4971, Fax: (408) 736-1919
Library, 665 W. Olive Ave., P.O. Box 3414, 94088-3714
(408) 730-7315
Police, P.O. Box 3707, 94086-3707 (408) 730-7100
Susanville (Lassen Co.), 66 N. Lassen St., 96130 (916) 257-2174,
Fax: (916) 257-4725
Chamber of Commerce, 84N. Lassen St., P.O. Box 338, 96130
(916) 257-4323

Susanville Library, Court House Annex, S. Roop St., 96130
(916) 257-8311, Fax: (916) 257-8115
Newspaper, *Lassen County Times,* 800 Main St., 96130
(916) 257-5321, Fax: (916) 257-0408
Police, 1801 Main St., 96130 (916) 257-5603
Sutter Creek (Amador Co.), #18 Main St., P.O. Box 366, 95685
(209) 267-5647, Fax: (209) 267-0639
Police, P.O. Box 366, 95685 (209) 267-5646
Swall Meadows (Mono Co.), 93514, Unincorporated
Chamber of Commerce, P.O. Box 247, Bridgeport 93517
(619) 924-3699
Sylmar (Los Angeles Co.), City of Los Angeles
Chamber of Commerce,13728 Foothill Blvd., 91342 (818) 367-5117,
Fax: (818) 362-0754
Library, 13059 Glenoaks Blvd., 91342 (818) 367-6102
Sylvia Park (Los Angeles Co.), Unincorporated
Taft (Kern Co.), 209 E. Kern St., 93268 (805) 763-1222, Fax: (805) 765-2480
Chamber of Commerce, 314 4th St., 93268 (805) 765-2165,
Fax: (805) 765-6639
Library, (see Bakersfield)
Newspaper, *Daily Midway Driller,* 800 Center St., P.O. Bin Z, 93268
(805) 763-3171, Fax: (805) 763-5638
Police, 320 Commerce Way, 93268 (805) 763-3101
Tahoe City (Placer Co.), 95730, Unincorporated
Chamber of Commerce, (see Lake Tahoe)
Library, P.O. Box 6570, 96145 (916) 583-3382
Newspaper, *Tahoe World,* P.O. Box 138, 95730 (916) 583-3487,
Fax: (916) 583-7109
Tarzana (Los Angeles Co.), City of Los Angeles
Chamber of Commerce, 18705 Ventura Blvd., 91356
(818) 343-3687, Fax: (818) 343-1134
Library, 18231 Ventura Blvd., 91356 (818) 343-1983
Tecopa (Inyo Co.), 92389, Unincorporated
Tehachapi (Kern Co.), 115 S. Robinson St., 93561, P.O. Box 668, 93581
(805) 822-2200, Fax: (805) 822-8559
Chamber of Commerce, 209 E. Tehachacpi Blvd., P.O. Box 401,
93561 (805) 822-4180, Fax: (805) 822-9036
Library, (see Bakersfield)
Newspaper, *Tehapachi News,* 411 N. Mill St., P.O. Box 230, 93561
(805) 822-6828, Fax: (805) 822-4053
Sheriff, P.O. Box 972, 93581 (805) 822-2222-
Tehama (Tehama Co.), 250 Cavalier Ave., P.O. Box 70, 96090
(916) 384-2406
Temecula (Riverside Co.), 43174 Business Park Dr., 92590 (909) 694-1989,
Fax: (909) 694-1999
Chamber of Commerce, 27450 Ynez Rd., #104, 92591
(909) 676-5090, Fax: (909) 694-0201
Temecula Library, 27533 Ynez Rd., 92390 (909) 676-5316,
Fax: (909) 699-1343
Newspaper, *The Californian,* 27450 Ynez Rd., Suite 300, 92591
(909) 676-4315, Fax: (909) 699-1467
Sheriff, 43172 Business Park Dr., 92390 (909) 694-1989

Temple City (Los Angeles Co.), 9701 Las Tunas Dr., P.O. Box 668, 91780 (818) 285-2171, Fax: (818) 285-8192
  Chamber of Commerce, 5827 N. Temple City Blvd., 91780-2163 (818) 286-3101
  Library, 5939 Golden West Ave., 91780 (818) 285-2136, Fax: (818) 285-2314
  Sheriff, 8838 E. Las Tunas Dr., 91780 (818) 285-7171
Templeton (San Luis Obispo Co.), 93465, Unincorporated
  Chamber of Commerce, P.O. Box 701, 93465 (805) 434-1789
Thermal (Riverside Co.), 92274, Unincorporated
  Chamber of Commerce, P.O. Box 284, 92274 (619) 399-0080
Thornton (San Joaquin Co.), 95686, Unincorporated
  Chamber of Commerce, P.O. Box 37, 95686 (209) 794-2156
  Library, 26341 N. Thornton Rd., 95686 (209) 794-2621
Thousand Oaks (Ventura Co.), 2400 Willow Lane, 91360, P.O. Box 1496, 91320 (805) 497-8611, Fax: (805) 499-3848
  Chamber of Commerce, 625 W. Hillcrest Dr., 91360 (805) 499-1993, Fax: (805) 498-7264
  Library, 1401 E. Janss Rd., 91362-2199 (805) 497-6282
  Newspaper, *News-Chronicle,* 2595 Thousand Oaks Blvd., P.O. Box 3129, 91359 (805) 496-3211, Fax: (805) 494-4523
  Sheriff, 800 S. Victoria Ave., Ventura, 93009 (805) 654-2314
Tiburon (Marin Co.), 1155 Tiburon Blvd., 94920 (415) 435-0956, Fax: (415) 435-2438
  Chamber of Commerce, 96-B Main St., P.O. Box 563, 94920 (415) 435-5633, Fax: (415) 435-1132
  Library, P.O. Bldg., Beach Rd., 94920-2343 (415) 435-1361, Fax: (415) 435-1786
  Newspaper, *The Ark,* Box 1054, 94920 (415) 435-2652, Fax: (415) 435-0849
  Police, 1155 Tiburon Blvd., 94920 (415) 435-7360
Toluca Lake (Los Angeles Co.), City of Los Angeles and Burbank
  Chamber of Commerce, P.O. Box 2312, 91610 (818) 761-6594
  Newspaper, *The Tolucan,* 10215 Riverside Dr., 91602 (818) 762-2171, Fax: (818) 980-1900
Topanga (Los Angeles Co.), 90290, Unincorporated
  Chamber of Commerce, P.O. Box 185, 90290 (213) 455-1419
Topanga Park (Los Angeles Co.), Unincorporated
Torrance (Los Angeles Co.), 3031 Torrance Blvd., 90503 (310) 618-5880, Fax: (310) 618-5891
  Chamber of Commerce, 3400 Torrance Blvd., #100, 90503 (310) 540-5858, Fax: (310) 540-7662
  Library, 3301 Torrance Blvd., 90503 (310) 618-5950
  Newspaper, *Daily Breeze,* 5215 Torrance Blvd., 90509 (310) 540-5511, Fax: (310) 540-6272
  Police, 3300 Civic Center Dr., 90503 (310) 328-3456
Tracy (San Joaquin Co.), 325 E. 10th St., 95376 (209) 836-2670, Fax: (209) 832-2625
  Chamber of Commerce, 223 E. 10th St., 95376 (209) 835-2131, Fax: (209) 833-9526

Tracy Library, 20 E. Eaton Ave., 95376 (209) 835-2221,
Fax: (209) 835-1745
Newspaper, *Tracy Press*, 145 W. 10th St., P.O. Box 419, 95378
(209) 835-3030, Fax: (209) 835-0655
Police, 400 E. 10th St., 95376 (209) 835-4550
Trinidad (Humboldt Co.), 409 Trinity St., P.O. Box 390, 95570
(707) 677-0223, Fax: (707) 677-3759
Chamber of Commerce, P.O. Box 356, 95570 (707) 677-0591
Police, P.O. Box 390, 95570 (707) 677-0133
Trona (San Bernardino Co.), 93562, Unincorporated
Community Services Council, P.O. Box 443, 93562 (619) 372-4842
Library, 82805 Mountain View St., 93562 (619) 372-5847
Newspaper, *Trona Argonaut*, 13193 Main St., 93562
(619) 372-4747, Fax: (619) 372-4447
Trousdale Estates (Los Angeles Co.), City of Beverly Hills
Truckee (Nevada Co.) 11570 Donner Pass Rd., 96161 (916) 582-7700,
Fax: (916) 582-7710
Chamber of Commerce, 12036 Donner Pass Rd., P.O. Box 2757,
96160 (916) 587-8808, Fax: (916) 587-2439
Library, 10075 Levone Ave., Suite 401, 96161 (916) 582-7846
Newspaper, *The Sierra Sun*, P.O. Box 2973, 95734 (916) 587-6061,
Fax: (916) 541-3880
Tujunga (Los Angeles Co.), City of Los Angeles
Chamber of Commerce, P.O. Box 571, 91043 (818) 352-4433
Library, 7771 Foothill Blvd., 91042 (818) 352-4481,
Fax: (818) 352-2501
Tulare (Tulare Co.), 411 E. Kern Ave., 93274 (209) 685-2300,
Fax: (209) 688-2452
Chamber of Commerce, 260 N. "L" St., 93274 (209) 686-1547,
Fax: (209) 686-4915
Library, 113 N. "F" St. 93274 (209) 685-2341, Fax: (209) 685-2345
Newspaper, *Advance-Register*, 388 E. Cross Ave., P.O. Box 30,
93275-0030 (209) 688-0521, Fax: (209) 688-7503
Police, 415 E. Kern St., 93274 (209) 688-2001
Tulelake (Siskiyou Co.), 470 "C" St., P.O. Box 847, 96134 (916) 667-5522,
Fax: (916) 667-5351
Chamber of Commerce, P.O. Box 592, 96134 (916) 667-5178
Library, P.O. Box 757, 96134 (916) 667-2291
Police, P.O. Box 400, 96134-0400 (916) 667-5284
Turlock (Stanislaus Co.), 900 N. Palm St., 95380, P.O. Box 1526, 95381-1526
(209) 669-0261, Fax: (209) 667-9406
Chamber of Commerce, 115 S. Golden State Blvd., 95380
(209) 632-2221, Fax: (209) 632-5289
Library, 550 Minaret Ave., 95380 (209) 667-1666
Newspaper, *Turlock Journal*, 138 S. Center, 95380 (209) 634-9141,
Fax: (209) 632-8813
Police, 250 Starr Ave., 95380 (209) 668-5550
Tustin (Orange Co.), 300 Centennial Way, 92680 (714) 573-3000,
Fax: (714) 832-0825
Chamber of Commerce, 399 El Camino Real, 92680 (714) 544-5341,
Fax: (714) 544-2083

Tustin Library, 345 E. Main, 92680 (714) 544-7725,
   Fax: (714) 832-4279
Newspaper, *Tustin News,* 649 S. "B" St., P.O. Box 486, 92681
   (714) 544-4110, Fax: (714) 544-9247
Police, 300 Centennial Way, 92680 (714) 544-5424
Twain Harte (Tuolumne Co.), 95383, Unincorporated
   Chamber of Commerce, Joaquin Gully Rd., P.O. Box 404, 95383
      (209) 586-4482
Twentynine Palms (San Bernardino Co.), 6136 Adobe Rd., P.O. Box 995,
   92277 (619) 367-6799, Fax: (619) 367-4890
   Chamber of Commerce, 6136 Adobe Rd., 92277 (619) 367-3445,
      (800) 533-7104, Fax: (619) 367-4890
   Library, 6078 Adobe Rd., 92277 (619) 367-9519
   Newspaper, *The Desert Trail,* P.O. Box 159, 92277 (619) 367-3577,
      Fax: (619) 367-1798
   Sheriff, 6527 White Feather Rd., Joshua Tree, 92252 (619) 366-4175
Twin Cities (Marin Co.), Unincorporated
   Police, 250 Doherty Dr., Larkspur, 94939 (415) 927-5150
Ukiah (Mendocino Co.), 300 Seminary Ave., 95482 (707) 463-6200,
   Fax: (707) 463-6204
   Chamber of Commerce, 495-E E. Perkins St., 95482 (707) 462-4705,
      Fax: (707) 462-0145
   Library, 105 Main St., 95482-4482 (707) 463-4491
   Newspaper, *Ukiah Daily Journal,* 590 S. School St., P.O. Box 749,
      95482 (707) 468-3500, Fax: (707) 468-5780
   Police, 300 Seminary Ave., 95482 (707) 463-6242
Union City (Alameda Co.), 34009 Alvarado-Niles Rd., 94587 (510) 471-3232,
   Fax: (510) 475-7318
   Chamber of Commerce, 32980 Alvarado-Niles Rd., 94587
      (510) 471-3115, Fax: (510) 471-6011
   Library, 34007 Alvarado-Niles Rd., 94587 (510) 471-6771,
      Fax: (415) 487-7241
   Police, 34009 Alvarado-Niles Rd., 94587 (510) 471-1365
Universal City (Los Angeles Co.), Unincorporated
   Chamber of Commerce, (see North Hollywood)
University of California Polices (see campus cities)
Upland (San Bernardino Co.), 460 N. Euclid Ave., 91786, P.O. Box 460,
   91785 (909) 931-4100, Fax: (909) 931-4123
   Chamber of Commerce, 433 N. Second Ave., 91786 (909) 931-4108,
      Fax: (909) 931-4184
   Library, 450 N. Euclid Ave., 91786 (909) 981-1033,
      Fax: (909) 920-0638
   Newspaper, *Inland Valley Daily Bulletin,* 2041 E. 4th St.,
      P.O. Box 4000, Ontario, 91761 (909) 987-6397
   Police, 1499 W. 13th St., 91786 (909) 946-7624
Vacaville (Solano Co.), 650 Merchant St., 95688 (707) 449-5100,
   Fax: (707) 449-5149
   Chamber of Commerce, 300 Main St., 95688 (707) 448-6424,
      (800) 799-6424, Fax: (707) 448-0424
   Vacaville Library, 680 Merchant St., 95688 (707) 448-2093,
      Fax: (707) 451-0987

Newspaper, *The Reporter,* 916 Cotting Lane, P.O. Box 1509, 95688
(707) 448-6401, Fax: (707) 447-8411
Police, 630 Merchant St., 95688 (707) 449-5200
Val Verde (Los Angeles Co.), City of Santa Clarita
Chamber of Commerce, (see Santa Clarita)
Valencia (Los Angeles Co.), City of Santa Clarita
Chamber of Commerce, (see Santa Clarita)
Library, 23743 W. Valencia Blvd., 91355 (805) 259-8942,
Fax: (805) 259-7187
Newspaper, *Santa Clarita Signal,* 24000 Creekside Rd.,
P.O. Box 801870, Santa Clarita, 91380-1870
(805) 259-1234, Fax: (805) 254-8068
Sheriff, 23740 Magic Mountain Pkwy., Valencia, 91355
(805) 255-1121
Valinda (Los Angeles Co.), Unincorporated
Vallejo (Solano Co.), 555 Santa Clara Ave., P.O. Box 3068, 94590
(707) 648-4527, Fax: (707) 648-4426
Chamber of Commerce, 2 Florida St., 94590 (707) 644-5551,
Fax: (707) 644-5590
Library, 505 Santa Clara St., 94590 (707) 553-5568,
Fax: (707) 553-5667
Newspaper, *Vallejo Times-Herald,* 440 Curtola Pkwy.,
P.O. Box 3188, 94590 (707) 644-1141,
Fax: (707) 643-0128
Police, P.O. Box 1031, 94590 (707) 648-4540
Valley Center (San Deigo Co.), 92082, Unincorporated
Chamber of Commerce, 28714 Valley Center Rd., #D, P.O. Box 793,
92082 (619) 749-8472
Library, 29115 Valley Center Rd., 92082-9699 (619) 749-1305
Van Nuys (Los Angeles Co.), City of Los Angeles
Chamber of Commerce, 14540 Victory Blvd., #100, 91411
(818) 989-0300, Fax: (818) 989-3836
Library, 6250 Sylmar Ave., 91401 (818) 989-8453,
Fax: (818) 904-3291
Newspaper, *Daily News,* 21221 Oxnard St., Woodland Hills, 91367
(818) 713-3000, Fax: (818) 713-0058
Venice (Los Angeles Co.), City of Los Angeles
Chamber of Commerce, 2904 Washington Blvd., #100,
P.O. Box 202, 90291 (310) 827-2366, Fax: (310) 301-2022
Library, 610 California Ave., 90291 (310) 821-1769
Ventura (Ventura Co.), 501 Poli St., 93001, P.O. Box 99, 93002
(805) 654-7800, Fax: (805) 652-0865
Chamber of Commerce, 785 S. Seaward Ave., 93001
(805) 648-2875, Fax: (805) 648-3535
County Library, 4274 Telegraph Rd., 93003 (805) 652-6289
Ventura Library, 800 S. Victoria Ave., 93003 (805) 652-6289,
Fax: (805) 652-6297
Newspaper, *Reporter,* 1583 SpinnakerDr., No. 213, 93001
(805) 658-2244, Fax: (805) 658-7803
Police, 1425 Dowell Dr., 93003-7802 (805) 339-4400
Verdugo City (Los Angeles Co.), City of Glendale
Chamber of Commerce, (see La Crescenta)

Vernon (Los Angeles Co.), 4305 Santa Fe Ave., 90058 (213) 583-8811,
   Fax: (213) 581-7924
   Chamber of Commerce, 3801 Santa Fe Ave., 90058 (213) 583-3313,
       Fax: (213) 583-0704
   Library, 4305 Santa Fe Ave., P.O. Box 805, 90058-0805
       (213) 583-8811
   Library, 4504 S. Central Ave., 90011 (213) 234-9106,
       Fax: (213) 485-8155
   Police, 4305 S. Santa Fe Ave., 90058 (213) 587-5171
Victorville (San Bernardino Co.), 14343 Civic Dr., 92392 (619) 955-5000,
   Fax: (619) 245-7243
   Chamber of Commerce, 14174 Greentree Blvd., P.O. Box 997,
       92392 (619) 245-6506, Fax: (619) 245-6506
   Library, 15011 Circle Dr., 92392 (619) 245-4222
   Newspaper, *Daily Press,* 13891 Park Ave., P.O. Box 1389, 92393
       (619) 241-7744, Fax: (619) 241-7145
   Sheriff, 14177 McArt St., 92392 (619) 241-2911
View Park (Los Angeles Co.), Unincorporated
Villa Park (Orange Co.), 17855 Santiago Blvd, 92667 (714) 998-1500,
   Fax: (714) 998-1508
   Library, Civic Center, 17865 Santiago Blvd., 92667 (714) 998-0861,
       Fax: (714) 998-2752
   Sheriff, P.O. Box 449, Santa Ana, 92702 (714) 647-1851
Visalia (Tulare Co.), 707 W. Acequia, 93291 (209) 738-3318,
   Fax: (209) 730-7043
   Chamber of Commerce, 720 W. Mineral King, 93291
       (209) 734-5876, Fax: (209) 734-7479
   Library, 200 W. Oak St., 93291-4993 (209) 733-6954,
       Fax: (209) 730-2524
   Newspaper, *Visalia Times-Delta,* 330 N. West St., 93279
       (209) 734-5821, Fax: (209) 733-0826
   Police, 303 S. Johnson St., 93291 (209) 738-3257
Vista (San Diego Co.), 600 Eucalyptus Ave., 92084, P.O. Box 1988,
   92085-1998 (619) 726-1340, Fax: (619) 945-7859
   Chamber of Commerce, 201 Washington St., 92084 (619) 726-1122,
       Fax: (619) 726-8654
   Library, 325 S. Melrose Dr., 92083-6686 (619) 940-4360
   Newspaper, *Vista Press,* 425 W. Vista Way, 92083 (619) 724-7161,
       Fax: (619) 726-3064
   Sheriff, 325 S. Melrose Dr., #210, 92083 (619) 940-4551
Walnut (Los Angeles Co.), 21201 La Puente Rd., 91789, P.O. Box 682,
   91788-0682 (909) 595-7543, Fax: (909) 595-6095
   Chamber of Commerce, 398 S. Lemon Creek Dr., #1, 91789
       (909) 595-6138, (909) 595-1695
   Library, 21155 La Puente Rd., 91789 (909) 595-0757,
       Fax: (909) 595-7553
   Sheriff, 21695 E. Valley Blvd., 91789 (818) 913-1715,
       (909) 595-2264
Walnut Creek (Contra Costa Co.), 1666 N. Main St., P.O. Box 8039, 94596
   (510) 943-5800, Fax: (510) 943-5897
   Chamber of Commerce, 1501 N. Broadway, #110, 94596
       (510) 934-2007, Fax: (510) 934-2404

Walnut Creek Library, 1644 N. Broadway, 94596-4297
(510) 646-6773
Newspaper, *Contra Costa Times,* 2640 Shadelands Dr.,
P.O. Box 5088, 94598 (510) 935-2525,
Fax: (510) 943-8362
Police, 1666 N. Main St., 94596 (510) 943-5844
Walnut Park (Los Angeles Co.), Unincorporated
Walteria (Los Angeles Co.), City of Torrance
Library, 3815 W. 242nd St., 90505 (310) 375-8418
Warner Center (Los Angeles Co.), City of Los Angeles
Wasco (Kern Co.), 746 8th St., P.O. Box 159, 93280 (805) 758-3003,
Fax: (805) 758-5411
Chamber of Commerce, 104 "F" St., P.O. Box 783, 93280
(805) 758-2746
Library, (see Bakersfield)
Newspaper, *Wasco Tribune,* P.O. Box Y, 93280 (805) 758-3063,
Fax: (805) 746-5571
Sheriff, 748 "F" St., 93280 (805) 758-5166
Waterford (Stanislaus Co.), 320 "E" St., P.O. Box 199, 95386
(209) 874-2328, Fax: (209) 874-9656
Chamber of Commerce, P.O. Box 159, 95386 (209) 874-9525
Library, 324 "E" St., 95386 (209) 874-2191
Police, P.O. Box 199, 95386 (209) 874-2349
Watsonville (Santa Cruz Co.), 250 Main St., 95076, P.O. Box 50000,
95077-5000 (408) 728-6005, Fax: (408) 761-0736
Chamber of Commerce, 444 Main St., P.O. Box 1748, 95077
(408) 724-3900, Fax: (408) 728-5300
Library, 310 Union St., 95076-4695 (408) 728-6040,
Fax: (408) 761-0736
Newspaper, *Register-Pajaronian,* 1000 Main St., P.O. Box 5055,
95077 (408) 724-0611, Fax: (408) 722-8386
Police, P.O. Box 1199, 95077 (408) 728-6110
Watts (Los Angeles Co.), City of Los Angeles
Library, 1501 E. 103rd St., 90002 (213) 567-2297,
Fax: (213) 485-8153
Weaverville (Trinity Co.), 96093, Unincorporated
Chamber of Commerce, 317 Main St., P.O. Box 517, 96093
(916) 623-6101, Fax: (916) 623-3753
Library, 211 N. Main St., P.O. Box 1226, 96093 (916) 623-1373
Newspaper, *Trinity Journal,* P.O. Box 340, 96093 (916) 623-2055
Weed (Siskiyou Co.), 550 Main St., P.O. Box 470, 96094 (916) 938-5020,
Fax: (916) 938-5005
Chamber of Commerce, 34 Main St., P.O. Box 366, 96094
(916) 938-4624
Library, 780 S. Davis St., P.O. Box 470, 96094 (916) 938-4769
Newspaper, *Weed Press,* 266 Main St., 96094 (916) 938-4747
Police, 550 Main St., 96094 (916) 938-4337
West Covina (Los Angeles Co.), 1444 W. Garvey Ave., 91790,
P.O. Box 1440, 91793 (818) 814-8400,
Fax: (818) 814-8406
Chamber of Commerce, 811 S. Sunset Ave., 91790 (818) 338-8496,
Fax: (818) 960-0511

West Covina Library, 1601 W. Covina Pkwy., 91790
  (818) 962-3541, Fax: (818) 962-1507
  Newspaper, *San Gabriel Valley Daily Tribune*, P.O. Box 1259,
    Covina, 91722 (818) 962-8811, Fax: (818) 962-8849
  Police, 1444 W. Garvey Ave., 91791 (818) 814-8501
West Hills (Los Angeles Co.), City of Los Angeles.
  Chamber of Commerce, P.O. Box 4643, 91308 (818) 884-7289
West Hollywood (Los Angeles Co.), 8611 Santa Monica Blvd., 90069
  (310) 854-7400, Fax: (310) 652-9930
  Chamber of Commerce, 9000 Sunset Blvd., #700, 90069
    (310) 858-8000, Fax: (310) 858-8103
  Library, 715 N San Vicente Blvd., 90069 (310) 652-5340,
    Fax: (310) 652-2580
  Sheriff, 720 N. San Vicente Blvd., 90069 (310) 855-8850,
    (213) 650-4142
West Los Angeles (Los Angeles Co.), City of Los Angeles
West Sacramento (Yolo Co.), 2101 Stone Blvd., P.O. Box 966, 95691
  (916) 373-5800, Fax: (916) 372-8765
  Chamber of Commerce, 1414 Merkley Ave., #1, P.O. Box 404,
    95691 (916) 371-7042, (800) 350-7210,
    Fax: (916) 371-7210
  Newspaper, *News Ledger*, 816 W. Acres Rd., P.O. Box 463, 95691
    (916) 371-8030, Fax: (916) 371-8055
  Police, 305 W. Third St., 95605 (916) 372-2461
Westchester (Los Angeles Co.), City of Los Angeles
  Chamber of Commerce, 5930 W. Century Blvd., 90045-5425
    (310) 645-5151, Fax: (310) 645-0130
  Library, 8946 Sepulveda Eastway, 90045 (213) 645-6082,
    Fax: (213) 485-8148
Westlake (Los Angeles Co.), City of Los Angeles
Westlake Village (Los Angeles Co.), 4374 Park Terrace Dr., 91361
  (818) 706-1613, Fax: (818) 706-1391
  Chamber of Commerce, 31838 Village Center Rd., 91360
    (818) 991-3101, (805) 496-5630, Fax: (818) 991-1754
  Library, 4363 Park Terrace Dr., 91361 (818) 865-9230,
    Fax: (818) 865-0724
  Newspaper, *Acorn*, 960 Westlake Blvd., Suite 207, 91361
    (818) 706-0206, Fax: (805) 379-1864
  Sheriff, 27050 Agoura Rd., Calabasas, 91301 (310) 456-6652
Westminster (Orange Co.), 8200 Westminster Blvd., 92683 (714) 898-3311,
  Fax: (714) 373-4684
  Chamber of Commerce, 14491 Beach Blvd., 92683 (714) 898-9648,
    Fax: (714) 373-1499
  Vietnamese Chamber of Commerce, 10451 Bolsa Ave., #211, 92683
    (714) 839-2257
  Library, 8180 13th St., 92683 (714) 893-5057, Fax: (714) 898-0229
  Newspaper, *Westminister Herald*, P.O. Box 428, 92684
    (714) 893-4501, Fax: (714) 893-4502
  Police, 8200 Westminster Ave., 92683 (714) 898-3311
Westmorland (Imperial Co.), 355 S. Center St., P.O. Box 699, 92281
  (619) 344-3411, Fax: (619) 344-5307
  Police, P.O. Box 267, 92281 (619) 344-3411

Westwood (Los Angeles Co.), City of Los Angeles
Westwood (Lassen Co.), 96137, Unincorporated
    Chamber of Commerce, P.O. Box 1235, 96137 (916) 256-2456,
        Fax: (916) 256-3693
Westwood Village (Los Angeles Co.), City of Los Angeles
Wheatland (Yuba Co.), 313 Main St., P.O. Box 395, 95692 (916) 633-2761,
        Fax: (916) 633-9102
    Police, P.O. Box 306 (95692 (916) 633-2821
Whittier (Los Angeles Co.), 13230 E. Penn St., 90602 (310) 945-8200,
        Fax: (310) 698-3201
    Chamber of Commerce, 8158 Painter Ave., P.O. Box 4188, 90607
        (310) 698-9554, Fax: (310) 693-2700
    Library, 7344 S. Washington Ave., 90602-1778 (310) 693-3813,
        Fax: (310) 696-2911
    Library, 11405 E. Rosehedge Dr., 90606 (310) 692-7742
    Newspaper, *Whittier Daily News*, P.O. Box 581, Covina, 90608
        (310) 698-0955, Fax: (310) 698-0450
    Police, 7315 S. Painter Ave., 90602 (310) 945-8250
Wildomar (Riverside Co.), Unincorporated
    Chamber of Commerce, P.O. Box 885, 92595 (909) 678-5883,
        Fax: (909) 678-4995
Williams (Colusa Co.), 810 Williams St., P.O. Box 310, 95987
        (916) 473-5389, Fax: (916) 473-2445
    Police, 688 7th St., 95987 (916) 473-2661
Willits (Mendocino Co.), 111 E. Commercial St., 95490 (707) 459-4601,
        Fax: (707) 459-1562
    Chamber of Commerce, 239 S. Main St., 95490-3591
        (707) 459-7910, Fax: (707) 459-7914
    Library, 390 E. Commercial St., P.O. Box 9, 95490 (707) 459-5908,
        Fax: (707) 459-7819
    Newspaper, *The Willits News*, 1424 S. Main St., P.O. Box 628,
        95490 (707) 459-4643, Fax: (707) 459-4537
    Police, 125 E. Commercial St., #150, 95490 (707) 459-6122
Willow Creek (Humboldt Co.), 95573, Unincorporated
    Chamber of Commerce, Hwy. 299 & Hwy. 96, P.O. Box 704, 95573
        (916) 629-2693, Fax: (916) 629-2178
    Library, Hwy. 299 & Hwy. 96, 95573 (916) 629-2146
    Newspaper, *The Kourier*, P.O. Box 355, 95573 (916) 629-2811
Willowbrook (Los Angeles Co.), Unincorporated
    Library, 11838 S. Wilmington Ave., Los Angeles, 90059
        (310) 564-5698, Fax: (310) 564-7709
Willows (Glenn Co.), 201 N. Lassen St., P.O. Box 864, 95988 (916) 934-7041,
        Fax: (916) 934-2225
    Chamber of Commerce, P.O. Box 1277, 95988 (916) 934-2841,
        Fax: (916) 934-2844
    Area Chamber of Commerce, 410 W. Sycamore St., 95988
        (916) 934-8150, Fax: (916) 934-2844
    Library, 201 N. Lassen, 95988 (916) 934-5156, Fax: (916) 934-2225
    Newspaper, *The Willows Journal*, P.O. Box 731, 95988
        (916) 934-5411, Fax: (916) 934-6815
    Police, 201 N. Lassen St., 95988 (916) 934-3456

Wilmington (Los Angeles Co.), City of Los Angeles
    Chamber of Commerce, 100 E. Water St., 90744 (310) 834-8586,
        Fax: (310) 834-8887
    Library, 1300 N. Avelan Blvd., 90744 (310) 834-1082
Windsor (Sonoma Co.), 9291 Old Redwood Hwy., P.O. Box 100, 95492
    (707) 838-1000
    Chamber of Commerce, 8499 Redwood Hwy., #202, P.O. Box 367,
        95492 (707) 838-7285, Fax: (707) 838-2778
Windsor Hills (Los Angeles Co.), Unincorporated
Winnetka (Los Angeles Co.), City of Los Angeles
    Chamber of Commerce, P.O. Box 2051, 91306
Winters (Yolo Co.), 318 First St., 95694 (916) 795-4910, Fax: (916) 795-4935
    Chamber of Commerce, 7 E. Main St., P.O. Box 423, 95694
        (916) 795-2329
    Library, 201 First St., 95694 (916) 795-4955
    Newspaper, *Winters Express,* 312 Railroad Ave., P.O. Box 608,
        95694 (916) 795-4551
    Police, 318-A First St., 95694 (916) 795-4561
Winton (Merced Co.), 95388, Unincorporated
    Chamber of Commerce, 7114 W. Myrtle Ave., P.O. Box 581, 95388
        (209) 358-4053
    Library, P.O. Box 38, 95388 (209) 358-3651
    Newspaper, *Winton Times,* 6950 Gerard St., P.O. Box 65, 95388
        (209) 358-5311, Fax: (209) 358-7108
Woodlake (Tulare Co.), 350 N. Valencia, 93286 (209) 564-8055,
        Fax: (209) 564-8776
    Library, 400 W. Whitney Ave., 93286 (209) 564-8424
    Police, 350 N. Valencia Blvd., 93286 (209) 564-3346
Woodland (Yolo Co.), 300 First St., 95695 (916) 661-5808,
        Fax: (916) 661-5844
    Chamber of Commerce, 520 Main St., 95695 (916) 662-7327,
        Fax: (916) 662-4086
    Library, 250 First St., 95695-3411 (916) 661-5982,
        Fax: (916) 666-5408
    Newspaper, *The Daily Democrat,* 711 Main St., P.O. Box 730,
        95695 (916) 662-5421, Fax: (916) 662-1288
    Police, 520 Court St., 95695 (916) 661-5900
Woodland Hills (Los Angeles Co.), City of Los Angeles
    Chamber of Commerce, 21600 Oxnard St., #S-520, P.O. Box 1,
        91367 (818) 347-4737, Fax: (818) 347-3321
    Library, 22200 Ventura Blvd., 91364 (818) 887-0160,
        Fax: (818) 904-3287
Woodside (San Mateo Co.), 2955 Woodside Rd., P.O. Box 620005, 94062
        (415) 851-6790, Fax: (415) 851-2195
    Library, 3140 Woodside Rd., 94062 (415) 851-0147,
        Fax: (415) 851-2695
    Sheriff, 401 Marshall St., Redwood City, 94063 (415) 368-3911
Woodside Village (Los Angeles Co.), City of West Covina
Wrightwood (San Bernardino Co.), 92397, Unincorporated
    Chamber of Commerce, P.O. Box 416, 92397 (619) 249-4320
    Library, 6014 Park Dr., 92397 (619) 249-4577

Yolo (Yolo Co.), 95697, Unincorporated
    Library, 37750 Sacramento St., P.O. Box 156, 95697 (916) 662-2363
Yorba Linda (Orange Co.), 4845 Casa Loma Ave., P.O. Box 87014,
    92686-8714 (714) 961-7100, Fax: (714) 993-7530
    Chamber of Commerce, 17670 Yorba Linda Blvd., P.O. Box 238,
    92686 (714) 993-9537, Fax: (714) 993-7764
    Library, 18181 Imperial Hwy., 92686 (714) 777-2873
    Police, #1 Civic Center Cir., Brea, 92621 (714) 990-7911
Yountville (Napa Co.), 6550 Yount St., 94599 (707) 944-8851,
    Fax: (707) 944-9619
    Chamber of Commerce, P.O. Box 2064, 94599 (707) 944-0904
    Library, Town Hall Bldg., 6548 Yount St., 94599 (707) 944-1888
    Sheriff, 1125 Third St., Napa 94558 (707) 253-4451
Yreka (Siskiyou Co.), 701 4th St., 96097 (916) 842-4386,
    Fax: (916) 842-3628
    Chamber of Commerce, 117 W. Miner St., 96097 (916) 842-1649
    Library, 719 4th St., 96097 (916) 842-8175, Fax: (916) 842-7001
    Newspaper, *Siskiyou Daily News,* 309 S. Broadway, P.O. Box 129,
    96097 (916) 842-5777, Fax: (916) 842-6787
    Police, 412 W. Miner St., 96097 (916) 841-2300
Yuba City (Sutter Co.), 1201 Civic Center Blvd., 95993 (916) 741-4609,
    Fax: (916) 741-4694
    Library, 750 Forbes Ave., 95991 (916) 741-7137,
    Fax: (916) 671-6539
    Newspaper, *Appeal-Democrat,* 1530 Ellis Lake Dr., Marysville
    95901 (916) 741-2345, Fax: (916) 741-1195
    Police, 1545 Poole Blvd., 95993 (916) 741-4667
Yucaipa (San Bernardino Co.), 34272 Yucaipa Blvd., 92399 (909) 797-2489,
    Fax: (909) 790-9203
    Chamber of Commerce, 35144 Yucaipa Blvd., #3, P.O. Box 45,
    92399 (909) 790-1841
    Library, 12040 5th St., 92399 (909) 790-3146, Fax: (909) 790-3151
    Newspaper, *Yucaipa News-Mirror,* P.O. Box 760, 92399
    (714) 797-9101, Fax: (714) 797-0502
    Sheriff, 34282 Yucaipa Blvd., 92399 (909) 790-3105
Yucca Valley (San Bernardino Co.), 57090 Twentynine Palms Hwy., 92284
    (619) 369-7207, Fax: (619) 369-0626
    Chamber of Commerce, 56300 Twentynine Palms Hwy., #D, 92284
    (619) 365-6323, Fax: (619) 365-0763
    Library, 57098 29 Palms Hwy., 92284 (619) 228-5455,
    Fax: (619) 228-5459
    Newspaper, *Hi-Desert Star,* 56445 29 Palms Hwy., P.O. Box 880,
    92286 (619) 365-3315, Fax: (619) 365-2650

THIS SPACE FOR RENT
To have your ad printed here in future printings,
Call (818) THE-NEWS

County Records
A county-by-county listing of offices.

Alameda County (01 or 60), 1225 Fallon St., Rm. 109, Oakland, 94612
    Assessor (510) 272-3755
    District Attorney, Rm. 900 (510) 272-6222, Fax: (510) 271-5157
    Library, 2400 Stevenson Blvd., Fremont, 94538 (510) 745-1400
    Recorder (510) 272-6363
    Registrar (510) 272-6933, 272-6973
    Sheriff, Rm. 103 (510) 272-6878
        Eden Township, 15001 Foothill, San Leandro, 94578
            (510) 667-7721, Fax: (510) 667-3626
    Superior Court (510) 272-6070
        Civil (510) 272-6737
        Criminal (510) 272-6767
        Hayward Branch, 24405 Amador St., 94544
            (510) 670-6344
        Pleasanton Branch, 5672 Stoneridge Dr., 94588
            (510) 551-6886
    Municipal Courts
        Alameda Municipal Court, 2233 Shoreline Dr., 94501
            (510) 268-4209
            Civil (510) 268-7479
            Criminal (510) 268-7483
            Traffic (510) 268-7478
        Berkeley-Albany Municipal Court, 2120 Martin Luther
            King Jr. Way, Berkeley, 94704 (510) 644-6976
            Civil/Small Claims, 2000 Center St., Room 202,
                Berkeley, 97404 (510) 644-6423,
                644-6933
            Criminal (510) 644-6917, 644-6919
            Traffic (510) 644-6872

Alameda County Municipal Courts Continued
  Fremont-Newark-Union City Municipal Court, 39439
    Paseo Padre Pkwy., Fremont, 94538
    (510) 795-2329, Fax: (510) 795-2349
    Civil (510) 795-2345
    Criminal (510) 795-2300
    Traffic (510) 795-2390
  Livermore-Pleasanton-Dublin Municipal Court, 5672
    Stoneridge Dr., Pleasanton, 94588
    (510) 463-0594, Fax: (510) 460-0153
    Civil (510) 551-6993, 463-0307,
      Fax: (510) 847-0863
    Criminal (510) 463-7947
    Small Claims (510) 551-6993, 463-0307
    Traffic (510) 551-6991, 463-7941
  Oakland-Piedmont Municipal Court, 661 Washington St.,
    3rd Floor, Rm. 320, Oakland, 94607
    (510) 268-7600
    Civil (510) 268-7724, Fax: (510) 268-7807
    Criminal (510) 268-7700, Fax: (510) 268-7705
    Small Claims (510) 268-7737
    Traffic (510) 268-7680, Fax: (510) 268-7695
  San Leandro-Hayward Municipal Court, 24405 Amador
    St., Hayward, 94544 (510) 670-5661
    Civil (510) 670-5650, Fax: (510) 670-5522
    Criminal (510) 670-5640, Fax: (510) 670-5953
    Traffic/Animal (510) 670-5630

Alpine County (02), County Courthouse, Main St., Markleeville, 96120
  Assessor, P.O. Box 155 (916) 694-2283
  County Clerk, P.O. Box 158 (916) 694-2281
  District Attorney, P.O. Box 248 (916) 694-2971,
    Fax: (916) 694-2956
  Library, P.O. Box 187 (916) 694-2120
  Recorder, P.O. Box 217 (916) 694-2286
  Registrar, P.O. Box 158 (916) 6c94-2281
  Sheriff, P.O. Box 278 (916) 694-2231
    Bear Valley, P.O. Box 5103, 95223 (209) 753-2321
  Superior Court, P.O. Box 276 (916) 692-2113
  Municipal Court, P.O. Box 206 (916) 694-2113,
    Fax: (916) 694-2491

Amador County (03), 108 Court St., Jackson, 95642
  Assessor (209) 223-6351
  County Clerk (209) 223-6463
  District Attorney, 708 Court St. (209) 223-6444,
    Fax: (209) 223-6304
  Library, 530 Sutter St. (209) 223-6400
  Recorder (209) 223-6468
  Registrar (209) 223-6464, 223-6465
  Sheriff, 700 Court St. (209) 223-6500
  Superior Court (209) 223-6463
  Municipal Court, 42-A Summit St. (209) 223-6358,
    Fax: (209) 223-4286

Butte County (04), 25 County Center Dr., Oroville, 95965
    Assessor (916) 538-7721
        Unsecured Property (916) 538-7716
    County Clerk (916) 538-7551
    District Attorney (916) 538-7411, Fax: (916) 538-7071
    Library, 1820 Mitchell, 95966 (916) 538-7642
    Recorder (916) 538-7691
    Registrar (916) 538-7761
    Sheriff, 33 County Center Dr. (916) 538-7321, Fax: (916) 538-2099
        Chico Substation, 33 County Center Dr., Oroville, 95965
            (916) 891-2973
    Superior Court, #1 Court St. (916) 538-7611
    Municipal Courts
        North County Municipal District
            Chico Branch, 655 Oleander Ave., 95926
                (916) 895-6502 Civil/Small Claims,
                196 Memorial Way (916) 891-2702
                Criminal 891-2703
                Traffic 891-2716
            Paradise Branch, 747 Elliot Rd., Paradise, 95969
                (916) 872-6347
        South County Municipal District
            Gridley Branch, 239 Sycamore St.,
                P.O. Box 1100, 95948 (916) 846-5701
            Oroville Branch, 1931 Arlin Rhine Dr., 95965
                (916) 538-7747
                Civil/Small Claims (916) 538-7838
                Criminal (916) 538-7747
                Traffic (916) 538-7747
Calaveras County (05), Government Center, San Andreas, 95249
        (209) 754-6303
    Assessor (209) 754-6356
    County Clerk (209) 754-6310
    District Attorney, 891 Mountain Ranch Rd. (209) 754-6330,
        Fax: (209) 754-6645
    Library, 46 Main St., P.O. Box 338 (209) 754-6510
    Recorder (209) 754-6372
    Registrar (209) 754-6375, 754-6376
    Sheriff, 891 Mountain Ranch Rd. (209) 754-6500,
        Fax: (209) 754-6581
    Superior Court, 891 Mountain Ranch Rd. (209) 754-6311
    Municipal Court (209) 754-6336
Colusa County (06), County Courthouse, 546 Jay St., Colusa, 95932
        (916) 458-0500
    Assessor, 547 Market St., (916) 458-0450
    County Clerk (916) 458-0500
    District Attorney, 547 Market St. (916) 458-2193,
        Fax: (916) 458-7851
    Library, 738 Market St. (916) 458-0671
    Recorder (916) 458-0500
    Registrar (916) 458-0500

Colusa County Sheriff, 929 Bridge St. (916) 458-2115
    Stonyford Substation, 4th Service Compound, Stonyford
        (916) 963-3144
Superior Court, 547 Market St. (916) 458-0430,
    Fax: (916) 458-0510
Municipal Court, 532 Oak St. (916) 458-0600, Fax: (916) 458-2904
Contra Costa County (07), 725 Court St., Martinez, 94553 (510) 646-4030,
    Fax: (510) 646-4098
Assessor, 834 Court St. (510) 313-7600
County Clerk (510) 646-2950
    Fictitious Names (510) 646-2976
    Marriage Licenses (510) 646-2976
District Attorney (510) 646-4500, Fax: (510) 646-2116
Library, 1750 Oak Park Blvd., Pleasant Hill, 94523 (510) 646-6423
Recorder, 730 Las Juantas, P.O. Box 350 (510) 646-2360
Registrar, 524 Main St. (510) 646-4160
Sheriff, 651 Pine St., 7th Floor (510) 646-2402, 646-2441
Superior Court, Courthouse, P.O. Box 911 (510) 646-2356
    Civil (510) 646-2950
    Criminal (510) 646-2048
    Divorce (510) 646-2981
    Probate (510) 646-2977
Municipal Courts
    Bay Municipal Court, 100 37th St., Richmond, 94805
        (510) 374-3800
        Civil (510) 374-3138
        Criminal (510) 374-3156, Fax: (510) 374-3785
        Small Claims (510) 374-3137
        Traffic (510) 374-3173
    Delta Municipal Court, 45 Civic Ave., P.O. 431,
        Pittsburgh, 94565
        Civil (510) 427-8159
        Criminal (510) 427-8173
        Traffic (510) 427-8170
    Mt. Diablo Municipal Court, 1950 Parkside, Concord,
        94519 (510) 646-5430
        Civil, 2970 Willow Pass Rd., Concord, 94519
            (510) 646-5410
        Criminal (510) 646-5415
        Small Claims (510) 646-5410
        Traffic (510) 646-5404
    Walnut Creek Municipal Court, 640 Ygnacio Valley Rd.,
        P.O. Box 5128, 94596 (510) 646-6763
        Civil (510) 646-6579
        Criminal (510) 646-6572
        Small Claims (510) 646-6579
        Traffic (510) 646-6572

Del Norte County (08), 450 "H" St., County Courthouse, Crescent City, 95531
    Assessor, 482 "G" St., #4 (707) 464-7200
    County Clerk (707) 464-7205, Fax: (707) 465-1470
    District Attorney (707) 464-7210, Fax: (707) 465-6609
    Library, 190 Price Mall (707) 464-9793
    Recorder, 457 "F" St. (707) 464-7216
    Registrar (707) 464-7205
    Sheriff, 650 5th St. (707) 464-4191
    Superior Court (707) 464-7217
    Municipal Court, 680 5th St. (707) 464-7240
El Dorado County (09), County Courthouse, 495 Main St., Placerville, 95667 (916) 621-6426
    Assessor, Government Center, 360 Fair Lane (916) 621-5719
    County Clerk, 360 Fair Lane (916) 621-5496, Fax: (916) 621-2147
    District Attorney, 515 Main St. (916) 621-6472, Fax: (916) 621-1280
    Library, 345 Fair Lane (916) 621-5540
    Recorder, 360 Fair Lane (916) 621-5490
    Registrar, 2850 Fairlane Court (916) 621-7480
    Sheriff, 300 Fair Lane (916) 621-5655
    Superior Court (916) 621-6426, Fax: (916) 622-9774
        S. Lake Tahoe Branch, 1354 Johnson Blvd., Suite 2, 96150 (916) 573-3060, Fax: (916) 544-6532
    Municipal Courts
        Cameron Park Municipal Court, 3321 Cameron Park Dr., Cameron Park, 95682 (916) 621-5867, Fax: (916) 672-2413
        Placerville Municipal Court, 1319 Broadway, 95667 (916) 621-6447
            Civil/Criminal (916) 621-6453
            Small Claims (916) 621-7470
            Traffic, 2850 Fairlane Court (916) 621-7470
        South Lake Tahoe Municipal Court, 1357 Johnson Blvd., Suite 1, 96150 (916) 573-3044, Fax: (916) 542-9102
Fresno County (10), Courthouse, 1100 Van Ness, Fresno, 93721 (209) 488-1625
    Assessor, Hall of Records, 2281 Tulare St., 2nd Floor (209) 488-3514
    County Clerk, Rm. 401, P.O. Box 1628, 93717 (209) 488-3375
        Fictitious Names (209) 488-3003
        Marriage Licenses, 2221 Kern St. (209) 488-3003
    District Attorney, 2220 Tulare St., Suite 1000 (209) 488-3133, Fax: (209) 488-1867
    Library, 2420 Mariposa St. (209) 488-3185
    Recorder, 2281 Tulare St., P.O. Box 766 (209) 488-3514, 488-3476
        Grantee/Grantor (209) 488-3471
        Vital Statistics (209) 488-3476
    Registrar, 2221 Kern St. (209) 488-3246
    Sheriff, 2200 Fresno St. (209) 488-3939, Fax: (209) 488-1899

Fresno County Superior Court, 1100 Van Ness Ave., Rm. 103
(209) 488-1625
    Civil & Probate (209) 488-3352
    Criminal (209) 488-2740
    Family Law (209) 488-3057

Municipal Courts
Consolidated Fresno Municipal Courts, County Courthouse, 1100 Van Ness, Rm. 200 (209) 488-3452
    Civil (209) 488-3453
    Criminal (209) 488-3388
    Small Claims (209) 488-3450
    Traffic (209) 488-3379
Caruthers Municipal Court, 2215 W. Tahoe, 93609 (209) 864-3160
Coalinga Municipal Court, 166 W. Elm St., 93210 (209) 935-2017, 935-9131
Firebaugh Municipal Court, 1325 "O" St., 93622 (209) 659-2011, 659-2012, 652-2013
Fowler Municipal Court, 106 S. Sixth St., 93623, P.O. Box 400, 93625 (209) 834-3215
Kerman Municipal Court, 719 S. Madera Ave., 93630 (209) 846-7371
Kingsburg Municipal Court, 1380 Draper St., 93631 (209) 897-2241
Parlier Municipal Court, 580 Tulare St., 93648 (209) 646-2815
Reedley-Dunlap Municipal Court, 815 "G" St., Reedley, 93654 (209) 638-3114, 888-2480
Riverdale Municipal Court, 3563 Henson St., 93656 (209) 867-3448
Sanger Municipal Court, 619-D "N" St., 93657 (209) 875-7158, 875-6824
Selma Municipal Court, 2117 Selma St., 93662 (209) 896-2123

Glenn County (11), 526 W. Sycamore St., Willows, 95988
Assessor (916) 934-6402
(916) 934-6525, Fax: (916) 934-6529
County Clerk (916) 934-6407, Fax: (916) 934-6419

Glenn County Continued
District Attorney, 540 W. Sycamore St., P.O. Box 430
(916) 934-6525, Fax: (916) 934-6529
Library, 201 N. Lassen St. (916) 934-5156
Recorder (916) 934-6412
Registrar (916) 934-6414
Sheriff, 543 W. Oak St. (916) 934-6431
    Orland Substation, County Rd. 200, 95988 (916) 865-1122
Superior Court (916) 934-6407
Municipal Courts
    Orland Branch, County Rd. 200, P.O. Box 577, 95988 (916) 865-1101
    Willows Branch, 543 W. Oak St., 95988 (916) 934-6446

Humboldt County (12), Courthouse, 825 5th St., Eureka, 95501
    Assessor (707) 445-7276
    County Clerk, Rm. 235 (707) 445-7503, Fax: (707) 445-7328
    District Attorney (707) 445-7411, Fax: (707) 445-7416
    Library, 421 "I" St. (707) 445-7284
    Recorder, Rm. 108 (707) 445-7593
    Registrar, 3033 "H" St. (707) 445-7678
    Sheriff 826 Fourth St. (707) 445-7505
        Garberville Substation, 648 Locust St., 95440
            (707) 923-2761, Fax: (707) 924-2914
        Hoopa Substation, P.O. Box 1247, 95546 (916) 625-4231,
            Fax: (916) 625-4904
    Superior Court (707) 445-7627
    Municipal Court
        Eureka Municipal District, Rm. 236
            Civil/Small Claims (707) 445-7431
            Criminal (707) 445-7231
            Traffic (707) 445-7605
        Eel River Municipal District
            Fortuna Branch, 777 9th St., 95540
                (707) 725-5121
            Garberville Branch, 483 Conger St., 95542
                (707) 923-2141
        Klamath-Trinity Municipal District
            Hoopa Branch, Courthouse, P.O. Box 698,
                95546 (916) 625-4204
        North Humboldt Municipal District
            Arcata Branch, 4605 Valley West Blvd.,
                P.O. Box 4747, 95521 (707) 822-0342

Imperial County (13), Courthouse, 939 W. Main St., El Centro, 92243
    Assessor, 940 W. Main St. (619) 339-4244
    County Clerk (619) 339-4217, Fax: (619) 352-7876
    District Attorney (619) 339-4331, Fax: (619) 352-4472
    Library, 1647 W. Main St. (619) 353-3500
    Recorder, 940 Main St., Rm. 206, P.O. Box 1560, 92244
        (619) 339-4272
    Registrar (619) 339-4226
    Sheriff, 328 Applestell Rd. (619) 339-6311, 339-6301,
        Fax: (619) 339-6348
        Bombay Beach Substation (619) 452-2051
        Brawley Substation, 388 Main St., 92227 (619) 344-2615
        Niland Substation, 218 E. First St. (619) 359-0607
        Ocotillo Substation, 1157 Imperial Hwy., 92259
            (619) 452-2051
        Palo Verde Substation (619) 854-3469
        Salton City Substation (619) 394-4414
        Winterhaven Substation, 513 Second Ave. (619) 572-0229
    Superior Court (619) 339-4374

Imperial County Municipal Courts
    Brawley Dept., 383 Main St., 92227 (619) 344-0710
    Calexico Dept., 415 E. 4th St., 92231 (619) 357-3726
    El Centro Dept., 939 Main St., 92243 (619) 339-4256
    Winterhaven Dept., 2124 Winterhaven Dr., P.O. Box 1087, 92283 (619) 572-0354

Inyo County (14), County Courthouse, 168 N. Edwards St., Independence, 93526 (619) 878-0366
  Assessor, P.O. Box J (619) 878-0302
  County Clerk, P.O. Box F (619) 878-0218
    Fictitious Names (619) 878-0218
    Marriage Licenses (619) 878-0218
  District Attorney, P.O. Box D (619) 878-0282, Fax: (619) 878-2383
  Library, P.O. Box K (619) 878-0260
  Recorder, P.O. Drawer F (619) 878-0222
    Grantee/Grantor (619) 878-0222
    Vital Statistics (619) 878-0222
  Registrar, P.O. Box F (619) 878-0224
  Sheriff P.O. Box S (619) 878-0383
    Bishop Substation, 301 W. Line St., 93514 (619) 873-7887
    Death Valley Station (619) 786-2238
    Independence Station, 101 E. Market (619) 878-0383, 878-2441
    Lone Pine Station (619) 878-5606
    Olancha Station (619) 764-2313
    Tecopa Shoshone Station (619) 852-4313
  Superior Court, P.O. Box U (619) 878-0298
  Municipal Courts
    Bishop Branch, 301 W. Line St., 93514 (619) 872-4971
    Independence Branch, 168 N. Edwards St., P.O. Box 518, 93526 (619) 878-0319

Kern County (15), Kern County Civic Center, 1115 Truxtun Ave., Bakersfield, 93301 (805) 861-2371
  Assessor, 7th Floor (805) 861-2311, Fax: (805) 326-1251
  County Clerk (805) 861-2621, Fax: (805) 324-6348
  District Attorney, 1215 Truxtun Ave., 4th Floor (805) 861-2421
  Library, 701 Truxtun Ave. (805) 861-2130
  Recorder, Hall of Records, 1655 Chester Ave. (805) 861-2181, Fax: (805) 631-9443
  Registrar (805) 861-2625, Fax: (805) 861-2574
  Sheriff, 1350 Norris Rd., 93308 (805) 861-7500
    Boron Station, 26949 Cote St. (619) 762-6666
    Buttonwillow Station, Mirasol & First Sts. (805) 764-5613
    Delano Station, 1122 Jefferson St. (805) 725-8534
    Frazier Park Station, I-5 & Tejon (805) 245-3440
    Glennville Station, P.O. Box 522 (805) 536-8322
    Kern Valley Station, 7046 Lake Isabella (619) 379-2641
    Lamont Station, 12022 Main St. (805) 845-2211
    Mojave Station, 1771 Hwy. 58 (805) 824-2471, Fax: (805) 824-9256
    Ridgecrest Station, 124 E. Coso St. (619) 375-4888, Fax: (619) 375-9884

A PUBLIC RECORDS PRIMER AND INVESTIGATOR'S HANDBOOK

Kern County Sheriff Continued
Rosamond Station, 2873 Diamond (805) 256-2511
Taft Substation, 315 Lincoln St. (805) 763-2481
Tehachapi City Station, 129 E. "F" St. (805) 822-2244,
(805) 822-3333, Fax: (805) 822-8559
Wasco Station, 748 "F" St. (805) 758-5166,
Fax: (805) 758-5411
Superior Court (805) 861-2437, 328-6300, Fax: (805) 328-6357
Municipal Courts
North Kern Municipal Court District
Delano-McFarland Branch, 1122 Jefferson St.,
Delano, 93215 (805) 725-8797,
861-2740, Fax: (805) 721-1237
Shafter-Wasco Branch, 325 Central Valley Hwy.,
Shafter, 93263 (805)746-3312,
861-2557, Fax: (805) 746-0545
East Kern Municipal Court District
Kern River Branch, 7046 Lake Isabella Blvd.,
Suite 214, Lake Isabella, 93240
(619) 379-3635, Fax: (619) 379-4544
Mojave Branch, 1773 Hwy. 58, 93501
(805) 824-2436, Fax: (805) 824-4408
Ridgecrest Branch, 132 E. Coso St., 93555
(619) 375-1396, Fax: (619) 375-2112
South Kern Municipal Court District
Arvin-Lamont Branch, 12022 Main St.,
P.O. Box 738, Lamont, 93241
(805) 861-2271, Fax: (805) 845-9142
Taft-Maricopa Branch, Southwest Regional
Courts Bldg., 311 N. Lincoln St., Taft,
93268 (805) 763-2401,
Fax: (805) 763-2439
West Kern Municipal Court District, 1215 Truxtun Ave.,
Bakersfield, 93301 (805) 861-3061,
Fax: (805) 861-2005
Civil: (805) 861-2401, Ext. 2605
Criminal: (805) 861-2400, Ext. 2606
Small Claims: (805) 861-2401, Ext. 2483
Traffic: (805) 861-3068, Ext. 2604
Kings County (16), Government Center, 1400 W. Lacey Blvd., Hanford,
93230
Assessor (209) 582-3211, Ext. 2469
County Clerk (209) 582-3211, Ext. 2438, Fax: (209) 583-1854
District Attorney (209) 582-0326, Fax: (209) 584-4127
Library, 401 N. Douty St. (209) 582-0261
Recorder (209) 582-3211, Ext. 2469
Registrar (209) 582-3211 Ext. 2439
Sheriff, P.O. Box 986, 93232 (209) 582-3211 Ext. 2795,
Fax: (209) 583-1553
Avenal Substation, 501 E. Kings St., P.O. Box 158, 93204
(209) 386-5361, Fax: (209) 583-1553
Superior Court (209) 582-3211, Ext. 2527, Fax: (209) 584-0319

Kings County Municipal Court
    Avenal Municipal Court, 501 E. Kings St., 93204
    (209) 386-5224, 386-5225
    Corcoran Municipal Court, 1000 Chittenden Ave., 93212
    (209) 992-5192, 992-5193
    Hanford Municipal Court, 1400 W. Lacey Blvd., 93230
    Civil: (209) 582-3211, Ext. 4202
    Criminal: (209) 582-3211, Ext. 4201
    Small Claims: (209) 582-3211, Ext. 4202
    Traffic (209) 582-3211, Ext. 2781
    Lemoore Municipal Court, 449 "C" St., P.O. Box 549, 93245 (209) 924-7757

Lake County (17), County Courthouse, 255 N. Forbes St., Lakeport, 95453
    Assessor (707) 263-2302
    County Clerk (707) 263-2374
    District Attorney (707) 263-2551, Fax: (707) 263-2328
    Library, 1425 N. High St. (707) 263-8816
    Recorder (707) 263-2293
    Registrar (707) 263-2372
    Sheriff, 375 Third St. (707) 263-2330, 263-2331, Fax: (707) 263-8927
    South Substation, Civic Center, 7000 Hwy. 53, Clearlake, 95422 (707) 994-6433, Fax: (707) 994-3541
    Superior Court (707) 263-2231, Fax: (707) 262-1327
    Municipal Courts
    North Lake Municipal Court, 255 N. Forbes St., Lakeport, 95453 (707) 263-2283, Fax: (707) 262-1327
    South Lake Municipal Court, 7000 Hwy. 53, P.O. Box 670, Clearlake, 95422 (707) 994-6598, 994-1625

Lassen County (18), Courthouse, 220 S. Lassen, Susanville, 96130
    Assessor (916) 251-8241
    County Clerk (916) 251-8124
    District Attorney, 220 S. Lassen (916) 251-8283, Fax: (916) 257-9089
    Library (916) 251-8127, 251-8276
    Recorder (916) 251-8234
    Registrar (916) 251-8217
    Sheriff, 200 S. Lassen (916) 251-8222, Fax: (916) 257-9363
    Superior Court (916) 251-8228, Fax: (916) 257-3480
    Municipal Court, 200 S. Lassen Civil/Small Claims (916) 251-8205, Fax: (916) 251-9061
    Criminal (916) 251-8206

Los Angeles County (19 or 70)
    Assessor, Map Book Library, Hall of Administration, 500 W. Temple St., Room 205, L.A. 90012 (213) 974-3211
    Regional Offices:
    Chatsworth, 9121 Oakdale Ave., Suite 200, 91311 (818) 701-4311
    Culver City, 4909 Overland Ave., 90230 (310) 202-3011
    Lancaster, 251 East Ave., K-6, 93535 (805) 940-6700

Los County Assessor Continued
    Lomita, 24330 Narbonne Ave., 90717 (310) 534-6100
    Long Beach, 5898 Cherry Ave., 90805 (310) 984-5111
    Newhall, 25129 The Old Rd., 91321 (805) 254-9550
    Norwalk, 12440 Firestone Blvd., #2000, 91650
        (310) 406-7525
    Pasadena, 988 S. Fair Oaks Ave., 91105 (818) 441-7100
    Santa Monica, 1444 9th St., 90401 (310) 458-5134
    South El Monte, 1441 Santa Anita Ave., 91733
        (818) 350-4695
    Van Nuys, 6640 Van Nuys Blvd., 91405 (818) 901-3404
    West Covina, 2934 E. Garvey Ave. S., #290, 91791
        (818) 859-6400
County Clerk, 12400 E. Imperial Hwy., Norwalk, 90650
    (310) 462-2636, 462-2716
    Fictitious Names Filings (310) 462-2177
    Marriage Licenses (310) 462-2195, 462-2137
    For outlying areas, see Superior Court Branches
District Attorney, 18-000 Criminal Courts Bldg., Rm. 18-709, 210 W. Temple St., L.A., 90012 (213) 974-3501
Library, 301 W. First St., L.A., 90012 (213) 629-3531, Ext. 323
Recorder, 12400 E. Imperial Hwy., Norwalk, 90650 (310) 462-2074
    Birth, Death & Marriage Records (24-hr. taped
        message) (310) 462-2137
    Public Information Counter (310) 462-2137, 462-2103
Registrar, 5557 Ferguson Dr., L.A., 90022 (310) 462-2748
    Campaign Reporting (310) 762-2339
    Elections (310) 462-2748, 462-2696
    News Media Representative (310) 462-2645
Sheriff, 4700 Ramona Blvd., Monterey Park, 91754-2169
    (213) 526-5430
    Booking Information (213) 780-2600
    Central Investigations Bureau (213) 974-6371
    Central Jail (213) 974-4911
    Detective Division (213) 526-5165, (310) 946-7883
    Headquarters Bureau (213) 526-5550
    Homicide Bureau (213) 890-5512
    Information Bureau (213) 526-5541
    Missing Persons (213) 890-5529
    Narcotics Bureau (310) 946-7101
    Vice Bureau (310) 946-7067
  Sheriff's Stations:
    Altadena, 780 E. Altadena Dr., 91002 (818) 798-1131
    Antelope Valley, 1010 W. Ave. "J", Lancaster, 93534
        (805) 948-8466
    Avalon, 215 Sumner Ave., P.O. Box 1551, 90704
        (310) 510-0174, Fax: (310) 510-2994
    Isthmus Facility, Two Harbors, Catalina Island
        (310) 510-0872
    Carson, 21356 S. Avalon Blvd., 90745 (310) 830-1123

Los Angeles County Sheriff Continued
Century, 11703 S. Alameda St., Lynwood, 90262
(213) 567-8121
91214 (818) 248-3464
East Los Angeles, 5019 E. Third St., L.A., 90022
(213) 264-4151
Industry, 150 N. Hudson Ave., City of Industry, 91744
(818) 330-3322, (909) 595-3649
Lakewood, 5130 N. Clark Ave., 90712 (310) 866-9061
Lennox, 4331 Lennox Blvd., Inglewood, 90304
(310) 671-7531
Lomita, 26123 S. Narbonne Ave., 90717 (310) 539-1661
Ext. 388
Lost Hills, 27050 Agoura Rd., Calabasas, 91301
(818) 878-1808
Marina Del Rey, Harbor Patrol, 13851 Fiji Way, 90292
(310) 823-7762
Norwalk, 12335 Civic Center Dr., 90650 (310) 863-8711
Palmdale, 1020 E. Palmdale Blvd., 93550 (805) 267-4308
Pico Rivera, 6631 Passons Blvd., 90660 (310) 949-2421
San Dimas, 122 N. San Dimas Ave., 91773
(818) 332-1184, (909) 599-1261
Santa Clarita Valley, 23470 W. Magic Mountain Pkwy.,
Valencia, 91355 (805) 255-1121,
(818) 984-0630
Gorman Substation, 49819 Gorman Post Rd., 93534
(805) 248-6093
Pyramid Lake Substation, Interstate 5, Hungry Valley
Offramp (805) 257-4362
Temple City, 8838 E. Las Tunas Dr., 91780
(818) 285-7171
Walnut, 21695 Valley Blvd., 91789 (818) 913-1715,
(909) 595-2264
West Hollywood, 720 N. San Vicente Blvd., L.A., 90069
(310) 855-8850, (213) 650-4142

Los Angeles County Continued
   Superior Court
      Central District
      Criminal Index, 210 W. Temple St., L.A., Rm. M-6, 90012
         (213) 974-5261, 974-5276
      Civil Index, 111 N. Hill St., Rm. 220, L.A., 90012
         (213) 974-5411, 974-5227
      Probate Index, 111 N. Hill St., Rm. 258, L.A., 90012
         (213) 974-5171

Los Angeles County civil cases with file numbers beginning with the letters "C" (Civil), "D" (Domestic, divorce, dissolution) or "P" (Probate) are located at 111 N. Hill Street, Los Angeles. If the "C","D" or "P" is preceded by two additional letters, the file is located at a branch court. **Criminal** cases for Central L.A. filings are located at the **Criminal Courts Building, 210 W. Temple St., L.A. 90012 (213) 974-5261**. Outlying criminal cases are located at the branch courts. All Central civil files filed more than five years ago are located at the **County Records Center, 222 N. Hill St., Room B212, L.A. 90012 (213) 974-1378**. Many branch files are also located there.

Newer files have a newer filing system that uses a two-letter prefix. The first letter designates the branch court (see individual branch listings). The second letter designates the type of file. Use the legend on the next page to determine the type of file. To be safe, call first.

Superior Court Case Codes:

A = Felony
B = NDA
C = Civil
D = Domestic (Divorce)
E = LPS
F = Paternity
G = Conciliation Court
H = H.C.
J = Delinquency
K = Dependency
L = RESL

M = Sanity
N = Abandonment
P = Probate
R = Criminal Appeal
S = Special Procedure
T = Adoption
V = Civil Appeal
W = Mental Health H.C.
X = Appel. H.C.
Y = D.A. Paternity

Superior Court Branch Courts

North Central (New code: "E", Old code: "NC" civil cases followed by "B"), 300 E. Olive Ave., Rm. 201, Burbank, 91502 (818) 500-3482

North Central (New code: "E", Old code: "NC" civil cases followed by "G"), 600 E. Broadway, Rm. 273, Glendale, 91205 (818) 500-3551

North (New Code: "M", Old code: "NO" civil cases), 1040 W. "J" Ave., Rm. 122, Lancaster, 93534 (805) 945-6476, 945-6451

Northeast (New code: "G", Old code: "NE" civil cases), 300 E. Walnut, Rm. 102, Pasadena, 91101 (818) 356-5691

North Valley (New code: "P:, Old code: "NV" civil cases), 900 Third St., Rm. 135, San Fernando, 91340 (818) 898-2651, 898-2664

Northwest (New code: "L", Old code: "NW" civil cases), 6230 Sylmar Ave., Rm. 107, Van Nuys, 91401 (818) 374-2170, 374-2208

South (New code: "N", Old code: "SO" civil cases), 415 W. Ocean, Rm. 401, Long Beach, 90802 (310) 491-5923, 491-5924

South Central (New code: "T", Old code: "SC" civil cases), 200 W. Compton Ave., Rm. 902, Compton, 90220 (310 603-7832, 603-7812

Southeast (New code: "V", Old code: "SE" civil cases), 12720 Norwalk Blvd., Rm. 101, Norwalk, 90650 (310) 807-7256, 807-7261

Southwest (New code: "Y", Old code: "SW" civil cases), 825 Maple Ave., Rm. 100, Torrance, 90503 (310) 222-8817, 222-8801, 222-8808

West (New code: "S", Old code: "WE" civil cases), 1725 Main, Rm. 101, Santa Monica, 90401 (310) 458-5283, 458-5285

East (New code: "K", Old code: "EA" civil cases), 400 Civic Center Dr., Rm. 101, Pomona, 91766 (909) 620-3002, 620-3023

County Records Center, 222 N. Hill St., Rm. 212, L.A., 90012 (213) 974-1378

Los Angeles County Municipal Courts:
Alhambra, 150 W. Commonwealth Ave., 91801
Civil (818) 308-5521
Criminal (818) 308-5525
Small Claims (818) 308-5523
Antelope, 1040 W. "J" Ave., Lancaster, 93534,
Fax: (805) 949-8628
Civil (805) 945-6351
Criminal (805) 945-6355
Small Claims (805) 945-6353
Bellflower, (see Los Cerritos)
Beverly Hills, 9355 Burton Way, 90210-3669
Civil/Small Claims (310) 288-1227
Criminal (310) 288-1236, 288-1352
Traffic (310) 288-1233, 288-1243
Burbank, 300 E. Olive Ave., 91502
Civil/Small Claims (310) 288-1227
Criminal (818) 500-3466
Catalina, 215 Sumner Ave., P.O. Box 677, Avalon, 90704-0677 (310) 510-0026, 510-1128
Citrus, 1427 West Covina Pkwy., West Covina, 91790
Civil (818) 813-3270
Criminal (818) 813-3239
Traffic (818) 813-3204
Compton, 200 W. Compton Blvd., 90220
Civil/Small Claims (310) 603-3480, 603-7172
Criminal (310) 603-7682
Traffic (310) 603-7698
Culver, 4130 Overland Ave., Culver City, 90230
Civil (310) 836-1664
Criminal (310) 836-1412
Small Claims (310) 836-5056
Traffic (310) 836-5062
Fax: (310) 836-8345
Downey, 7500 E. Imperial Hwy., 90242
Civil/Small Claims (818) 500-3461
Criminal (310) 803-7051
Traffic (310) 803-7046, 803-7048
East Los Angeles, 214 S. Fetterly Ave., L.A., 90022
Civil/Small Claims (213) 780-2017
Criminal (213) 780-2025
Traffic (213) 780-2086
El Monte, (see Rio Hondo)
Glendale, 600 E. Broadway, 91206
Civil (818) 500-3539
Criminal (818) 500-3541
Small Claims (818) 500-3538
Traffic (818) 500-3546
Hermosa Beach, (see South Bay)
Huntington Park, (see San Antonio)

Los Angeles County Municipal Courts Continued
Inglewood, One Regent St., 90301
Civil/Small Claims (310) 419-5127
Criminal (310) 419-5120
Traffic (310) 419-5132, 419-5309
Lancaster, (see Antelope)
Long Beach, 415 W. Ocean Blvd., 90802
Civil (310) 491-6234
Criminal (310) 491-6226
Small Claims (310) 491-6238
Traffic (310) 491-6211
Los Angeles Central Civil, 110 N. Grand Ave., L.A., 90012 (213) 974-6120, 974-6140, 974-6271
Small Claims (213) 974-6131, 974-6305
Los Angeles Central Criminal, 5th Floor, 210 W. Temple St., L.A., 90012 (213) 974-6141
Central Arraignment, 429 Bauchet St., Rm. 210, L.A., 90012 (213) 974-6151
Hollywood Branch, 5925 Hollywood Blvd, Rm. 102, 90028
Criminal (213) 856-5747
Metropolitan Branch, 1945 S. Hill St., L.A., 90007
Traffic (213) 744-4022, 744-4036
Baldwin Hills Ticket Payment Office, 3650 Martin Luther King Jr. Blvd., Suite 183C, L.A., 90008 (213) 298-3657
San Pedro Branch, 505 S. Centre Ave., 90731
Civil (310) 519-6015
Criminal (310) 519-6018
Small Claims (310) 519-6014
Traffic (310) 519-6215
Valley Division, 14400 Erwin Street Mall, Van Nuys, 91401
Civil 374-3060
Criminal (818) 374-2628
Traffic (818) 374-2630
San Fernando Branch, 900 Third St., 91340
Criminal (818) 898-2407
Small Claims, 911 First St. (818) 898-2425
Traffic (818) 898-2405
West Valley Ticket Payment Office, 21201 Victory Blvd., Suite 120, Canoga Park, 91303
(818) 887-4351
West Los Angeles Branch, 1633 Purdue Ave., L.A., 90025
Criminal (310) 312-6547
Robertson Branch, 3000 Robertson Blvd., L.A., 90034 (310) 558-7725
Small Claims (310) 558-7724
Traffic (310) 558-7719

Los Angeles County Municipal Courts Continued
  Los Cerritos, 10025 E. Flower St., Bellflower, 90706
    Civil (310) 804-8008
    Criminal (310) 804-8015
    Small Claims (310) 804-8008
    Traffic (310) 804-8023
  Malibu, 23525 Civic Center Way, 90265
    Civil (310) 317-1312
    Criminal (310) 317-1331
    Small Claims (310) 317-1309
  Calabasas, 5030 N. Parkway Calabasas, 91302
    Small Claims (818) 222-1800
    Traffic (818) 222-1148
  Manhattan Beach, (see South Bay)
  Newhall, 23747 W. Valencia Blvd., Valencia, 91355 Civil
    (805) 253-7312
    Criminal (805) 253-7308
    Small Claims (805) 253-7309
    Traffic (805) 253-7312
  North Hollywood, (see Los Angeles-Valley)
  Pasadena, 200 N. Garfield Ave., 91101
    Civil/Small Claims (818) 356-5448
    Criminal (818) 356-5254
  Pomona, 350 W. Mission Blvd., 91766
    Civil/Small Claims (909) 620-3213
    Criminal (909) 620-3219
    Traffic (909) 620-3207
  Redondo Beach, (see South Bay)
  Rio Hondo, 11234 E. Valley Blvd., El Monte, 91731 Civil
    (818) 575-4116
    Criminal (818) 575-4121
    Small Claims (818) 575-4125
    Traffic (818) 575-4112
  San Antonio, (see Southeast)
  Santa Anita, 300 W. Maple Ave., Monrovia, 91016-3390
    Civil/Small Claims (818) 301-4050
    Criminal (818) 301-4051
    Traffic (818) 301-4069
  Santa Monica, 1725 Main St., 90401
    Civil (310) 260-3706
    Criminal (310) 260-3517
    Small Claims (310) 260-3705
    Traffic (310) 260-3505
  Sherman Oaks, (see Los Angeles-Valley)
  South Bay, 825 Maple Ave., Torrance, 90503
    (310) 222-6500, 222-6501
  Southeast
    Huntington Park, 6548 Miles Ave., 90255
      Civil (213) 586-6365
      Criminal (213) 586-6363
      Small Claims (213) 586-6359
      Traffic (213) 586-6355

Los Angeles County Municipal Courts Continued
  South Gate, 8640 California Ave., 90280
    Civil/Small Claims (213) 563-4018
    Criminal (213) 563-4012
    Traffic (213) 563-4012
  Tarzana, (see Los Angeles-Valley)
  Torrance, (see South Bay)
  Van Nuys, (see Los Angeles-Valley)
  West Covina, (see Citrus)
  West Los Angeles, (see Los Angeles-West L.A.)
  Whittier, 7339 S. Painter Ave., 90602
    Civil/Small Claims (310) 907-3127
    Criminal (310) 907-3113
    Traffic (310) 907-3134
  Woodland Hills, (see Los Angeles-Valley)
Madera County (20), County Government Center, 209 W. Yosemite Ave., Madera, 93637 (209) 675-7703
  Assessor (209) 675-7710
  County Clerk (209) 675-7721, Fax: (209) 673-3302
  District Attorney (209) 675-7726, Fax: (209) 673-0430
  Library, 121 N. "G" St. (209) 675-7871
  Recorder (209) 675-7724
  Registrar (209) 675-7720
  Sheriff, 216 W. Sixth St. (209) 675-7769
  Superior Court (209) 675-7907, 675-7721, Fax: (209) 675-0701
  Municipal Courts
    Borden Municipal Court, 14241 Road 28, Madera, 93638
      (209) 675-7786, Fax: (209) 673-0542
    Chowchilla Municipal Court, 141 S. Second St., 93610
      (209) 665-4861, Fax: (209) 665-3185
    Madera Municipal Court, 209 W. Yosemite Ave., 93637
      (209) 675-7734, Fax: (209) 675-7618
    Sierra Municipal Court, 40601 Rd., #274, Bass Lake, 93604 (209) 642-3235, Fax: (209) 642-3445
Marin County (21), Hall of Justice, 3501 Civic Center Dr., 94903, P.O. Box E, San Rafael, 94913
  Assessor, Rm. 202 (415) 499-7194
  County Clerk, Rm. 151 (415) 499-6416, Fax: (415) 499-7184
  District Attorney, Rm. 183 (415) 499-6450, Fax: (415) 499-3719
  Library, Civic Center Administration Bldg., (415) 499-6058
  Recorder, Rm. 290
    Grantee-Grantor (415) 499-6092, 499-6093
    Vital Statistics (415) 499-6094
  Registrar, Rm. 152 (415) 499-6456
  Sheriff, Rm. 167 (415) 499-7282
  Superior Court (415) 499-6407
  Municipal Court, Rm. 191 (415) 499-6244
Mariposa County (22), 5088 Bullion St., P.O. Box 247, Mariposa, 95338
  Assessor, Hall of Records, P.O. Box 35 (209) 966-2332
  County Clerk (209) 966-2007, Fax: (209) 742-6860
  District Attorney, P.O. Box 748 (209) 966-3626,
    Fax: (209) 966-5681

Mariposa County Continued
    Library, P.O. Box 106 (209) 966-2140
    Recorder, P.O. Box 156 (209) 966-5719
    Registrar (209) 966-2005
    Sheriff, P.O. Box 276 (209) 966-3615
        Boating Substation, La Grange, 95311 (209) 852-2532
    Superior Court (209) 966-2005, Fax: (209) 742-6860
    Municipal Court, P.O. Box 316 (209) 966-5711,
        Fax: (209) 742-6860

Mendocino County (23), 100 State and Perkins Sts., Ukiah, 95482
    Assessor (707) 463-4311
    County Clerk, P.O. Box 148 (707) 463-4370, Fax: (707) 463-4257
    District Attorney, P.O. Box 1000 (707) 463-4211,
        Fax: (707) 463-4687
    Library, 105 N. Main St. (707) 463-4493
    Recorder, P.O. Box 148
        Grantee/Grantor (707) 463-4376
        Vital Statistics (707) 463-4253
    Registrar, P.O. Box 148 (707) 463-4371
    Sheriff, 951 Low Gap Rd., (707) 463-4411, 463-4517
        Willits Station, 125 E. Commercial, #200, 95490
            (707) 459-6111, Fax: (707) 459-7840
        Ft. Bragg Station, 700 S. Franklin, #B, 95437
            (707) 964-6308, Fax: (707) 961-2662
    Superior Court (707) 463-4482, 462-4481, 463-4664, 462-4571,
        Fax: (707) 468-3459
    Municipal Courts
        Anderson Municipal Court, Veteran Bldg., Hwy. 128,
            P.O. Box 336, Boonville, 94515 (707) 895-3329
        Arena Municipal Court, 24000 S. Hwy. One (VFW Hall),
            P.O. Box 153, Point Arena, 95468
            (707) 882-2116
        Long Valley Municipal Court, P.O. Box 157, Leggett,
            95585 (707) 925-6460, Fax: (707) 925-6225
        Round Valley Municipal Court, 76270 Grange St.,
            P.O. Box 25, Covelo, 95428 (707) 983-6446
        Ten Mile River Municipal Court, 700 S. Franklin St., Fort
            Bragg, 95437 (707) 964-3192
        Ukiah Municipal Court, Courthouse, Rm. 210,
            P.O. Box 337, 95482 (707) 463-4486,
            Fax: (707) 463-4655
        Willits Municipal Court, 125 E. Commercial St., Rm. 100,
            95490 (707) 459-5554, 459-7800,
            Fax: (707) 459-7818

Merced County (24), County Courts Building, 2222 "M" St., Merced, 95340
    Assessor (209) 385-7631
    County Clerk (209) 385-7501 Fax: (209) 725-3535
    District Attorney, 21st and "M" Sts.,
        (209) 385-7381,Fax: (209) 385-7473
    Library, 2100 "O" St. (209) 385-7643
    Recorder (209) 385-7627
    Registrar (209) 385-7541

Merced County Continued
    Sheriff, 700 W. 22nd St., Rm. 1 (209) 385-7360,
        Fax: (209) 385-7659
        Los Banos Station, 445 "I" St., 93635 (209) 385-7340
    Superior Court, 627 W. 21st. St. (209) 385-7531
    Municipal Courts
        Los Banos Branch, 445 "I" St., 93635 (209) 826-6500,
            Fax: (209) 826-8108
        Merced Branch, 670 W. 22nd St., 95340
            Civil (209) 385-7337
            Criminal (209) 385-7335
            Small Claims (209) 385-7337
            Traffic (209) 385-7561 445 "I" St., Los Banos,
                93635 (209) 826-6500
Modoc County (25), County Courthouse, 204 Court St., P.O. Box 131, Alturas, 96101
    Assessor (916) 233-6218
    County Clerk, Rm. 204, P.O. Box 131 (916) 233-6200,
        Fax: (916) 233-2434
    District Attorney, P.O. Box 1171 (916) 233-6212
    Library, 212 W. Third St. (916) 233-6326
    Recorder, Rm. 107 (916) 233-6205, 233-6204
    Registrar, P.O. Box 131 (916) 233-6200
    Sheriff, 102 Court St., P.O. Drawer 460 (916) 233-4416,
        Fax: (916) 233-4971
    Superior Court (916) 233-6222
    Municipal Court, 205 South East St. (916) 233-6517,
        Fax: (916) 233-6500
Mono County (26), County Courthouse, P.O. Box 537, Bridgeport, 93517
    Assessor (619) 932-5204, 932-5207
    County Clerk (619) 932-5241, Fax: (619) 932-7520
    District Attorney, P.O. Box 617 (619) 932-5223,
        Fax: (619) 932-5283
    Library, P.O. Box 398 (619) 932-7482
    Recorder (619) 932-5240
    Registrar (619) 932-5241
    Sheriff, 100 Bryant St., P.O. Box 616, (619) 932-5279,
        Fax: (619) 932-7435
    Superior Court (619) 932-5239
    Municipal Courts
        Bridgeport Branch, P.O. Box 494, 93517 (619) 932-5203
        Mammoth Lakes Branch, P.O. Box 1037, 93546
            (619) 924-5444
Monterey County (27), County Courthouse, Executive Office, 240 Church St., P.O. Box 414, Salinas, 93902
    Assessor, 2nd Floor (408) 755-5035
    County Clerk, P.O. Box 1819 (408) 755-5030, Fax: (408) 757-5792
    District Attorney, Rm. 101 (408) 755-5070, Fax: (408) 755-5068
    Library, 550 Harcourt St., Seaside, 93955 (408) 899-2055
    Recorder, P.O. Box 29 (408) 755-5041
    Registrar, 370 S. Main St., P.O. Box 1848 (408) 755-5085

Monterey County Continued
  Sheriff, 1414 Natividad Rd., 93906 (408) 755-3702,
    Fax: (408) 755-8828
    King City Station, 250 Franciscan Way, 93930
      (408) 385-8312, Fax: (408) 385-8376
    Monterey Station, 1200 Aguajito Rd., 93940
      (408) 647-7702, Fax: (408) 647-7888
  Superior Court (408) 755-5030, 755-5031
    Monterey Branch, 1200 Aquajito Rd., Monterey, 93940
      (408) 647-7730, 647-7731
    Salinas Branch, 240 Church St., Rm. 320, 93902
      (408) 755-5060, Fax: (408) 757-5792
  Municipal Courts
    King City Branch, 250 Franciscan Way, P.O. Box 647,
      93930 (408) 385-8335, Fax: (408) 385-8383
    Monterey Branch, 1200 Aquajito Rd., P.O. Box 751,
      93940 (408) 647-7750
      Civil (408) 647-7730
      Criminal (408) 647-7752
      Small Claims (408) 647-7751
      Traffic (408) 647-7753
    Salinas Branch, P.O. Box 1409, 93902
      Criminal (408) 755-5052
      Small Claims (408) 755-5051
      Traffic (408) 755-5053
      Fax: (408) 755-5483
Napa County (28), County Courthouse, 825 Brown St., Napa, 94559
  Assessor, 1127 First St., Rm. 128, 94558 (707) 253-4466
  County Clerk, P.O. Box 880 (707) 253-4481
  District Attorney, 931 Parkway Mall, P.O. Box 720
    (707) 253-4211, Fax: (707) 253-4041
  Library, 1150 Division St. (707) 253-4241
  Recorder, 900 Combs St., Rm. 116, P.O. Box 298 (707) 253-4246
  Registrar, 900 Combs St., Rm. 256, P.O. Box 5779 (707) 253-4321
  Sheriff, 1125 Third St., First Floor, (707) 253-4501, Fax: (707) 253-
    American Canyon Station, 2185 Elliot Dr., 94589
      (707) 648-0171
    Santalina Station, 1199 Big Tree Rd., 94573
      (707) 963-5944
    Yountville Station, 6550 Yount St. (707) 944-9228
  Superior Court (707) 253-4366, Fax: (707) 253-4229
  Municipal Court, 825 Brown St. (707) 253-4573,
    Fax: (707) 253-4229
Nevada County (29), 201 Church St., Nevada City, 95959
  Assessor, 950 Maidu Ave., 95959-6100, P.O. Box 6100
    (916) 265-1232
  County Clerk, P.O. Box 6126, (916) 265-1293.
    Fax: (916) 265-1715
  District Attorney, 201 Church St., Courthouse Annex
    (916) 265-1301, Fax: (916) 265-7217
  Library, 207 Mill St., Grass Valley, 95945 (916) 273-4117

Nevada County Continued
  Recorder, 950 Maidu Ave., P.O. Box 6100, 95959-6100
    (916) 265-1221, 265-1702
  Registrar (916) 265-1298
  Sheriff, Administrative Center, 950 Maidu Ave., P.O. Box 6100,
    95959-6100 (916) 265-1471, Fax: (916) 265-1709
  Superior Court (916) 265-1475
    Personnel (916) 265-1225
  Municipal Courts
    Nevada-City Division, Courthouse Annex, 201 Church St.
      (916) 265-1311, Fax: (916) 265-1779
    Truckee Municipal Court, 10775 Levon Ave., Suite 301,
      96161 (916) 582-7866, Fax: (916) 582-7875

Orange County (30), 700 Civic Center Drive W., P.O. Box 838, Santa Ana,
    92702
  Assessor, 12 Civic Center Plaza, P.O. Box 149, 92701
    (714) 834-2727
  County Clerk, Rm. D-100 (714) 834-2200
  District Attorney, P.O. Box 808 (714) 834-3636,
    Fax: (714) 734-5706
  Library, 14361 Yale Ave., Irvine, 92714 (714) 551-7151
  Recorder, 630 N. Broadway, Rm. 101, P.O. Box 638, 92701
    (714) 834-2500
  Registrar, 1300 S. Grand Ave., 92705 (714) 567-7601,
    Fax: (714) 567-7627
  Sheriff, 550 N. Flower P.O. Box 449 (714) 647-7000
    Laguna Niguel Station, 30331 Crown Valley Pkwy., 92677
      (714) 249-5200, Fax: (714) 831-8416
    Stanton Station, 11100 Cedar St., 90680 (714) 891-2481,
      Fax: (714) 893-3207
  Superior Court P.O. Box 1994 (714) 834-3734,
    Fax: (714) 834-6171
  Municipal Courts
    Central Orange Judicial District, 700 Civic Center Drive
      West, P.O. Box 1138, Santa Ana, 92702
      (714) 834-3575, Fax: (714) 953-9032
    Harbor Judicial District, 4601 Jamboree Rd., Suite 104,
      Newport Beach, 92660-2595 (714) 476-4699
    North Orange Judicial District, 1275 N. Berkeley Ave.,
      P.O. Box 5000, Fullerton, 92635 (714) 773-4400
      Civil/Small Claims (714) 773-4421
      Criminal (714) 773-4451
      Traffic (Recording) (714) 773-4603
    South Orange Judicial District, 30143 Crown Valley Pkwy,
      Laguna Niguel, 92677-2098 (714) 249-5000
    Annex, 23141 Moulton Pkwy., 2nd Floor, Laguna Hills,
      92653-1206
      Civil (714) 472-6964
      Small Claims (714) 472-6968
      Fax: (714) 472-6977
      Traffic (714) 472-6900, Fax: (714) 472-6905

Orange County Municipal Court Continued
   West Orange Judicial District, 8141 13th St., Westminster, 92683
      Civil/Small Claims (714) 896-7191,
         Fax: (714) 896-7219
      Criminal (714) 896-7351, Fax: (714) 896-7219
      Traffic (Recording) (714) 896-7225,
         Fax: (714) 896-7290
Placer County (31), 101 Maple St., Auburn, 95603
   Assessor, 145 Fulweiler Ave. (916) 889-4300
   County Clerk, 11960 Heritage Oaks Plaza, Suite 15, P.O. Box 5228, 95604 (916) 889-7983
   District Attorney, 11562 "B" St. (916) 889-7000,
      Fax: (916) 889-7129
   Library, 350 Nevada St. (916) 889-4115
   Recorder, 11960 Heritage Oaks Plaza, Suite 15, P.O. Box 5228, 95604 (916) 889-7983
      Vital Statistics (916) 889-7948
      Fictitious Names (916) 889-7948
   Registrar, 11544 "C" Ave. (916) 889-7088
   Sheriff, 11500 "A" Ave., 95603, P.O. Box 6990, 95604
      (916) 889-7800, Fax: (916) 889-7899
      (916) 581-6305, Fax: (916) 581-6377
   Superior Court, 4th Floor (916) 889-6550
      Civil (916) 889-6553
      Criminal (916) 889-7982
      Domestic (916) 889-6555, 889-6560
      Probate (916) 889-6557
   Municipal Courts
      Administrator (916) 889-7400
      Dept. 1, 11546 "B" Ave., Auburn, 95603 (916) 889-7407
      Dept. 2, 300 Taylor St., Suite 10, Roseville, 95678
         (916) 784-6419
         Traffic (916) 652-7212
      Dept. 3
         Colfax Branch, 10 Culver St., P.O. Box 735, 95713 (916) 346-8721
         Foresthill Branch, 24580 Main St.,
            P.O. Box 267, 95631 (916) 367-2302
         Lincoln Branch, 453 "G" St., 95648
            (916) 645-8955
         Loomis Branch, 3877 Shawn Way, P.O. Box 44, 95650 (916) 652-7212
   Municipal Courts
      Tahoe Municipal Court,
         2501 N. Lake Blvd., P.O. Box 5669, Tahoe City, 96145 (916) 581-6337
Plumas County (32), 520 W. Main St., P.O. Box 10686, Quincy, 95971
   Assessor, P.O. Box 11016 (916) 283-6380
   County Clerk, P.O. Box 10207 (916) 283-6305,
      Fax: (916) 283-6415

Plumas County Continued
    District Attorney, P.O. Box 10716 (916) 283-6303,
        Fax: (916) 283-6340
    Library, 445 Jackson St., P.O. Box 10270 (916) 283-6310
    Recorder, P.O. Box 10207 (916) 283-6218
    Registrar, P.O. Box 10207 (916) 283-6305
    Sheriff, 1400 E. Main St., P.O. Box 1106 (916) 283-6300,
        Fax: (916) 283-6344
    Superior Court (916) 283-6297
    Municipal Courts
        Chester Branch, P.O. Box 722, 96020 (916) 258-2646
        Greenville Branch, P.O. Box 706, 95947 (916) 284-7213
        Portola Branch, P.O. Box 1054, 96122 (916) 832-4286
        Quincy Branch, P.O. Box 10628, 95971 (916) 283-6232,
            Fax: (916) 283-6415

Riverside County (33), County Courthouse, 4050 Main St., Riverside, 92502
    Assessor, 4080 Lemon St., Riverside, 92501-3659 (909) 275-6200,
        Fax: (909) 275-6238
        Blyth Branch, 160 N. Broadway, 92225-1608
            (619) 921-7888, Fax: (619) 922-3306
        Hemet Branch, 880 N. State St., 92543-1496
            (909) 766-2500, Fax: (909) 766-2503
        Palm Springs Branch, 3255 Tahquitz Canyon Way, Rm.
            114, 92262-6962 (619) 778-2400,
            Fax: (619) 778-2413
        Riverside Office (909) 275-6250
    County Clerk, 3470 12th St., 92501, P.O. Box 751, Riverside,
        92502-0751 (909) 275-1950, Fax: (909) 682-3350
    District Attorney, 4075 Main St., Riverside, 92501 (909) 275-5400,
        Fax: (909) 275-5682
    Library, 3021 Franklin, Riverside, 92507 (909) 782-5211
    Recorder, 4080 Lemon St., P.O. Box 751, Riverside, 92502
        Grantor/Grantee (909) 275-1906
        Birth, Death, Marriage (909) 275-1959
    Registrar, 1260 Palmyrita Ave., Riverside, 92507 (909) 275-8700,
        Fax: (909) 275-8733
    Sheriff, 4050 Main St., P.O. Box 512, Riverside, 92502
        (909) 275-2400, Fax: (909) 275-2428
        Banning Station, 155 E. Hayes St., 92220 (909) 849-6744
        Blythe Station, 260 N. Spring, 92225 (619) 922-6121,
            Fax: (619) 922-7603
        Indio Station, 46-209 Oasis St., Rm. 302, 92201
            (619) 863-8255, Fax: (619) 863-8919
        Lake Elsinore Station, 117 S. Langstaff, 92330
            (909) 674-3172, Fax: (909) 245-1060

Riverside Sheriffs Continued
    Lake Hemet/Mountain Substation, 56570 Hwy. 74,
        Mountain Center, 92561 (909) 766-2400
    Southwest County, 30755-A Auld Rd., Murrieta, 92563
        (909) 696-3131, Fax: (909) 696-3056
Superior Court, 4100 Main St., Riverside, 92501 (909) 275-5536,
    Fax: (909) 275-5537
    Civil, 4050 Main St. (909) 275-1950
    Criminal (909) 275-1433
    Family Law, 4164 Brockton Ave., 92501 (909) 275-1940
    Juvenile, 9991 County Farm Rd., 92503 (619) 358-4137,
        Fax: (909) 358-4124
    Indio Branch, 46-209 Oasis St., Rm. 104, 92201
        Civil/Small Claims (619) 863-8729
        Criminal/Juvenile (619) 863-8206
        Family Law (619) 863-8209
        Probate (619) 863-8207
    Palm Springs Branch (courtroom only - for records see
        Indio Branch above), 3255 E. Tahquitz Canyon
        Way, 92262 (619) 778-2175
Municipal Courts
    Corona Judicial District, 505 S. Buena Vista Ave., Rm.
        201, 91720-1997
        Civil/Small Claims (909) 272-5620
        Criminal (909) 272-5630
        Traffic (909) 272-5634
    Desert Judicial District
      Blythe Branch, County Administrative Center, 260 N.
        Spring St., 92225
        Civil/Small Claims (619) 922-8129
        Criminal/Traffic (619) 922-8128
      Indio Branch, County Administrative Center, 82-675
        Hwy. 111, P.O. Drawer BBB, 92201-2552
        Civil (619) 863-8203
        Criminal (619) 863-8204
        Small Claims (619) 863-8208
        Traffic (619) 863-8201
      Palm Springs Branch, County Administrative Center,
        3255 E. Tahquitz Canyon Way, 92262,
        P.O. Box 2728, 92263-2728 (619) 778-2160,
        Fax: (619) 778-2165
        Civil (619) 778-2175
        Small Claims (619) 778-2170
        Traffic (619) 778-2166
    Mt. San Jacinto Judicial District, 155 E. Hays St., Banning,
        92220
        Civil/Small Claims (909) 849-4793
        Criminal (909) 849-4791
        Traffic (909) 849-8009

Riverside County Municipal Courts Continued
    Three Lakes Judicial District
        Lake Elsinore Branch, 117 S. Langstaff, Lake Elsinore, 92330 (909) 674-3161
        Perris Branch, 227 N. "D" St., 92370 (909) 940-6866, Fax: (909) 940-6870
            Criminal (909) 940-6840
            Small Claims (909) 940-6820
            Traffic (909) 940-6830
        Temecula Branch, Walter P. Abraham Administrative Center, 41002 County Center Dr., 92591-2037 (909) 694-5174, Fax: (909) 940-6810
            Civil/Small Claims (909) 694-5160

Sacramento County (34), 720 9th St., Sacramento, 95814
    Assessor, 700 "H" St., Rm. 3650 (916) 440-8522, 440-5669
    County Clerk, Rm. 101 (916) 440-5522
    District Attorney, 901 "G" St., Rm. 261 (916) 440-6637, 440-6217, Fax: (916) 440-8540
    Library, 828 "I" St. (916) 440-5926
    Recorder, 600 8th St., Rm. 2720, P.O. Box 839 (916) 440-6334
    Registrar, 3700 Branch Center Rd., 95827 (916) 366-2051, 366-2658, Fax: (916) 366-4116
    Sheriff, 711 "G" St. P.O. Box 988, 95812 (916) 440-7146, Fax: (916) 440-5332
    Superior Court (916) 440-5522
    Municipal Courts
        Sacramento Branch, 720 9th St., Rm. 606, 95814
            Civil (916) 440-9723
            Felonies (916) 440-7736
            Misdemeanors (916) 440-6402
            Small Claims, (916) 386-7181
            Traffic (916) 386-7157
        South Sacramento Municipal Court
            Elk Grove Branch District, 8978 Elk Grove Blvd., 95824 (916) 685-9825, Fax: (916) 685-4689
            Walnut Grove-Isleton Judicial District, 14177 Market St., P.O. Box 371, 95690 (916) 776-1416, Fax: (916) 776-1624
            Galt Branch, 301 Civic Dr., 95632 (209) 745-1577, Fax: (209) 745-6176

San Benito County (35), County Courthouse, Rm. 103, 440 5th St., Hollister, 95023
    Assessor (408) 637-5561
    County Clerk, Rm. 206 (408) 637-3786, Fax: (408) 636-2939
    District Attorney, 419 4th St. (408) 636-4120, Fax: (408) 636-4126
    Recorder, Rm. 206 (408) 637-3786
    Registrar, Rm. 206 (408) 637-3786
    Sheriff, P.O. Box 700, 95024-0700 (408) 636-4080
    Superior Court, Rm. 206 (408) 637-2835
    Municipal Court, Rm. 103 (408) 637-3741

San Bernardino County (36), 351 N. Arrowhead Ave., San Bernardino, 92415-0240
   Assessor, Hall of Records, 172 W. Third St., 92415-0310 (909) 387-8307
   County Clerk, 5th Floor (909) 387-3921
      Fictitious Name Filings (909) 387-3927
      Marriage Licenses (909) 387-8334
   District Attorney, 316 N. Mountain View Ave., 92415-0004 (909) 387-8309, Fax: (909) 387-6313
   Library, 104 W. 4th St., 92415-0035 (909) 387-5719, 387-5721
   Recorder, 222 W. Hospitality Lane, 92415-0018 (909) 387-8306
   Registrar, 777 E. Rialto Ave. (909) 387-8300
   Sheriff, 655 E. Third St., 92415-0061 (909) 387-3500, 884-8129, Fax: (909) 387-3688
      Apple Valley Station, 22521 Shawnee Rd., 92307 (619) 240-7400, Fax: (619) 240-7499
      Barstow Station, 225 E. Mt. View, 92311 (619) 256-4838, Fax: (619) 256-4870
      Big Bear Station, 477 Summit Blvd., P.O. Box 2803, 92315 (909) 866-0100, Fax: (909) 866-0110
      Chino Hills Station, 13843 Peyton Dr., 91709 (909) 590-1621, Fax: (909) 590-0458
      Colorado River Station, 111 Bailey Ave., Needles, 92363 (619) 326-9200, Fax: (619) 326-9211
      Fontana Station, 17780 Arrow Blvd., 92335 (909) 829-3728, Fax: (909) 829-3721
      Hesperia Station, 15776 Main St., 92345 (619) 947-1500, Fax: (619) 947-1598
      Highland Station, 27215 E. Baseline, 92346 (909) 425-9793, Fax: (909) 425-0693
      Lucerne Valley Substation (619) 248-7655
      Morongo Basin Station, 6527 White Feather Rd., Joshua Tree, 92252 (619) 366-4175, Fax: (619) 366-4224
      Parker Substation (619) 663-3600
      Phelan Substation, 4050 Phelan Rd., P.O. Box 292000, 92371 (619) 868-1006, Fax: (619) 249-3149
      Rancho Cucamonga Station, 10510 Civic Center Dr., 91730 (909) 989-6611, Fax: (909) 941-8491
      Tona Substation, 13215 Market St., 93562 (619) 372-4096, Fax: (619) 372-4097
      Twin Peaks Station, P.O. Box 384, 26010 Hwy 189, 92391 (909) 336-0600, Fax: (909) 337-4893
      Victorville City Station, 14177 McArt, Victorville, 92392 (619) 241-2911, Fax: (619) 241-2181
      Victor Valley Station, 14455 Civic Dr., Victorville, 92392 (619) 243-8720, Fax: (619) 243-8711
      Wrightwood Substation, 6025 Park Dr., 92397 (619) 249-3213, Fax: (619) 249-3149
      Yucaipa Station, 34282 Yucaipa Blvd., 92399 (909) 790-3105, Fax: (909) 790-3111

San Bernardino County Superior Court, 172 W. Third St., 2nd Floor, San Bernardino, 92415-0302 (909) 387-6500, Fax: (909) 387-6650
Juvenile Court, 900 E. Gilbert St., San Bernardino, 92415-0942 (909) 387-7536
Desert District, 14455 Civic Dr., Victorville, 92392
   (619) 243-8672
   Civil (619) 243-8672
   Criminal (619) 243-8638
   Juvenile Traffic (619) 243-8683
   Fax: (619) 243-8790
East Desert District, 6527 White Feather Rd., Joshua Tree, 92252 (619) 366-4110, Fax: (619) 366-4156
West District, 8303 W. Haven Ave., Rancho Cucamonga, 91730
   Civil (909) 945-4393, Fax: (909) 945-4154
   Family Law (909) 945-4136

Superior and Municipal (Trial) Courts
Central Division, 351 N. Arrowhead Ave., San Bernardino, 92415
   Civil/Small Claims (909) 885-0139
   Criminal/Traffic (909) 384-1888
Valley Division, 17780 Arrow Blvd., Fontana, 92333
   Civil/Small Claims (909) 884-5766
   Criminal/Traffic (909) 829-2434
East Division, 216 Brookside Ave., Redlands, 92373
   Civil (909) 798-8541
   Criminal/Traffic (909) 798-8542
   Fax: (909) 798-8588
West Valley Division, 8303 Haven Ave., Rancho Cucamonga, 91730
   Civil (909) 945-4393
   Criminal/Traffic (909) 885-2584
   Fax: (909) 944-4507
Barstow Division, 235 E. Mountain View, 92311
   Civil (619) 256-4817, Fax: (619) 256-4711
   Criminal (619) 256-4785, Fax: (619) 256-4884
   Small Claims (619) 256-4755
   Traffic (619) 256-4758
Chino Division, 13260 Central Ave., 91710
   Civil/Small Claims (909) 465-5266
   Criminal (909) 465-5262
   Traffic (909) 465-5260
   Fax: (909) 465-5306
Morongo Basin Division, 6527 White Feather Rd., Joshua Tree, 92252 (619) 366-4100, 366-4105, Fax: (619) 366-4156
Victorville Division, 14455 Civic Dr., 92392
   Civil/Small Claims (619) 243-8627
   Criminal (619) 243-8631
   Traffic (619) 243-8632
   Fax: (619) 243-8794

San Bernardino County Municipal Courts
Bear Valley Municipal Court, 477 Summit Blvd.,
P.O. Box 2806, Big Bear Lake, 92315
(909) 866-0150, Fax: (909) 866-0160
Crest-Forest Municipal Court, 26010 Hwy. 189,
P.O. Box 394, Twin Peaks, 92391
(909) 336-0620
Needles-Calzona Municipal Court, 1111 Baily Ave.,
Needles, 92363 (619) 326-9245
Trona Municipal Court, 13207 Market St., P.O. Box 534,
93562 (619) 372-5276

San Diego County (37 or 80), 220 W. Broadway, San Diego, 92101
Assessor, 1600 Pacific Coast Hwy. (619) 236-3771, 531-5507,
Fax: (619) 557-4056
County Clerk (619) 237-0502, 557-4155
District Attorney (619) 531-4040, Fax: (619) 237-1351
Library, 5555 Overland Ave., Bldg. 15, 92123-1296
(619) 694-2414
Recorder, 1600 Pacific Coast Hwy., Rm. 260 (619) 237-0502
Grantee/Grantor, 1600 Pacific Hwy. 92101 (619) 237-0502
Birth, Death, Marriage (619) 237-0502
Registrar, 5201 Ruffin Rd., 92123 (619) 570-1061
Sheriff, 9621 Rich Mowen Court, 92123 (619) 974-2222
Alpine Substation, 1347 Tavern Rd., 91901 (619) 579-4137
Borrego Office, 610 Palm Canyon Rd., 92004 (619) 767-5656
Jacumba Office, P.O. Box 1117, 393919 Hwy. 94, Boulevard,
91905-0217 (619) 766-4585
Campo Substation, 378 Sheraton Rd., 92006 (619) 478-5378
Dulzura Office, P.O. Box 306, 92007 (619) 468-3268
Encinitas Sheriff's Station, 175 N. El Camino Real, 92024
(619) 753-1252
Fallbrook Substation, 127 E. Hawthorne, 92028 (619) 723-6050
Imperial Beach Sheriff's Station, 845 Imperial Beach Blvd., 91945
(619) 498-2400
Julian Substation, 1485 Hollow Glen Rd., 92036 (619) 765-0503
Lemon Grove Substation, 3240 Main St., 91945 (619) 441-4100,
Fax: (619) 441-4020
Pauma/Valley Center Substation, 28205 Lake Wohlford, 92082
(619) 749-1303, 749-1309
Pine Valley Substation, 28848 Old Hwy. 80, P.O. Box 312, 92062
(619) 473-8774, Fax: (619) 473-8367
Poway Substation, 12935 Pomerado Rd., 92064 (619) 738-2532,
Fax: (619) 748-7954
Ramona Substation, 1424 Montecito Rd., 92065 (619) 789-9157,
Fax: (619) 788-9077
Ranchita Office, 37550 Montezuma Valley Rd., 92066
(619) 782-3353
Santee Sheriff's Station, 8811 Cuyamaca St., 92071
(619) 258-3100, Fax: (619) 258-3096
Vista Sheriff's Station, 325 S. Melrose Dr., #210, 92083-6627
(619) 940-4551, Fax: (619) 630-9366

San Diego County Sheriffs Stations Continued
   Warner Springs Office, 25402 Oak Grove Truck Trail,
      P.O. Box 26, 92086-0026 (619) 782-3353
   Superior Court, 220 W. Broadway, 92101
      Records (619) 531-3151
      Older Records (619) 531-3244
   El Cajon Branch, 250 E. Main St., 92020
      Civil (619) 441-4622
      Criminal (619) 441-4370
   South Bay Branch, 500 3rd Ave., Chula Vista, 92010
      (619) 691-4801, 531-3489
   Vista Branch, 325 S. Melrose, Suite 100, 92083
      Records (619) 940-4442
Municipal Courts
   San Diego Judicial District, County Courthouse, 220 W.
      Broadway, 92101-3877
      Civil 1409 4th Ave., 92101 (619) 687-2180,
         Fax: (619) 687-2160
      Criminal (619) 531-3040, Fax: (619) 685-6525
      Traffic, 8950 Clairmont Mesa Blvd., 92123
         (619) 565-2234, Fax: (619) 694-3197
   North County Judicial District
      Vista Office, 325 S. Melrose Dr., 92083-6693
         Criminal (619) 940-4644
      Escondido Branch, 600 E. Valley Parkway, 92025-3098
         (619) 740-4005
   El Cajon Judicial District, 250 E. Main St., 92020
      Civil (619) 441-4734
      Criminal (619) 441-4275
   South Bay Judicial District
      Chula Vista Branch, 500 Third Ave., 91910
         Civil (619) 691-4639
         Criminal/Traffic (619) 691-4726
         Small Claims (619) 691-4439
San Francisco City/County (38 or 90), City Hall, 400 Van Ness, San
   Francisco, 94102 (415) 554-5150
Assessor, Rm. 101 (415) 554-5500
County Clerk, Rm. 317 (415) 554-4165, 554-4175,
   Fax: (415) 554-4179
District Attorney, 880 Bryant St., Rm. 322, 94103 (415) 553-1752,
   Fax: (415) 553-9054
Library, Civic Center, Larkin and McAllister Sts. (415) 557-4400
Recorder, Rm. 167 (415) 554-4176
Registrar, Rm. 158 (415) 554-4375, 554-4397
Sheriff, Rm. 333 (415) 554-7225
Superior Court (415) 554-5151
   Civil Division, Rm. 317 (415) 554-4170
   Criminal Division, Hall of Justice, 850 Bryant St., #306,
      94103 (415) 553-9361
   Divorce (415) 554-4168
   Probate (415) 554-4162

A PUBLIC RECORDS PRIMER AND INVESTIGATOR'S HANDBOOK 253

San Francisco, Municipal Court, Rm. 303 (415) 554-4521
   Civil, Rm. 300 (415) 554-4532
   Criminal, Hall of Justice, 850 Bryant St., Rm. 201, 94103
     (415) 553-9395
   Small Claims, Rm. 164 (415) 554-4566
   Traffic, Hall of Justice, 850 Bryant St., Rm. 101, 94103
     (415) 553-9457
San Joaquin County (39), County Courthouse, 222 E. Weber Ave., Rm. 303, Stockton, 95202 (209) 468-2355
   Assessor, 24 S. Hunter St., Rm. 303 (209) 468-2630
   County Clerk (209) 468-2362
   District Attorney, Rm. 202, P.O. Box 990, 94201 (209) 468-2400, Fax: (209) 465-0371
   Library, 605 N. El Dorado St., 95201 (209) 937-8415
   Recorder, 24 S. Hunter, Rm. 304, P.O. Box 1968, 95201
     (209) 468-3939
   Registrar, Rm. 202, P.O. Box 810, 95201 (209) 468-2885
   Sheriff, 7000 Michael Calnis Blvd., French Camp, 95231,
     P.O. Box 201058, 95202 (209) 468-4310
   Superior Court, County Courthouse, 222 E. Weber Ave., Rm. 303
     (209) 468-2355
     Civil (209) 468-2873
     Criminal (209) 468-2369
     Divorce (209) 468-2355
     Probate (209) 468-2843
   Municipal Courts
     Stockton Municipal District, 222 E. Weber Ave.
       (209) 462-2926, 468-2972
       Civil (209) 468-2933
       Criminal (209) 468-2935
       Small Claims (209) 2949
       Traffic (209) 468-2920
     Lodi Judicial District, 230 W. Elm St., Box 1030, 95240
       (209) 333-6750, 333-6753
       Civil (209) 333-6755
       Criminal (209) 333-6750
       Small Claims (209) 333-6755
       Traffic (209) 333-6752
     Eastern Department
       Manteca-Ripon-Escalon Municipal Court, 315 E.
         Center St., Manteca, 95336
         (209) 239-6427
         Civil (209) 239-9188
         Criminal (209) 239-1316
         Small Claims (209) 239-9188
     Western Department
       Tracy Branch, 475 E. 10th St., 95376
         (209) 831-5909
         Civil (209) 831-5902
         Criminal (209) 831-5900
         Small Claims (209) 831-5902
         Traffic (209) 831-5913

San Luis Obispo County (40), County Government Center, San Luis Obispo, 93408
    Assessor, Rm. 100 (805) 781-5643
    County Clerk, Rm. 385 (805) 781-5243
    District Attorney, Rm. 450 (805) 781-5800, Fax: (805) 781-4307
    Library, 995 Palm St., (805) 781-5994
    Recorder, Rm. 102
        Grantor/Grantee (805) 781-5080
        Vital Statistics (805) 781-5088
    Registrar, 1009 Monterey St. (805) 781-5228
    Sheriff, 1575 Kansas Ave., P.O. Box 32, 93406 (805) 781-4540, 781-4550, Fax: (805) 781-1228
        Arroyo Grande Station (805) 473-7100
        Los Osos Station (805) 528-6083
        Templeton Station (805) 237-3000
    Superior Court, Rm. 385 (805) 781-5241
    Municipal Courts
        Grover City Dept., 214 S. 16th St., 93433
            Civil (805) 473-7077
            Criminal (805) 473-7072
            Small Claims (805) 473--7077
            Traffic (805) 473-7070
        Paso Robles Dept., 549 10th St., 93446
            Civil (805) 237-3079
            Criminal (805) 237-3080
            Small Claims (805) 237-3077
            Traffic (805) 237-3070
        San Luis Obispo Dept., 1050 Monterey St., Rm. 220 (805) 781-5695
            Civil (805) 781-5675
            Criminal (805) 781-5670
            Small Claims (805) 781-5677
            Traffic (805) 781-5696

San Mateo County (41), Hall of Justice and Records, 401 Marshall St., Redwood City, 94063 (415) 363-4000
    Assessor, 280 Middlefield Rd., (415) 363-4500
    County Clerk (415) 363-4713
        Fictitious Names (415) 363-4212
        Marriage Licenses (415) 363-4212
    District Attorney (415) 363-4636, Fax: (415) 363-4873
    Library, 25 Tower Rd., San Mateo, 94402 (415) 312-5228
    Recorder (415) 363-4213
    Registrar, 40 Tower Rd., San Mateo, 94402 (415) 312-5222
    Sheriff, (415) 364-1811.
        Half Moon Bay Station (415) 363-4365
    Superior Court (415) 363-4711, 363-4766, Fax: (415) 363-4194

San Mateo County Municipal Courts
  Northern Branch, 1050 Mission Rd., South San Francisco, 94080 (415) 877-5700, 877-5772,
  Fax: (415) 877-5703
  Criminal (415) 877-5708
  Small Claims (415) 877-5480
  Traffic (415) 877-5333
  Southern Branch, 750 Middlefield Rd., Redwood City, 94063 (415) 363-4516
  Criminal (415) 363-4300
  Small Claims (415) 363-4303
  Traffic (415) 363-4300
  Central Branch, 800 N. Humboldt St., San Mateo, 94401
  (415) 573-2616
  Civil (415) 573-2611
  Small Claims (415) 573-2605
  Traffic (415) 573-2622

Santa Barbara County (42), 1100 Anacapa St., Santa Barbara, 93101
  Assessor (805) 568-2550
  County Clerk, 2nd Floor (805) 568-2220, Fax: (805) 568-2219
    Fictitious Names (805) 568-2250
    Marriage Licenses (805) 568-2250
  District Attorney, 1105 Santa Barbara St. (805) 568-2300,
    Fax: (805) 568-2398
  Library, 40 E. Anapamu St. (805) 962-7653
  Recorder, P.O. Box 159, 93102-0159 (805) 568-2250
    Vital Statistics (805) 568-2250
  Registrar, P.O. Box 159, 93102-0159 (805) 568-2200
  Sheriff, 4434 Calle Real, P.O. Box 6427, 93102-6427
    (805) 681-4100, Fax: (805) 681-5346
    Lompoc Station, 751 Burston Mesa Rd., 93436
      (805) 737-7737
    New Cuyama Station, 215 Newsome, P.O. Box 269, 93254
      (805) 766-2310
    Santa Maria Station, 812-A W. Foster Rd., 93455
      (805) 936-6150
    Solvang Station, 1745 Mission Dr., 93463 (805) 686-1000
  Superior Court (805) 568-2220, 568-2737
  Municipal Courts
    Lompoc Judicial District, 115 Civic Center Plaza, 93436
      (805) 737-7790
    Santa Barbara Judicial District, 118 E. Figueroa St., 93101
      (805) 568-2735, Fax: (805) 681-2847
      Civil (805) 568-2740
      Criminal (805) 568-2780
      Small Claims (805) 568-2740
      Traffic (805) 568-2770

Santa Barbara Municipal Courts Continued
  Santa Maria Judicial District, 312-M E. Cook St., 93454
    (805) 346-7551, Fax: (805) 681-7591
    Civil (805) 346-7564, 346-7565
    Criminal, (805) 346-7566
    Small Claims, (805) 346-7563
    Traffic, (805) 346-7590
  Solvang Municipal Court, 1745 Mission Dr.,
    P.O. Box 228, Solvang, 93464 (805) 686-5040
Santa Clara County (43), 191 N. First St., San Jose, 95113
  Assessor, 70 W. Hedding St., 95110 (408) 299-3227
  County Clerk (408) 299-2964
  District Attorney, 70 W. Hedding, W. Wing, 95110
    (408) 299-7400, Fax: (408) 998-1562
  Library, 180 W. San Carlos St., (408) 277-4815
  Recorder, 70 W. Hedding St., 95110 (408) 299-2481
  Registrar, 1553 Berger Dr., Bldng. 1, P.O. Box 1147, 95801
    (408) 299-2161
  Sheriff, 1005 Timothy Dr., 95133-1057 (408) 299-2622, 299-2005,
    Fax: (408) 998-0636
    San Jose Station, 41 N. First St., 95113 (408) 299-2432,
      Fax: (408) 299-2685
    Saratoga Station, 14374 Saratoga Ave., 95070
      (408) 867-9715
  Superior Court, (408) 299-2964
    Civil (408) 299-2964
    Criminal, 115 Terraine St., 95110 (408) 299-2974
    Juvenile, 840 Guadelupe Pkwy., 95110 (408) 299-4749
    Palo Alto Branch, 270 Grant Ave., 94306 (415) 324-1595
  Municipal Courts
    Gilroy-Morgan Hill, 7350 Rosanna St., 95020
      (408) 842-3939
      Civil/Small Claims (408) 842-6299
      Criminal (408) 847-2442
      Traffic (408) 842-3949
    Los Gatos, 14205 Capri Dr., 95030
      Civil (408) 866-8331
      Traffic (408) 378-3408
      Small Claims (408) 866-8331
    Palo Alto, 270 Grant Ave., 94306 (415) 378-3408
      Criminal (415) 324-2228
      Small Claims (415) 324-0391
      Traffic (415) 323-5167
    San Jose, 200 W. Hedding St., 95110 (408) 299-4971
      Criminal (408) 299-2281
      Traffic, 935 Ruff Dr., 95110 (408) 299-7950
    Santa Clara, 1095 Homestead Rd., 95050
      Civil (408) 249-2690
      Criminal (408) 249-4823

Santa Clara County Municipal Courts Continued
  Sunnyvale, 605 W. El Camino Real, 94087
    Civil (408) 739-1502
    Criminal (408) 739-1503
    Traffic (408) 739-1677
Santa Cruz County (44), Government Center, 701 Ocean St., Rm. 110, Santa Cruz, 95060 (408) 454-2020
  Assessor, Rm. 130 (408) 454-2002
  County Clerk, Rm. 110 (408) 454-2380
    Fictitious Names, Rm. 210-D (408) 454-2474
  District Attorney, Rm. 250 (408) 454-2400
  Library, 224 Church St. (408) 429-3526
  Recorder, Rm. 230 (408) 454-2800
  Registrar, Rm. 210 (408) 454-2060
  Sheriff, 701 Ocean St., Rm. 340, (408) 454-2414, Fax: (408) 454-2353
  Superior Court (408) 454-2020
  Municipal Courts
    Sunnyvale Branch, 605 W. El Camino Real, Rm. 120
      Civil (408) 454-3090
      Criminal (408) 454-2155
      Small Claims/Traffic (408) 445-2070
    Watsonville Branch, 1430 Freedom Blvd., 95076 (408) 763-8060, Fax: (408) 763-8069
Shasta County (45), 1500 Court St., Redding, 96001
  Assessor, Rm. 115 (916) 225-5501
  County Clerk, Downtown Redding Mall, 1643 Market St. (916) 225-5378
  District Attorney, 1525 Court St. (916) 245-6310, Fax: (916) 245-6345
  Library, 1855 Shasta St. (916) 225-5769
  Recorder, Rm. 102 (916) 225-5671
  Registrar, P.O. Box 880, 96099 (916) 225-5731
  Sheriff, 1525 Court St., 2nd Floor (916) 245-6025, Fax: (916) 245-6054
    Burney Division (916) 335-4511, Fax: (916) 245-6074
    City of Shasta Lake Station (916) 245-6096
    Knighton Station (916) 245-6083
    Lakehead Station (916) 238-8648
    Shingletown Station (916) 474-5242
  Superior Court, Rm. 300 (916) 225-5631, 225-5641
  Municipal Courts
    Anderson Branch, 1925 W. Howard St., 96007 (916) 365-2563
    Burney Branch, 20509-C Shasta St., P.O. Box 66, 96013 (916) 335-3571
    Redding Branch, 1545 West St., 96001, P.O. Box 270, 96099 (916) 225-5331
      Civil (916) 225-5431
      Criminal (916) 225-5136
      Small Claims (916) 225-5703
      Traffic (916) 225-5316

Sierra County (46), Courthouse Square, P.O. Box 95, Downieville, 95936
    Assessor, P.O. Box 8 (916) 289-3283
    County Clerk, Courthouse Drawer D (916) 289-3295,
        Fax: (916) 289-3300
    District Attorney, P.O. Box 457 (916) 289-3269
    Library, Hwy. 49, Senior Center
    Recorder, Courthouse Drawer D (916) 289-3295
    Registrar, Courthouse Drawer D (916) 289-3295
    Sheriff, P.O. Box 66 (916) 289-3234
        Loyalton Station (916) 939-4479
    Superior Court (916) 289-3698, Fax: (916) 289-3318
    Municipal Court, P.O. Box 401 (916) 289-3215
Siskiyou County (47), 311 4th St., Yreka, 96097
    Assessor (916) 842-8036
    County Clerk, Courthouse, P.O. Box 338 (916) 842-8084,
        Fax: (916) 842-8093
    District Attorney, P.O. Box 986 (916) 842-8125
    Library, 719 4th St. (916) 842-8175
    Recorder, Courthouse, P.O. Box 8 (916) 842-8065
    Registrar, Courthouse, P.O. Box 338 (916) 842-8086
    Sheriff, 311 Lane St. (916) 842-8317
    Superior Court (916) 842-8082, 842-8330
    Municipal Courts Courts
        Dorris-Tulake Judicial District
            Doris Division, 324 Pine St., P.O. Box 828,
                96023 (916) 397-3161
            Tulelake Division, P.O. Box 873, 96134
                (916) 667-5218
        Western Judicial District
            Fort Jones Division, Yreka, 96097
                (916) 842-8182
            Happy Camp Division, P.O. Box 807, 96039
                (916) 493-2327
            Yreka Division, Courthouse, Rm. 5,
                P.O. Box 1034, 96097 (916) 842-8182,
                Fax: (916) 842-8178
        Southeastern Judicial District, 550 Main St., P.O. Box 530,
            Weed, 96094 (916) 938-2718
            Civil/Small Claims (916) 938-3897
            Criminal/Traffic (916) 938-2718
Solano County (48), Hall of Justice, North Wing, 600 Union Ave., P.O. Caller
    5000, Fairfield, 94533
    Assessor (707) 421-6200
    County Clerk, 600 Texas St. (707) 421-7485, Fax: (707) 421-6311
    District Attorney (707) 421-6800, Fax: (707) 421-7986
    Recorder, Courthouse, 580 Texas St. (707) 4219-6290
    Registrar, Hall of Justice, P.O. Box 1 (707) 421-6675
    Sheriff, 430 Union Ave. (707) 421-7000, Fax: (707) 421-7952
    Superior Court (707) 421-6470

Solano County Municipal Courts
  Northern Solano Judicial District, 530 Union Ave., #200,
    Fairfield, 94533 (707) 421-7400
    Civil (707) 421-7435
    Criminal (707) 421-7440
    Traffic (707) 421-7460
  Vallejo-Benicia Municipal Court, 321 Tuolomne St.,
    Vallejo, 94590 (707) 553-5064,
    Fax: (707) 553-5661
Sonoma County (49), Hall of Justice, 600 Administration Dr., Santa Rosa, 95403
  Assessor, 585 Fiscal Dr. (707) 527-1888
  County Clerk, Hall of Justice, Rm. 101J, P.O. Box 11187, 95406
    (707) 527-3800
    Fictitious Names (707) 527-3800
    Marriage Licenses (707) 527-3800
  District Attorney, Hall of Justice, Rm. 103J (707) 527-2311,
    Fax: (707) 527-2762
  Library, Third & "E" Sts., 95404-4479 (707) 545-0831
  Recorder, 585 Fiscal Dr., Rm. 103F, Box 6124, 95406
    (707) 527-2651
  Registrar, 435 Fiscal Dr., P.O. Box 1419, 95406 (707) 527-1800
  Sheriff, Rm. 103J (707) 527-2751
  Superior Court, Hall of Justice, Rm. 100J (707) 527-1160,
    527-2100, Fax: (707) 527-1165
  Municipal Court, Hall of Justice, Rm. 102J (707) 527-1100,
    527-2300
Stanislaus County (50), 1100 "I" St., Modesto, 95354
  Assessor, P.O. Box 1068, 95353 (209) 525-6461
  County Clerk, 912 11th St. (209) 558-6419
    Marriage Licenses (209) 558-6419
  District Attorney, P.O. Box 442, 95353 (209) 525-5577,
    Fax: (209) 525-5545
  Library, 1500 "I" St. (209) 558-7808
  Recorder, 912 11th St.
    Grantee/Grantor (209) 558-6310
    Birth/Death/Marriage (209) 558-6312
  Registrar, 912 11th St. (209) 558-6313
  Sheriff (209) 525-7933, Fax: (209) 525-5255
  Superior Court, P.O. Box 1011, 95353 (209) 558-6000
  Municipal Courts
    Ceres Divison, 2744 Second St., 95351 (209) 558-6000
    Modesto Divison, 1100 "I" St, P.O. Box 828, 95353
      (209) 558-6000, 558-6486
    Turlock Division, 300 Star Ave., 95380 (209) 558-6000
Sutter County (51), County Administrative Bldg., 463 Second St., Yuba City, 95991
  Assessor, 212 Bridge St. (916) 741-7160
  County Clerk, 433 Second St. (916) 741-7120
  District Attorney, 446 Second St. (916) 741-7330,
    Fax: (916) 741-7337
  Library, 750 Forbes Ave. (916) 741-7137

Sutter County Recorder (916) 741-7134
Registrar, 433 Second St. (916) 741-7122
Sheriff, 1077 Civic Center Blvd., 95993 (916) 741-7307,
    Fax: (916) 741-7318
    Live Oak Station, 9867 "O" St., 95953 (916) 695-2122
    Pleasant Grove Station, 3058 Hawsley, 95668
        (916) 655-3556
Superior Court (916) 741-7352
    Municipal Court, County Courthouse, 463 Second St.
    (916) 741-7362
    Civil/Small Claims (916) 741-7351, 741-7352
    Criminal, 466 Second St. (916) 741-7360
    Traffic (916) 741-7350

Tehama County (52), 633 Washington St., P.O. Box 250, Red Bluff, 96080
Assessor, New Annex Courthouse (916) 527-5931
County Clerk (916) 527-6441
District Attorney, P.O. Box 519 (916) 527-3053,
    Fax: (916) 527-4735
Recorder (916) 527-3350
Registrar, P.O. Box 250 (916) 527-8190
Sheriff, P.O. Box 729 (916) 529-7900
Superior Court, P.O. Box 310 (916) 527-6441
Municipal Courts
    Corning Municipal Court, 720 Hoag St, 96021
        (916) 824-4601
    Red Bluff Municipal Court, 445 Pine St., P.O. Box 1170,
    96080 (916) 527-3563

Trinity County (53), 101 Court St., P.O. Box 1258, Weaverville, 96093
Assessor, P.O. Box 1255 (916) 623-1257
County Clerk, P.O. Box 1258 (916) 623-1222, Fax: (916) 623-3762
    Fictitious Names (916) 623-1215
    Marriage Licenses (916) 623-1215
District Attorney, P.O. Box 310 (916) 623-1304,
    Fax: (916) 623-2865
Library, 211 N. Main St., P.O. Box 1226 (916) 623-1373
Recorder, P.O. Box 1258 (916) 623-1215
Registrar, P.O. Box 1258 (916) 623-1220
Sheriff, 101 Memorial Dr., P.O. Box 1228, (916) 623-1370
    Hayfork Station (916) 628-5634
Superior Court (916) 623-1208
Municipal Courts
    Weaverville Branch, 101 Court St., P.O. Box 1258, 96093
        (916) 623-1208
    Hayfork and Southern Trinity Branch (916) 628-5240

Tulare County (54), County Civic Center, Visalia, 93291
Assessor (209) 733-6361
County Clerk, Rm. 203 (209) 733-6374
    Fictitious Names, (209) 733-6374, 733-6375
    Marriage Licenses (209) 733-6518
    Vital Statistics (209) 733-6418
District Attorney, Rm. 202 (209) 733-6411, Fax: (209) 730-2658

Tulare County Library, 200 W. Oak, 93291-4993 (209) 733-6954
Recorder, Rm. 203 (209) 733-6374
Registrar, Rm. 201 (209) 733-6278
Sheriff, 2404 W. Burrel St. (209) 733-6220, Fax: (209) 733-6180
    Orosi Station, 41414 Rd. 128, 93647 (209) 591-5810
    Pixley Station, 161 N. Pine (707) 685-2666
    Porterville Station, 379 N. Third St., 93257
        (209) 782-4700, Fax: (209) 782-4709
Superior Court (209) 733-6348
Municipal Courts
    Central Division
        Exeter Branch, 125 "B" St., 93321
        (209) 592-2177
        Lindsay Branch, 251 E. Honolulu St., 93247-2566
        (209) 562-4436
        Woodlake Branch, 350 N. Valencia Blvd., 93266-1297
        (209) 564-8969
    Dinuba Divison, 920 S. College Ave., 93618
        (209) 591-5815
    Porterville Division, 87 E. Morton Ave., 93257
        (209) 782-4710
        Civil/Small Claims (209) 782-4726
        Criminal (209) 782-4726
        Traffic (209) 782-6830
    Tulare-Pixley Division, 425 E. Kern St., 93274,
        P.O. Box 1136, 93275 (209) 685-2550
    Visalia Division, County Civic Center, #124, 93291
        (209) 733-6830
Tuolumne County (55), 41 W. Yaney Ave., Sonora, 95370 (Mailing address, 2 S. Green St., Sonora, 95370)
Assessor (209) 533-5535
County Clerk, 2 S. Green St. (209) 533-5555
    Fictitious Names (209) 533-5570
    Marriage License (209) 533-5570
District Attorney, 2. S. Green St. (209) 533-5655,
    Fax: (209) 533-5503
Library, 480 Greenley Rd. (209) 533-5507
Recorder, 2 S. Green St. (209) 533-5531
Registrar, 2 S. Green St. (209) 533-5570
Sheriff, 28 N. Lower Sunset Dr. (209) 533-5815
Superior Court (209) 533-5675
    Civil (209) 533-5555
    Criminal (209) 533-5563
Municipal Courts
    Central Municipal Court, 9 N. Washington St., Sonora,
        95370 (209) 532-2671
        Criminal (209) 533-5671
        Traffic (209) 533-5673
    West Municipal Court, 18250 Main St., P.O. Box 535,
        Jamestown, 95327 (209) 984-5661

Ventura County (56), 800 S. Victoria Ave., Ventura, 93009
   Assessor (805) 654-2181
   County Clerk (805) 654-2266, Fax: (805) 654-2424
   District Attorney (805) 654-2500, Fax: (805) 654-2850
   Library, 4274 Telegraph Rd. (805) 652-6289
   Recorder (805) 654-2292
   Registrar (805) 654-2781
   Sheriff (805) 654-2381
        Camarillo County Patrol, 670 Palm Dr., 93010
           (805) 482-9844
        East County Patrol (805) 494-8200
        West County Patrol (805) 524-2233
        Ojai Station, 403 S. Ventura St., 93023 (805) 646-1414
   Superior Court
        Civil (805) 654-2265
        Criminal (805) 654-2240
        Family (805) 654-2261
        Probate (805) 654-2264
        Traffic (805) 654-2611
        East Valley, 3855-F Alamo St., Simi Valley, 93063
           Civil/Family Law(805) 582-8086
           Criminal/Traffic (805) 582-8080
           Probate (805) 582-8066
   Municipal Court, P.O. Box 6489, Ventura, 93006-6489
        Civil (805) 654-2609
        Criminal (805) 654-2611
        Small Claims (805) 654-2610
        Traffic (805) 654-2611
Yolo County (57), 725 Court St., Rm. 200, Woodland, 95695
   Assessor, 625 Court St., Rm. 104 (916) 666-8135
   County Clerk, Rm. 105 (916) 666-8130. Fax: (916) 666-8109
   District Attorney, 204 4th St., Rm. 308, P.O. Box 1247
        (916) 666-8180, Fax: (916) 666-8185
   Library, 373 N. College St. (916) 666-8005
   Recorder, 625 Court St., Rm. 105 (916) 666-8130
   Registrar, 625 Court St., Rm. B-05, P.O. Box 1820 (916) 666-8133
   Sheriff, 41793 Gibson Rd. 95776 (916) 668-5280,
        Fax: (916) 668-5238
   Municipal & Superior Courts, 725 Court St., Rm. 111
        (916) 666-8050
        Civil, P.O. Box 2175 (916) 666-8170, Fax: (916) 666-8592
        Criminal, P.O. Box 2177 (916) 666-8050
        Small Claims, P.O. Box 2175 (916) 666-8052
        Traffic, 725 Main St., #310, P.O. Box 2205
           (916) 666-8065
Yuba County (58), 215 5th St., Marysville, 95901 (916) 741-6258
   Assessor, 935 14th St. (916) 741-6221
   County Clerk, 935 14th St. (916) 741-6341, Fax: (916) 742-6285
   District Attorney (916) 741-6201, Fax: (916) 749-7901
   Library, 303 Second St. (916) 741-6241
   Recorder, 935 14th St. (916) 741-6547
   Registrar, 935 14th St. (916) 741-6545

Yuba County Sheriff, 215 5th St., P.O. Box 1389 (916) 741-6355,
    Fax: (916) 741-6445
    Yuba Station (916) 675-2881
Superior Court (916) 741-6456, Fax: (916) 634-7681
Municipal Courts
    Civil (916) 741-6351
    Criminal (916) 741-6353
    Fax: (916) 634-7687

THIS SPACE FOR RENT
To have your ad printed here in future printings,
Call (818) THE-NEWS

The California Public Records Act
Government Code Section 6250 et seq.

6250. Legislative findings and declarations
In enacting this chapter, the Legislature, mindful of the right of individuals to privacy, finds and declares that access to information concerning the conduct of the people's business is a fundamental and necessary right of every person in this state.

6251. Short title. This chapter shall be known and may be cited as the California Public Records Act.

6252. Definition of terms
As used in this chapter:
(a) "State agency" means every state office, officer, department, division, bureau, board, and commission of other state body or agency, except those agencies provided for in Article IV (except Section 20 thereof) or Article VI of the California Constitution.
(b) "Local agency" includes a county; city, whether general law or chartered; city and county; school district; municipal corporation; district; political subdivision; or any board, commission or agency thereof; other local public agency; or nonprofit organizations of local governmental agencies and officials which are supported solely by public funds.
(c) "Person" includes any natural person, corporation, partnership, firm, or association.
(d) "Public records" includes any writing containing information relating to the conduct of the public's business prepared, owned, used, or retained by any state or local agency regardless of physical form or characteristics. "Public records" in the custody of or maintained by the Governor's office means any writing prepared on or after January 6, 1975.
(e) "Writing" means handwriting, typewriting, printing, photostating, photographing, and every other means of recording upon any form of communication or representation, including letters, words, pictures, sounds or symbols, or combination thereof, and all papers, maps, magnetic or paper tapes, photographic films and prints, magnetic or punched cards, discs, drums, and other documents.
(f) "Member of the public" means any person, except a member, agent, officer, or employee of a federal, state, or local agency acting within the scope of his or her membership, agency, office, or employment.

6253. Times when records are open to inspection; Establishment of written guidelines for accessibility of records
(a) Public records are open to inspection at all times during the office hours of the state or local agency and every person has a right to inspect any public record, except as

hereafter provided. Every agency may adopt regulations stating the procedures to be followed when making its records available in accordance with this section.
The following state and local bodies shall establish written guidelines for accessibility of records. A copy of these guidelines shall be posted in a conspicuous public place at the offices of such bodies, and a copy of the guidelines shall be available upon request free of charge to any person requesting that body's records:
Department of Motor Vehicles
Department of Consumer Affairs
Department of Transportation
Department of Real Estate
Department of Corrections
Department of the Youth Authority
Department of Justice
Department of Insurance
Department of Corporations
Secretary of State
State Air Resources Board
Department of Water Resources
Department of Parks and Recreation
San Francisco Bay Conservation and Development Commission
State Board of Equalization
State Department of Health Services
Employment Development Department
State Department of Social Services
State Department of Mental Health
State Department of Developmental Services
State Department of Alcohol and Drug Abuse
Office of Statewide Health Planning and Development
Public Employees' Retirement System
Teachers' Retirement Board
Department of Industrial Relations
Department of General Services
Department of Veterans Affairs
Public Utilities Commission
California Coastal Commission
State Water Quality Control Board
San Francisco Bay Area Rapid Transit District
All regional water quality control boards
Los Angeles County Air Pollution Control District
Bay Area Air Pollution Control District
Golden Gate Bridge, Highway and Transportation District
(b) Guidelines and regulations adopted pursuant to this section shall be consistent with all other sections of this chapter and shall reflect the intention of the Legislature to make such records accessible to the public. The guidelines and regulations adopted pursuant to this section shall not operate to limit the hours public records are open for inspection as prescribed in subdivision (a).
6253.1. Stricter standards permitted
Except as otherwise prohibited by law, a state or local agency may adopt requirements for itself which allow greater access to records than prescribed by the minimum standards set forth in this chapter.
6253.5. Inspection of election petitions
Notwithstanding the provisions of Sections 6252 and 6253, statewide, county, city, and district initiative, referendum, and recall petitions, petitions circulated pursuant to Section 5091 of the Education Code, petitions for the reorganization of school districts submitted pursuant to Article 1 (commencing with Section 35700) of Chapter 4 of Part 21 of the Education Code, petitions for the reorganization of community college districts submitted pursuant to part 46 (commencing with Section 74000) of the Education Code, and all memoranda prepared by the county clerks in the examination of

such petitions indicating which registered voters have signed particular petitions shall not be deemed to be public records and shall not be open to inspection except by the public officer or public employees who have the duty of receiving, examining or preserving such petitions or who are responsible for preparation of such memoranda and, if the petition is found to be insufficient, by the proponents of the petition and such representatives of the proponents as may be designated by the proponents in writing in order to determine which signatures were disqualified and the reasons therefor; provided, however, that the Attorney General, the Secretary of State, the Fair Political Practices Commission, a district attorney, and a city attorney shall be permitted to examine such material upon approval of the appropriate superior court.

If the proponents of a petition are permitted to examine the petition and memoranda, such examination shall commence not later than 21 days after certification of insufficiency.

As used in this section "proponents of the petition" means the following:

(a) For statewide initiative and referendum measures, the person or persons who submit a draft of a petition proposing the measure to the Attorney General with a request that he prepare a title and summary of the chief purpose and points of the proposed measure.

(b) For other initiatives and referenda on measures, the person or persons who publish a notice of intention to circulate petitions, or, where publication is not required, who filed petitions with the clerk.

(c) For recall measures, the person or persons defined in Section 29711 of the Elections Code.

(d) For petitions circulated pursuant to Section 5091 of the Education Code, the person or persons having charge of the petition who submit the petition to the county superintendent of schools.

(e) For petitions circulated pursuant to Article 1 (commencing with Section 35700) of Chapter 4 of Part 21 of the Education Code, the person or persons designated as chief petitioners under Section 35701 of the Education Code.

(f) For petitions circulated pursuant to Part 46 (commencing with Section 74000) of the Education Code, the person or persons designated as chief petitioners under Sections 74102, 74133, and 74152 of the Education Code.

6253.6. Requests for bilingual election materials

(a) Notwithstanding the provisions of Sections 6252 and 6253, information compiled by public officers or public employees revealing the identity of persons who have requested bilingual ballots or ballot pamphlets, made in accordance with any federal or state law, or other data that would reveal the identity of the requester, shall not be deemed to be public records and shall not be provided to any person other than public officers or public employees who are responsible for receiving those requests and processing the same.

(b) Nothing contained in subdivision (a) shall be construed as prohibiting any person who is otherwise authorized by law from examining election materials, including, but not limited to, affidavits of registration, provided that requests for bilingual ballots or ballot pamphlets shall be subject to the restrictions contained in subdivision (a).

6254. Records exempt from disclosure requirements

Except as provided in Section 6254.7, nothing in this chapter shall be construed to require disclosure of records that are any of the following:

(a) Preliminary drafts, notes, or interagency or intra-agency memoranda which are not retained by the public agency in the ordinary course of business, provided that the public interest in withholding those records clearly outweighs the public interest in disclosure.

(b) Records pertaining to pending litigation to which the public agency is a party, or to claims made pursuant to Division 3.6 (commencing with Section 810) until the pending litigation or claim has been finally adjudicated or otherwise settled.

(c) Personnel, medical, or similar files, the disclosure of which would constitute an unwarranted invasion of personal privacy.

(d) Contained in or related to:

(1) Applications filed with any state agency responsible for the regulation or supervision or the issuance of securities or of financial institutions, including, but not

limited to banks, savings and loan associations, industrial loan companies, credit unions, and insurance companies.
(2) Examination, operating, or condition reports prepared by, on behalf of, or for the use of any state agency referred to in paragraph (1).
(3) Preliminary drafts, notes, or interagency or intra-agency communications prepared by, on behalf of, or for the use of any state agency referred to in paragraph (1).
(4) Information received in confidence by any state agency referred to in paragraph (1).
(e) Geological and geophysical data, plant production data, and similar information relating to utility systems development, or market or crop reports, which are obtained in confidence from any person.
(f) Records of complaints to, or investigations conducted by, or records of intelligence information or security procedures of the office of the Attorney General and the Department of Justice, and any state or local police agency, or any investigatory or security files compiled by any other state or local police agency, or any investigatory or security files compiled by any other state or local agency for correctional, law enforcement or licensing purposes, except that state and local law enforcement agencies and the California Highway Patrol shall disclose the names and addresses of persons involved in, or witnesses other than confidential informants to, the incident, the description of any property involved, the date, time, and location of the incident, the statements of all witnesses, other than confidential informants, to the victims of an incident, or an authorized representative thereof, an insurance carrier against which a claim has been or might be made, and any person suffering bodily injury or property damage or loss as the result of the incident caused by arson, burglary, fire, explosion, larceny, robbery, vandalism, vehicle theft, or a crime of violence as defined by subdivision (c) of Section 13960, unless the disclosure would endanger the safety of a witness or other person involved in the investigation, disclosure would endanger the successful completion of the investigation or a related investigation. However, nothing in this division shall require the disclosure of that portion of those investigative files which reflect the analysis or conclusions of the investigating officer.
Other provisions of this subdivision notwithstanding, state and local law enforcement agencies shall make public the following information, except to the extent that disclosure of a particular item of information would endanger the safety of a person involved in an investigation or would endanger the successful completion of the investigation or a related investigation:
(1) The full name, current address, and occupation of every individual arrested by the agency, the individual's physical description including date of birth, color of eyes and hair, sex, height and weight, the time and date of arrest, the time and date of booking, the location of the arrest, the factual circumstances surrounding the arrest, the amount of bail set, the time and manner of release or the location where the individual is currently being held, and all charges the individual is being held upon, including any outstanding warrants from other jurisdictions and parole or probation holds.
(2) The time, substance, and location of all complaints or requests for assistance received by the agency and the time and nature of the response thereto, including, to the extent the information regarding crimes alleged or committed or any other incident investigated is recorded, the time, date and location of occurrence, the time and date of the report, the name, age, and current address of the victim, except that the address of the victim of any crime defined by Section 261, 264, 264.1, 273a, 273d, 273.5, 286, 288, 288a, 289, 422.6, 422.7, or 422.75 of the Penal Code shall not be disclosed, the factual circumstances surrounding the crime or incident, and a general description of any injuries, property or weapons involved. The name of a victim of any crime defined by Section 261, 264, 264.1, 273a, 273d, 273.5, 286, 288, 288a, 289, 422.6, 422.7, or 422.75 of the Penal Code may be withheld at the victim's request, or at the request of the victim's parent or guardian if the victim is a minor. When a person is the victim of more than one crime, information disclosing that the person is a victim of a crime defined by Section 261, 264, 264.1, 273a, 273d, 286, 288, 288a, 289, 422.6, 422.7, or 422.75 of the Penal Code may be deleted at the request of the victim, or the victim's parent or guardian if the victim is a minor, in making the report of the crime, or of any

crime or incident accompanying the crime, available to the public in compliance with the requirements of this paragraph.

(g) Test questions, scoring keys, and other examination data used to administer a licensing examination, examination for employment, or academic examination, except as provided for in Chapter 3 (commencing with Section 99150) of Part 65 of the Education Code.

(h) The contents of real estate appraisals or engineering or feasibility estimates and evaluations made for or by the state or local agency relative to the acquisition of property, or to prospective public supply and construction contracts, until all of the property has been acquired or all of the contract agreement obtained. However, the law of eminent domain shall not be affected by this provision.

(i) Information required from any taxpayer in connection with the collection of local taxes which is received in confidence and the disclosure of the information to other persons would result in unfair competitive disadvantage to the person supplying the information.

(j) Library circulation records kept for the purpose of identifying the borrower of items available in libraries, and library and museum materials made or acquired and presented solely for reference or exhibition purposes. The exemption in this subdivision shall not apply to records of fines imposed on the borrowers.

(k) Records the disclosure of which is exempted or prohibited pursuant to federal or state law, including, but not limited to, provisions of the Evidence Code relating to privilege.

(l) Correspondence of and to the Governor or employees of the Governor's office or in the custody of or maintained by the Governor's legal affairs secretary, provided that public records shall not be transferred to the custody of the Governor's legal affairs secretary to evade the disclosure provisions of this chapter.

(m) In the custody of or maintained by the Legislative Counsel.

(n) Statements of personal worth or personal financial data required by a licensing agency and filed by an applicant with the licensing agency to establish his or her personal qualification for the license, certificate, or permit applied for.

(o) Financial data contained in applications for financing under Division 27 (commencing with Section 44500) of the Health and Safety Code, where an authorized officer of the California Pollution Control Financing Authority determines that disclosure of such financial data would be competitively injurious to the applicant and such data is required in order to obtain guarantees from the United States Small Business Administration. The California Pollution Control Financing Authority shall adopt rules for review of individual requests for confidentiality under this section and for making available to the public those portions of an application which are subject to disclosure under this chapter.

(p) Records of state agencies related to activities governed by Chapter 10.3 (commencing with Section 3512) of Division 4 of Title 1, Chapter 10.5 (commencing with Section 3525) of Division 4 of Title 1, and Chapter 12 (commencing with Section 3560) of Division 4 of Title 1, which reveal a state agency's deliberative processes, impressions, evaluations, opinions, recommendations, meeting minutes, research, work products, theories, or strategy, or which provide instruction, advice, or training to employees who do not have full collective bargaining and representative rights under the above chapters. Nothing in this subdivision shall be construed to limit the disclosure duties of a state agency with respect to any other records relating to the activities governed by the employee relations acts referred to in this division.

(q) Records of state agencies related to activities governed by Articles 2.6 (commencing with Section 14081), 2.8 (commencing with Section 14087.5), and 2.91 (commencing with Section 14089) of Chapter 7 of Part 3 of Division 9 of the Welfare and Institutions Code, which reveal the special negotiator's deliberative processes, discussions, communications, or any other portion of the negotiations with providers of health care services, impressions, opinions, recommendations, meeting minutes, research, work product, theories, or strategy, or which provide instruction, advice or training to employees.

Except for the portion of a contract containing the rate of payment, contracts for inpatient services entered into pursuant to these articles, on or after April 1, 1984, shall be open to inspection one year after they are fully executed. In the event that a contract for inpatient services which is entered into prior to April 1, 1984, is amended on or after April 1, 1984, the amendment, except for any portion containing the rates of payment, shall be open to inspection one year after it is fully executed. If the California Medical Assistance Commission enters into contracts with health care providers for other than inpatient hospital services, those contracts shall be open to inspection one year after they are fully executed.

Three years after a contract or amendment is open to inspection under this subdivision, the portion of the contract or amendment containing the rates of payment shall be open to inspection.

Notwithstanding any other provision of law, the entire contract or amendment shall be open to inspection by the Joint Legislative Audit Committee. The Joint Legislative Audit Committee shall maintain the confidentiality of the contracts and amendments until such time as a contract or amendment is fully open to inspection by the public.

(r) Records of Native American graves, cemeteries, and sacred places maintained by the Native American Heritage Commission.

(s) A final accreditation report of the Joint Commission on Accreditation of Hospitals which has been transmitted to the State Department of Health Services pursuant to subdivision (b) of Section 1282 of the Health and Safety Code.

(t) Records of a local hospital district, formed pursuant to Division 23 (commencing with Section 32000) of the Health and Safety Code, which relate to any contract with an insurer or nonprofit hospital service plan for inpatient or outpatient services for alternative rates pursuant to Section 10133 or 11512 of the Insurance Code. However, the record shall be open to inspection within one year after the contract is fully executed.

(u) Information contained in applications for licenses to carry concealed weapons issued by the sheriff of a county or the chief or other head of a municipal police department which indicates when or where the applicant is vulnerable to attack or which concerns the applicant's medical or psychological history or that of members of his or her family.

(v) Residence addresses contained in licensure applications and registration applications for collection agencies as may be required by the Bureau of Collection and Investigative Services of the Department of Consumer Affairs pursuant to Section 6876.2, 6877, 6878, and 6894.3 of the Business and Professions Code.

(w) (1) Records of the Major Risk Medical Insurance Program related to activities governed by Part 6.3 (commencing with Section 12695), and Part 6.5 (commencing with Section 12700), of Division 2 of the Insurance Code, and which reveal the deliberative processes, discussions, communications, or any other portion of the negotiations with health plans, or the impressions, opinions, recommendations, meeting minutes, research, work product, theories, or strategy of the board or its staff, or records that provide instructions, advice, or training to employees.

(2)(A) Except for the portion of a contract that contains the rates of payment, contracts for health coverage entered into pursuant to Part 6.3 (commencing with Section 12695), or Part 6.5 (commencing with Section 12700), of Division 2 of the Insurance Code, on or after July 1, 1991, shall be open to inspection one year after they have been fully executed.

(B) In the event that a contract for health coverage that is entered into prior to July 1, 1991, is amended on or after July 1, 1991, the amendment, except for any portion containing the rates of payment shall be open to inspection one year after the amendment has been fully executed.

(3) Three years after a contract or amendment is open to inspection pursuant to this subdivision, the portion of the contract or amendment containing the rates of payment shall be open to inspection.

(4) Notwithstanding any other provision of law, the entire contract of amendments to a contract shall be open to inspection by the Joint Legislative Audit Committee. The Joint Legislative Audit Committee shall maintain the confidentiality of the contracts and

amendments thereto, until the contract or amendments to a contract is open to inspection pursuant to paragraph (3).

Nothing in this section prevents any agency from opening its records concerning the administration of the agency to public inspection, unless disclosure is otherwise prohibited by law.

Nothing in this section prevents any health facility from disclosing to a certified bargaining agent relevant financing information pursuant to Section 8 of the National Labor Relations Act.

6254.1. Exemption of residence or mailing address

(a) Except as provided in Section 6254.7, nothing in this chapter requires disclosure of records that are the residence address of any person contained in the records of the Department of Housing and Community Development, if the person has requested confidentiality of that information, in accordance with Section 18081 of the Health and Safety Code.

(b) Nothing in this chapter requires the disclosure of the residence or mailing address of any person in any record of the Department of Motor Vehicles except in accordance with Section 1808.21 of the Vehicle Code.

6254.2. Disclosure of pesticide safety and efficacy information; Trade secrets; Affirmation of requester; Action for wrongful disclosure; Effect of invalidation of federal law

(a) Nothing in this chapter exempts from public disclosure the same categories of pesticide safety and efficacy information that are disclosable under paragraph (1) of subsection (d) of Section 10 of the Federal Insecticide, Fungicide, and Rodenticide Act (7 U.S.C. Sec. 136h(d)(1)), if the individual requesting the information is not an employee or agent specified in subdivision (h).

(b) The Director of Food and Agriculture, upon his or her initiative, or upon receipt of a request pursuant to the California Public Records Act (Chapter 3.5 (commencing with Section 6250) of Division 7 of Title 1) for the release of data submitted and designated as a trade secret by a registrant or applicant, shall determine whether any or all of the data so submitted is a properly designated trade secret. In order to assure that the interested public has an opportunity to obtain and review pesticide safety and efficacy data and to comment prior to the expiration of the public comment period on a proposed pesticide registration, the director shall provide notice to interested persons when an application for registration enters the registration evaluation process.

(c) If the director determines that the data is not a trade secret, the director shall notify the registrant or applicant by certified mail.

(d) The registrant or applicant shall have 30 days after receipt of this notification to provide the director with a complete justification and statement of the grounds on which the trade secret privilege is claimed. This justification and statement shall be submitted by certified mail.

(e) The director shall determine whether the data is protected as a trade secret within 15 days after receipt of the justification and statement or, if no justification and statement is filed, within 45 days of the original notice. The director shall notify the registrant or applicant and any party who has requested the data pursuant to the California Public Records Act of that determination by certified mail. If the director determines that the data is not protected as a trade secret, the final notice shall also specify a date, not sooner than 15 days after the date of mailing of the final notice, when the data shall be available to any person requesting information pursuant to subdivision (a).

(f) "Trade secret" means data that is nondisclosable under paragraph (1) of subsection (d) of Section 10 of the Federal Insecticide, Fungicide, and Rodenticide Act.

(g) This section shall be operative only so long as, and to the extent that, enforcement of paragraph (1) of subsection (d) of Section 10 of the Federal Insecticide, Fungicide, and Rodenticide Act has not been enjoined by federal court order, and shall become inoperative if an unappealable federal court judgment or decision becomes final that holds that paragraph invalid, to the extent of the invalidity.

(h) The Director of Food and Agriculture shall not knowingly disclose information submitted by an applicant or registrant pursuant to Article 4 (commencing with Section 12811) of Chapter 2 of Division 7 of the Food and Agricultural Code to any employee or agent of any business or other entity engaged in the production, sale, or distribution of pesticides in countries other than the United States or in other countries in addition to the United States, or to any other person who intends to deliver this information to any foreign or multi-national business or entity, unless the applicant or registrant consents to this disclosure. To implement this subdivision, the director shall require the following affirmation to be signed by the person who requests information pursuant to this section:

Affirmation of Status

This affirmation is required by Section 6254.2 of the Government Code.

I have requested access to information submitted by an applicant or registrant under the California Food and Agricultural Code. I hereby affirm all of the following:

(1) I do not seek access to the information for purposes of delivering it or offering it for sale to any business or other entity engaged in the production, sale, or distribution of pesticides in countries other than the United States or in other countries in addition to the United States, or to the agents or employees of such a business or entity.

(2) I will not purposefully deliver or negligently cause the data to be delivered to such a business or entity or its agents or employees.

I am aware that I may be subject to criminal penalties under Section 118 of the Penal Code if I make any statement of material facts knowing that the statement is false or if I willfully conceal any material fact.

Name

Signature

Organization

Address

Date

Request No.

Client, if you are requesting access on behalf of someone other than the organization or affiliation listed above.

(i) Notwithstanding any other provision of this section, the Director of Food and Agriculture may disclose information submitted by an applicant or registrant to any person in connection with a public proceeding conducted under law or regulation, if the director determines that the information is needed to determine whether a pesticide, or any ingredient of any pesticide, causes unreasonable adverse effects on health or the environment.
(j) The director shall maintain records of the names of persons to whom data is disclosed pursuant to this section and the persons or organizations they represent and shall inform the applicant or registrant of the names and the affiliation of these persons.
(k) Section 118 of the Penal Code applies to any affirmation made pursuant to this section.
(l) Any officer or employee of the state or former officer or employee of the state who, because of this employment or official position, obtains possession of, or has access to, material which is prohibited from disclosure by this section, and who, knowing that

disclosure of this material is prohibited by this section, willfully discloses the material in any manner to any person not entitled to receive it, shall, upon conviction, be punished by a fine of not more than ten thousand dollars ($10,000), or by imprisonment in the county jail for not more than one year, or by both fine and imprisonment. For purposes of this subdivision, any contractor with the state who is furnished information pursuant to this section, or any employee of any contractor, shall be considered an employee of the state.

(m) This section does not prohibit any person from maintaining a civil action for wrongful disclosure of trade secrets.

(n) The director may limit an individual to one request per month pursuant to this section if the director determines that a person has made a frivolous request within the past 12-month period.

6254.25. Applicability of work-product privilege to memoranda submitted to state body or legislative body regarding pending litigation

Nothing in this chapter or any other provision of law shall require the disclosure of a memorandum submitted to a state body or to the legislative body of a local agency by its legal counsel pursuant to subdivision (q) of Section 11126 or Section 54956.9 until the pending litigation has been finally adjudicated or otherwise settled. The memorandum shall be protected by the attorney work-product privilege until the pending litigation has been finally adjudicated or otherwise settled.

6254.3. Confidentiality of state employee home addresses and telephone numbers

(a) The home addresses and home telephone numbers of state employees shall not be deemed to be public records and shall not be open to public inspection, except that disclosure of that information may be made as follows:

(1) To an agent, or a family member of the individual to whom the information pertains.

(2) To an officer or employee of another state agency when necessary for the performance of its official duties.

(3) To an employee organization pursuant to regulations adopted by the Public Employment Relations Board, except that the home addresses and home telephone numbers of state employees performing law enforcement-related functions shall not be disclosed.

(4) To an agent or employee of a health benefit plan providing health services or administering claims for health services to state employees and their enrolled dependents, for the purpose of providing the health services or administering claims for employees and their enrolled dependents.

(b) Upon written request of any employee, a state agency shall not disclose the employee's home address or home telephone number pursuant to paragraph (3) of subdivision (a) and a state agency shall remove the employee's home address and home telephone number from any mailing list maintained by the agency, except if the list is used exclusively by the agency to contact the employee.

6254.4. Voter information concerning public employees; Confidentiality by request

(a) The home address, telephone number, occupation, and precinct number of any active or retired judge or court commissioner, any active or retired district attorney or assistant district attorney, any active or retired public defender or assistant public defender, or any active or retired peace officer as defined in Section 830.1, subdivision (a), (b), (d), or (e) of Section 830.2, or Section 830.5, of the Penal Code, provided the peace officer is employed by the Department of Corrections or the California Youth Authority, or of the spouse or children of a peace officer living with the peace officer, appearing in any record of any voter registration affidavit is confidential if the person requests confidentiality of that information at the time of registration or reregistration, and shall not be disclosed to any person, except to any other governmental agency or to any person engaged in the business of examining public records and files for the primary purpose of reporting those portions of the public records which impart constructive notice under the laws relating to land and land titles, and except as prohibited by Section 1808.4 of the Vehicle Code, or pursuant to Section 615 of the Elections Code. Confidentiality granted under this section shall apply only to records prepared or generated on or after the date that the voter is granted confidentiality.

(b) A person who requests confidentiality of the information specified in subdivision (a) shall register or reregister to vote by means of a confidential affidavit of registration form which shall be prescribed by the Secretary of State and which shall be attested to under penalty of perjury by the affiant that he or she is a person entitled to confidential treatment pursuant to this section.
(c) For purposes of this section, "home address" means only street address and does not include an individual's city or post office address. Any record shall be open to public inspection to the extent otherwise provided by law if the address if completely obliterated or otherwise removed from the record.

6254.5. Disclosure of otherwise exempt records
Notwithstanding any other provisions of the law, whenever a state or local agency disclosed a public record which is otherwise exempt from this chapter, to any member of the public, this disclosure shall constitute a waiver of the exemptions specified in Sections 6254, 6254.7, or other similar provisions of law. For purposes of this section, "agency" includes a member, agent, officer, or employee of the agency acting within the scope of his or her membership, agency, office, or employment.
This section, however, shall not apply to disclosures:
(a) Made pursuant to the Information Practices Act (commencing with Section 1798 of the Civil Code) or discovery proceedings.
(b) Made through other legal proceedings.
(c) Within the scope of disclosure of a statute which limits disclosure of specified writings to certain purposes.
(d) Not required by law, and prohibited by formal action of an elected legislative body of the local agency which retains the writings.
(e) Made to any governmental agency which agrees to treat the disclosed material as confidential. Only persons authorized in writing by the person in charge of the agency shall be permitted to obtain the information. Any information obtained by the agency shall only be used for purposes which are consistent with existing law.
(f) Of records relating to a financial institution or an affiliate thereof, if the disclosures are made to the financial institution or affiliate by a state agency responsible for the regulation or supervision of the financial institution or affiliate.

6254.6. Confidentiality of identity of employers providing private industry wage data for salary setting purposes
Whenever a city and county or a joint powers agency, pursuant to a mandatory statute or charter provision to collect private industry wage data for salary setting purposes, or a contract entered to implement that mandate, is provided this data by the federal Bureau of Labor Statistics on the basis that the identify of private industry employers shall remain confidential, the identify of the employers shall not be open to the public or be admitted as evidence in any action or special proceeding.

6254.7. Air pollution data; Housing code violations; "Trade secrets"
(a) All information, analyses, plans, or specifications that disclose the nature, extent, quantity, or degree of air contaminants or other pollution which any article, machine, equipment, or other contrivance will produce, which any air pollution control district or any other state or local agency or district requires any applicant to provide before such applicant builds, erects, alters, replaces, operates, sells, rents, or uses such article, machine, equipment, or other contrivance, are public records.
(b) All air or other pollution monitoring data, including data compiled from the stationary sources, are public records.
(c) All records of notices and orders directed to the owner of any building of violations of housing or building codes, ordinances, statutes, or regulations which constitute violations of standards provided in Section 1941.1 of the Civil Code, and records of subsequent action with respect to such notices and orders, are public records.
(d) Except as otherwise provided in subdivision (e) and Chapter 3 (commencing with Section 99150) of Part 65 of the Education Code, trade secrets are not public records under this section. "Trade secrets," as used in this section, may include, but are not limited to, any formula, plan, pattern, process, tool, mechanism, compound, procedure, production data, or compilation of information which is not patented, which is known only to certain individuals within a commercial concern who are using it to fabricate,

produce, or compound an article of trade or a service having commercial value and which gives its user an opportunity to obtain a business advantage over competitors who do not know or use it.

(e) Notwithstanding any other provision of law, all air pollution emission data, including those emission data which constitute trade secrets as defined in subdivision (d) are public records. Data used to calculate emission data are not emission data for the purposes of this subdivision and data which constitute trade secrets and which are used to calculate emission data are not public records.

6254.8. Employment contracts between state or local agency and public official or employee; Public record

Every employment contract between a state or local agency and any public official or public employee is a public record which is not subject to the provisions of Sections 6254 and 6255.

6254.9. Computer software developed by government agency

(a) Computer software developed by a state or local agency is not itself a public record under this chapter. The agency may sell, lease, or license the software for commercial or noncommercial use.

(b) As used in this section, "computer software" includes computer mapping systems, computer programs, and computer graphics systems.

(c) This section shall not be construed to create an implied warranty on the part of the State of California or any local agency for errors, omissions, or other defects in any computer software as provided pursuant to this section.

(d) Nothing in this section is intended to affect the public record status of information merely because it is stored in a computer. Public records stored in a computer shall be disclosed as required by this chapter.

(e) Nothing in this section is intended to limit any copyright productions.

6254.10. Archaeological site information

Nothing in this chapter requires disclosure of records that relate to Archaeological site information maintained by the Department of Parks and Recreation, the State Historical Resources Commission, or the State Lands Commission.

6254.11. Disclosure of records on volatile organic compounds or chemical substances

Nothing in this chapter requires the disclosure of records that relate to volatile organic compounds or chemical substances information received or compiled by an air pollution control officer pursuant to Section 42203.2 of the Health and Safety Code.

6255. Withholding records from inspection; Justification; Public interest

The agency shall justify withholding any record by demonstrating that the record in question is exempt under express provisions of this chapter or that on the facts of the particular case the public interest served by not making the record public clearly outweighs the public interest served by disclosure of the record.

6256. Right to copy of identifiable public records; Time limits

Any person may receive a copy of any identifiable public record or copy thereof. Upon request, an exact copy shall be provided unless impracticable to do so. Computer data shall be provided in a form determined by the agency. Each agency, upon any request for a copy of records shall determine within 10 days after the receipt of such request whether to comply with the request and shall immediately notify the person making the request of such determination and reasons therefor.

6256.1. Extension of time for determination in unusual circumstances; Reasons

In unusual circumstances, as specified in this section, the time limit prescribed in Section 6256 may be extended by written notice by the head of the agency to the person making the request setting forth the reasons for the extension and the date on which a determination is expected to be dispatched. No such notice shall specify a date that would result in an extension for more than 10 working days.

As used in this section, "unusual circumstances" means, but only to the extent reasonably necessary to the proper processing of the particular request:

(a) The need to search for and collect the requested records from field facilities or other establishments that are separate from the office processing the request.

(b) The need to search for, collect, and appropriately examine a voluminous amount of separate and distinct records which are demanded in a single request.
(c) The need for consultation, which shall be conducted with all practicable speed, with another agency having a substantial interest in the determination of the request or among two or more components of the agency having substantial subject matter interest therein.

6256.2. Delay in access; Prohibition; Notification of denial; Name of person responsible

Nothing in this chapter shall be construed to permit an agency to delay access for purposes of inspecting public records. Any notification of denial of any request for records shall set forth the names and titles or positions of each person responsible for the denial.

6257. Fees, Records containing exempt and nonexempt material; Provision of segregable portions

Except with respect to public records exempt by express provisions of law from disclosure, each state or local agency, upon any request for a copy of records, which reasonably describes an identifiable record, or information produced therefrom, shall make the records promptly available to any person, upon payment fees covering direct costs of duplication, or a statutory fee, if applicable. Any reasonably segregable portion of a record shall be provided to any person requesting such record after deletion of the portions which are exempt by law.

6258. Enforcement of rights; Proceedings for injunctive or declaratory relief; Writ of mandate

Any person may institute proceedings for injunctive or declarative relief or writ of mandate in any court of competent jurisdiction to enforce his or her right to inspect or to receive a copy of any public record or class of public records under this chapter. The times for responsive pleadings and for hearings in these proceedings shall be set by the judge of the court with the object of securing a decision as to these matters at the earliest possible time.

6259. Order to show cause; In camera inspection; Reviewability of determination; Costs and attorney fees

(a) Whenever it is made to appear by verified petition to the superior court of the county where the records or some part thereof are situated that certain public records are being improperly withheld from a member of the public, the court shall order the officer or person charged with withholding the records to disclose the public record or show cause why he or she should not do so. The court shall decide the case after examining the record in camera, if permitted by subdivision (b) of Section 915 of the Evidence Code, papers filed by the parties and any oral argument and additional evidence as the court may allow.
(b) If the court finds that the public official's decision to refuse disclosure is not justified under Section 6254 or 6255, he or she shall order the public official to make the record public. If the judge determines that the public official was justified in refusing to make the record public, he or she shall return the item to the public official without disclosing its content with an order supporting the decision refusing disclosure.
(c) In an action filed on or after January 1, 1991, an order of the court, either directing disclosure by a public official or supporting the decision of the public official refusing disclosure, is not a final judgment or order within the meaning of Section 904.1 of the Code of Civil Procedure from which an appeal may be taken, but shall be immediately reviewable by petition to the appellate court for the issuance of an extraordinary writ. Upon entry of any order pursuant to this section, a party shall, in order to obtain review of the order, file a petition within 10 days after service upon him or her of a written notice of entry of the order, or within such further time not exceeding 20 days as the trial court may for good cause allow. If the notice is served by mail, the period within which to file the petition shall be increased by five days. A stay of an order or judgment shall not be granted unless the petitioning party demonstrates it will otherwise sustain irreparable damage and probable success on the merits. Any person who fails to obey the order of the court shall be cited to show cause why he or she is not in contempt of court.

(d) The court shall award court costs and reasonable attorney fees to the plaintiff should the plaintiff prevail in litigation filed pursuant to this section. The costs and fees shall be paid by the public agency of which the public official is a member or employee and shall not become a personal liability of the public official. If the court finds that the plaintiff's case is clearly frivolous, it shall award court costs and reasonable attorney fees to the public agency.

6260. Effect of chapter on prior rights and proceedings
The provisions of this chapter shall not be deemed in any manner to affect the status of judicial records as it existed immediately prior to the effective date of this section, nor to affect the rights of litigants, including parties to administrative proceedings, under the laws of discovery of this state, nor to limit or impair any rights of discovery in a criminal case.

6261. Itemized statement of total expenditures and disbursement of any agency
Notwithstanding Section 6252, an itemized statement of the total expenditures and disbursements of any agency provided for in Article VI of the California Constitution shall be open for inspection.

6262. Disclosure of licensing complaint and investigation records on request of district attorney
The exemption of records of complaints to, or investigations conducted by, any state or local agency for licensing purposes under subdivision (f) of Section 6254 shall not apply when a request for inspection of such records is made by a district attorney.

6263. Inspection or copying of public records on request of district attorney
A state or local agency shall allow an inspection of any public record or class of public records not exempted by this chapter when requested by a district attorney.

6264. Petition by district attorney to require disclosure
The district attorney may petition a court of competent jurisdiction to require a state or local agency to allow him to inspect or receive a copy of any public record or class of public records not exempted by this chapter when the agency fails or refuses to allow inspection or copying within 10 working days of a request. The court may require a public agency to permit inspection or copying by the district attorney unless the public interest or good cause in withholding such records clearly outweighs the public interest in disclosure.

6265. Disclosure of records to district attorney; Status of records
Disclosure of records to a district attorney under the provisions of this chapter shall effect no change in the status of the records under any other provision of law.

6267. Registration and circulation records of library supported by public funds
All registration and circulation records of any library which is in whole or in part supported by public funds shall remain confidential and shall not be disclosed to any person, local agency, or state agency except as follows:
(a) By a person acting within the scope of his or her duties within the administration of the library.
(b) By a person authorized, in writing, by the individual to whom the records pertain, to inspect the records.
(c) By order of the appropriate superior court.
As used in this section, the term "registration records" includes any information which a library requires a patron to provide in order to become eligible to borrow books and other materials, and the term "circulation records" includes any information which identifies the patrons borrowing particular books and other material.
This section shall not apply to statistical reports of registration and circulation nor to records of fines collected by the library.

6268. Transfer of public records in custody or control of Governor upon leaving office
Public records, as defined in Section 6252, in the custody or control of the Governor when he or she leaves office, either voluntarily or involuntarily, shall, as soon as is practical, be transferred to the State Archives. Notwithstanding any other provisions of law, the Governor, by written instrument, the terms of which shall be made public, may restrict public access to any of the transferred public records, or any other writings he or

she may transfer, which have not already been made accessible to the public. With respect to public records, public access, as otherwise provided for by this chapter, shall not be restricted for a period greater than 50 years or the death of the Governor, whichever is later, nor shall there be any restriction whatsoever with respect to enrolled bill files, press releases, speech files, or writings relating to applications for clemency or extradition in cases which have been closed for a period of at least 25 years. Subject to any restrictions permitted by this section, the Secretary of State, as custodian of the State Archives, shall make all such public records and other writings available to the public as otherwise provided for in this chapter.

Except as to enrolled bill files, press releases, speech files, or writings relating to applications for clemency or extradition, this section shall not apply to public records or other writings in the direct custody or control of any Governor who held office between 1974 and 1988 at the time of leaving office, except to the extent that that Governor may voluntarily transfer those records or other writings to the State Archives.

Notwithstanding any other provision of law, the public records and other writings of any Governor who held office between 1974 and 1988 may be transferred to any educational or research institution in California provided that with respect to public records, public access, as otherwise provided for by this chapter, shall not be restricted for a period greater than 50 years or the death of the Governor, whichever is later. No records or writings may be transferred pursuant to this paragraph unless the institution receiving them agrees to maintain, and does maintain, the materials according to commonly accepted archival standards. No public records transferred shall be destroyed by that institution without first receiving the written approval of the Secretary of State, as custodian of the State Archives, who may require that the records be placed in the State Archives rather than being destroyed. An institution receiving those records or writings shall allow the Secretary of State, as custodian of the State Archives, to copy, at state expense, and to make available to the public, any eand all public records, and inventories, indices, or finding aids relating to those records, which the institution makes available to the public generally. Copies of those records in the custody of the State Archives shall be given the same legal effect as is given to the originals.

Index

990, IRS Form, 105
A Public Records Odyssey, 74
Abstracts of judgments, 83
Accession number, 116
Accountants, 91
Acupuncturists, 92
Addresses, 68, 82, 84, 106, 109
Affidavit in support of search warrant, 85
Affidavit, voter, 22
Agent for Service of Process, 44, 107
Air Reserve, 119
Airplanes, 23, 31, 69, 81, 115
Alarms, security permits, 21
Alcoholic Beverage Control, 89
Alimony, 27
Allied Health Committees, 92
Animal Regulation, 14, 21, 78
Appliance repair persons, 28
Architects, 28, 91
Armed Service Locators, 113
Army National Guard, 120
Arraignments, 28
Arrest records, 21
Arrest report information, 97, 268
Articles of Incorporation, 29
Articles of Organization, 108
Assessor, 14, 22, 23, 49, 58, 59, 69, 81
Assessor's Parcel Number, 81
Assets, 30, 69
Associations, 71
Athletic Commission, 91
Attorney General, California, 22
Auctioneers, 89
Audiology, 92
Automobile dealerships, 106
Automobile manufacturers, 106
Automotive Repair, 91
Awards, military, 118
Bail information, 21
Ballot measures, 21, 22, 79
Bank assets, 30
Banking Department, State, 29, 90
Bankruptcy information, 30, 69, 116, 125
Bar Association, 110
Barbers, 91
Behavioral Scientists, 91
Bellicosity, 34
Belligerence (see Bellicosity), 34
Best man, 82
Bill of Rights, U.S., 19
Birth certificates, 14, 23, 24, 29, .55, 82, 110
Blood tests for marriages, 23
Board of Equalization, 22, 28, 96
Boating and Waterways Dept., 90
Boats, 23, 69, 81, 106, 115
Boles, Kenny, 47
Bride's maid, 82
Brokers, boat and yacht, 90
Building permits, 20, 43, 77
Bulk mail permits, 30
Burial information, 31
Business permits, 21
Business permits and licenses, 21, 77
Buyer of property, 24
CA-1, tax return, 105
California Highway Patrol, 97
California Public Records Act, 265
Campaign contributions, 20, 22, 29, 80, 116
Campaign Disclosure Statement, 80
CD-ROM, 67, 68, 71
CDB Infotek, 68
Cemetery Board, 91
Census records, 117
Chamber of commerce, 14, 15
Chambers of commerce, 42
Change of address information, 126
Charitable Trusts, 105
Child support, 27
Children, 84
Chiropractic Examiners, 91

CHP, 97
City attorney, 27
City directories, 73
City elections, 78
City hall, 43
City records, 77
Civil case files, 27, 69, 84, 85, 116, 125
Civil service members, retired, 122
Collateral, 29, 109
Columbo move, 38
Commercial database, 67
Commissioner, court, 28
Commissions, 30
Compliment, how to, 37
Confidential marriages, 23, 83
Conflict of interest statement, 30, 80
Constitution, U.S., 19
Consumer Affairs, Dept. of, 28, 90
Contact Lens, 92
Contractors, 28, 77, 91
Contracts, 83
Contributions, campaign, 20, 21, 22
Cook, Victor, 73
Coolidge, President Calvin, 15
Corporations, 26, 29, 70, 94, 107
Corrections, State Dept. of, 29
Cosmetologists, 91
Counties, listings of, 223
County Clerk, 26
County clerk, 26, 83
County Codes, 86
County recorder, 82
Court of Appeals, 95
Criminal case files, 27, 69, 84, 116, 125
Criminal histories, 94
Databases, 16, 67, 68, 69, 74
Dataquick real estate database, 44, 69
Date of birth, 24
DBAs, 84
Death certificates, 23, 24, 82, 110
Death records, 31

Deceased persons, 26
Deed of trust, 24
Deeds, 24, 83
Demolition permits, 20, 77
Dentists, 28, 91
Department of Motor Vehicles, 28, 68, 69, 105
DIALOG, 70
Disbarrments of attorneys, 110
Disclosure Inc., 122
Dismantling yards, 106
District Attorney, 27
District attorney, 27
Divorce files, 26, 84, 110
DMV (see also Department of Motor Vehicles), 28
Dogs, licenses, 21
Driver's license number, 13, 25, 109, 125
Drivers license information, 28, 105
Driving instructors, 106
Driving schools, 106
DWC Authorization Number, 111
Elections, 29, 78
Elections, city, 21
Elections, federal, 31
Electrical permits, 77
Electronic and Appliance Repairs, 91
Embalmers, 91
Employment, places of, 24, 84
ENG News Service, 74
ENG Productions, 74
Engineers, 93
Equalization Board, 96
Exclusive News Group, 74
Excuses by records curators, 35
Executives, 70, 122
Exemption, homeowner's, 22
Exhibits, civil case, 26
FAA, 115
FAA (See Federal Aviation Administration), 31, 115
Fair Political Practices Commission, 29, 96
FBI, 65
FEC, 116

Federal Aviation Administration, 31, 115
Federal Communications Commission, 31
Federal court, 30
Federal Election Commission, 31, 116
Federal identification number, 109
Federal Records Centers, 116
Fictitious name statements, 26, 37, 38, 68, 69, 84
Financial information, 84, 125
Financing statement, 109
Fines, overdue book, 21
Fingerprints, 25
FRC location number, 116
Freedom of Information Act, 19
Funeral directors, 28, 91
Gale Research Inc., 71
Garage sale permits, 21
Genealogical libraries, 117, 127
Genealogists, 75
General partnerships, 26
Geologists, 28, 91
Geophysicists, 91
Gifts, records of, 30
GKL Corporate/Search, Inc., 75
Governor, 22
Grading permits, 20, 77
Grand Tour, Grand Tea, 24
Grandparents, 26
Grant deeds, 83
Grantor-Grantee, 23, 24, 25, 43, 83
Guide Dogs for the Blind, 92
Guns, 42
Haines and Company, Inc., 64, 75
Hairdressers, 28
Hearing Aid Dispensers, 92
Hinckley, John, 41, 42
Home Furnishings, 92
Homeowner's exemptions, 22
Homeowners exemptions, 81
Horticulture, 15
How to Locate and Investigate People, 74
Humane Society, 78
Income tax, 20

Income tax information, 30
Index (you're already there!), 279
Indictments, 27
Info AmeriCall, 69
Information Superhighway, 16
Injuries, on the job, 110
Insurance, Dept. of, 29, 104
IRS form 990, 105
IRSC, 69
Jackson, Michael, 45, 46, 47
Jennings, Jan, 75
Judges, 28
Judgments, civil, 27
Justice court (doesn't exist), 85
Justice Department, 105
Kitchen Cabinet, Reagan's, 43, 44
Land Surveyors, 93
Landscape Architects, 92
Last will and testament, 26
Legal description, 81
Legal references, 70
Lessor retailers, vehicle, 106
Lexis-Nexis, 70
Library cards, 21
Library, public, 15, 65
Licenses, business, 21
Licenses, pet, 21
Liens, 25
Liens, mechanics, 25
Limited Liability Companies, 29, 108
Limited partnerships, 26, 29, 108
LLC, 108
LLC-1, 108
LLC-12, 108
Loans, records of, 30
Locksmiths, 46
Los Angeles Times Index, 65
Magazines, 64
Manufacturer's Identification Code, vessels, 115
Maps, 80
Marriage certificates, 23, 24, 29, 68, 69, 82, 110
Marriage licenses, 26, 83
Mead Data Central, 70
Mechanics licenses, 28
Mechanics liens, 25, 83

Medical Board, 92
Medical records, 20
Metered mail, 30, 126
Michael Jackson, 48
Military discharge papers, 83
Military duty assignments, 118
Military records, 30, 113, 117, 119
Minerals, oil and gas brokers, 107
Ministers, 24
Modem, 67
Morgue, newspaper, 14
Motorcycles, 28, 106
Municipal court, 27, 28, 85
Municipal records, 77
Municipalities, listed, 131
National Archives, 116
National Guard, 30
National Personnel Records Center, 30, 117, 120
National Telephone Directory, 71
Naturalization files, 125
Neighbors, 63
Neverland, 45, 46
News media resources, 64
Newspapers, 64, 70
Newspaper morgues, 65
Nexis, 71
Nexis/Lexis, 108
Next of kin, 84
Notaries' bonds, 83
Notary public, 25, 30, 109
Notary's log book, 25, 26, 109
Nurses, 28
Nurses, registered, 93
Nursing Homes, 92
Occupations, 79, 82
Office of Personnel Management, 122
Optometrists, 92
OSHA, 68
Osteopathic Board, 107
PACs (Political Action Committee), 21
PACs (Political Action Committees, 79, 116
PACs (Political Action Committees), 80

Parents, 26, 82
Parents, identifying, 24
Parker, Dorothy, 15
Parolees, 94
Patience Deficit Syndrome, 35
Permit mail, 126
Permits, business, 21
Persistence, 15
Personnel Services, 92
Pets, 78
Pets, licenses, 21
Pharmacists, 92
Photograph, 118
Physical Therapists, 92
Physician's Assistant, 92
Physicians, 92
Pilots' licenses, 31, 115
Place of birth, 24
Plumbing permits, 77
Podiatrists, 92
Police Department, 21
Political action committees, 21, 22, 96, 116
Political campaigns, 79
Political candidates, 96, 116
Polling places, 22, 80
Post office box applications, 30, 125
Powers of attorney, 25, 83
Precinct listings, 22, 80
Prisoner information, 29
Prisons, 94
Privacy, 20, 76
Privacy Rights Clearing House, 76
Private investigators, 28, 93
Private vehicle registrations services, 106
Probate files, 26, 59, 84
probate files, 68
Probation of attorneys, 110
Probation reports, 84
Professional licenses, 28
Property assets, 30, 69, 81, 84
Property tax, 20, 69, 81
ProPhone, 71
Psychiatric Technicians, 93
Psychologists, 28, 92
Public Records Act, 19, 265

Public records curators, 33, 35, 36
Public Records defined, 19
Public Reprovals, attorneys, 110
Quint, Barbara, 74
Quitclaim deeds, 83
Rabies vaccinations, 21, 78
Radio operator licenses, 31
Radio transcripts, 65
Rand Corporation, 74
Reader's Guide to Periodic Literature, 65
Reagan, Nancy, 43, 45
Reagan, Ronald, 41, 42, 43, 45
Real estate agents, 107
Real estate brokers, 107
Real Estate Department, 29, 107
Reciprocal Enforcement Support Law, 27, 84
Reconveyances, 25, 83
Recorder, 14, 23, 24, 25, 49, 82, 83
Reference librarians, 52, 64
Registered Dispensing Opticians, 92
Registered Nurses, 93
Registrar of Voters, 14, 22, 79
Registry of Charitable Trusts, 105
Religious affiliations, 24
Request for Military Information, 117
Resale permits, 28, 96
RESL, 27, 84
Respiratory therapists, 92
Return, search warrant, 85
Reverse phone Directories, 63
Reverse phone directories, 64, 68, 71, 73, 75
Reverse phone directory, 52
Sales tax, 96
Search warrants, 45, 85, 125
Searcher Magazine, 74
SEC, 31, 122
Secretary of State, 22, 25, 26, 29, 30, 44, 75, 107
Securities and Exchange Commission, 31, 122
Security alarm permits, 21
Seller of property, 24

Serial number, military, 118
Service number, military, 118
Sherman Foundation Library, 73
Ship brokers, 90
Shorthand Reporters, 93
Signature samples, 79
Slumlord properties, 77
Small claims court, 27, 85
Social Security Administration, 31, 123
Social Security information, 20, 123
Social Security number, 13, 29, 68, 118
Social Security Numbers by State, 124
Speech Pathologists, 92
Standard & Poor's Register, 70
Standard Form 180, 117
State Assembly, 22
State Bar Association, 110
State Senate, 22
Statement of Economic Interest, 30
Statement of Economic Interests, 30, 80
Statement of Information, LLC, 109
Statement of Officers, 29, 44, 107
Statewide offices, 89
Stock assets, 30
Straw parties, 81
Structural Pest Control, 93
Superior court, 28, 84
Suspensions of attorneys, 110
Swimming pools, 20
Tax Collector, 23
Tax Court, U.S., 30
Tax liens, 83
Tax preparers, 28, 93
Tax returns, non-profits, 105
Tax, income, 20
Tax, property, 20
Telephone Directories, 63
Telephone directories, 73
Telephone numbers, 79
Television transcripts, 65

Thinking, the process of, 12, 15, 16, 17
Thumb print, 109
Traffic citations, 106
Traffic court, 27, 28, 85
Traffic schools, 106
Trailers, 28, 106
Trucks, 28
Trust deeds, 24, 83
U. S. Coast Guard, 115
U.S. Air Force, 114, 119, 120
U.S. Army, 113, 119, 120, 121
U.S. Coast Guard, 114, 119, 121
U.S. District Court, 30, 116, 125
U.S. Marine Corps, 114, 121
U.S. Naval Reserve, 120
U.S. Navy, 114, 120, 121
U.S. Postal Service, 125
UCC, 29, 69, 108, 109
UCC financing statements, 83
Uniform Commercial Code, 29, 109
Unlisted phone numbers, 63, 79
Unsecured property, 23, 81
Vaccinations, rabies, 21
Vehicle registration, 28, 105, 106
Vehicle verifiers, 106
Vehicles, 84
Vessels for hire, 90
Veterinarians, 28, 93
Vital Records, 23
Vital statistics, 29, 82, 110
Vocational Nurse, 93
Voters, Registrar of, 22, 79
Voting records, 22, 43, 49, 78
Welfare information, 20
Will, last and testament, 26, 84
Wing numbers, 115
Witnesses, wedding, 82
Workers Compensation Appeals Board, 29, 110
Yachts, 90
Yearbooks, school, 15
Yellow pages, 64

Pssst!

Got a great story that needs to be told?

You're in luck. There's an investigative reporter who'd love to hear from you. And he'll handle everything.

Even if you remain anonymous.

Don Ray
P.O. Box 4375
Burbank, CA 91503-4375
(818) THE-NEWS

Ps. I never give up my sources!

Don Ray in Person!
Bring the expert to you!

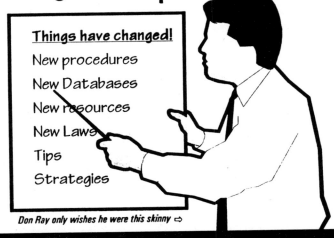

Things have changed!
- New procedures
- New Databases
- New resources
- New Laws
- Tips
- Strategies

Don Ray only wishes he were this skinny ⇨

Don Ray can train,
He can entertain!
Book 'em today.

Thousands of criminal investigatiors, journalists, private investigators, genealogists and librarians have improved their investigative skills while smiling through Don Ray's lively, humorous and energetic presentations.

To book him, Call (818) THE-NEWS.